Get the eBook FREE!

(PDF, ePub, Kindle, and liveBook all included)

We believe that once you buy a book from us, you should be able to read it in any format we have available. To get electronic versions of this book at no additional cost to you, purchase and then register this book at the Manning website.

Go to https://www.manning.com/freebook and follow the instructions to complete your pBook registration.

That's it!
Thanks from Manning!

WebAssembly in Action

WebAssembly in Action

WITH EXAMPLES USING C++ AND EMSCRIPTEN

C. GERARD GALLANT

MANNING
SHELTER ISLAND

Manning Publications Co.
20 Baldwin Road
PO Box 761
Shelter Island, NY 11964

Acquisitions editor:	Brian Sawyer
Development editor:	Toni Arritola
Technical development editor:	Ian Lovell
Review editor:	Ivan Martinović
Production editor:	Anthony Calcara
Copy editor:	Rebecca Deuel-Gallegos
Proofreader:	Tiffany Taylor
Technical proofreader:	Arno Bastenof
Typesetter:	Dottie Marsico
Cover designer:	Marija Tudor

ISBN 9781617295744
Printed in the United States of America

brief contents

v

contents

preface

Compared to my friends, I was a late bloomer when it came to programming. I only discovered it in high school by chance because I needed another computer course, and my guidance counselor suggested Computer Ed. I was expecting to learn about how computers work, but, much to my surprise, the course was about programming. It didn't take long before I was hooked, and I adjusted my career direction from one dealing with building architecture to one in software architecture.

In 2001, I landed a job with Dovico Software helping it maintain and improve its C++ client/server application. The winds of change were blowing, and in 2004, Dovico decided to switch to a software-as-a-service model, and I moved to the web application product. I still helped maintain the C++ applications, but my core focus became web development with C# and JavaScript. These days, I still do web development, but my focus has shifted to the architecture side of things—building APIs, working with databases, and exploring new technologies.

I enjoy being able to give back to the developer community through blogs and public speaking. In September 2017, I was asked if I'd be interested in giving a presentation at a local user group. As I was browsing for ideas on what I could talk about, I ran across an article from PSPDFKit that talked about a technology called WebAssembly (https://pspdfkit.com/blog/2017/webassembly-a-new-hope/).

I had read about Google's Native Client (PNaCI) technology, in which C or C++ compiled code could run in the Chrome web browser at near-native speeds. I'd also read about Mozilla's asm.js technology, where you could compile C or C++ code to a subset of JavaScript and have it run really fast in browsers that supported it. In browsers that didn't support asm.js, it would still run, but at normal speed, because it's just JavaScript. Somehow, this was the first I'd heard of WebAssembly.

WebAssembly takes the improvements that asm.js brought and aims to address its shortcomings. Not only can you write code in a number of different languages and compile it into something that works safely in a browser, but it's already available in all major desktop and mobile browsers! It's also available outside the browser, in places like Node.js! I was blown away by its potential and spent every spare moment from then on digging into the technology and blogging about it.

Late in 2017, my blog posts were noticed by Manning Publications, and I was contacted to see if I would be interested in writing a book about WebAssembly. At first, the book was going to cover multiple languages as well as show you how to work with the technology from both a backend and frontend developer perspective. By the first review, however, it became obvious that the book wasn't focused enough, so we decided that it would be best to narrow the scope to the C++ programming language and focus more on backend developers.

The WebAssembly community and working groups haven't been sitting still while I've been working on this book. In fact, several advancements to the technology are in the works. Recently, the ability to use multithreaded WebAssembly modules in the desktop version of Google Chrome became possible without the need to turn on a developer flag! WebAssembly has the potential to help bring web development to a whole new level, and I'm excited to see where things go.

acknowledgments

I was told that writing a book took work and time, but I wasn't expecting it to take as much work as it did! With help from my editors and reviewers, and feedback from those who purchased an early copy, I believe this has turned out to be a great book that will help you get started with WebAssembly.

I need to thank a lot of people who made this book possible. First and foremost, I need to thank my family for their patience with me as I worked long into the evenings and on weekends and holidays, and even used up some vacation time to meet deadlines. My wife Selena and my girls Donna and Audrey—I love you all very much!

Next, thank you to my first editor at Manning, Kevin Harreld, who helped me get up and running with writing this book. Kevin later accepted a job at another company, giving me the opportunity and pleasure to work with Toni Arritola for the remainder of the book. Toni, thank you for your patience while working with me, your professionalism, your honesty where you didn't beat around the bush and told it like it was, and your desire for quality.

Thank you to everyone at Manning who has played a role in this book, from marketing to production. Your tireless work is appreciated.

Thank you to all the reviewers who took time out of their busy lives to read this book at the various stages of its development and gave constructive feedback, including Christoffer Fink, Daniel Budden, Darko Bozhinovski, Dave Cutler, Denis Kreis, German Gonzalez-Morris, James Dietrich, James Haring, Jan Kroken, Jason Hales, Javier Muñoz, Jeremy Lange, Jim Karabatsos, Kate Meyer, Marco Massenzio, Mike Rourke, Milorad Imbra, Pavlo Hodysh, Peter Hampton, Reza Zeinali, Ronald Borman, Sam Zaydel, Sander Zegveld, Satej Kumar Sahu, Thomas Overby Hansen, Tiklu Ganguly, Timothy R. Kane, Tischliar Ronald, Kumar S. Unnikrishnan, Viktor Bek, and Wayne Mather.

Special thanks to my technical editor, Ian Lovell, who gave lots of invaluable feedback throughout the process, and my technical proofreader, Arno Bastenhof, who gave the code one last review before the book went into production.

And finally, a huge thank you to the browser makers that have worked together to bring a technology to market that will benefit the web for years to come. Thank you to the many people around the world continuing to work on improving WebAssembly and extend its reach. The possibilities are enormous for this technology, and I can't wait to see where WebAssembly takes us.

about this book

WebAssembly in Action was written to help you understand what WebAssembly is, how it works, and what you can and can't do with it. It leads you through the various options for how you can build a WebAssembly module depending on your needs. It starts with simple examples and builds up to more advanced topics, like dynamic linking, parallel processing, and debugging.

Who should read this book

WebAssembly in Action is for developers with a basic understanding of C or C++, Java-Script, and HTML. While there's WebAssembly information online, some of it is out-of-date and typically doesn't go into a lot of detail or cover advanced topics. This book presents the information in an easy-to-follow format that will help both beginner and expert developers create and interact with WebAssembly modules.

How this book is organized

This book has 13 chapters that are divided into four parts.

Part 1 explains what WebAssembly is and how it works. It also introduces you to the Emscripten toolkit, which you'll use throughout this book to create WebAssembly modules:

- Chapter 1 discusses what WebAssembly is, the problems it solves, and how it works. It also explains what makes it secure, which languages can be used to create WebAssembly modules, and where the modules can be used.
- Chapter 2 explains how a WebAssembly module is structured and what each section of the module is responsible for.

- Chapter 3 introduces you to the Emscripten toolkit and teaches you about the different output options available when creating a WebAssembly module. You're also introduced to the WebAssembly JavaScript API.

Part 2 leads you through the process of creating a WebAssembly module and interacting with it in a web browser:

- Chapter 4 teaches you how to take an existing C or C++ codebase and adjust it so that it can also be compiled into a WebAssembly module. You'll also learn how to interact with the module from your web page's JavaScript.
- Chapter 5 teaches you how to adjust the code you built in chapter 4 so that the WebAssembly module can now call into your web page's JavaScript code.
- Chapter 6 walks you through the process of modifying the WebAssembly module to work with function pointers passed to the module from your JavaScript code. This allows your JavaScript to specify functions on-demand and take advantage of JavaScript promises.

Part 3 introduces advanced topics like dynamic linking, parallel processing, and working with WebAssembly modules in places other than a web browser:

- Chapter 7 introduces you to the basics of dynamic linking, in which two or more WebAssembly modules can be linked together at runtime to act as one.
- Chapter 8 takes what you learned in chapter 7 and expands on it, teaching you how to create multiple instances of the same WebAssembly module and have each instance dynamically link to another WebAssembly module on-demand.
- Chapter 9 teaches you about web workers and pthreads. In this chapter, you'll learn how to prefetch WebAssembly modules as needed in a background thread of your browser using web workers. You'll also learn how to do parallel processing in a WebAssembly module using pthreads.
- Chapter 10 demonstrates that WebAssembly isn't limited to a web browser. In this chapter, you'll learn how to use several of your WebAssembly modules in Node.js.

Part 4 digs into debugging and testing:

- Chapter 11 teaches you about the WebAssembly text format by having you build a card-matching game.
- Chapter 12 extends the card-matching game to show you the various options that are available to debug a WebAssembly module.
- Chapter 13 teaches you how to write integration tests for your modules.

Each chapter builds on what was learned in the previous chapters, so it's best if they're read in order. Developers should read chapters 1, 2, and 3 in sequence to understand what WebAssembly is, how it works, and how to use the Emscripten toolkit. Appendix A is also important so that you can get the tooling set up properly in order to follow along with the code in this book. The first two parts of the book cover the core concepts. The rest—the advanced and debugging topics—can be read based on your needs.

About the code

This book contains many source code examples in both numbered listings and inline with normal text. To distinguish it from normal text, the code is formatted with a `fixed-width font like this`. Also, if code has changed from a previous example, the change is indicated **in bold**.

In some cases, the code shown in the book has been reformatted with line breaks and indentation to accommodate the page space available. In rare cases where there still isn't enough room, listings will use a line-continuation marker (➡). In the book's text, annotations highlight important concepts rather than the use of comments.

The source code for this book is available for download from the publisher's website at www.manning.com/books/webassembly-in-action.

liveBook discussion forum

Purchase of *WebAssembly in Action* includes free access to a private web forum run by Manning Publications where you can make comments about the book, ask technical questions, and receive help from the author and from other users. To access the forum, go to https://livebook.manning.com/#!/book/webassembly-in-action/discussion. You can also learn more about Manning's forums and the rules of conduct at https://livebook.manning.com/#!/discussion.

Manning's commitment to our readers is to provide a venue where a meaningful dialogue between individual readers and between readers and the author can take place. It isn't a commitment to any specific amount of participation on the part of the author, whose contribution to the forum remains voluntary (and unpaid). We suggest you try asking the author some challenging questions lest his interest stray! The forum and the archives of previous discussions will be accessible from the publisher's website as long as the book is in print.

Other online resources

Need additional help?

- Emscripten has a lot of documentation available for many different tasks: https://emscripten.org.
- The Emscripten community is very active, with frequent releases. If you find an issue with Emscripten itself, you can check to see if someone has filed a bug report or knows how to work around the issue you're having: https://github.com/emscripten-core/emscripten.
- Stack Overflow is also a great website to ask questions or help others: https://stackoverflow.com/questions.

about the author

C. GERARD GALLANT received a Microsoft Certified Professional certificate in 2013 for completing the Programming in IITML5 with JavaScript and CSS3 specialist exam. He blogs regularly on Blogger.com and DZone.com.

about the cover illustration

The figure on the cover of *WebAssembly in Action* is captioned "Fille Lipparotte," or a girl from the Lipparotte. The illustration is taken from a collection of dress costumes from various countries by Jacques Grasset de Saint-Sauveur (1757–1810), titled *Costumes Civils Actuels de Tous les Peuples Connus,* published in France in 1788. Each illustration is finely drawn and colored by hand. The rich variety of Grasset de Saint-Sauveur's collection reminds us vividly of how culturally apart the world's towns and regions were just 200 years ago. Isolated from each other, people spoke different dialects and languages. In the streets or in the countryside, it was easy to identify where they lived and what their trade or station in life was just by their dress.

The way we dress has changed since then, and the diversity by region, so rich at the time, has faded away. It is now hard to tell apart the inhabitants of different continents, let alone different towns, regions, or countries. Perhaps we have traded cultural diversity for a more varied personal life—certainly for a more varied and fast-paced technological life.

At a time when it is hard to tell one computer book from another, Manning celebrates the inventiveness and initiative of the computer business with book covers based on the rich diversity of regional life of two centuries ago, brought back to life by Grasset de Saint-Sauveur's pictures.

Part 1

First steps

This part of the book will introduce you to WebAssembly and the process of creating a WebAssembly module.

In chapter 1, you'll learn what WebAssembly is, the problems it solves, what makes it secure, and which programming languages you can use with it.

In chapter 2, I'll introduce the internal structure of a WebAssembly module, so you can see what each section's purpose is.

Then, in chapter 3, you'll learn about the different output options available with the Emscripten toolkit by creating your first WebAssembly modules. I'll also introduce you to the WebAssembly JavaScript API.

Meet WebAssembly

This chapter covers

- What WebAssembly is
- The problems that WebAssembly solves
- How WebAssembly works
- What makes WebAssembly secure
- The languages you can use to create a WebAssembly module

When it comes to web development, one thing that's top of mind for most web developers is performance, from how fast the web page loads to how responsive it is overall. A number of studies have shown that if your web page doesn't load within three seconds, 40% of your visitors will leave. That percentage increases for every additional second it takes your page to load.

How long it takes your web page to load isn't the only issue. According to one Google article, if a web page has poor performance, 79% of visitors say they're less likely to purchase from that website again (Daniel An and Pat Meenan, "Why marketers should care about mobile page speed" [July 2016], http://mng.bz/MOlD).

As web technologies have advanced, there's been a push to move more and more applications to the web. This has presented developers with another challenge, because web browsers support only one programming language: JavaScript.

Having a single programming language across all browsers is good in one sense—you only have to write your code once, and you know that it will run in every browser. You still have to test in each browser you intend to support, because vendors sometimes implement things slightly differently. Also, sometimes one browser vendor won't add a new feature at the same time other vendors do. Overall, though, having one language to support is easier than having four or five. The downside of browsers supporting only JavaScript, however, is that the applications we want to move to the web aren't written in JavaScript—rather, they're written in languages like C++.

JavaScript is a great programming language, but we're now asking it to do more than it was originally designed to do—heavy computations for games, for example— and we're asking it to run really fast.

1.1   What is WebAssembly?

As browser makers looked for ways to improve JavaScript's performance, Mozilla (which makes the Firefox browser) defined a subset of JavaScript called asm.js.

1.1.1   Asm.js, the forerunner to WebAssembly

Asm.js brought the following advantages:

- You don't write asm.js directly. Instead, you write your logic using C or C++ and convert it into JavaScript. Converting code from one language to another is known as *transpiling*.
- Faster code execution for high computations. When a browser's JavaScript engine sees a special string called the `asm pragma` statement (`"use asm";`), it acts as a flag, telling the browser that it can use the low-level system operations rather than the more expensive JavaScript operations.
- Faster code execution from the very first call. Type-hints are included to tell JavaScript what type of data a variable will hold. For example, a | 0 would be used to hint that the variable `a` will hold a 32-bit integer value. This works because a bitwise OR operation of zero doesn't change the original value, so there are no side effects to doing this.

  These type-hints serve as a promise to the JavaScript engine indicating that, if the code declares a variable as an integer, it will never change to a string, for example. Consequently, the JavaScript engine doesn't have to monitor the code to find out what the types are. It can simply compile the code as it's declared.

The following code snippet shows an example of asm.js code:

```
function AsmModule() {            Flag telling JavaScript that the
  "use asm";               ◁──── code that follows is asm.js
  rcturn {
    add: function(a, b) {          Type-hint indicating that the
      a = a | 0;             ◁──── parameter is a 32-bit integer
      b = b | 0;
      return (a + b) | 0;    ◁──┐ Type-hint indicating that the
    }                            return value is a 32-bit integer
  }
}
```

Despite asm.js's advantages, it still has some shortcomings:

- All the type-hints can make the files really large.
- The asm.js file is a JavaScript file, so it still has to be read in and parsed by the JavaScript engine. This becomes an issue on devices like phones because all that processing slows load time and uses battery power.
- To add additional features, browser makers would have to modify the JavaScript language itself, which isn't desirable.
- JavaScript is a programming language and wasn't intended to be a compiler target.

1.1.2 From asm.js to MVP

As browser makers looked at how they could improve on asm.js, they came up with a WebAssembly minimum viable product (MVP) that aimed to take asm.js's positive aspects while addressing its shortcomings. In 2017, all four major browser vendors (Google, Microsoft, Apple, and Mozilla) updated their browsers with support for the MVP, which is sometimes referred to as Wasm:

- WebAssembly is a low-level assembly-like language that can run at near-native speeds in all modern desktop browsers as well as many mobile browsers.
- WebAssembly files are designed to be compact and, as a result, can be transmitted and downloaded fast. The files are also designed in such a way that they can be parsed and initialized quickly.
- WebAssembly is designed as a compile target so that code written in languages such as C++, Rust, and others can now run on the web.

Backend developers can leverage WebAssembly to improve code reuse or bring their code to the web without having to rewrite it. Web developers also benefit from the creation of new libraries, improvements to existing libraries, and the opportunity to improve performance in computationally heavy sections of their own code. Although WebAssembly's primary use is in web browsers, it's also designed with portability in mind, so you can use it outside the browser as well.

1.2 What problems does it solve?

The WebAssembly MVP addresses the following asm.js issues.

1.2.1 Performance improvements

One of the biggest issues that WebAssembly aims to solve is performance—from how long it takes to download your code to how quickly the code executes. With programming languages, rather than writing code in the machine language that the computer's processor understands (1s and 0s, or native code), you usually write something that's closer to a human language. While it's easier to work with code that's abstracted from your computer's fine details, computer processors don't understand your code, so when it comes time to run it, you have to convert what you wrote into machine code.

JavaScript is what's known as an *interpreted programming language*—that is, it reads the code you wrote as it's executing and translates those instructions into machine code on the fly. With interpreted languages, there's no need to compile the code ahead of time, which means it starts running sooner. The downside, however, is that the interpreter has to convert the instructions to machine code every time the code is run. If your code is doing a loop, for example, each line of that loop has to be interpreted every time the loop is executed. Because a lot of time isn't always available during the interpretation process, optimizations aren't always possible either.

Other programming languages, like C++, aren't interpreted. With these types of languages, you need to convert the instructions to machine code ahead of time using special programs called compilers. With compiled programming languages, it takes a bit of time up front to convert the instructions to machine code before you can run them, but the advantage is that there's more time to run optimizations on the code; once it's compiled to machine code, it doesn't have to be compiled again.

Over time, JavaScript has gone from simply being a glue language that ties components together, where it was only expected to be short-lived, to a language now used by many websites to do complex processing; it can easily involve hundreds to thousands of lines of code; and, with the rise of single-page applications, this code can often be long-lived. The internet has gone from websites that just displayed some text and a few pictures to very interactive websites and even sites that are called web applications because they're similar to desktop applications but run in a web browser.

As developers continued to push JavaScript's limits, some noticeable performance issues came to light. Browser makers decided to try to find a middle ground in which you get the advantages of an interpreter, where the code starts running as soon as it gets called, but you also have code that runs faster when it's being executed. To make the code faster, browser makers introduced a concept called JIT (just-in-time) compiling, in which the JavaScript engine monitors the code as it runs; if a section of code is used enough times, the engine will attempt to compile that section into machine code so that it can bypass the JavaScript engine and use the lower-level system methods instead, which are much faster.

The JavaScript engine needs to monitor the code several times before it gets compiled to machine code because JavaScript is also a dynamic programming language. In JavaScript, a variable can hold any type of value. For example, a variable can hold an integer initially but later be assigned a string. Until the code is run a few times, a browser doesn't know what to expect. Even when compiled, the code still needs to be monitored, because there's a chance that something will change and the compiled code for that section will need to be thrown out and the process started again.

1.2.2 *Faster startup times compared with JavaScript*

As with asm.js, WebAssembly isn't designed to be written by hand, and it's not intended to be read by humans. When code is compiled to WebAssembly, the resulting bytecode is represented in a binary format, rather than a text format, which reduces the file size, allowing it to be transmitted and downloaded fast.

The binary file is designed in such a way that module validation can be made in a single pass. The file's structure also allows for different sections of the file to be compiled in parallel.

By implementing JIT compilation, browser makers have made a lot of progress in improving JavaScript performance. But the JavaScript engine can compile JavaScript to machine code only after code has been monitored several times. WebAssembly code, on the other hand, is statically typed, which means the types of values that the variables will hold are known ahead of time. Because of this, WebAssembly code can be compiled to machine code from the beginning, without having to be monitored first—performance improvements are seen from the first time the code is run.

Since the MVP's initial release, browser makers have found ways to further improve WebAssembly's performance. One such improvement was the introduction of something they call *streaming compilation,* which is the process of compiling the WebAssembly code to machine code as the file is being downloaded and received by the browser. Streaming compilation allows for a WebAssembly module to be initialized as soon as it finishes downloading, which speeds up the module's startup time considerably.

1.2.3 *Ability to use languages other than JavaScript in the browser*

Up until this point, for a language other than JavaScript to be able to target the web, the code had to be converted to JavaScript, which wasn't intended to be a compiler target. WebAssembly, on the other hand, was designed to be a compiler target from the beginning, so developers who want to use a particular language for web development will be able to do so without having to transpile their code into JavaScript.

Because WebAssembly isn't tied to the JavaScript language, improvements can be made to the technology more easily and without worrying about interfering with how JavaScript works. This independence should result in the ability to improve WebAssembly much faster.

For the WebAssembly MVP, C and C++ were given focus as languages that could target WebAssembly, but Rust has since added support, and several other languages are also experimenting with it.

1.2.4 *Opportunity for code reuse*

Being able to take code written in languages other than JavaScript and compile it to WebAssembly gives developers more flexibility when it comes to code reuse. Now, something that would have had to be rewritten in JavaScript can be used on the desktop or server and run in the browser.

1.3   *How does it work?*

As figure 1.1 illustrates, with JavaScript, the code is included in the website and is interpreted as it runs. Because JavaScript variables are dynamic, looking at the add function in the illustration, it's not obvious what type of values you're dealing with. The variables a and b could be integers, floats, strings, or even a combination in which one variable could be a string and the other a float, for example.

The only way to know what the types are for sure is to monitor the code as it executes, which is what the JavaScript engine does. Once the engine is satisfied that it knows the variable's types, it can convert that section of code into machine code.

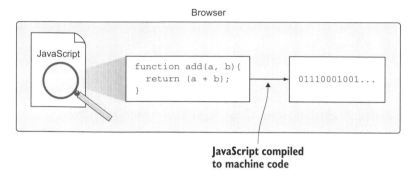

Figure 1.1   JavaScript compiled to machine code as it executes

WebAssembly isn't interpreted but, rather, is compiled into the WebAssembly binary format by a developer ahead of time, as figure 1.2 shows. Because the variable types are all known ahead of time, when the browser loads the WebAssembly file, the JavaScript engine doesn't need to monitor the code. It can simply compile the code's binary format into machine code.

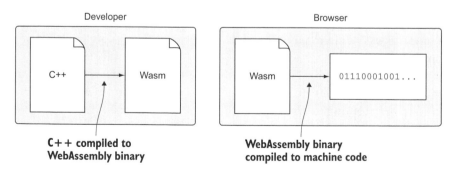

Figure 1.2   C++ being turned into WebAssembly and then into machine code in the browser

1.3.1 Overview of how compilers work

In section 1.2.1, we talked briefly about how developers write code in a language that's closer to a human language, but computer processors understand only machine language. As a result, the code you write has to be converted into machine code in order to execute. What I didn't mention is that each type of computer processor has its own type of machine code.

It would be inefficient to compile each programming language directly to each version of machine code. Instead, what usually happens is shown in figure 1.3, in which a part of the compiler, referred to as the *frontend*, converts the code you wrote into an intermediate representation (IR). Once the IR code has been created, the *backend* part of the compiler takes this IR code, optimizes it, and then turns it into the desired machine code.

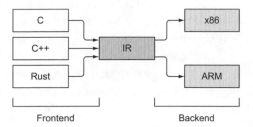

Frontend   Backend

Figure 1.3 Compiler frontend and backend

Because a browser can run on a number of different processors (from desktop computers to smartphones and tablets, for example), distributing a compiled version of the WebAssembly code for each potential processor would be tedious. Figure 1.4 shows what you do instead, which is take the IR code and run it through a special compiler that converts it into a special binary bytecode and places that bytecode in a file with a .wasm extension.

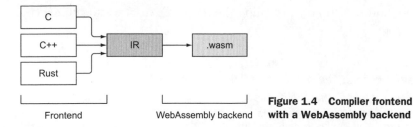

Frontend   WebAssembly backend

Figure 1.4 Compiler frontend with a WebAssembly backend

The bytecode in your Wasm file isn't machine code yet. It's simply a set of virtual instructions that browsers that support WebAssembly understand. As figure 1.5 shows, when the file is loaded into a browser that supports WebAssembly, the browser verifies that everything is valid; the bytecode is then compiled the rest of the way into the machine code of the device the browser is running on.

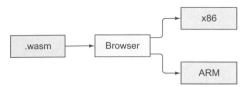

Figure 1.5   **Wasm file loaded into a browser and then compiled to machine code**

1.3.2   *Loading, compiling, and instantiating a module*

At the time of writing, the process of downloading the Wasm file into the browser and having the browser compile it is done using JavaScript function calls. There's a desire to allow WebAssembly modules to interact with ES6 modules in the future, which would include the ability for WebAssembly modules to be loaded though a special HTML tag (`<script type="module">`), but this isn't yet available. (ES is shorthand for ECMAScript, and 6 is the version. ECMAScript is the official name for JavaScript.)

Before the WebAssembly module's binary bytecode can be compiled, it needs to be validated to make sure that the module is structured correctly, that the code can't do anything that isn't permitted, and that it can't access memory that the module doesn't have access to. Checks are also made at runtime to ensure that the code stays within the memory that it has access to. The Wasm file is structured so that validation can be made in a single pass to ensure that the validation process, compilation to machine code, and then instantiation occur as quickly as possible.

Once a browser has compiled the WebAssembly bytecode into machine code, the compiled module can be passed to a web worker (we'll dig into web workers in chapter 9, but, for now, know that web workers are a way to create threads in JavaScript) or to another browser window. The compiled module can even be used to create additional instances of the module.

Once a Wasm file has been compiled, it has to be instantiated before it can be used. *Instantiation* is simply the process of receiving any import objects that are needed, initiating the module's elements, calling the start function if a start function was defined, and then finally returning the module's instance to the execution environment.

> **WebAssembly vs. JavaScript**
>
> Up until now, the only language allowed to run within the JavaScript virtual machine (VM) was JavaScript. When other technologies were tried over the years, like plug-ins, they needed to create their own sandboxed VM, which increased both the attack surface and the use of computer resources. For the first time ever, the JavaScript VM is being opened up to allow WebAssembly code to also run in the same VM. This has several advantages. One of the biggest is that the VM has been heavily tested and hardened against security vulnerabilities over the years. If a new VM was created, it would undoubtedly have some security issues to iron out.

WebAssembly is being designed as a complement to JavaScript and not as a replacement. Although we'll likely see some developers try to create entire websites using only WebAssembly, this probably won't be the norm. There will be times when JavaScript will still be the better choice. There will also be times when a website may need to include WebAssembly for access to faster calculations or for lower-level support. For example, SIMD (single instruction, multiple data)—the ability to process multiple data with a single instruction—was being built into the JavaScript of several browsers, but browser vendors decided to deprecate the JavaScript implementation and make SIMD support available only via WebAssembly modules. As a result, if your website needs SIMD support, you'll need to include a WebAssembly module to communicate with.

When programming for a web browser, you basically have two main components: the JavaScript VM, which the WebAssembly module runs in, and Web APIs (for example, DOM, WebGL, web workers, and so on). Being an MVP, there are some things missing from WebAssembly. Your WebAssembly module can communicate with JavaScript but isn't yet able to talk directly to any of the Web APIs. A post-MVP feature is being worked on that will give WebAssembly direct access to Web APIs. In the meantime, modules can interact with Web APIs indirectly by calling into JavaScript and having JavaScript perform the action needed on the module's behalf.

1.4 Structure of a WebAssembly module

WebAssembly currently has only four available value types:

- 32-bit integers
- 64-bit integers
- 32-bit floats
- 64-bit floats

Boolean values are represented using a 32-bit integer, where 0 is `false` and a `nonzero` value is `true`. All other value types, such as strings, need to be represented in the module's linear memory.

The main unit of a WebAssembly program is called the *module*, a term used for both the binary version of the code and the compiled version in the browser. A WebAssembly module isn't something you're expected to create by hand, but having a basic understanding of how the module is structured, and how it works under the hood, can come in handy because you interact with certain aspects of it during initialization and over the module's lifetime.

Figure 1.6 is a basic representation of a WebAssembly file's structure. You'll learn about a module's structure in more detail in chapter 2, but, for now, I'll give you a quick overview.

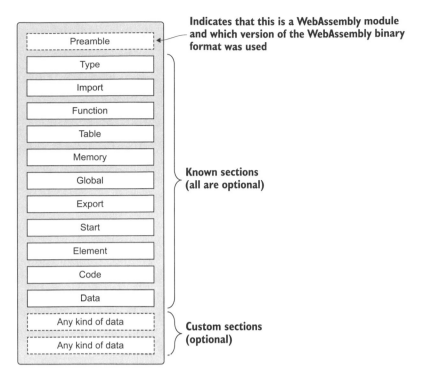

Figure 1.6   A basic representation of a WebAssembly file's structure

A Wasm file starts with a section called the *preamble*.

1.4.1   *Preamble*

The preamble contains a magic number (0x00 0x61 0x73 0x6D, which is \0asm) that distinguishes a WebAssembly module from an ES6 module. This magic number is then followed by a version (0x01 0x00 0x00 0x00, which is 1) that indicates which version of the WebAssembly binary format was used to create the file.

Only one version of the binary format exists at the moment. One of the goals with WebAssembly is to keep everything backward-compatible as new features are being added and to avoid having to increase the version number. If a feature ever arises that can't be implemented without breaking things, then the version number will be increased.

Following the preamble, a module can have several *sections*, but each section is optional, so you could technically have an empty module with no sections. You'll learn about one use case for an empty module in chapter 3 when you implement feature detection to check if WebAssembly is supported in a web browser.

Two types of sections are available: *known* sections and *custom* sections.

1.4.2 Known sections

Known sections can be included only once and must appear in a specific order. Each known section has a specific purpose, is well-defined, and is validated when the module is instantiated. Chapter 2 goes into more detail about known sections.

1.4.3 Custom sections

A custom section provides a way to include data inside the module for uses that don't apply to the known sections. Custom sections can appear anywhere in the module (before, in between, or after the known sections) any number of times, and multiple custom sections can even reuse the same name.

Unlike with known sections, if a custom section isn't laid out correctly, it won't trigger a validation error. Custom sections can be loaded lazily by the framework, which means the data they contain might not be available until some point after the module's initialization.

For the WebAssembly MVP, a custom section called "name" was defined. The idea with this section is that you could have a debug version of your WebAssembly module, and this section would hold the names of the functions and variables in text form for use when debugging. Unlike with other custom sections, this section should appear only once and only after the Data section.

1.5 WebAssembly text format

WebAssembly has been designed with the web's openness in mind. Just because the binary format isn't designed to be written or read by humans doesn't mean that WebAssembly modules are a way for developers to try to hide their code. Actually, quite the opposite is true. A text format that uses *s-expressions* has been defined for WebAssembly that corresponds to the binary format.

> **INFO** Symbolic expression, or s-expression, was invented for the Lisp programming language. An s-expression can be either an atom or an ordered pair of s-expressions that allow you to nest s-expressions. An atom is a symbol that's not a list: foo or 23, for example. A list is represented by parentheses, and can be empty or can hold atoms or even other lists; each item is space delimited: () or (foo) or (foo (bar 132)), for example.

This text format will enable View Source for the code in a browser, for example, or it can be used for debugging. You can even write s-expressions by hand and, by using a special compiler, compile the code into the WebAssembly binary format.

Because the WebAssembly text format will be used by browsers when you choose to View Source and for debugging purposes, having a basic understanding of the text format will be useful. For example, since all sections of a module are optional, you could define an empty module using the following s-expression:

```
(module)
```

If you were to compile the (module) s-expression into the WebAssembly binary format and look at the resulting binary values, the file would contain only the preamble bytes :0061 736d (the magic number) and 0100 0000 (the version number).

> **LOOKING AHEAD**   In chapter 11, you'll create a WebAssembly module using only the text format so that you'll have a better idea of what you're looking at if you ever need to debug a module in a browser, for example.

1.6   *How is WebAssembly secure?*

One way that WebAssembly is secure is that it's the first language to ever share the JavaScript VM, which is sandboxed from the runtime and has had years of hardening and security tests to make it secure. WebAssembly modules don't have access to anything that JavaScript doesn't have access to and will also respect the same security policies, which include enforcing things like same-origin policy.

Unlike a desktop application, a WebAssembly module doesn't have direct access to a device's memory. Instead, the runtime environment passes the module an ArrayBuffer during initialization. The module uses this ArrayBuffer as linear memory, and the WebAssembly framework checks to make sure that the code is operating within the bounds of the array.

A WebAssembly module doesn't have direct access to items, such as function pointers, that are stored in the Table section. The code asks the WebAssembly framework to access an item based on its index. The framework then accesses the memory and executes the item on the code's behalf.

In C++, the execution stack is in memory along with the linear memory and, although the C++ code isn't supposed to modify the execution stack, it's possible to do so using pointers. WebAssembly's execution stack is also separate from the linear memory and isn't accessible by the code.

> **MORE INFO**   If you would like more information about WebAssembly's security model, you can visit the following website: https://webassembly.org/docs/security.

1.7   *What languages can I use to create a WebAssembly module?*

To create the MVP, WebAssembly's initial focus was on the C and C++ languages, but languages like Rust and AssemblyScript have since added support. It's also possible to write code using the WebAssembly text format, which uses s-expressions, and compile that into WebAssembly using a special compiler.

Right now, WebAssembly's MVP doesn't have garbage collection (GC), which limits what some languages can do. GC is being worked on as a post-MVP feature, but, until it arrives, several languages are experimenting with WebAssembly by either compiling their VM to WebAssembly or, in some cases, by including their own garbage collector.

The following languages are experimenting with or have WebAssembly support:

- C and C++.
- Rust is aiming to be the programming language of choice for WebAssembly.
- AssemblyScript is a new compiler that takes TypeScript and turns it into WebAssembly. Converting TypeScript makes sense, considering that it's typed and already transpiles to JavaScript.
- TeaVM is a tool that transpiles Java to JavaScript but can now also generate WebAssembly.
- Go 1.11 added an experimental port to WebAssembly that includes a garbage collector as part of the compiled WebAssembly module.
- Pyodide is a port of Python that includes the core packages of Python's scientific stack: Numpy, Pandas, and matplotlib.
- Blazor is an experimental effort from Microsoft to bring C# to WebAssembly.

MORE INFO The following GitHub repository maintains a curated list of languages that compile to, or have their VMs in, WebAssembly. The list also indicates where the language stands in its support of WebAssembly: https://github.com/appcypher/awesome-wasm-langs.

For learning WebAssembly in this book, we'll use C and C++.

1.8 Where can I use my module?

In 2017, all the modern browser makers released versions of their browsers that support WebAssembly's MVP; these include Chrome, Edge, Firefox, Opera, and Safari. Several mobile web browsers also support WebAssembly, including Chrome, Firefox for Android, and Safari.

As mentioned at the beginning of this chapter, WebAssembly was designed with portability in mind so that it can be used in multiple locations, not just in a browser. A new standard called WASI (WebAssembly Standard Interface) is being developed to ensure WebAssembly modules will work consistently across all supported systems. The following article gives a good overview of WASI: Lin Clark, "Standardizing WASI: A system interface to run WebAssembly outside the web" (March 27, 2019), http://mng.bz/gVJ8.

MORE INFO If you'd like to learn more about WASI, the following GitHub repository has a curated list of related links and articles: https://github.com/wasmerio/awesome-wasi.

One nonbrowser location that supports WebAssembly modules is Node.js, starting with version 8. Node.js is a JavaScript runtime built using Chrome's V8 JavaScript engine that allows JavaScript code to be used server-side. Similar to how many developers see WebAssembly as an opportunity to use code that they're familiar with in the browser, rather than JavaScript, Node.js lets developers who prefer JavaScript also use it on the server side. To demonstrate using WebAssembly outside the browser, chapter 10 will show you how to work with your WebAssembly module in Node.js.

WebAssembly isn't a replacement for JavaScript but is rather a complement to it. There are times when using a WebAssembly module will be a better choice and times when using JavaScript will be better. Running in the same VM as JavaScript lets both technologies leverage each other.

WebAssembly will open the door for developers who are proficient in languages other than JavaScript to make their code available on the web. It will also allow web developers who might not know how to code in languages like C or C++ to gain access to newer and faster libraries and potentially those with features not available in current JavaScript libraries. In some cases, WebAssembly modules might be used by libraries to speed up execution of certain aspects of the library; other than having faster code, the library would work the same as it always has.

The most exciting thing about WebAssembly is that it's already available in all major desktop browsers, in several major mobile browsers, and even outside the browser in Node.js.

Summary

As you saw in this chapter, WebAssembly brings a number of performance improvements as well as improvements in language choice and code reuse. Some key improvements that WebAssembly brings are the following:

- Transmission and download times are faster because of smaller file sizes due to the use of binary encoding.
- Due to the way Wasm files are structured, they can be parsed and validated quickly. Also because of how they're structured, portions of the files can be compiled in parallel.
- With streaming compilation, WebAssembly modules can be compiled as they're being downloaded so that they're ready to be instantiated the moment the download completes, speeding up load time considerably.
- Code execution is faster for things like computations due to the use of machine-level calls rather than the more expensive JavaScript engine calls.
- Code doesn't need to be monitored before it's compiled to determine how it's going to behave. The result is that code runs at the same speed every time it runs.
- Being separate from JavaScript, improvements can be made to WebAssembly faster because they won't impact the JavaScript language.
- You can use code written in a language other than JavaScript in a browser.
- There's an increased opportunity for code reuse by structuring the WebAssembly framework in such a way that it can be used in the browser and outside it.

A look inside
WebAssembly modules

2

This chapter covers

- Descriptions of a WebAssembly module's known and custom sections

In this chapter, you'll learn about the different sections of a WebAssembly module and their purposes. I'll offer more detail as you proceed through this book, but it's helpful to have a basic understanding of how modules are structured and how the different sections work together.

Some benefits of a module's different sections and how they're designed are

- *Efficiency*—The binary bytecode can be parsed, validated, and compiled in a single pass.
- *Streaming*—Parsing, validation, and compilation can begin before all the data has been downloaded.
- *Parallelization*—It's possible for the parsing, validation, and compilation to be performed in parallel.
- *Security*—The module doesn't have direct access to the device memory, and items like function pointers are called on your code's behalf.

17

Figure 2.1 represents the basic structure of the WebAssembly binary bytecode. Although you'll interact with the various sections when working with WebAssembly modules, the compiler is responsible for creating the sections as needed and placing them in the proper order based on your code.

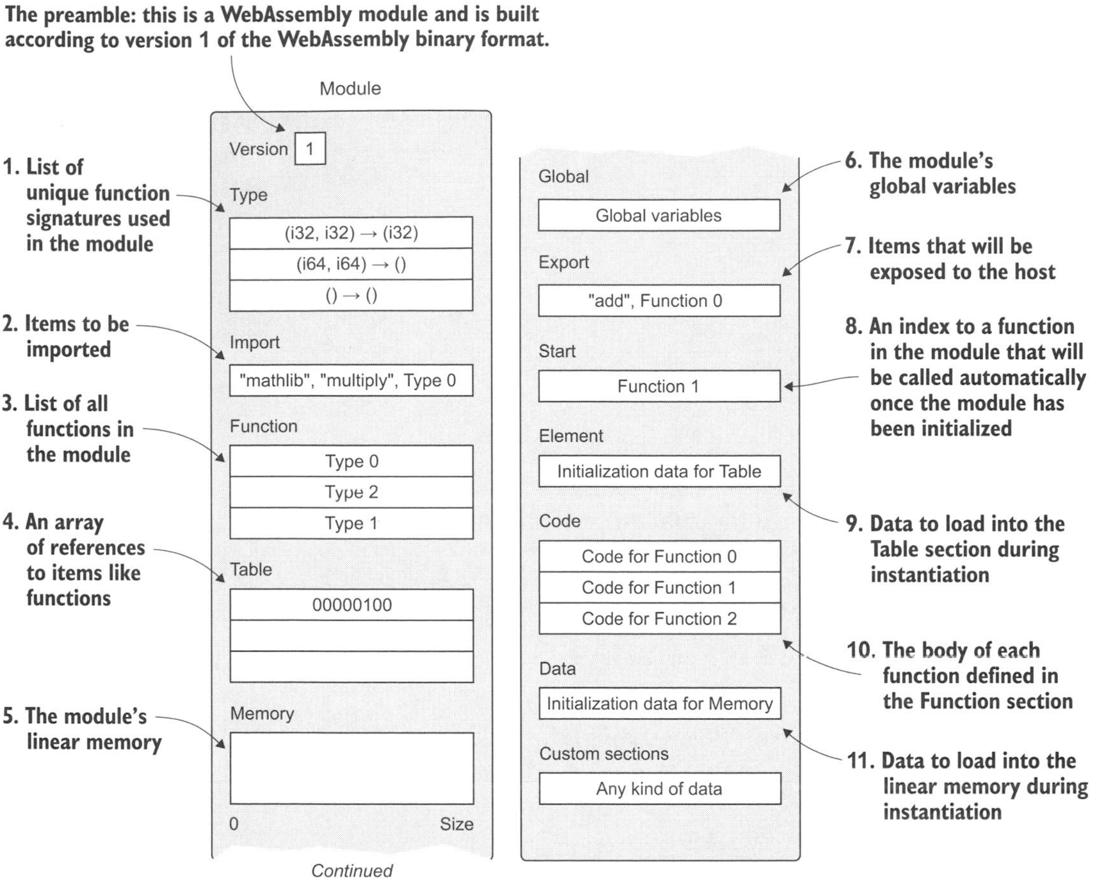

The preamble: this is a WebAssembly module and is built according to version 1 of the WebAssembly binary format.

Module

Version | 1 |

1. List of unique function signatures used in the module

Type

| (i32, i32) → (i32) |
| (i64, i64) → () |
| () → () |

2. Items to be imported

Import

| "mathlib", "multiply", Type 0 |

3. List of all functions in the module

Function

| Type 0 |
| Type 2 |
| Type 1 |

4. An array of references to items like functions

Table

| 00000100 |
| |
| |

5. The module's linear memory

Memory

| |
| |

0   Size

Global

| Global variables |

6. The module's global variables

Export

| "add", Function 0 |

7. Items that will be exposed to the host

Start

| Function 1 |

8. An index to a function in the module that will be called automatically once the module has been initialized

Element

| Initialization data for Table |

Code

| Code for Function 0 |
| Code for Function 1 |
| Code for Function 2 |

9. Data to load into the Table section during instantiation

Data

| Initialization data for Memory |

10. The body of each function defined in the Function section

Custom sections

| Any kind of data |

11. Data to load into the linear memory during instantiation

Continued

Figure 2.1   The basic structure of the WebAssembly binary bytecode, highlighting the known and custom sections

WebAssembly modules can have several sections, but each section is optional. You could technically have an empty module with no sections. As introduced in chapter 1, the two types of available sections are

- Known sections
- Custom sections

Known sections have a specific purpose, are well-defined, and are validated when the WebAssembly module is instantiated. Custom sections are used for data that doesn't apply to the known sections and won't trigger a validation error if the data isn't laid out correctly.

The WebAssembly bytecode starts with the preamble, which indicates that the module is a WebAssembly module and that it's version 1 of the WebAssembly binary format. After the preamble, you have the known sections, which are all optional. The figure shows the custom sections at the end of the module, but, in reality, they can be placed before, in between, or after the known sections. As with known sections, custom sections are also optional.

Now that you've seen a high-level representation of a WebAssembly module's basic structure, let's take a closer look at each of the known sections.

2.1 Known sections

If a known section is included, it can be included at most one time, and known sections must appear in the order presented here.

Section	Description
Type	The *Type* section declares a list of all unique function signatures that will be used in the module, including those that will be imported. Multiple functions can share the same signature.

Figure 2.2 is an example of a Type section holding three function signatures:

- The first has two 32-bit integer (i32) parameters and a 32-bit integer (i32) return value.
- The second has two 64-bit integer (i64) parameters but no return value.
- The third doesn't accept any parameters or return a value.

Section	Description
Import	The *Import* section declares all the imports that will be used in the module, which can include Function, Table, Memory, or Global imports. Imports are designed so that modules can share code and data, but still allow for the modules to be compiled and cached separately. The imports are provided by the host environment when the module is instantiated.
Function	The *Function* section is a list of all the functions in the module. The position of the function declaration in this list represents the index of the function body in the Code section. The value listed in the Function section indicates the index of the function's signature in the Type section.

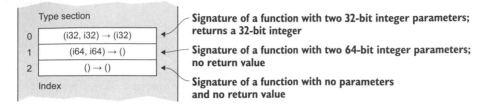

Figure 2.2   A Type section holding three function signatures. The signature at index 0 receives two 32-bit integer parameters and returns a 32-bit integer value. The signature at index 1 receives two 64-bit integer parameters but doesn't have a return value. The signature at index 2 doesn't receive any parameter values and doesn't have a return value.

Figure 2.3 shows an example of how the Type, Function, and Code sections are related. If you look at the Function section in the diagram, the value of the second function is the index to the function signature that doesn't have any parameters or return value. The index of the second function points to the matching index in the code section.

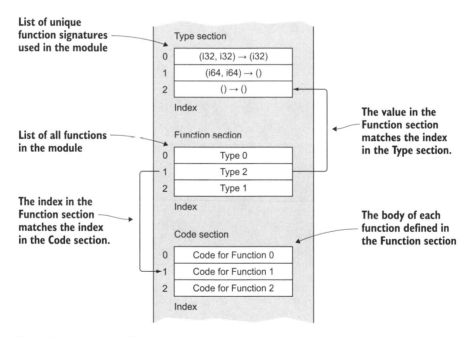

Figure 2.3   Example of how the Type, Function, and Code sections work together

Function declarations are separated from the function bodies to allow for parallel and streaming compilation of each function in the module.

Section	Description
Table	The *Table* section holds a typed array of references, like functions, that can't be stored in the module's linear memory as raw bytes. This section provides one of the core security aspects of WebAssembly by giving the WebAssembly framework a way to map objects in a secure way. Your code doesn't have direct access to the references stored in the table. Instead, when your code wants to access the data referenced in this section, it asks for the framework to operate on the item at a specific index in the table. The WebAssembly framework then reads the address stored at that index and performs the action. When dealing with functions, for example, this enables the use of function pointers by specifying the table index.

Figure 2.4 shows the WebAssembly code asking for the item at index 0 in the Table section to be called. The WebAssembly framework reads the memory address at that index and then executes the code at that memory location.

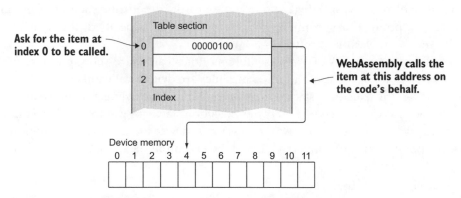

Figure 2.4 Example of an item in the Table section being called

A table is given an initial size and, optionally, a maximum size. For tables, the size is the number of elements in the table. It's possible to ask a table to grow by a specified number of elements. If a maximum number of elements is specified, the system will prevent the table from growing past that point. If a maximum isn't specified, however, the table will be allowed to grow without restriction.

Section	Description
Memory	The *Memory* section holds the linear memory used by the module instance.

The Memory section is also a core security aspect of WebAssembly because WebAssembly modules don't have direct access to the device's memory. Instead, as figure 2.5 shows, the environment that instantiates the module passes in an ArrayBuffer that a module instance uses as linear memory. As far as the code is concerned, this linear memory

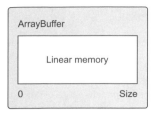

Figure 2.5   ArrayBuffer is used as linear memory by WebAssembly modules.

acts just like the heap in C++, but every time the code tries to access this memory, the framework verifies that the request is within the bounds of the array.

A module's memory is defined as WebAssembly pages that are 64 KB each (1 KB is 1,024 bytes, so one page holds 65,536 bytes). When the environment specifies how much memory the module can have, it specifies the initial number of pages and, optionally, the maximum number of pages. If the module needs more memory, you can request that the memory grow by a specified number of pages. If a maximum number of pages is specified, the framework will prevent the memory from growing past that point. If a maximum number of pages isn't specified, the memory will be allowed to grow without restriction.

Multiple instances of WebAssembly modules can share the same linear memory (ArrayBuffer), which is useful when modules are dynamically linked.

In C++, the execution stack is in memory along with the linear memory; although the C++ code isn't supposed to modify the execution stack, it's possible to do so using pointers. In addition to code not having access to the device memory, WebAssembly has taken security a step further and has separated the execution stack from the linear memory.

Section	Description
Global	The *Global* section allows for the definition of global variables for the module.
Export	The *Export* section holds a list of all objects that will get returned to the host environment once the module has been instantiated (the portions of the module that the host environment can access). This can include Function, Table, Memory, or Global exports.
Start	The *Start* section declares the index of the function that's to be called after the module has been initialized but before the exported functions are callable. The start function can be used as a way to initialize global variables or memory. If specified, the function can't be imported. It must exist within the module.
Element	The *Element* section declares the data that gets loaded into the module's Table section during instantiation.
Code	The *Code* section holds the body of each function declared in the Function section; each function body must appear in the same order as it was declared. (See figure 2.3 for a depiction of how Type, Function, and Code sections work together.)
Data	The *Data* section declares the data that gets loaded into the module's linear memory during instantiation.

In chapter 11, you'll learn about the WebAssembly text format, which is the text equivalent of the module's binary format. It's used by browsers for debugging the module if source maps aren't available. The text format can also be useful if you need to inspect your generated modules to see how the compiler created them to determine why something isn't working as expected. The text format uses the same names for sections that you learned in this chapter, but they're sometimes abbreviated (`func` instead of function, for example).

A module can also include custom sections as a way to include data that doesn't apply to the known sections defined in this chapter.

2.2 Custom sections

Custom sections can appear anywhere in the module (before, in between, or after the known sections), any number of times; multiple custom sections can even reuse the same name.

Unlike with known sections, if a custom section isn't laid out correctly, it won't trigger a validation error. Custom sections can be loaded lazily by the framework, which means the data they contain might not be available until some point after the module's initialization.

One use case for custom sections is the "name" section that was defined for the WebAssembly MVP. The idea with this section is that function and variable names could be placed here in text form to aid in debugging. Unlike normal custom sections, however, this section should only appear once if included and must appear after the Data known section.

Summary

In this chapter, you learned about the known and custom sections of a WebAssembly module to gain a better understanding of what the sections are responsible for and how they work together. This understanding will help you as you interact with the WebAssembly modules and when you work with the WebAssembly text format. In particular, you learned that

- WebAssembly module sections, and how they're designed, are one reason for many of WebAssembly's features and advantages.
- A compiler handles generating the WebAssembly module's sections and placing them in the proper order.
- All sections are optional, so it's possible to have an empty module.
- If specified, known sections can appear only once and must appear in a specific order.
- Custom sections can be placed before, in between, or after known sections and are used to specify data that doesn't apply to the known sections.

Creating your first WebAssembly module

This chapter covers

- An overview of the Emscripten toolkit
- Creating a module using Emscripten and Emscripten's HTML template
- Creating a module with Emscripten JavaScript plumbing code and letting this code handle loading the module
- Creating a module without the Emscripten JavaScript plumbing code and then loading the module yourself
- Feature detection to test if WebAssembly is available

In this chapter, you'll write some C code and then use the Emscripten toolkit to compile it into a WebAssembly module. This will let us look at three approaches we can use with the toolkit to create WebAssembly modules. Just to give you an idea of what's possible using thc toolkit, some of the items that have been ported to Web-Assembly using Emscripten include the Unreal Engine 3, SQLite, and AutoCAD.

3.1 *The Emscripten toolkit*

The Emscripten toolkit is currently the most mature toolkit available to compile C or C++ code into WebAssembly bytecode. It was originally created to transpile such code into asm.js. When work started on the WebAssembly MVP, Emscripten was chosen because it uses the LLVM compiler, and the WebAssembly working group already had experience with LLVM from its work with Google's Native Client (PNaCl). Emscripten can still be used to transpile C and C++ code into asm.js, but you'll be using it to compile the code you write into WebAssembly modules.

As described in chapter 1, compilers typically have a frontend section, which takes the source code and converts it to an intermediate representation (IR), and a backend to convert the IR into the desired machine code, as figure 3.1 shows.

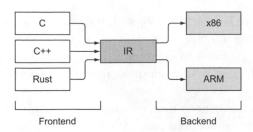

Figure 3.1   Compiler frontend and backend

I mentioned that Emscripten uses the LLVM compiler—this compiler toolchain currently has the most WebAssembly support, and the nice thing with LLVM is that there are a number of frontends and backends you can plug into it. The Emscripten compiler uses Clang, which is similar to the GCC in C++, as the frontend compiler to convert the C or C++ code into an LLVM IR, as figure 3.2 shows. Emscripten then takes the LLVM IR and converts it into a binary bytecode, which is simply a virtual set of instructions that browsers that support WebAssembly understand. This might sound a bit intimidating at first, but, as you'll see in this chapter, the process of compiling C or C++ code into a WebAssembly module is a simple command in a console window.

Before you continue, please see appendix A to install Emscripten and ensure you have all the tools you'll need to use in this book. Once you have the necessary tools installed, you can continue to the next section.

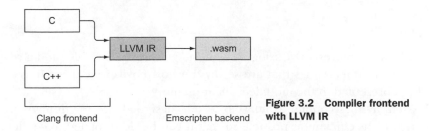

Figure 3.2   Compiler frontend with LLVM IR

3.2   *WebAssembly modules*

When the WebAssembly file is loaded by a browser that supports WebAssembly, the browser will check to ensure that everything is valid. If everything checks out with the file, the browser will compile the bytecode the rest of the way into the device's machine code, as figure 3.3 shows.

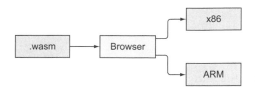

Figure 3.3   **The WebAssembly file is loaded into a browser and compiled to machine code.**

Both the WebAssembly binary file and the compiled object in the browser are referred to as *modules*. Although you can create an empty module, it won't be of much use, so most modules will have at least one function to do some sort of processing. A module's functions can be built-in, can be imported from other modules' exports, or can even be imported from JavaScript.

WebAssembly modules have several sections that Emscripten will populate based on your C or C++ code. Under the hood, sections start with a section ID followed by the section's size and then the content itself. Chapter 2 provides more information about module sections. All the sections are optional, which is why you can have an empty module.

The Start section points to the index of a function that's part of the module (not imported). The function referenced will be called automatically before any of the module's exports are callable by the JavaScript. If you include a main function in your C or C++ code, Emscripten will set it up as the module's start function.

A WebAssembly module receives memory to use from the host in the form of an ArrayBuffer. As far as the module is concerned, the buffer acts just like the heap in C or C++, but every time the module interacts with the memory, the WebAssembly framework verifies that the request is within the bounds of the array.

WebAssembly modules only support four data types:

- 32-bit integers
- 64-bit integers
- 32-bit floats
- 64-bit floats

Boolean values are represented using a 32-bit integer, where 0 is false and a nonzero value is true. All other values that are set by the host environment, such as strings, need to be represented in the module's linear memory.

WebAssembly files contain a binary bytecode designed not for humans to read but rather to be as efficient as possible so that it can be downloaded, compiled, and instantiated quickly. At the same time, WebAssembly modules aren't intended to be black boxes that developers can use to hide their code. WebAssembly has been designed with the web's openness in mind, so the WebAssembly binary format has an equivalent WebAssembly text format representation. We can see this text format by going into the browser's developer tools.

WebAssembly modules have several advantages:

- They're designed to be a compile target, which JavaScript wasn't designed for. This will allow improvements to be made to WebAssembly over time without impacting JavaScript.
- They're designed to be portable, meaning that they can also be used in places other than web browsers. Node.js is currently another place you can use WebAssembly modules.
- WebAssembly files use a binary format so that they are as compact as possible and can be transmitted and downloaded quickly.
- Files are structured to allow validation to happen in a single pass, which speeds up startup time.
- Using the latest WebAssembly JavaScript API functions, the file can be compiled to machine code as it's being downloaded so that it's ready to be used as soon as the download completes.
- Because of JavaScript's dynamic nature, code needs to be monitored several times before it gets compiled to machine code. WebAssembly bytecode, on the other hand, is compiled to machine code right away. The result is that the first call to a function is just as fast as the tenth call, for example.
- Because it's compiled ahead of time, the compiler can make optimizations to the code before it even reaches the browser.
- WebAssembly code runs almost as fast as native code. Because WebAssembly has checks to make sure the code is behaving properly, there's a slight performance reduction compared to running pure native code.

3.2.1 When would you not use a WebAssembly module?

Although WebAssembly has a lot of advantages, it's not the right choice in every case. JavaScript will be a better choice under certain circumstances:

- If the logic is simple, the extra work to set up a compiler toolchain and write something in another language might not be worth the effort.
- Although this issue is being worked on and will change, at the moment, WebAssembly modules don't have direct access to the *DOM* or any Web APIs.

DEFINITION The DOM, or Document Object Model, is an interface representing the various aspects of a web page, which gives JavaScript code a way to interact with the page.

3.3   *Emscripten output options*

You can create WebAssembly modules in several ways depending on your goals. You can instruct Emscripten to generate the WebAssembly module file and, depending on the options specified in the command line, Emscripten can also include a *JavaScript plumbing file* and an HTML file.

> **DEFINITION**   A JavaScript plumbing file is a JavaScript file that Emscripten generates. The file's contents can vary depending on the command-line arguments given. The file has code that will automatically download the WebAssembly file and have it compiled and instantiated in the browser. The JavaScript also contains numerous helper functions to make it easier for the host to talk with the module and vice versa.

You can use the three following approaches to create a module with Emscripten:

- *Ask Emscripten to generate the WebAssembly module, JavaScript plumbing file, and HTML template file.*

  Having Emscripten generate an HTML file isn't typical for production but is useful if you're learning about WebAssembly and want to focus on the compiling of C or C++ before digging into the details of what's involved with loading and instantiating a module. This method is also useful if you wish to experiment with portions of code as a way to debug or prototype things. With this approach, you can simply write the C or C++ code, compile it, and then open the generated HTML file in your browser to see the results.

- *Ask Emscripten to generate the WebAssembly module and the JavaScript plumbing file.*

  This is typically the approach used for production because you can add the generated JavaScript file to a new or existing HTML page simply by including a reference to the file. This JavaScript file will automatically download and have the module instantiated when the HTML page is loaded. The JavaScript file also has several helper functions to make the interactions between the module and your JavaScript easier.

  Both the HTML template approach and this approach will include any standard C library items in the module if your code uses them. If your code doesn't use a standard C library function, but you need it included in the module, you can use flags to tell Emscripten to include the functions that you need.

- *Ask that Emscripten generate only the WebAssembly module.*

  This approach is meant for *dynamically linking* two or more modules at runtime, but it can also be used to create a minimalist module that contains no standard C library support or JavaScript plumbing file.

> **DEFINITION**   This will be covered in more detail in chapters 7 and 8, but, for now, dynamic linking of WebAssembly modules is the process of joining two or more modules together at runtime, where the unresolved symbols in one module (a function, for example) resolve to symbols existing in another module.

If your code needs to pass anything more than integers or floats between the module and JavaScript, then it will need memory management. Unless you have a standard library equivalent to the `malloc` and `free` functions, I don't recommend this approach for this scenario. The module's linear memory is really an array buffer passed to the module during instantiation, so the memory issues won't affect the browser or your OS but could lead to bugs that are difficult to track down.

Aside from dynamic linking, this approach is useful for learning how to manually download, compile, and instantiate a module using the WebAssembly JavaScript API, which the Emscripten plumbing code does for you. Knowing what the WebAssembly JavaScript API functions do will make it easier to understand some examples you may find online.

Because Emscripten is not the only compiler available that can create WebAssembly modules (Rust has one, for example), you might, in the future, want to use a third-party module that doesn't have code to load itself. You may need to manually download and have a module instantiated at some point.

3.4 Compiling C or C++ with Emscripten and using the HTML template

Suppose you've been asked to write some logic that will determine what prime numbers exist in a certain number range. You could write the code using JavaScript, but you've read that one of the main areas where WebAssembly shines is with calculations, so you've decided to use WebAssembly for this project.

You'll need to integrate the project into an existing website, but you'll want to create the WebAssembly module first to verify that everything is working as expected before moving on. You'll create the logic using C and then compile it to a WebAssembly module using Emscripten. Conveniently, as figure 3.4 shows, Emscripten can generate the JavaScript needed to download and compile the WebAssembly module and can also create an HTML file from a template.

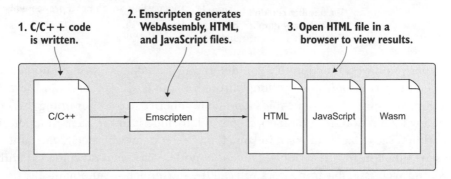

Figure 3.4   Emscripten generating the WebAssembly, JavaScript, and HTML files

The first thing you'll need to do is create a folder where you'll keep your files: WebAssembly\Chapter 3\3.4 html_template\.

> **NOTE**   This book has adopted the Windows convention for representing file separators. *Nix users will need to replace the \ characters with /.

As figure 3.5 shows, the first step of the process is to create the C or C++ code. Create a file called calculate_primes.c, and then open it. The first thing you'll need to do is include a header file for the standard C library, the C standard input and output library, and the Emscripten library:

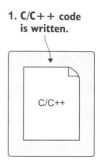

1. C/C++ code is written.

Figure 3.5   Step 1 is to create the C or C++ code.

```
#include <stdlib.h>
#include <stdio.h>
#include <emscripten.h>
```

The next step is to write a helper function called `IsPrime`, which will accept as a parameter an integer value that you'll check to see if it's a prime number. If it is, the function will return `1`. Otherwise, the function will return `0` (zero).

A prime number is any number that can only be divided evenly by 1 and itself. Other than 2, even numbers are never prime numbers, so the function can skip those. Also, since checking any number higher than the number's square root would be redundant, your code can skip those numbers too, which will make the logic a bit more efficient. Based on this, you can create the following function in the calculate_primes.c file:

```
int IsPrime(int value) {
  if (value == 2) { return 1; }                          <-- 2 is a prime number.
  if (value <= 1 || value % 2 == 0) { return 0; }        <-- 1 or less and even numbers
                                                             (other than 2) aren't primes.
  for (int i = 3; (i * i) <= value; i += 2) {            <-- Loops from 3 to the square root of
    if (value % i == 0) { return 0; }                        the value; only checks odd numbers
  }                                                      <-- The value can be divided evenly by the
                                                             loop value, so it's not a prime number.
  return 1;        <-- The number couldn't be divided
}                      evenly by any number you
                       checked. It's a prime number.
```

Now that you have a function that can determine if a value is a prime number or not, you need to write some code to loop through a range of numbers, call the `IsPrime` function, and output the value if it's a prime number. The code for doing this doesn't need any interaction from JavaScript, so you'll include it in the `main` function. When Emscripten sees a `main` function in your C or C++ code, it will specify this function as the start function for the module. Once the module has been downloaded and compiled, the WebAssembly framework will call the start function automatically.

You'll use the `printf` function in your `main` function to pass strings to Emscripten's JavaScript code. This code will then take the strings received and display them in the text box on the web page as well as in the console window of the browser's developer tools. In chapter 4, you'll write code in which the module will talk to JavaScript code, which will give you a better understanding of how the interaction with JavaScript works.

Following your `IsPrime` function, you can write the code shown in the following listing to loop from 3 to 100,000 to find out which of those numbers are prime numbers.

Listing 3.1   The `main` function in calculate_primes.c

```
...

int main() {
  int start = 3;
  int end = 100000;

  printf("Prime numbers between %d and %d:\n", start, end);

  for (int i = start; i <= end; i += 2) {
    if (IsPrime(i)) {
      printf("%d ", i);
    }
  }
  printf("\n");

  return 0;
}
```

Annotations:
- **Starts with an odd number to allow the following loop to be more efficient** (points to `int start = 3;`)
- **Tells the JavaScript code what the range is** (points to the `printf` line)
- **Loops through the range of numbers but only checks the odd numbers** (points to the `for` loop)
- **If the current value is a prime number, tells the JavaScript code the value** (points to `if (IsPrime(i))`)

Figure 3.6 shows the next step of the process, in which you'll ask the Emscripten compiler to take your C code and convert it into a WebAssembly module. In this case, you'll also want Emscripten to include the JavaScript plumbing file as well as the HTML template file.

To compile your C code into a WebAssembly module, you need to use the console window to run the `emcc` command, which is the Emscripten compiler. Rather than having to specify a file path for the files you want Emscripten to compile, it's easier if

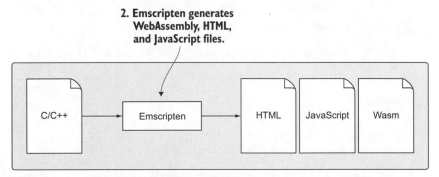

Figure 3.6   Emscripten is asked to compile the C code into a WebAssembly file to generate the JavaScript plumbing file and HTML file.

you navigate to the WebAssembly\Chapter 3\3.4 html_template\ folder. Open a console window, and navigate to this folder.

The cmcc command accepts a number of inputs and flags. Although their order doesn't matter, in general, you should include the input files first. In this case, you should place calculate_primes.c after emcc.

By default, if you don't include an output file name, Emscripten won't generate an HTML file and will instead generate a WebAssembly file with the name a.out.wasm and a JavaScript file with the name a.out.js. To specify an output file, you'll need to use the -o flag (hyphen and lowercase o) followed by the file name you want. To have Emscripten include the HTML template, you'll need to specify a file name with a .html extension.

Run the following command to generate the WebAssembly module, JavaScript plumbing file, and HTML template. Note that this might take a couple of minutes if this is your first time running the Emscripten compiler because it will also be creating some common resources for the compiler to reuse. These resources will be cached so that subsequent compiles will be much faster:

```
emcc calculate_primes.c -o html_template.html
```

> **MORE INFO**   There are several optimization flags available on Emscripten's website at https://emscripten.org/docs/optimizing/Optimizing-Code.html. Emscripten recommends starting out with no optimizations when you first port your code. Not specifying an optimization flag at the command line defaults to -O0 (capital O followed by zero). You should debug and fix any issues that might exist in your code before you start turning on optimizations. Depending on your needs, you would then adjust the optimization flags from -O0 to -O1, -O2, -Os, -Oz, and -O3.

If you look in the folder where you have the calculate_primes.c file, you should now see the three other files that are highlighted in figure 3.7.

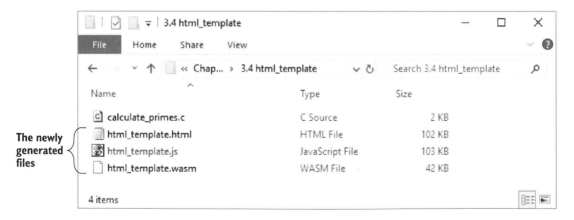

Figure 3.7   The newly generated HTML, JavaScript, and WebAssembly files

The html_template.wasm file is your WebAssembly module. The html_template.js file is the generated JavaScript file, and the third file is your HTML file, html_template .html.

As figure 3.8 shows, the final step of the process is to view the web page to verify that the WebAssembly module is behaving as expected.

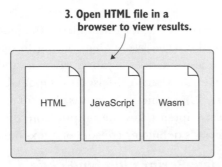

3. Open HTML file in a browser to view results.

HTML JavaScript Wasm

Figure 3.8   You can now open the HTML file in a web browser to view the results.

If you're using Python for your local web server, navigate to the WebAssembly\Chapter 3\3.4 html_template\ folder and start up the web server. Open a web browser, and type the following address into the address box (depending on your web server, you might not need the :8080 portion of the address):

```
http://localhost:8080/html_template.html
```

You should see the HTML page that was generated, as shown in figure 3.9.

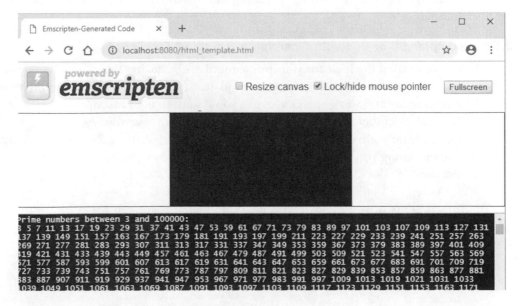

Figure 3.9   The HTML page running in Google Chrome

TIP   Python needs to be installed in order to install the Emscripten toolkit, which is convenient because Python can also run a local web server. If you wish to use a different web server for the examples in this book, you can, but you'll need to ensure that the WebAssembly *media type* is present. Instructions for how to start up a local web server using Python can be found in appendix A. The media type that browsers expect when loading a WebAssembly module is also mentioned in this appendix.

The HTML file created by Emscripten directs any `printf` output from the module to a text box so that you can see output on the page rather than having to open the browser's developer tools. The HTML file also includes a canvas element above the text box that allows for WebGL output. WebGL is an API based on OpenGL ES 2.0 that enables web content to render 2D and 3D graphics to a canvas element.

In a later chapter, you'll learn how Emscripten takes the output from the call to `printf` and directs that output to the browser's debugger console or a text box.

3.5   *Having Emscripten generate the JavaScript plumbing code*

Being able to ask Emscripten to include an HTML template file can be helpful if you want to try out code quickly or verify that the logic in a module is sound before moving on. When it comes to production code, however, you don't typically use the HTML template file. Instead, you ask Emscripten to compile your C or C++ code into a WebAssembly module and generate the JavaScript plumbing file. Then, you either create a new web page or edit an existing one and include a reference to the JavaScript file. Once the JavaScript file reference is part of the web page, when the page loads, the file will handle downloading and instantiating the WebAssembly module automatically.

3.5.1   *Compiling C or C++ with Emscripten-generated JavaScript*

You've verified the logic for your prime numbers by having Emscripten build the WebAssembly module with the HTML template. Now that the WebAssembly module's logic is ready and working as expected, you'll want to tell Emscripten to generate only the WebAssembly module and the JavaScript plumbing file. As figure 3.10 shows, you'll create your own HTML file and then reference the generated JavaScript file. The first thing you'll need to do is create a folder where you'll keep your files for this section: WebAssembly\Chapter 3\3.5 js_plumbing\.

As figure 3.11 shows, the first step is creating the C or C++ code. Listing 3.2 shows the contents of the calculate_primes.c file that you created for use with the HTML template. Copy this file to your 3.5 js_plumbing folder.

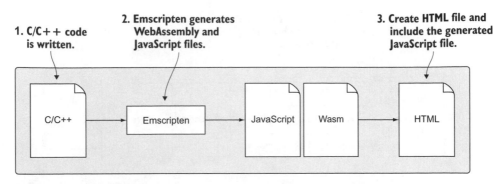

1. C/C++ code is written.

2. Emscripten generates WebAssembly and JavaScript files.

3. Create HTML file and include the generated JavaScript file.

Figure 3.10 Emscripten is asked to generate the WebAssembly and JavaScript plumbing files. You then create the HTML file and include a reference to the generated JavaScript file.

Listing 3.2   Code in calculate_primes.c

```c
#include <stdlib.h>
#include <stdio.h>
#include <emscripten.h>

int IsPrime(int value) {
  if (value == 2) { return 1; }
  if (value <= 1 || value % 2 == 0) { return 0; }

  for (int i = 3; (i * i) <= value; i += 2) {
    if (value % i == 0) { return 0; }
  }

  return 1;
}

int main() {
  int start = 3;
  int end = 100000;

  printf("Prime numbers between %d and %d:\n", start, end);

  for (int i = start; i <= end; i += 2) {
    if (IsPrime(i)) {
      printf("%d ", i);
    }
  }
  printf("\n");

  return 0;
}
```

1. C/C++ code is written.

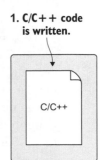

Figure 3.11   Step 1 is to create the C or C++ code.

Now that you have your new C file, figure 3.12 shows the next step of the process, in which you'll ask the Emscripten compiler to take your C code and convert it into a

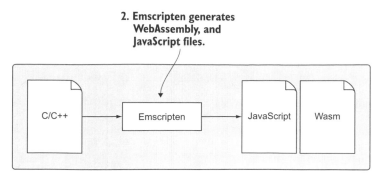

Figure 3.12   Emscripten is asked to compile the C code into a WebAssembly file and to generate the JavaScript plumbing file.

WebAssembly module. You'll also want Emscripten to include the JavaScript plumbing file but not the HTML template file.

To compile your C code into a WebAssembly module, you'll need to open a console window and navigate to the WebAssembly\Chapter 3\3.5 js_plumbing\ folder. The command to use here is similar to the one that you used when asking for the HTML template to be included. In this case, you want only the WebAssembly and JavaScript files generated. You don't want the HTML file, so you'll need to modify the output file name to have a .js extension rather than a .html extension. Run the following command to have Emscripten build the WebAssembly module and JavaScript file:

```
emcc calculate_primes.c -o js_plumbing.js
```

If you look in the folder where you copied the calculate_primes.c file, you should now see two new files, pointed out in figure 3.13.

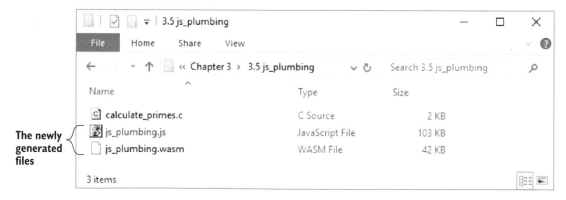

Figure 3.13   The newly generated JavaScript and WebAssembly files

Now that you have the WebAssembly module and generated JavaScript file, figure 3.14 shows the next step, in which you'll create an HTML file and include the generated JavaScript file. The JavaScript file that Emscripten generated handles the loading and instantiation of the WebAssembly module, so simply including a reference to that file in an HTML page is all you need to gain access to the module's features.

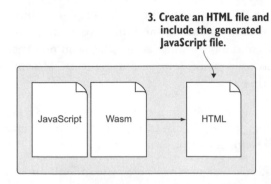

3. Create an HTML file and include the generated JavaScript file.

Figure 3.14   An HTML file is modified, or a new one is created, to reference the generated JavaScript file.

3.5.2   Creating a basic HTML web page for use in browsers

For developers who may be strong with languages like C or C++ but have never really worked with HTML pages, I'll briefly introduce the elements of an HTML page, which you'll build in a moment to use for your examples in this chapter. If you already understand the basics of HTML pages, you can skip ahead to the next section, "Creating your HTML page."

HTML BASICS

The first thing every HTML page needs is a DocType declaration that tells the browser which version of HTML is being used. HTML 5 is the latest version and the one you'll want to use, so the DocType for HTML 5 is written as <!DOCTYPE html>.

   For the most part, HTML is a series of tags similar to XML. XML is used to describe data, whereas HTML is used to describe presentation. HTML tags are similar to the DocType declaration just mentioned and usually consist of opening and closing tags surrounding content that can also include other tags.

   After the DocType declaration, an HTML page starts with an html tag, which holds all the page content. Within the html tags are the head and body tags.

   The head tag is where you can include metadata about the page, like a title or the file's character encoding. The character encoding that's typically used for HTML files is UTF-8, but you can also use other encodings. You can also include link tags in the head tag to include references to files for things like the styles to use for the look of the page content.

   The body tag is where you place all the content for the page. As with the head tag, the body tag can also include file references.

Script tags are used to include JavaScript code by including an src attribute, which tells the browser where to find a code file. This is still in the works, but browser makers want to allow WebAssembly modules to be included in a web page by simply including a script tag in the page, similar to <script type="module">.

Script tags can be placed in either the head or body tag, but, until recently, it was considered best practice to place script tags at the end of the body tag. This was because the browser would pause DOM construction until the script was downloaded, and a web page felt more responsive if it showed something before the pause rather than showing a white screen briefly at the beginning. Script tags can now include an async attribute, which tells the browser to continue building the DOM while downloading the script file at the same time.

> **MORE INFO**   The following web page explains in more detail why script tags were recommended at the end of the body tag: Ilya Grigorik, "Adding Interactivity with JavaScript," Google Developers, http://mng.bz/xld7.

The browser doesn't need the whitespace in an HTML file. The indents and linefeeds in an HTML file are optional and are included for readability.

CREATING YOUR HTML PAGE

The following HTML (listing 3.3) is a basic web page for your WebAssembly file, which you should place in the WebAssembly\Chapter 3\3.5 js plumbing\ folder and name js_plumbing.html. The web page in this listing simply includes a reference to the JavaScript file that Emscripten generated. Because the JavaScript file handles the loading and instantiation of the WebAssembly module for you, all you have to do is include a reference to the file.

Listing 3.3   The HTML for js_plumbing.html

```
<!DOCTYPE html>
<html>
  <head>
    <meta charset="utf-8"/>
  </head>
  <body>
    HTML page I created for my WebAssembly module.

    <script src="js_plumbing.js"></script>        ⟵──┐  The JavaScript file handles
  </body>                                              loading and instantiating the
</html>                                                WebAssembly module for you.
```

VIEWING YOUR HTML PAGE

If you open a web browser and type the following into the address box, you should see a page displayed similar to the one in figure 3.15:

```
http://localhost:8080/js_plumbing.html
```

Figure 3.15   The HTML page that you created, running in Google Chrome

While looking at the web page in the browser, you might be asking yourself, where's the text showing all the prime numbers that I saw when I used the HTML template approach in section 3.4?

When you asked Emscripten to generate the HTML template in section 3.4, Emscripten placed all the `printf` output into a text box on the web page; but, by default, it directs all such output to the console of the browser's developer tools. To display these tools, press F12.

Each browser's developer tools are a bit different, but they all have a way to view console output. As you can see in figure 3.16, the text from the `printf` call in your module is being output to the console window in the browser's developer tools.

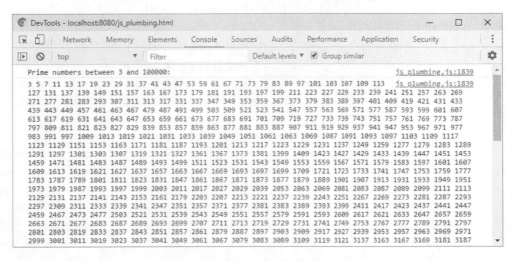

Figure 3.16   The console window in Google Chrome's developer tools showing the list of prime numbers

3.6   Having Emscripten generate only the WebAssembly file

Figure 3.17 shows the third scenario that we're going to cover when creating a Web-Assembly module with Emscripten. Here, you'll ask Emscripten to only compile your C or C++ code to WebAssembly and to not generate any other files. In this case, you'll not only have to create an HTML file, but you'll also have to write the JavaScript code necessary to download and instantiate the module.

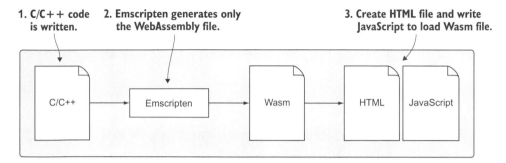

Figure 3.17   Emscripten being requested to generate only the WebAssembly file. You then create the necessary HTML and JavaScript code to download and instantiate the module.

You can create a WebAssembly module this way by telling Emscripten that you want to create a side module. A side module is actually intended for use with dynamic linking in which multiple modules can be downloaded and then linked together at runtime to work as one unit. This is similar to dependent libraries in other languages. We'll talk about dynamic linking later in the book; for this scenario, we're not asking for a side module to do dynamic linking. You'll be asking Emscripten to create a side module because, when you do, Emscripten doesn't include any of the standard C library functions with your code in the WebAssembly module, and it doesn't create a Java-Script plumbing file.

You might want to create a side module for several reasons:

- You wish to implement dynamic linking in which multiple modules will be downloaded and linked together at runtime. In this case, one of your modules will be compiled as a main module and will have the standard C library functions. I explain the differences between main modules and side modules in chapter 7, when you'll dig into dynamic linking, but both side modules and main modules fall into the three scenarios that you're looking at in this chapter.
- The logic in your module doesn't need the standard C library. Be careful here because if you're passing anything other than an integer or float between the JavaScript code and the module, memory management is needed, which will require some form of the standard C library functions `malloc` and `free`. Memory management issues will impact only your module, given that the module's

memory is only an array buffer passed to it by JavaScript, but the bugs that can arise may prove difficult to track down.

- You wish to learn how to download the module and have it compiled and instantiated by the browser, which is a useful skill to have, given that Emscripten isn't the only compiler that creates WebAssembly modules. Several examples on the internet show modules being loaded manually, so being able to create a module that you can load manually is helpful if you wish to follow along. There is also a chance that, at some point in the future, you'll want to work with a third-party module that has no JavaScript plumbing file.

3.6.1   *Compiling C or C++ as a side module with Emscripten*

As figure 3.18 shows, your first step will be to create some C code. Create a folder where you'll keep your files for this section: Web-Assembly\Chapter 3\3.6 side_module\.

1. C/C++ code is written.

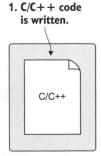

Because your C code won't have access to the printf function, you'll need a simple C file as a replacement for the examples used so far. You're going to build a function called Increment that accepts an integer, adds 1 to the value received, and then returns the result to the caller. In this case, the caller will be a JavaScript function. Place the following code into a file called side_module.c:

```
int Increment(int value) {
  return (value + 1);
}
```

Figure 3.18   Step 1 is to create the C or C++ code.

Now that you have your C code, you can move on to the next step, which is to ask Emscripten to generate only the WebAssembly file, as figure 3.19 shows. To compile the code as a side module, you'll need to include the -s SIDE_MODULE=2 flag as part of the emcc command line. The -s SIDE_MODULE=2 flag tells Emscripten that you don't want things like the standard C library functions included in the module or the Java-Script plumbing file generated.

You'll also need to include the -O1 optimization flag (capital letter O and the number 1). If you don't specify an optimization flag, Emscripten will use the default -O0 (capital letter O and the number 0), which indicates to not do any optimizations. Not

2. Emscripten generates only the WebAssembly file.

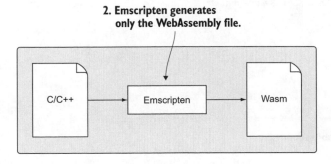

Figure 3.19   Have Emscripten generate only the WebAssembly file.

including any optimizations in this scenario will cause link errors to be thrown if you try to load your module—the module is expecting several functions and global variables, but your code won't be providing them. Adding any optimization flag other than -O0 will fix the issue by removing the extra imports, so you go with the next optimization flag level of -O1. (The letter O is case-sensitive and must be uppercase.)

You need to specify that you want your Increment function exported so that it can be called by JavaScript code. To indicate this to the Emscripten compiler, you can include the function's name in the -s EXPORTED_FUNCTIONS command-line array. Emscripten adds an underscore character in front of the functions when it generates the WebAssembly file, so you'll need to include the underscore character when including the function name in the exported array: _Increment.

> **TIP** In this case, you need to specify only one function in the EXPORTED_
> FUNCTIONS command-line array. If you need to specify multiple functions,
> don't include a space in between the comma and the next function, or you'll
> receive a compilation error. If you do want to include a space between the
> function names, you need to wrap the command-line array in double quotes,
> as follows: -s "EXPORTED_FUNCTIONS=['_Increment', '_Decrement']".

Finally, the output file that you specify needs to have the .wasm extension. In your first scenario, you specified an HTML file, and in your second, you specified a JavaScript file. In this case, you specify a WebAssembly file. If you don't specify a file name, Emscripten will create a file with the name a.out.wasm.

You can compile your Increment code into a WebAssembly module by opening a command-line window, navigating to the folder where you saved your C file, and then running the following command:

```
emcc side_module.c -s SIDE_MODULE=2 -O1
    -s EXPORTED_FUNCTIONS=['_Increment'] -o side_module.wasm
```

If you look in the folder where you have the side_module.c file, you should now see just the one new file that's highlighted in figure 3.20.

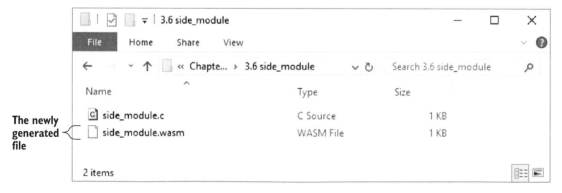

The newly generated file

Figure 3.20   The newly generated WebAssembly file

3.6.2 *Loading and instantiating in a browser*

Now that you know how to create the Wasm file itself, you need to create an HTML file and write the JavaScript code to request this file from the server and have the module instantiated.

PROMISES AND ARROW FUNCTION EXPRESSIONS

When working with many of the JavaScript functions that we're about to cover, the functions typically operate asynchronously through the use of promises. When you call an asynchronous function, it will return a `Promise` object that will be called later when the action either is fulfilled (succeeded) or was rejected (there was an error).

The `Promise` object has a `then` method, which accepts two parameters that are callback functions. The first parameter will be called when the action is fulfilled and the second if the action was rejected.

With the following example, I include both a function to call when the request is fulfilled and one to call if there is an error:

```
asyncFunctionCall.then(onFulfilled, onRejected);  ◁─┐
```
Passes in callback functions to be called when the promise is fulfilled or rejected

Both the fulfilled and rejected functions accept a single parameter. The function that calls the fulfilled function can pass any data it wants for the fulfillment parameter value. The rejected parameter value is a string containing the rejected reason.

In the previous example, you passed in function pointers to be called when the `then` method is fulfilled or rejected. Rather than having a separate function somewhere else in the code, you can always create anonymous functions, as in the following example:

```
asyncFunctionCall.then(function(result) {   ◁─┐
    ...
}, function(reason) {   ◁─┐
    ...
});
```
An anonymous function for if the promise is fulfilled
An anonymous function for if the promise is rejected

Often when working with promises, you'll see this taken a bit further using arrow function expressions, which have a shorter syntax compared to normal functions, as in the following example:

```
asyncFunctionCall.then((result) => {   ◁─┐
    ...
}, (reason) => {   ◁─┐
    ...
});
```
Using an arrow function expression for the fulfilled function
Using an arrow function expression for the rejected function

When there is only the one parameter, the parentheses are optional. For example, the `(result) => {}` function could be written as `result => {}`. If there are no parameters, then parentheses are used: `() => {}`.

For the body of the arrow function expression, if a return value is expected and curly braces are used, then an explicit return statement is required:

```
(value1, value2) => { return value1 + value2 }
```

If the body of the arrow function expression is wrapped in parentheses or nothing at all, then there is an implicit return, as follows:

```
(value1, value2) => value1 + value2
```

If you're interested only in finding out if the action was fulfilled, you don't have to specify the second parameter in the then method for the rejection.

If, on the other hand, you have an action in which you're interested only if there was an issue, you can specify null for the first parameter and then a callback for the rejection. Typically, however, if you're interested only if there was an error, you'd use the catch method. This method accepts one parameter, a callback function that will be called if the action was rejected.

Both the then and catch methods return promises, which allows several asynchronous operations to be chained together. This makes working with several asynchronous operations that are dependent on each other much easier because the next then method will be called only once the one before it is fulfilled:

```
asyncFunctionCall.then(result =>
  asyncFunctionCall2()        ◁————————  asyncFunctionCall2 also
).then(result => {                       returns a promise.

}).catch((err) => {           ◁————————  asyncFunctionCall2 fulfilled

});                           ◁————————  One of the calls in the chain was
                                         rejected. Log or display the error.
```

JAVASCRIPT OBJECT SHORTHAND

Some functions that you'll be using in upcoming examples accept objects as parameters. You can create an object in JavaScript using new Object(), but there is also a shorthand way of creating objects using curly braces, as in the following example, which creates an empty object:

```
const person = {};
```

Within the object, you can include name/value pairs, with each pair separated by a comma. The name/value pair itself is separated by a colon, and the value can be a string, number, object, array, true, false, or null. String values are wrapped in single or double quotes. The following is an example of a name/value pair:

```
age: 21
```

Creating objects in this manner makes things easier because the object can be declared and initialized in one step. Once you've defined the JavaScript object, you can access the properties using dot notation, as follows:

```
const person = { name: "Sam Smith", age: 21 };
console.log("The person's name is: " + person.name);
```

AN OVERVIEW OF THE WEBASSEMBLY JAVASCRIPT API

Browsers that support WebAssembly have something known as the WebAssembly JavaScript API. This API is a WebAssembly namespace with several functions and objects that are used to compile and instantiate a module; interact with aspects of the module, like its memory, to pass strings back and forth between the module and Java-Script, for example; and handle error conditions.

When using Emscripten's generated JavaScript file, it handles the process of down-loading the WebAssembly file for you. It then interacts with the WebAssembly Java-Script API to have the WebAssembly module compiled and instantiated.

In this section, you'll see how the API is used so that you can interact with it to manually load the WebAssembly module that you built in section 3.6.1.

> **INFO** Most modern desktop and mobile browsers, including Edge, Firefox, Chrome, Safari, and Opera, support WebAssembly. You can view a detailed list at the following website: https://caniuse.com/#search=WebAssembly.

Before you can do anything with a WebAssembly module, you need to first ask for the WebAssembly file to be downloaded. To request the file, you'll use the `fetch` Java-Script method. This method lets JavaScript make HTTP-related calls asynchronously. If you only need to pull data, rather than pass data to the server, for example, then you need to specify only the first parameter, which is the URI of the file you want to download, and the `fetch` method will return a `Promise` object. For example, if the Wasm file is sitting in the same folder on the server where the HTML file was down-loaded from, then you will only need to specify the file name for the URI, as follows:

```
fetch("side_module.wasm")
```

The `fetch` method accepts a JavaScript object as an optional second parameter to control numerous settings in relation to the request, such as the content type of the data if you're passing data to the server. For this book, you won't be using the optional second parameter, referred to as `init`, but if you need to know the details of the `init` object, they are available on the MDN Web Docs site at http://mng.bz/ANle.

Once you've fetched the WebAssembly file, you need a way to compile and then instantiate it; for this, the `WebAssembly.instantiateStreaming` function is the recom-mended approach because the module gets compiled to machine code as the byte-code is being downloaded by the `fetch` method. Compiling the module as it's being downloaded speeds up load time because the module is ready to be instantiated as soon as it finishes downloading.

The `instantiateStreaming` function accepts two parameters. The first is a `Response` object, or a `Promise` object that will fulfill with a `Response` object, represent-ing the source of a Wasm file. Because the `fetch` method returns a `Response` object, you can simply include the method call as the first parameter of `instantiateStream-ing`. The second parameter is an optional JavaScript object, which we'll discuss shortly, in which you pass the module any data that it's expecting, such as imported functions or global variables.

The `instantiateStreaming` function returns a `Promise` object that, if fulfilled, will hold a `module` property and an `instance` property. The `module` property is a `WebAssembly.Module` object, and the `instance` property is a `WebAssembly.Instance` object. The `instance` property is the object that we're interested in because it holds an `exports` property, which contains all the items the module exports.

The following is an example of using the `WebAssembly.instantiateStreaming` function to load the module you created in section 3.6.1:

The Promise object from the fetch call is passed as the first parameter.
The instance object is where you can access the exported function.

```
WebAssembly.instantiateStreaming(fetch("side_module.wasm"),
  importObject).then(result => {
  const value = result.instance.exports._Increment(17);    <───
  console.log(value.toString());
});
```

The `instantiateStreaming` function was added to browsers after the WebAssembly MVP was first released, so there's a chance that some browsers that support WebAssembly won't support `instantiateStreaming`. It's best to use feature detection to check and see if `instantiateStreaming` is available before trying to use it. At the end of this chapter, section 3.7 shows you how to test to see if this function is available. If it's not, you should use the older `WebAssembly.instantiate` function.

> **TIP** MDN Web Docs (formerly the Mozilla Developer Network) has an article about the `instantiateStreaming` function and includes an up-to-date browser compatibility table toward the bottom of the page: http://mng .bz/ZeoN.

As when calling `instantiateStreaming`, with the `instantiate` function, you can also use `fetch` to download the contents of the WebAssembly file. But, unlike with `instantiateStreaming`, you can't pass the `Promise` object directly into the `instantiate` function. Instead, you need to wait for the `fetch` request to be fulfilled, convert the data into an ArrayBuffer, and then pass that ArrayBuffer into the `instantiate` function. As with the `instantiateStreaming` function, the `instantiate` function also accepts an optional second parameter JavaScript object for the module's imports.

The following is an example of using the `WebAssembly.instantiate` function:

Passes the ArrayBuffer to the instantiate function

```
fetch("side_module.wasm").then(response =>     <───
  response.arrayBuffer()                  <───
).then(bytes =>
  WebAssembly.instantiate(bytes, importObject)
).then(result => {
  const value = result.instance.exports._Increment(17);   <───
  console.log(value.toString());
});
```

Asks for the WebAssembly file to be downloaded

Asks for the file's data to be turned into an ArrayBuffer

You now have access to the instantiated module: result.instance.

In chapter 9, you'll work with just a compiled module (not instantiated) by passing it from a web worker. You'll also work with the `WebAssembly.compileStreaming` and `WebAssembly.compile` functions at that time. For now, the `compileStreaming` and `compile` functions work the same as the `instantiateStreaming` and `instantiate` functions but only return the compiled module.

Note that there is a `WebAssembly.Module` function that can compile a module and a `WebAssembly.Instance` function to instantiate a compiled module, but these two functions aren't recommended because the calls are synchronous. The `instantiate-Streaming`, `instantiate`, `compileStreaming`, and `compile` functions are asynchronous and are the recommended functions to use instead.

As mentioned earlier, the optional JavaScript object (often called `importObject`) can be passed as a second parameter to the `instantiateStreaming` and `instantiate` functions to provide the module with anything it needs to import. This object can include memory, a table, global variables, or function references. You'll work with these imports as you work with the various examples throughout this book.

WebAssembly modules can include a Memory section that indicates how many pages of memory it would like initially and, optionally, the maximum number of pages it would like. Each page of memory holds 65,536 bytes or 64 KB. If the module indicates that the memory needs to be imported, then it's up to your JavaScript code to provide it as part of the `importObject` that gets passed to the `instantiateStreaming` or `instantiate` function.

> **MORE INFO** One WebAssembly security feature is that the module can't allocate its own memory or resize it directly. Instead, the memory used by WebAssembly modules is provided by the host in the form of a resizable ArrayBuffer when the module is instantiated.

To pass memory to the module, the first thing that you need to do is create an instance of the `WebAssembly.Memory` object to include as part of the `importObject`. The `WebAssembly.Memory` object accepts a JavaScript object as part of its constructor. The first property of the JavaScript object is `initial`, which indicates how many pages of memory should be initially allocated for the module. The JavaScript object can optionally include a `maximum` property, which indicates the maximum number of pages a WebAssembly's memory is allowed to grow. You'll see more details about growing memory later.

The following is an example of how you create a `WebAssembly.Memory` object and pass it to a module:

```
const importObject = {
  env: {
    memory: new WebAssembly.Memory({initial: 1, maximum: 10})    ◁──────┐
  }                                            One page of memory initially
};                                             and only allowed to grow to a
                                                    maximum of 10 pages
WebAssembly.instantiateStreaming(fetch("test.wasm"),
  ➡ importObject).then(result => { ... });
```

CREATING THE JAVASCRIPT TO FETCH AND INSTANTIATE THE MODULE

You're going to write some JavaScript code to load in the side_module.wasm file that you created in section 3.6.1, and you'll use the `WebAssembly.instantiateStreaming` function. In section 3.6.1, you asked Emscripten to create the module as a side module so that Emscripten wouldn't include any of the standard C library functions in the Wasm file and wouldn't create a JavaScript plumbing file. Although we don't intend to use it this way in this chapter, because the side module approach with Emscripten is really intended for dynamically linking two or more modules together at runtime, Emscripten adds imports to the module that you'll need to provide when you call `instantiateStreaming`.

You'll need to define a JavaScript object, which you'll call `importObject`, that has a child object called `env`, which in turn contains a `__memory_base` property that the module wants to import. This `__memory_base` property will simply hold a value of zero because you won't be dynamically linking this module.

Once you have your `importObject` created, you can call the `instantiateStreaming` function, passing in the result of the `fetch` method for the Wasm file as the first parameter and the `importObject` as the second parameter. The `instantiateStreaming` function returns a promise, so you'll set up a handler for the success callback, which will be called once the module has been downloaded, compiled, and instantiated. At that point, you can access the exported elements of the WebAssembly module instance and call your `_Increment` function, passing in a value of 17. Your `_Increment` function takes the value that's passed in, adds 1 to it, and returns the new value. The `console.log` call that you'll include will output the result to the browser's console window and display the number 18 in this case.

The following is the JavaScript code that's needed to load and instantiate your module.

Listing 3.4   The JavaScript to load and instantiate side_module.wasm

```
const importObject = {
  env: {
    __memory_base: 0,
  }
};

WebAssembly.instantiateStreaming(fetch("side_module.wasm"),
  importObject).then(result => {
  const value = result.instance.exports._Increment(17);
  console.log(value.toString());
});
```

CREATING A BASIC HTML PAGE

In your Chapter 3\3.6 side_module\ folder, create a side_module.html file, and then open it with your favorite editor. As you can see in listing 3.5, the HTML that you're going to use to load the WebAssembly file is almost identical to what you used in the js_plumbing.html file in section 3.5.2, except that here, rather than referencing a JavaScript file, you're going to take the JavaScript code that you wrote in listing 3.4 and add it to the script block in listing 3.5.

Listing 3.5   An HTML page for the WebAssembly module named side_module.html

```html
<!DOCTYPE html>
<html>
  <head>
    <meta charset="utf-8"/>
  </head>
  <body>
    HTML page I created for my WebAssembly module.

    <script>
      const importObject = {
        env: {
          __memory_base: 0,
        }
      };

      WebAssembly.instantiateStreaming(fetch("side_module.wasm"),
        importObject).then(result => {
        const value = result.instance.exports._Increment(17);
        console.log(value.toString());
      });
    </script>
  </body>
</html>
```

Open a web browser and type `http://localhost:8080/side_module.html` into the address box. Then press F12 to open the browser's developer tools to see that the HTML page that you just created output the number 18, as figure 3.21 shows.

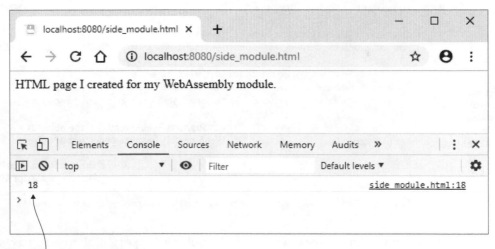

The result of passing 17 to the
module's `Increment` function

Figure 3.21   The HTML page that you created, showing the result of the call to the `Increment` function

3.7 *Feature detection: How to test if WebAssembly is available*

With new technologies, some browser vendors will sometimes implement a feature before other browser vendors. Not everybody upgrades their browsers to the latest version as frequently as we'd like, either, so even if the user is using a browser from a vendor that has implemented a feature, they might not be using a version of the browser that supports this feature. If there's a chance that your users will be using a browser where a feature you need won't exist, then it's considered best practice to check for the feature before trying to use it.

WebAssembly is a new enough technology that not all browsers—or all versions of Node.js—currently in use support it. It's also possible that a browser may support WebAssembly but not allow the module you request to be loaded and instantiated due to security checks with things like Content Security Policy (CSP), which is an added layer of security to try to prevent things like cross-site scripting (XSS) and data injection attacks. Because of this, simply checking if the WebAssembly JavaScript object exists isn't enough. The following function can be used to detect if the browser or Node.js supports WebAssembly.

Listing 3.6 JavaScript to test if WebAssembly is supported

Wraps in a try/catch just in case a CompileError or LinkError is thrown

Checks to see that the WebAssembly JavaScript API object exists

Compiles a minimal module with just the magic number ('\0asm') and version (1)

Checks whether the result is a WebAssembly .Module JavaScript API object

WebAssembly isn't supported.

Supports WebAssembly if the object is a WebAssembly.Instance JavaScript API object

If the result is a WebAssembly .Module JavaScript API object

```javascript
function isWebAssemblySupported() {
  try {
    if (typeof WebAssembly === "object") {
      const module = new WebAssembly.Module(new Uint8Array([0x00, 0x61,
        0x73, 0x6D, 0x01, 0x00, 0x00, 0x00]));
      if (module instanceof WebAssembly.Module) {
        const moduleInstance = new WebAssembly.Instance(module);
        return (moduleInstance instanceof WebAssembly.Instance);
      }
    }
  } catch (err) {}

  return false;
}

console.log((isWebAssemblySupported() ? "WebAssembly is supported":
  "WebAssembly is not supported"));
```

Now that you know how to test if WebAssembly is supported, there's still a chance that the browser or Node.js won't support the latest feature. For example, `WebAssembly.instantiateStreaming` is a new JavaScript function that can be used instead of the `WebAssembly.instantiate` function, but `instantiateStreaming` was created after the MVP was released. As a result, the `instantiateStreaming` function might not exist in every browser that supports WebAssembly. To test to see if a JavaScript function exists, you can do the following:

```
if (typeof WebAssembly.instantiateStreaming === "function") {
  console.log("You can use the WebAssembly.instantiateStreaming
➥ function");
} else {
  console.log("The WebAssembly.instantiateStreaming function is not
➥ available. You need to use WebAssembly.instantiate instead.");
}
```

When it comes to feature detection, you generally test for the function you want to use first and fall back to alternatives if the function isn't available. In our case, `instantiateStreaming` is preferred because it compiles the code as the module is being downloaded; but if it's not available, then `instantiate` will still work. The `instantiate` function just doesn't have the same performance improvements that `instantiateStreaming` does.

Now: how can you use what you learned in this chapter in the real world?

Real-world use cases

The following are some possible use cases for what you've learned in this chapter:

- You can use Emscripten's HTML Template output option to quickly create proof-of-concept code or test out a WebAssembly feature independently of your web page. Using the `printf` function, you can output information to the text box on the web page and the console of the browser's developer tools to verify that things are working as expected. Once you have the code working in a test environment, you can implement it in your main code base.
- You can use the WebAssembly JavaScript API to do feature detection to determine if WebAssembly is supported.
- Other examples include a calculator or a unit converter (Celsius to Fahrenheit or centimeters to inches, for example).

Exercises

You can find the solutions to these exercises in appendix D.

1 Which four data types does WebAssembly support?
2 Add a `Decrement` function to the side module you created in section 3.6.1.
   a The function should have an integer return value and an integer parameter. Subtract 1 from the value received, and return the result to the calling function.
   b Compile the side module, and then adjust the JavaScript to call the function and display the result to the console

Summary

As you saw in this chapter, the Emscripten toolkit uses the LLVM compiler toolchain to convert C or C++ code into an LLVM IR. Emscripten then converts the LLVM IR into WebAssembly bytecode. WebAssembly-supported browsers load the WebAssembly file, and, if everything checks out, the bytecode gets compiled the rest of the way into the device's machine code.

The Emscripten toolkit gives you flexibility depending on your needs, allowing you to create modules in several different ways:

- You can create a module but also have the HTML and JavaScript files generated for you. This is a useful approach when someone wants to learn about creating WebAssembly modules before having to learn about the HTML and JavaScript side of things. It's also useful when you need to test something quickly and not have to create the HTML and JavaScript as well.

- You can create a module and also have the JavaScript file generated for you. Here, you are responsible for creating your own HTML file. This gives you the flexibility to either create a new custom HTML page or simply add the generated JavaScript file reference to an existing web page. This would be the typical method used for production code.

- Finally, you can create only the module. Here you're responsible for creating your own HTML file as well as the JavaScript needed to download and instantiate the module. This approach can be useful in learning the details surrounding the WebAssembly JavaScript API.

Part 2

Working with modules

Now that you know what WebAssembly is, and have been introduced to the Emscripten toolkit, this part of the book will guide you through creating WebAssembly modules that your JavaScript code can interact with and vice versa.

In chapter 4, you'll learn how to take an existing C or C++ codebase and adjust it so that it can also be compiled into a WebAssembly module. You'll learn how to interact with your new module from your web page's JavaScript.

Chapter 5 teaches you how to adjust the code from chapter 4 so that the WebAssembly module can call into your web page's JavaScript.

Chapter 6 takes calling into the JavaScript code of your web page to another level by passing JavaScript function pointers to the WebAssembly module. This allows your JavaScript to specify functions on demand and take advantage of JavaScript promises.

Reusing your existing C++ codebase

This chapter covers

- Adjusting a C++ codebase so that it can also be compiled by Emscripten
- Exporting WebAssembly functions so that they can be called by JavaScript
- Calling a WebAssembly function using Emscripten helper functions
- Passing strings and arrays to the WebAssembly module via the module's memory

Typically, when people talk about the advantages of WebAssembly, it's from the standpoint of performance. But WebAssembly brings another advantage to the table—code reuse. Rather than writing the same logic multiple times for each target environment (desktop, website, and others), WebAssembly lets you reuse the same code in multiple locations.

Imagine a scenario in which a company already has a desktop point-of-sale application written in C++ but wants to add an online solution. The company

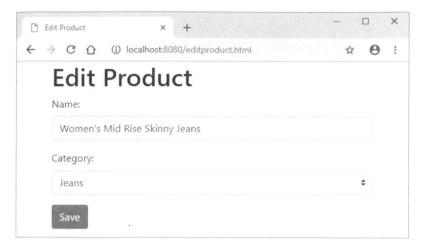

Figure 4.1   The Edit Product page that you'll be building

decides that the first part of the website it should build is the Edit Product web page shown in figure 4.1. The new website will also use Node.js for the server-side logic, but I'll leave the discussion of working with Node.js for a later chapter.

Because the company has existing C++ code, it would like to take advantage of WebAssembly to extend its validation code to both the browser and Node.js. This will ensure that all three locations are validating the data in the exact same way, all while using a single codebase, which makes maintainability easier. As figure 4.2 shows, the steps for building this website and incorporating the validation logic are as follows:

1   Modify the C++ code so that it can be compiled by Emscripten.
2   Ask Emscripten to generate the WebAssembly and JavaScript plumbing files.
3   Create the web page and then write the JavaScript code necessary to interact with the WebAssembly module.

Why would you want to validate the user's input twice? Why not skip validation in the browser and just validate the data on the server? You want to validate the data in the browser first, rather than just on the server, for a few reasons:

- Mainly, the user may not be physically near the server. The farther away they are, the longer it takes for the data to reach the server and for a response to be returned. If the user is on the other side of the world, this delay is noticeable, so validating what you can in the browser makes the website more responsive for the user.
- Validating as much as you can in the browser also reduces the amount of work the server needs to do. If the server doesn't have to respond as often per user, it can handle more users at once.

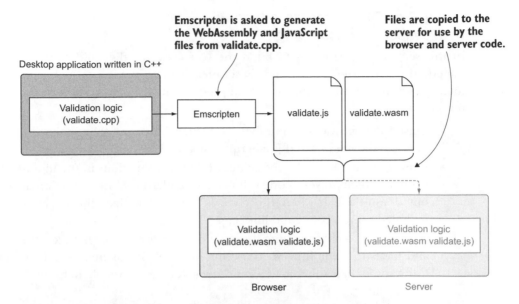

Figure 4.2 The steps needed to turn the existing C++ logic into a WebAssembly module for use in a browser and by the server-side code. I discuss the server aspect, Node.js, in a later chapter.

As helpful as it is to validate user data in the browser, you can't assume that the data is perfect when it reaches the server; there are ways to get around the browser's validation checks. You don't want to risk adding bad data to a database—whether submitted inadvertently or intentionally by the user. Regardless of how good the validation is in the browser, the server-side code must always validate the data it receives.

Figure 4.3 shows how the validation will work in the web page that you're about to build. When the user enters some information and then clicks the Save button, validation checks will be performed to ensure the data is as expected. If there's an issue with the data, the web page will display an error message. Once the issue is corrected, the user can click the Save button again. If there are no issues with the data, then the information will be passed to the server.

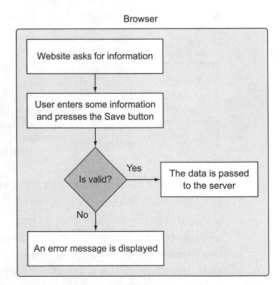

Figure 4.3 How validation will work in the browser

4.1   Using C or C++ to create a module with Emscripten plumbing

In this section, you're going to build the C++ code for the validation logic; you'll include the standard C library and Emscripten helper functions, which is the recommended way to build a module for use in production. This approach is recommended for a few reasons:

- Emscripten provides a number of helper functions that make interactions between the module and JavaScript easier.
- Emscripten also includes the standard C library functions in the module if your code uses them. If your code will need a standard C library function at runtime but doesn't use it when the code is being compiled, the function can be included using a command-line flag.
- If you need to pass anything more than integers or floats between the module and JavaScript, you'll need to use the module's linear memory. The standard C library includes the `malloc` and `free` functions, which help with memory management.

You'll see the approach to building a WebAssembly module that doesn't include the standard C library or Emscripten helper functions later in this chapter.

4.1.1   Making the C++ modifications

The first thing you'll need to do is create a folder where you'll keep your files for this section of the chapter: WebAssembly\Chapter 4\4.1 js_plumbing\source\.

As figure 4.4 shows, the first step toward building a website that reuses the C++ validation code is to modify the code so that it can also be compiled by Emscripten.

Desktop application written in C++

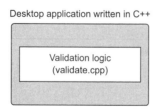

Validation logic
(validate.cpp)

Figure 4.4   The first step of the process in reusing C++ code is to adjust the code so that it can be compiled by Emscripten.

EMSCRIPTEN'S CONDITIONAL COMPILATION SYMBOL AND HEADER FILE

In many cases, when you use C or C++ code that's part of an existing solution to create a WebAssembly module, you'll need to add some things to the code for everything to work together. For example, when the code is compiled for a desktop application, it doesn't need the Emscripten header file; you'll need a way to include that header file, but only when the code is being compiled by Emscripten.

Fortunately, Emscripten includes a conditional compilation symbol, __EMSCRIPTEN__, that you can use to detect whether Emscripten is compiling the solution. If needed, you can also include an else condition with the conditional compilation symbol check to include header files that are needed when code isn't being compiled by Emscripten.

Create a file called validate.cpp, and open it. Add the header files for the standard C library and the string library. Because this code is part of an existing solution, you'll need to add the header file for the Emscripten library, but you'll need to wrap it in a conditional compilation symbol check to make sure it gets included only if Emscripten is compiling the code:

```
#include <cstdlib>
#include <cstring>

#ifdef __EMSCRIPTEN__          <———  Symbol is present when the code
  #include <emscripten.h>      <———  is being compiled by Emscripten
#endif
                                      Emscripten library's
                                      header file
```

> **INFO** Several C header files have been deprecated or are no longer supported in C++. An example is stdlib.h. You should now use cstdlib instead of stdlib.h. For the complete list of header file changes, you can visit https://en.cppreference.com/w/cpp/header.

THE EXTERN "C" BLOCK

In C++, function names can be overloaded, so to make sure the name is unique when compiled, the compiler mangles it by adding information to it about the function's parameters. The compiler changing function names when the code is compiled is a problem for external code that wants to call a specific function, because that function's name no longer exists.

You'll want to tell the compiler to not modify the names of the functions that the JavaScript code will be calling. To do this, you need to include an extern "C" block around the functions. All the functions that you'll be adding to this file are placed within this block. Add the following to the validate.cpp file:

```
#ifdef __cplusplus
extern "C" {          <———  So the compiler doesn't rename the
#endif                       functions within these curly braces


                             Your WebAssembly functions
                      <———   will be placed here.
#ifdef __cplusplus
}
#endif
```

THE VALIDATEVALUEPROVIDED FUNCTION

The Edit Product web page that you'll be building will have a product name field and category drop-down list that you'll need to validate. Both the name and selected category will be passed to the module as strings, but the category ID will hold a numeric value.

You'll create two functions, ValidateName and ValidateCategory, to validate the product name and selected category. Because both functions need to ensure that a value was provided, you'll create a helper function called `ValidateValueProvided` that will accept the following parameters:

- The value that was passed to the module from the web page.
- The appropriate error message from the module based on whether the function is being called by `ValidateName` or `ValidateCategory`. If a value isn't provided, this error message will be placed into the third parameter's return buffer.
- The buffer to put the error message into if the value isn't provided.

Place the following code within the `extern "C"` curly braces of the validate.cpp file:

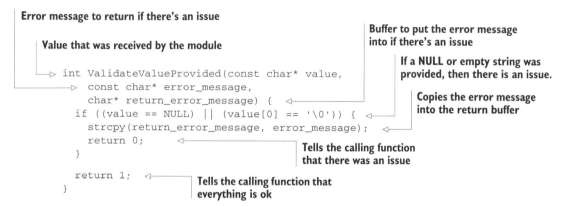

Error message to return if there's an issue

Value that was received by the module

Buffer to put the error message into if there's an issue

If a NULL or empty string was provided, then there is an issue.

Copies the error message into the return buffer

```
int ValidateValueProvided(const char* value,
    const char* error_message,
    char* return_error_message) {
  if ((value == NULL) || (value[0] == '\0')) {
    strcpy(return_error_message, error_message);
    return 0;
  }
  return 1;
}
```

Tells the calling function that there was an issue

Tells the calling function that everything is ok

THE VALIDATENAME FUNCTION

You'll now create the `ValidateName` function, which receives the following parameters:

- The user-entered product name
- A maximum-length value for the name
- A pointer to a buffer, to which you'll add an error message if there's an issue with the validation

The function will verify two things:

- Was a product name provided? You'll verify this by passing the name to the `ValidateValueProvided` helper function.
- You'll also verify that the length of the name provided doesn't exceed the maximum length value, by using the standard C library function `strlen`.

If either validation check fails, you'll place the appropriate error message into the return buffer and exit the function, returning 0 (error). If the code runs to the end of the function, there were no validation issues, so a 1 (success) message is returned.

You'll also add the `EMSCRIPTEN_KEEPALIVE` declaration to the `ValidateName` function and wrap it in a conditional compilation symbol check to make sure it's included only if Emscripten is compiling the code. In chapter 3, you added functions from the module to an Emscripten command-line flag called `EXPORTED_FUNCTIONS` so that the JavaScript code could interact with those functions. The `EMSCRIPTEN_KEEPALIVE` declaration automatically adds the associated function to the exported functions so that you don't have to explicitly specify it at the command line.

The code in the next listing is the `ValidateName` function. Add it after the `Validate-ValueProvided` function in validate.cpp.

Listing 4.1   `ValidateName` function in validate.cpp

```
...
#ifdef __EMSCRIPTEN__
    EMSCRIPTEN_KEEPALIVE
#endif
int ValidateName(char* name,
    int maximum_length,
    char* return_error_message) {
  if (ValidateValueProvided(name,
    "A Product Name must be provided.",
    return_error_message) == 0) {
    return 0;
  }

  if (strlen(name) > maximum_length) {
    strcpy(return_error_message, "The Product Name is too long.");
    return 0;
  }

  return 1;
}
```

- **Adds the function to the list of exported functions**
- **Product name passed to the module**
- **Maximum length allowed for the name**
- **Buffer in which to put the error message if there's an issue**
- **If the value wasn't specified, then return an error.**
- **If the value exceeds the maximum length, then return an error.**
- **Tells the caller that everything was ok**

THE ISCATEGORYIDINARRAY FUNCTION

Before you create the `ValidateCategory` function, you'll create a helper function to simplify the function's logic. This helper function will be called `IsCategoryIdInArray` and will receive the following parameters:

- The user-selected category ID
- A pointer to an array of integers holding the valid category IDs
- The number of items in the array of valid category IDs

The function will loop through the items in the array to check whether the user-selected category ID is actually in the array. If so, a 1 (success) code is returned. If the category ID isn't found, a 0 (error) code is returned.

Add the following `IsCategoryIdInArray` function to the validate.cpp file after the `ValidateName` function:

- **Category ID passed to the module**
- **Pointer to an array of integers holding the valid category IDs**
- **Number of items in the valid_category_ids array**
- **Converts the string received into an integer**

```
int IsCategoryIdInArray(char* selected_category_id,
    int* valid_category_ids,
    int array_length) {
  int category_id = atoi(selected_category_id);
```

```
for (int index = 0; index < array_length; index++) {     ◁──── Loops through the array
  if (valid_category_ids[index] == category_id) {     ◁─┐
    return 1;                                            │
  }                           If the ID is in the array, then exit
}                             the function, telling the caller
                                    that the ID was found.

return 0;   ◁─┐
}             │ Tells the caller that the category ID
              │ wasn't found in the array
```

THE VALIDATECATEGORY FUNCTION

The final function that you need to create is ValidateCategory, which will receive the following parameters:

- The user-selected category ID
- A pointer to an array of integers holding the valid category IDs
- The number of items in the array of valid category IDs
- A pointer to a buffer, to which you'll add an error message if there's an issue with the validation

The function will verify three things:

- Was a category ID provided? You'll verify this by passing the ID to the Validate-ValueProvided helper function.
- Was a pointer to the valid category IDs array provided?
- Is the user-selected category ID in the array of valid IDs?

If any of the validation checks fail, you'll place the appropriate error message into the return buffer and exit the function, returning 0 (error). If the code runs to the end of the function, there were no validation issues, so a 1 (success) message is returned.

Add the ValidateCategory function, shown in the following listing, below the IsCategoryIdInArray function in the validate.cpp file.

Listing 4.2   The ValidateCategory function

```
...                              Selected category ID
                                 passed to the module
#ifdef __EMSCRIPTEN__                                    Pointer to an array of integers
  EMSCRIPTEN_KEEPALIVE                                   holding the valid category IDs
#endif
int ValidateCategory(char* category_id,     ◁─┘
    int* valid_category_ids,     ◁──────────────────────┐  Number of items in the
    int array_length,     ◁─────────────────────────────┘  valid_category_ids array
    char* return_error_message) {     ◁─────────┐
  if (ValidateValueProvided(category_id,        │ Buffer to put the error message
    "A Product Category must be selected.",      into if there's an issue
    return_error_message) == 0) {     ◁─┐
    return 0;                           │ If a value isn't received,
  }                                       return an error.

  if ((valid_category_ids == NULL) || (array_length == 0)) {     ◁───┐
    strcpy(return_error_message,                                      │
      "There are no Product Categories available.");       If the array wasn't
                                                           specified, then
                                                           return an error.
```

```
    return 0;
  }

  if (IsCategoryIdInArray(category_id, valid_category_ids,
      array_length) == 0) {
    strcpy(return_error_message,
        "The selected Product Category is not valid.");
    return 0;
  }

  return 1;
}
```

If the selected category ID isn't found in the array, then return an error.

Tells the caller that everything was ok

4.1.2 Compiling the code into a WebAssembly module

Now that the C++ code has been modified so that it can also be compiled by Emscripten, you can move to the next step and have Emscripten compile the code into WebAssembly, as figure 4.5 shows.

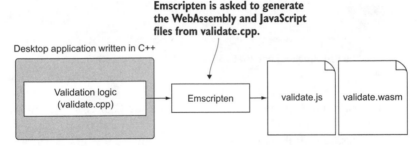

Emscripten is asked to generate the WebAssembly and JavaScript files from validate.cpp.

Desktop application written in C++

Validation logic (validate.cpp) → Emscripten → validate.js   validate.wasm

Figure 4.5   The second step of the process in reusing C++ code is to ask Emscripten to generate both the WebAssembly and JavaScript files.

When you write the JavaScript code to interact with the module, you'll use the `ccall` and `UTF8ToString` Emscripten helper functions (for details on the `ccall` function, see appendix B). To ensure that these functions are included in the generated JavaScript file, you'll need to specify them when compiling the C++ code. To do this, you'll use the `EXTRA_EXPORTED_RUNTIME_METHODS` command-line array to specify the functions.

NOTE   When including functions, remember that function names are case-sensitive. The `UTF8ToString` function, for example, must have a capital `UTF`, `T`, and `S`.

To compile the code into a WebAssembly module, you need to open a command prompt, navigate to the folder where you saved the validate.cpp file, and then run the following command:

```
emcc validate.cpp -o validate.js
  -s EXTRA_EXPORTED_RUNTIME_METHODS=['ccall','UTF8ToString']
```

4.1.3   Creating the web page

Now that you've modified the C++ code and compiled it into a WebAssembly module, you'll need to build the Edit Product page for the website, shown in figure 4.6.

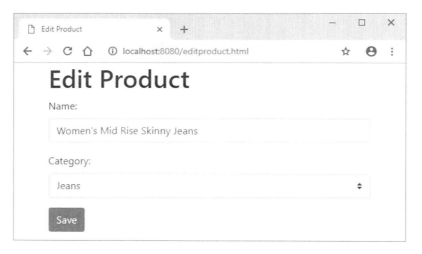

Figure 4.6   The Edit Product page that you'll be building and validating

TIP   Some of you may be strong with languages like C or C++ but not have ever really worked with HTML. If you'd like to familiarize yourself with HTML basics, the following website has some really good tutorials: www.w3schools.com/html.

For a more professional-looking web page, instead of styling everything manually, you'll be using Bootstrap. This popular framework for web development includes a number of design templates to help make development easier and faster. For this book, you'll simply point to the files that are hosted on the *CDNs*, but Bootstrap can be downloaded and included with your web page. The instructions for downloading Bootstrap are included in appendix A.

INFO   A CDN, or *content delivery network*, is geographically distributed with a goal of serving the file or files needed as close to the device requesting them as possible. This distribution speeds up the process of downloading the files, which improves website load times.

In the WebAssembly\Chapter 4\4.1 js_plumbing\ folder, create a folder called frontend and then create a file in the frontend folder called editproduct.html. Open the editproduct.html file in your favorite text editor, and enter the HTML shown in the following listing.

Listing 4.3 HTML of the Edit Product page (editproduct.html)

```html
<!DOCTYPE html>
<html>
  <head>
    <title>Edit Product</title>
    <meta charset="utf-8"/>
    <meta name="viewport" content="width=device-width, initial-scale=1">
    <link rel="stylesheet"
      href="https://maxcdn.bootstrapcdn.com/bootstrap/4.1.0/css/W3Schools
      bootstrap.min.css">
    <script
      src="https://ajax.googleapis.com/ajax/libs/jquery/3.3.1/W3Schools
      jquery.min.js"></script>
    <script
      src="https://cdnjs.cloudflare.com/ajax/libs/popper.js/1.14.0/umd/
      W3Schools popper.min.js"></script>
    <script
      src="https://maxcdn.bootstrapcdn.com/bootstrap/4.1.0/js/W3Schools
      bootstrap.min.js"></script>
  </head>
  <body onload="initializePage()">
    <div class="container">
      <h1>Edit Product</h1>

      <div id="errorMessage" class="alert alert-danger" role="alert"
        style="display:none;"></div>

      <div class="form-group">
        <label for="name">Name:</label>
        <input type="text" class="form-control" id="name">
      </div>

      <div class="form-group">
        <label for="category">Category:</label>
        <select class="custom-select" id="category">
          <option value="0"></option>
          <option value="100">Jeans</option>
          <option value="101">Dress Pants</option>
        </select>
      </div>

      <button type="button" class="btn btn-primary"
        onclick="onClickSave()">Save</button>
    </div>

    <script src="editproduct.js"></script>
    <script src="validate.js"></script>
  </body>
</html>
```

4.1.4   *Creating the JavaScript that will interact with the module*

Figure 4.7 shows the next step of the process, in which you'll copy the files generated by Emscripten, validate.js and validate.wasm, to the folder where you have the editproduct.html file. You'll then create an editproduct.js file that will bridge the gap between the user interacting with the web page and the code interacting with the module.

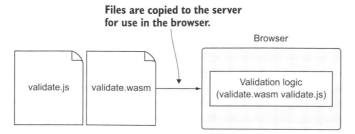

Figure 4.7   The third step of the process in reusing C++ code is to copy the generated files to where the HTML file is and build the JavaScript code to interact with the module.

Copy the validate.js and validate.wasm files from the WebAssembly\Chapter 4\4.1 js_plumbing\source\ folder to the WebAssembly\Chapter 4\4.1 js_plumbing\frontend\ folder. In the frontend folder, create a file called editproduct.js, and then open it.

Rather than include code to talk to the server, you'll simulate having received data from the server by creating a JavaScript object named `initialData`. This object will be used to initialize the controls when the web page is displayed. Add the JavaScript object to the editproduct.js file:

```
const initialData = {                    ◁──────┐  Simulated data received
  name: "Women's Mid Rise Skinny Jeans",         │  from the server
  categoryId: "100",
};
```

When you call the module's `ValidateName` function, it will want to know the maximum length that the product name can be. To specify this value, you'll use the constant `MAXIMUM_NAME_LENGTH`. You'll also have an array of valid category IDs, `VALID_CATEGORY_IDS`, for use when validating the user's category ID selection. Add the following snippet after the `initialData` object in the editproduct.js file:

```
const MAXIMUM_NAME_LENGTH = 50;          ◁──────┐  Maximum length a
const VALID_CATEGORY_IDS = [100, 101];   ◁──┐   │  name is allowed to be
                                            │
                                            └  List of valid category IDs
                                               that can be selected
```

In the HTML of the editproduct.html page, you specified that an `initializePage` function be called when the web page has loaded. This function call lets you populate the controls on the page with the data from the `initialData` object.

Within the `initializePage` function, you first populate the product name field with the `name` value in the `initialData` object. Next, loop through the category drop-down list to find the item in the list that matches the `categoryId` value in the `initialData` object. If you find the matching `category` ID value, you set the selection of the desired item in the list by passing the item's index to the `selectedIndex` property. Add the following `initializePage` function to the editproduct.js file:

```
function initializePage() {
  document.getElementById("name").value = initialData.name;

  const category = document.getElementById("category");
  const count = category.length;                                    Gets the count of
  for (let index = 0; index < count; index++) {                     how many items are
    if (category[index].value === initialData.categoryId) {         in the drop-down
      category.selectedIndex = index;
      break;                                                        Loops through each
    }                                                               item in the category list
  }
}
```

If a match is found, select that item in the list and exit the loop.

The next function you need to add to the editproduct.js file is `getSelectedCategoryId`. This returns the selected item's ID from the category list and is called when the user clicks the Save button:

```
function getSelectedCategoryId() {
  const category = document.getElementById("category");
  const index = category.selectedIndex;
  if (index !== -1) { return category[index].value; }    If there is a selected item
                                                          in the list, then return
  return "0";          Nothing was selected, so          that item's value.
}                      you return zero for the ID.
```

You'll now need to create the `setErrorMessage` function, which is used to present an error message to the user. You'll do this by populating a section of the web page with the string received from the WebAssembly module. If an empty string is passed to the function, it's a signal to hide the error section on the website. Otherwise, the error section is shown. The following snippet is the `setErrorMessage` function to add to the editproduct.js file:

```
function setErrorMessage(error) {
  const errorMessage = document.getElementById("errorMessage");
  errorMessage.innerText = error;
  errorMessage.style.display = (error === "" ? "none" : "");
}
```

The HTML for the Save button on the web page has an `onclick` event specified to trigger the `onClickSave` function when a user clicks the button. In the `onClickSave` function, you'll grab the user-entered values and pass them to the `validateName` and `validateCategory` JavaScript functions. If either validation function indicates that there was an issue, the error message from the module is retrieved from the module's memory and displayed to the user.

> **TIP**   You could give the JavaScript functions any name, but I've named them so that they match the function in the module that they call. The `validate-Name` JavaScript function, for example, calls the `ValidateName` module function.

As described in previous chapters, WebAssembly modules support only four basic data types (32-bit integers, 64-bit integers, 32-bit floats, and 64-bit floats). For more complex data types like strings, you need to use the module's memory.

Emscripten has a `ccall` helper function that exists to help call a module's functions and will help with the memory management of strings if those strings are expected to last only for the call's duration. In this case, you'll pass a string buffer to the module so that it can be populated with the appropriate validation error if there's an issue with the user's input. Because the memory for the string needs to last longer than just the call to the `ValidateName` or `ValidateCategory` module function, you'll need to handle memory management manually in the `onClickSave` function. To do this, the Emscripten plumbing code provides access to the `malloc` and `free` standard C library functions via `_malloc` and `_free`, respectively, so that you can allocate and free the module's memory.

Aside from allocating and freeing the memory, you also need to be able to read the string from the module's memory. To do this, you'll use Emscripten's `UTF8ToString` helper function. This function accepts a pointer and reads the string from that memory location.

The next listing is the `onClickSave` function that you need to add to the editproduct .js file after the `setErrorMessage` function.

Listing 4.4   The `onClickSave` function in editproduct.js

Reserves 256 bytes of the module's memory for an error message

Grabs the user-entered values from the web page

```
...

function onClickSave() {
  let errorMessage = "";
  const errorMessagePointer = Module._malloc(256);

  const name = document.getElementById("name").value;
  const categoryId = getSelectedCategoryId();

  if (!validateName(name, errorMessagePointer) ||
      !validateCategory(categoryId, errorMessagePointer)) {
    errorMessage = Module.UTF8ToString(errorMessagePointer);
  }
```

Checks to see if the Name and Category ID are valid

Grabs the error message from the module's memory

```
Module._free(errorMessagePointer);  ◁─────────────┐   Releases the memory that
                                                      │   was locked by _malloc
setErrorMessage(errorMessage);  ◁───┐
if (errorMessage === "") {           │   Displays the error
                                     │   message if there was one
         ◁───┐
    }         │   There were no issues. The
}             │   data can be passed to the
              │   server to be saved.
```

TALKING TO THE MODULE: VALIDATENAME

The first function in the WebAssembly module that you'll want to call has the following signature in C++:

```
int ValidateName(char* name,
    int maximum_length,
    char* return_error_message);
```

To call the `ValidateName` function in the module, you'll be using the `ccall` Emscripten helper function. For details on the parameters to the `ccall` function, see appendix B. Your `ccall` function will be passed the following values for the parameters:

- `'ValidateName'`, indicating the function name that you want to call.
- `'number'`, for the return type because the function returns an integer.
- An array with the values `'string'`, `'number'`, and `'number'` indicating the data types of the parameters.

  The first parameter of `ValidateName` is the `char*` pointer for the user-entered product name. In this case, the string being temporary is acceptable, so you'll let the `ccall` function handle the memory management for you by specifying `'string'` for that parameter.

  The second parameter is expecting an `int`, so you'll simply specify a `'number'` type.

  The third parameter is where things can get a little confusing. That `char*` pointer parameter is the return message if there's an error. You need that pointer to be long-lived so that you can return it to the calling JavaScript function. Rather than letting the `ccall` function handle the string's memory management in this case, you handle it in the `onClickSave` function. You simply want to pass the string as a pointer, and to pass a pointer, you need to specify the parameter type as `'number'`.

- An array holding the value that the user entered for a product name, the constant value for the maximum length the product name can be, and a buffer to hold any error messages that might be returned.

The following code snippet is the `validateName` function that you need to add to the editproduct.js file after the `onClickSave` function:

```
                                                    Name of the function you're
                                                    calling in the module
function validateName(name, errorMessagePointer) {
  const isValid = Module.ccall('ValidateName',  ◁───┘
       'number',  ◁────────── Return type of the function
```

Array of parameter types

```
   ['string', 'number', 'number'],
   [name, MAXIMUM_NAME_LENGTH, errorMessagePointer]);
   return (isValid === 1);
}
```

Array holding the values for the parameters

Returns true if the integer is 1 and false if not

TIP   In this case, the code to call the module's `ValidateName` function is straightforward. As you'll see in future examples, the code can be more involved. It's recommended that the code for each WebAssembly function that's called be kept in its own JavaScript function to make maintainability easier.

TALKING TO THE MODULE: VALIDATECATEGORY

You're now going to write the `validateCategory` JavaScript function to call the module's `ValidateCategory` function. The `ValidateCategory` function has the following signature in C++:

```
int ValidateCategory(char* category_id,
    int* valid_category_ids,
    int array_length,
    char* return_error_message);
```

The `ValidateCategory` function is expecting an array pointer of integers, but the `ccall` function's array parameter type is for only 8-bit values (see appendix B for more information about these parameters). Because the module's function is expecting an array of 32-bit integers, you need to manually allocate memory for the array and free it after the call to the module returns.

A WebAssembly module's memory is simply a typed array buffer. Emscripten provides several views that allow you to view the memory in different ways so that you can work with different data types more easily. Because the module expects an array of integers, you'll use the `HEAP32` view.

To allocate enough memory for the array pointer, your call to `Module._malloc` needs to multiply the number of items in the array by the number of bytes for each item that's placed in the `Module.HEAP32` object. For this, you'll use the constant `Module.HEAP32.BYTES_PER_ELEMENT`, which holds a value of 4 for the `HEAP32` object.

Once you have the memory allocated for the array pointer, you can use the `HEAP32` object's `set` method to copy the array's contents into the module's memory:

- The first parameter is the array, `VALID_CATEGORY_IDS`, to be copied to the WebAssembly module's memory.
- The second parameter is an index for where the `set` method should start writing the data in the underlying array (the module's memory). In this case, because you're working with the 32-bit view of the memory, each index refers to one of the groupings of 32 bits (4 bytes). As a result, you need to divide the memory address by four.

The final JavaScript function that you need to add to the end of the editproduct.js file is the `validateCategory` function in the next listing.

Listing 4.5   The `validateCategory` function in editproduct.js

Gets the number of bytes per
element for the HEAP32 object

Allocates enough memory
for each item of the array

```
...

function validateCategory(categoryId, errorMessagePointer) {
  const arrayLength = VALID_CATEGORY_IDS.length;
  const bytesPerElement = Module.HEAP32.BYTES_PER_ELEMENT;
  const arrayPointer = Module._malloc((arrayLength *
      bytesPerElement));
  Module.HEAP32.set(VALID_CATEGORY_IDS,
      (arrayPointer / bytesPerElement));

  const isValid = Module.ccall('ValidateCategory',
      'number',
      ['string', 'number', 'number', 'number'],
      [categoryId, arrayPointer, arrayLength, errorMessagePointer]);

  Module._free(arrayPointer);

  return (isValid === 1);
}
```

Copies the
array's elements
into the module's
memory

Calls the
ValidateCategory
function in the
module

Frees the memory that
was allocated for the array

Returns true if the integer
is 1 and false if not

4.1.5   Viewing the results

Now that you have the completed JavaScript code, you can open your browser and type `http://localhost:8080/editproduct.html` into the address box to see the web page you just built. You can test the validation by removing all the text from the Name field and then clicking the Save button. An error should display on the web page (figure 4.8).

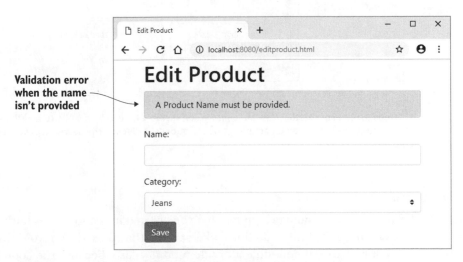

Validation error
when the name
isn't provided

Figure 4.8   Edit Product page's Name validation error

4.2   *Using C or C++ to create a module without Emscripten*

Suppose you want to have Emscripten compile the C++ code and not include any of the standard C library functions or generate the JavaScript plumbing file. As convenient as the Emscripten plumbing code is, it hides a lot of the details of working with a WebAssembly module. This approach is useful for learning because you'll get a chance to directly work with things like the JavaScript WebAssembly API.

Typically, production code uses the process discussed in section 4.1, in which Emscripten includes the standard C library functions your code uses in the generated module. In that process, Emscripten also generates a JavaScript plumbing file that handles loading and instantiating the module and includes helper functions such as ccall to make interacting with the module easier.

As you can see in figure 4.9, the process in this section is similar to that in section 4.1, except that you'll be asking Emscripten to generate only the WebAssembly file and not the JavaScript plumbing file.

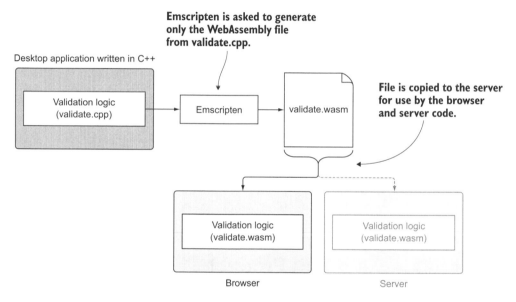

Figure 4.9   Steps for turning existing C++ logic into WebAssembly for use by a website and the server-side code but without any generated Emscripten JavaScript code. I discuss the server aspect, Node.js, in a future chapter.

4.2.1   *Making the C++ modifications*

Although the code in the validate.cpp file that you created in section 4.1 is fairly basic, it uses some standard C library functions, like strlen, that Emscripten won't include when you ask it to create the module as a side module. Also, because the code needs to pass pointers to values placed in memory, you need a way to flag that memory as

Desktop application written in C++

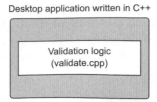

Validation logic
(validate.cpp)

Figure 4.10   Your first step is to create your own versions of the standard C library functions you need so that the code can be compiled by Emscripten.

locked to prevent the C or JavaScript code from overwriting the values in that section of memory until the code is finished with the memory.

Because you won't have access to the `malloc` and `free` standard library functions, your first step (figure 4.10) will be to implement your own.

THE HEADER FILE FOR THE SIDE MODULE'S SYSTEM FUNCTIONS

Create the folder WebAssembly\Chapter 4\4.2 side_module\source\. In the source folder, create a file called side_module_system_functions.h and open it with your editor. Add the following snippet to the file to define the function signatures for the functions that you're about to create:

```
#pragma once

#ifndef SIDE_MODULE_SYSTEM_FUNCTIONS_H_
#define SIDE_MODULE_SYSTEM_FUNCTIONS_H_

#include <stdio.h>

void InsertIntoAllocatedArray(int new_item_index, int offset_start,
    int size_needed);

int create_buffer(int size_needed);
void free_buffer(int offset);

char* strcpy(char* destination, const char* source);
size_t strlen(const char* value);

int atoi(const char* value);

#endif // SIDE_MODULE_SYSTEM_FUNCTIONS_H_
```

THE IMPLEMENTATION FILE FOR THE SIDE MODULE'S SYSTEM FUNCTIONS

Now create the side_module_system_functions.cpp file in the source folder, and open it with your editor. You'll be creating a simple replacement for the standard C library's `malloc` and `free` functions. The `malloc` function finds the first available memory location that's big enough for the requested memory size. It then flags that block of memory so that it doesn't get used by other code requests for memory. Once the code is finished with the memory block, it calls the standard C library's `free` function to release the lock.

You'll use an array to handle allocating chunks of memory for 10 concurrent requests, which is more than enough for this validation code. You should always have at least one page of memory that is 65,536 bytes (64 KB), so the memory allocations will happen within this block.

At the beginning of the side_module_system_functions.cpp file, add the includes for the C standard input and output library and Emscripten header file. Add the opening extern "C" block, and then add the constants for the memory size and the maximum number of concurrent memory blocks that will be allowed:

```
#include <stdio.h>
#include <emscripten.h>

#ifdef __cplusplus
extern "C" {
#endif

const int TOTAL_MEMORY = 65536;
const int MAXIMUM_ALLOCATED_CHUNKS = 10;
```

Following the constants, add the current_allocated_count variable that will indicate how many blocks of memory are currently allocated. Add a definition for an object, MemoryAllocated, which will hold the start of the memory that's allocated and how long the block of memory is. Then create the array that will hold the objects that indicate which blocks of memory are in use:

```
int current_allocated_count = 0;

struct MemoryAllocated {
  int offset;
  int length;
};

struct MemoryAllocated
  AllocatedMemoryChunks[MAXIMUM_ALLOCATED_CHUNKS];
```

Your next step is to create a function that will accept an index for where it will insert a new memory block in the AllocatedMemoryChunks array. Any items in the array from that index to the end of the array will be moved one spot toward the end of the array. The function will then place the memory block's start location (offset) and memory block size at the requested location in the array. Place the code in the following listing after the AllocatedMemoryChunks array in the side_module_system_functions.cpp file.

Listing 4.6   The InsertIntoAllocatedArray function

```
...

void InsertIntoAllocatedArray(int new_item_index, int offset_start,
    int size_needed) {
  for (int i = (MAXIMUM_ALLOCATED_CHUNKS - 1); i > new_item_index; i--){
    AllocatedMemoryChunks[i] = AllocatedMemoryChunks[(i - 1)];
  }

  AllocatedMemoryChunks[new_item_index].offset = offset_start;
  AllocatedMemoryChunks[new_item_index].length = size_needed;

  current_allocated_count++;
}
```

Now, create a simplified version of the `malloc` function called `create_buffer`. When you include string literals in C++ code and compile the code into a WebAssembly module, Emscripten has these string literals loaded into the module's memory automatically when the module is instantiated. Because of this, the code will need to leave room for the strings and will only start allocating memory at byte 1,024. The code will also increase the size of the memory requested so that it's a multiple of 8.

The first thing the code will do is loop through the currently allocated memory to see if there's room in between the allocated blocks to fit the requested memory size. If so, the new allocated block will be inserted into the array at that index. If there isn't enough room for the requested memory size between the existing allocated memory blocks, then the code will check to see if there's room following the currently allocated memory.

The code will return the memory offset of where the memory block has been allocated if it was successful in finding a spot. Otherwise, it will return 0 (zero), which will indicate an error given that the code will only start allocating memory at byte 1,024.

Add the code from the next listing to the side_module_system_functions.cpp file.

Listing 4.7 Simplified version of the `malloc` function

```
...

EMSCRIPTEN_KEEPALIVE
int create_buffer(int size_needed) {
  if (current_allocated_count == MAXIMUM_ALLOCATED_CHUNKS) { return 0; }

  int offset_start = 1024;
  int current_offset = 0;
  int found_room = 0;

  int memory_size = size_needed;
  while (memory_size % 8 != 0) { memory_size++; }      ⟵  Increases the size so that the next offset is a multiple of 8

  for (int index = 0; index < current_allocated_count; index++) {   ⟵  Is there room in between the currently allocated memory blocks?
    current_offset = AllocatedMemoryChunks[index].offset;
    if ((current_offset - offset_start) >= memory_size) {
      InsertIntoAllocatedArray(index, offset_start, memory_size);
      found_room = 1;
      break;                          Room wasn't found between the
    }                                 currently allocated memory blocks.

    offset_start = (current_offset + AllocatedMemoryChunks[index].length);
  }

  if (found_room == 0) {        ⟵
    if (((TOTAL_MEMORY - 1) - offset_start) >= size_needed) {   ⟵
      AllocatedMemoryChunks[current_allocated_count].offset = offset_start;
      AllocatedMemoryChunks[current_allocated_count].length = size_needed;
      current_allocated_count++;
      found_room = 1;
    }                                    Is there room between the
  }                                      last memory block and the
                                         end of the module's memory?
```

```
    if (found_room == 1) { return offset_start; }
    return 0;
}
```

Your `free` function equivalent will be called `free_buffer`. In this function, you'll simply loop through the array of allocated memory blocks until you find the offset that was passed in by the caller. Once you find that array item, you'll shift all items after it by one position toward the beginning of the array. Add the code in the next listing after the `create_buffer` function.

Listing 4.8   Simplified version of the `free` function

```
...

EMSCRIPTEN_KEEPALIVE
void free_buffer(int offset) {
  int shift_item_left = 0;

  for (int index = 0; index < current_allocated_count; index++) {
    if (AllocatedMemoryChunks[index].offset == offset) {
      shift_item_left = 1;
    }

    if (shift_item_left == 1) {
      if (index < (current_allocated_count - 1)) {
        AllocatedMemoryChunks[index] = AllocatedMemoryChunks[(index + 1)];
      }
      else {
        AllocatedMemoryChunks[index].offset = 0;
        AllocatedMemoryChunks[index].length = 0;
      }
    }
  }

  current_allocated_count--;
}
```

The following snippet continues the side_module_system_functions.cpp file, in which you create a version of the system library functions `strcpy` and `strlen`:

```
char* strcpy(char* destination, const char* source) {
  char* return_copy = destination;
  while (*source) { *destination++ = *source++; }
  *destination = 0;

  return return_copy;
}

size_t strlen(const char* value) {
  size_t length = 0;
  while (value[length] != '\0') { length++; }

  return length;
}
```

The next listing continues the side_module_system_functions.cpp file to create a version of the system library function `atoi`.

Listing 4.9 The version of `atoi`

```
...

int atoi(const char* value) {
  if ((value == NULL) || (value[0] == '\0')) { return 0; }

  int result = 0;
  int sign = 0;

  if (*value == '-') { sign = -1; ++value; }

  char current_value = *value;
  while (current_value != '\0') {
    if ((current_value >= '0') && (current_value <= '9')) {
      result = result * 10 + current_value - '0';
      ++value;
      current_value = *value;
    }
    else {
      return 0;
    }
  }

  if (sign == -1) { result *= -1; }
  return result;
}
```

Annotations:
- **Flag if the first character is a negative sign. Move to the next byte.**
- **Loop until you reach the null terminator.**
- **If the current character is a number. . .**
- **Move the pointer to the next byte.**
- **. . . convert current_value to an integer. Add it to the result.**
- **If you found a non-numeric character, then exit, returning zero.**
- **If you have a negative number, then flip the value to negative.**

Finally, add the closing extern `"C"` curly brace at the end of your side_module_system_functions.cpp file, as shown in the following snippet:

```
#ifdef __cplusplus
}
#endif
```

Now that you've completed the side_module_system_functions.cpp file, copy the validate .cpp file from the WebAssembly\Chapter 4\4.1 js_plumbing\source\ folder and place it in the WebAssembly\Chapter 4\4.2 side_module\source\ folder.

Open the validate.cpp file, and remove the includes for the cstdlib and cstring files. Then, add an include for the new side_module_system_functions.h header file before the ValidateValueProvided function and within the extern `"C"` block.

WARNING The include for the header file must be placed within the extern `"C"` block. This is because you'll be asking the Emscripten compiler to compile two .cpp files. Although both files' functions are within extern `"C"` blocks, the Emscripten compiler still assumes that function calls in the validate.cpp file are being compiled to a C++ file, where the functions have been mangled. The compiler won't see the mangled function names in the generated module and will assume that they need to be imported instead.

The following snippet shows the modifications to the validate.cpp file:

```
#ifdef __EMSCRIPTEN__
  #include <emscripten.h>
#endif
```

```
#ifdef __cplusplus
extern "C" {
#endif

#include "side_module_system_functions.h"
```

Important: place the header file within the extern "C" block.

4.2.2   Compiling the code into a WebAssembly module

Now that you've created the C++ code, the next step is to have Emscripten compile the code into a WebAssembly module but without the JavaScript plumbing code, as figure 4.11 shows.

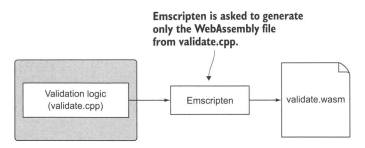

Emscripten is asked to generate only the WebAssembly file from validate.cpp.

Validation logic (validate.cpp) → Emscripten → validate.wasm

Figure 4.11   The second step of the process is to ask Emscripten to generate only the WebAssembly file. Emscripten won't generate the JavaScript plumbing file in this case.

To compile the C++ code into a WebAssembly module, open a command prompt, navigate to the folder where you saved the C++ files, and run the following command:

```
emcc side_module_system_functions.cpp validate.cpp -s SIDE_MODULE=2
⇒ -O1 -o validate.wasm
```

4.2.3   Creating the JavaScript that will interact with the module

Now that you have the WebAssembly module, you can see the next step in figure 4.12. Within the WebAssembly\Chapter 4\4.2 side_module\ folder, create a folder called frontend, and copy the editproduct.html and editproduct.js files from WebAssembly\ Chapter 4\4.1 js_plumbing\frontend\ into it.

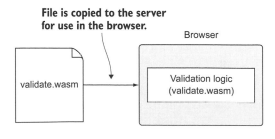

File is copied to the server for use in the browser.

Browser

validate.wasm → Validation logic (validate.wasm)

Figure 4.12   The third step of the process is to copy the generated file to where the HTML file is and build the JavaScript code to interact with the module.

Then, copy validate.wasm from WebAssembly\Chapter 4\4.2 side_module\ source\ to the new frontend folder.

The first thing you need to do is open the editproduct.html file and remove the validate.js JavaScript file reference at the bottom. The end of the editproduct.html file should now look like the following snippet:

```
  </div>

  <script src="editproduct.js"></script>
</body>
</html>
```

Next, make a few changes to the editproduct.js file (listing 4.10): add two global variables before the `initializePage` function, called `moduleMemory` and `moduleExports`. The `moduleMemory` variable keeps a reference to the module's `WebAssembly.Memory` object so that you can read and write to memory.

Because you don't have access to Emscripten's plumbing code, you also don't have a `Module` object. Instead, you'll use the global object reference, `moduleExports`, which you'll receive when you instantiate the module. The `moduleExports` reference will allow you to call all the exported functions in the module. You'll also add the code at the end of the `initializePage` function to load and instantiate the module.

Listing 4.10　Modifications to `initializePage` in editproduct.js

```
...

let moduleMemory = null;        ⟵——— Adds two new global variables
let moduleExports = null;

function initializePage() {
  ...

  moduleMemory = new WebAssembly.Memory({initial: 256});   ⟵┐
                                                   Places the reference to
  const importObject = {                           the module's memory in
    env: {                                          the global variable
      __memory_base: 0,
      memory: moduleMemory,
    }
  };

  WebAssembly.instantiateStreaming(fetch("validate.wasm"),  ⟵─────┐
  ➥ importObject).then(result => {                    Downloads and
    moduleExports = result.instance.exports;   ⟵┐     instantiates the
  });                                           │     module
}                               Keeps a reference to the
                                instantiated module's exports

...
```

The Emscripten compiler puts an underscore character before each function in the module, which is why you'll see the module's functions, like `create_buffer`, prefixed with an underscore character in listing 4.11.

The next function you need to modify is onClickSave, where you'll replace the call to Module._malloc with moduleExports._create_buffer, the call to Module.UTF8To-String with getStringFromMemory, and the Module._free call with moduleExports._free_buffer. The changes to the onClickSave function are indicated in bold in the following listing.

Listing 4.11   Edit of the onClickSave function in editproduct.js

```
...
function onClickSave() {                    Replaces Module._malloc with
  let errorMessage = "";                    moduleExports._create_buffer
  const errorMessagePointer = moduleExports._create_buffer(256);   ◁

  const name = document.getElementById("name").value;
  const categoryId = getSelectedCategoryId();

  if (!validateName(name, errorMessagePointer) ||
      !validateCategory(categoryId, errorMessagePointer)) {
    errorMessage = getStringFromMemory(errorMessagePointer);   ◁
  }                                                                Replaces
                                                                  Module.UTF8ToString
  moduleExports._free_buffer(errorMessagePointer);   ◁           with a helper function
                                                                  to read the string from
  setErrorMessage(errorMessage);                                  memory
  if (errorMessage === "") {              Replaces Module._free with
    ◁                                     moduleExports._free_buffer
  }          There were no issues with
}            the validation. The data
...          can be saved.
```

The memory that you passed to the WebAssembly module during initialization was provided via a WebAssembly.Memory object that you kept a reference to in the moduleMemory variable. Under the hood, the WebAssembly.Memory object is holding an ArrayBuffer object, which serves as the bytes for the module to simulate actual machine memory. You can access the underlying ArrayBuffer object held by the moduleMemory reference by accessing the buffer property.

As you'll recall, the Emscripten plumbing code has objects like HEAP32 that allow you to view the module's memory (the ArrayBuffer) in different ways so that you can work with different types of data more easily. Without access to Emscripten's plumbing code, you don't have access to objects like HEAP32, but, fortunately, those objects are simply referencing JavaScript objects like Int32Array, which you do have access to.

You need to create a helper function called getStringFromMemory that will read the strings that the module returns to the JavaScript code from the module's memory. Strings in C or C++ are placed in memory as an array of 8-bit characters, so you'll use the Uint8Array JavaScript object to access the module's memory starting at the offset specified by a pointer. Once you have the view, loop through the items in the array, reading in one character at a time until you reach the null-terminator character.

After the `onClickSave` function in the editproduct.js file, you need to add the `get-StringFromMemory` helper function, shown in the following listing.

Listing 4.12   The `getStringFromMemory` function in editproduct.js

```
...

function getStringFromMemory(memoryOffset) {
  let returnValue = "";

  const size = 256;
  const bytes = new Uint8Array(moduleMemory.buffer, memoryOffset, size);

  let character = "";
  for (let i = 0; i < size; i++) {
    character = String.fromCharCode(bytes[i]);
    if (character === "\0") { break; }

    returnValue += character;
  }

  return returnValue;
}
```

Annotations:
- **Gets the section of memory starting at the offset and ending 256 characters later**
- **Loops through the bytes one byte at a time**
- **Converts the current byte into a character**
- **If the current character is the null-terminator, then you're done reading in the string.**
- **Adds the current character to the return string before looping to the next character**

Now that you can read a string from the module's memory, you'll need to create a function that will let you write a string to the module's memory. Similar to the `get-StringFromMemory` function, the `copyStringToMemory` function starts by creating a `Uint8Array` object to manipulate the module's memory. You'll then use the JavaScript `TextEncoder` object to turn a string into an array of bytes. Once you have this array of bytes from the string, you can call the `Uint8Array` object's `set` method, passing in the array of bytes for the first parameter and the offset for where to start writing those bytes as the second parameter.

The following is the `copyStringToMemory` function, which you need to add to the editproduct.js file after the `getStringFromMemory` function:

```
function copyStringToMemory(value, memoryOffset) {
  const bytes = new Uint8Array(moduleMemory.buffer);
  bytes.set(new TextEncoder().encode((value + "\0")),
      memoryOffset);
}
```

Modify the `validateName` function to first allocate memory for the product name that the user entered. Copy the string value into the module's memory at the pointer's memory location by calling the `copyStringToMemory` function. Then call the module's `_ValidateName` function; afterward, free the memory that was allocated for the name pointer.

The following code snippet shows the modification to the `validateName` function:

```
function validateName(name, errorMessagePointer) {
  const namePointer = moduleExports._create_buffer(
```

```
        (name.length + 1));
    copyStringToMemory(name, namePointer);

    const isValid = moduleExports._ValidateName(namePointer,
        MAXIMUM_NAME_LENGTH, errorMessagePointer);

    moduleExports._free_buffer(namePointer);

    return (isValid === 1);

}
```

The last item that you need to modify is the validateCategory function. You'll allocate memory for the category ID and then copy the ID to the pointer's memory location.

The function will allocate the memory needed for the items in the VALID_CATEGORY_IDS global array and then copy each array item into the module's memory, similar to the approach you used with the Emscripten plumbing code. The difference is that you don't have access to the Emscripten HEAP32 object—but that object is simply a reference to the Int32Array JavaScript object, which you can access.

Once the array's values are copied into the module's memory, the code calls the module's _ValidateCategory function. When the function returns, the code frees the memory that was allocated for the array and string pointers. The following listing shows the modified validateCategory function.

Listing 4.13   validateCategory

Allocates memory for the category ID   Copies the ID to the
                                                         module's memory

```
...
                                                                          Allocates
function validateCategory(categoryId, errorMessagePointer) {              memory for each
    const categoryIdPointer = moduleExports._create_buffer(               item in the array
➥    (categoryId.length + 1));
    copyStringToMemory(categoryId, categoryIdPointer);  ◁                 Gets an
                                                                          Int32Array
    const arrayLength = VALID_CATEGORY_IDS.length;                        view of the
    const bytesPerElement = Int32Array.BYTES_PER_ELEMENT;                 memory and
    const arrayPointer = moduleExports._create_buffer(                    then copies in
➥    (arrayLength * bytesPerElement));              ◁                     the array's
                                                                          values
    const bytesForArray = new Int32Array(moduleMemory.buffer);  ◁
    bytesForArray.set(VALID_CATEGORY_IDS, (arrayPointer / bytesPerElement));

    const isValid = moduleExports._ValidateCategory(categoryIdPointer,
➥    arrayPointer, arrayLength, errorMessagePointer);  ◁         Calls the
                                                                 _ValidateCategory
    moduleExports._free_buffer(arrayPointer);  ◁                 function in the module
    moduleExports._free_buffer(categoryIdPointer);

    return (isValid === 1);                          Frees the memory
}                                                    that was allocated
```

4.2.4 *Viewing the results*

Now that you've revised the code, you can open a web browser and type `http://localhost:8080/editproduct.html` into the address box to see the web page. You can test the validation by adding more than 50 characters to the Name field and then clicking the Save button, which should display a validation error, as figure 4.13 shows.

Validation error when the name is too long →

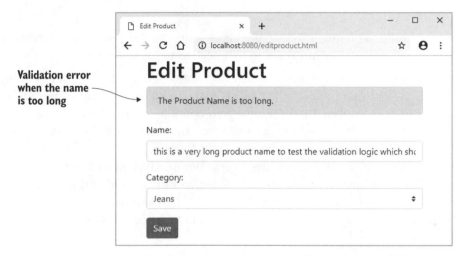

Figure 4.13 Edit Product page's Name validation error when the name entered is too long

Now: how can you use what you learned in this chapter in the real world?

Real-world use cases

The following are some possible use cases for what you've learned in this chapter:

- You can adjust one of your existing C++ codebases, or take a portion of the codebase, and compile it to WebAssembly so that it can be run in the browser.
- If you have JavaScript code that calls the server or a third-party API and receives large amounts of text data in return, you could create a WebAssembly module that parses the string for the data that your web page needs.
- If you have a website that allows users to upload a photo, you could create a WebAssembly module that accepts the file's bytes in order to resize or compress the photo before uploading. This would save bandwidth, which would help the user reduce data usage and would reduce processing on the server.

Exercises

You can find the solutions to these exercises in appendix D.

1 What two options are there to have Emscripten make your functions visible to the JavaScript code?
2 How do you prevent function names from being mangled when compiled so that your JavaScript code can use the expected function name?

Summary

In this chapter, you dug into the code-reuse aspect of WebAssembly by creating a web page that accepted user information that needed to be validated:

- By using the conditional compilation symbol __EMSCRIPTEN__ and placing functions within an extern "C" block, you can adjust existing code so that it can also be compiled by the Emscripten compiler. This allows a single C or C++ codebase, which might be part of a desktop application, for example, to also be available for use in a web browser or in Node.js.
- By including the EMSCRIPTEN_KEEPALIVE declaration with a function, you can have the function automatically added to Emscripten's list of functions that it will make visible to the JavaScript code. By using this declaration, you don't need to include the function in the command line's EXPORTED_FUNCTIONS array when compiling the module.
- You can call the module's functions using the ccall Emscripten helper function.
- To pass anything other than an integer or float between the module and JavaScript code requires interactions with the module's memory. The Emscripten-generated JavaScript code provides a number of functions that help with this.

Creating a WebAssembly module that calls into JavaScript

5

This chapter covers

- Calling into JavaScript directly using Emscripten's toolkit
- Calling into JavaScript without Emscripten's toolkit

In chapter 4, you created a WebAssembly module that your JavaScript code called into using Emscripten's ccall helper function. You passed a buffer as a parameter to the module's function so that, if there was an issue, an error message could be returned by placing it into the buffer. If there was an issue, your JavaScript read the string from the module's memory and then displayed the message to the user, as figure 5.1 shows.

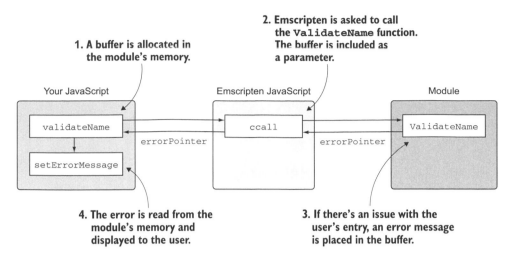

Figure 5.1   **How the JavaScript code currently interacts with the module's functions**

Imagine that rather than passing a buffer to the module's function if there's an issue, the module can just pass the error message directly to your JavaScript, as figure 5.2 shows.

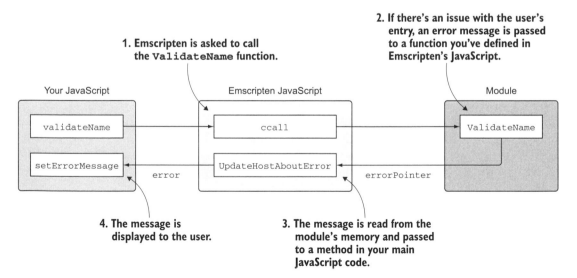

Figure 5.2   **The module calling a function in the JavaScript code**

When using the Emscripten toolkit, you can interact with JavaScript code from your module in three ways:

1 Use `Emscripten` macros. These include the `emscripten_run_script` series of macros, the `EM_JS` macro, and the `EM_ASM` series of macros.
2 Add custom JavaScript to Emscripten's JavaScript file that you can call into directly.
3 Use function pointers in which the JavaScript code specifies a function for the module to call into. We'll look at this approach in chapter 6.

With any way of interacting with JavaScript from a module, one approach may work better than another in certain circumstances:

1 Emscripten's macros can be quite helpful when debugging or when you need only the odd interaction with the JavaScript code. As the complexity of the macro code or number of interactions with JavaScript increases, you might consider separating the macro code out of your C or C++ code. You would do this so that both your module's code and the web page code can be more easily maintained.

Under the hood, when the `EM_JS` and `EM_ASM` series of macros are used, the Emscripten compiler creates the necessary functions and adds them to the generated Emscripten JavaScript file. When the WebAssembly module calls the macros, it's really calling the generated JavaScript functions.

INFO More about Emscripten's macros, including how to use them, can be found in appendix C.

2 As you'll see in this chapter, calling into JavaScript directly is easy and will simplify your website's JavaScript somewhat. If you plan to make function calls from the JavaScript function you place in Emscripten's generated JavaScript, you need some knowledge of the main JavaScript code. If you're supplying the module to a third party, they'll need clear instructions on setting things up correctly so that there are no errors because, for example, a function doesn't exist.

WARNING If you plan to use this approach and also target Node.js, then the JavaScript code you add to the generated JavaScript file must be self-contained. You'll work with Node.js in chapter 10 and will see this in more detail then, but, basically, because of the way Node.js loads the Emscripten JavaScript file, the code within the file can't call into your main JavaScript code.

3 In chapter 6, you'll see that using function pointers gives you a lot more flexibility because the module doesn't need to know what functions exist in your JavaScript code. Instead, the module will just call the JavaScript function that you provide it. The added flexibility of function pointers comes with a bit more complexity because it requires more code in your JavaScript to make everything work.

Rather than letting Emscripten generate the JavaScript functions for you using macros, you can define your own JavaScript to be included in Emscripten's JavaScript file. You'll be looking into this approach in this chapter.

For this scenario, you're going to modify the validation module that you created in chapter 4 so that, if there's an issue with the validation, you won't pass the error message back to the calling function by using a parameter. What you'll do instead is the following (figure 5.3):

1 If there's an issue with the user's entry, have the module call a JavaScript function that you'll place in Emscripten's generated JavaScript file.

2 The JavaScript function will accept a pointer from the module and, from that, will read the error message from the module's memory.

3 It will then pass the message to your web page's main JavaScript, which will handle updating the UI with the error received.

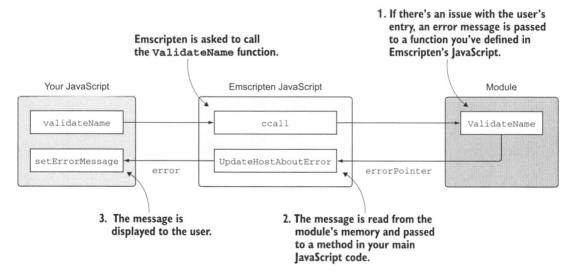

Figure 5.3   How the module and JavaScript will be reworked to allow the module to call back to the JavaScript

5.1 Using C or C++ to create a module with Emscripten plumbing

Let's revise the C++ validation logic that you created in chapter 4 so that it can talk to the JavaScript code. You'll include the standard C library and Emscripten helper functions, which is the recommended way to build a module for use in production. We'll look at the other approach to building a WebAssembly module that doesn't include the standard C library or Emscripten helper functions later in this chapter.

As figure 5.4 shows, the steps to build the module will be similar to what you saw in chapter 4:

1 Modify the C++ code so that it no longer receives a string buffer and instead calls a JavaScript function if there's an issue with the validation.
2 Define the JavaScript code that you want included in Emscripten's generated JavaScript file.
3 Ask Emscripten to generate the WebAssembly and JavaScript plumbing files.
4 Copy the generated files for use in the browser.
5 Create the web page, and then write the JavaScript code necessary to interact with the WebAssembly module.

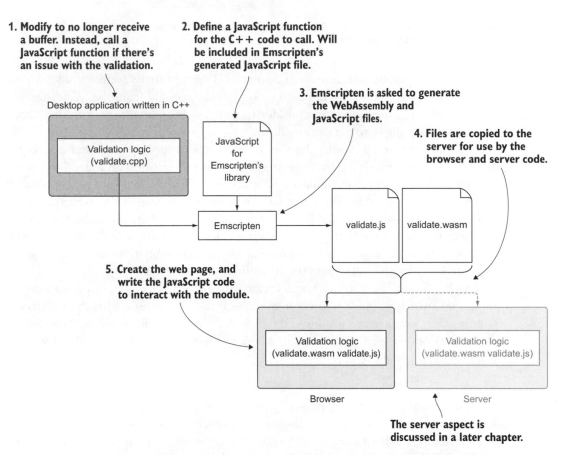

Figure 5.4   Steps for turning C++ logic, as well as some JavaScript that needs to be included in Emscripten's JavaScript file, into a WebAssembly module for use in a browser and by the server-side code. I discuss the server aspect, Node.js, in a later chapter.

5.1.1 Adjusting the C++ code

You can see in figure 5.5 that the first step of the process is to modify the C++ code so that it no longer receives a string buffer. Instead, the code will call a JavaScript function, passing it the error message if there's a problem with the validation.

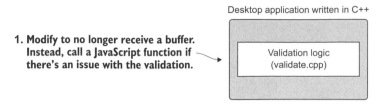

1. Modify to no longer receive a buffer. Instead, call a JavaScript function if there's an issue with the validation.

Desktop application written in C++

Validation logic (validate.cpp)

Figure 5.5   Step 1 is to modify the C++ code so that it passes the error message to a JavaScript function.

In your WebAssembly folder, create a Chapter 5\5.1.1 EmJsLibrary\source\ folder for the files that you'll use in this section. Copy the validate.cpp file from the WebAssembly\ Chapter 4\4.1 js_plumbing\source\ folder to your newly created source folder. Open the validate.cpp file in your favorite editor.

In a moment, you'll modify the C++ code to call a function that's defined in the JavaScript code. Because the function isn't part of the C++ code, you'll need to tell the compiler what the function signature is by including the `extern` keyword in front of the signature. Doing this allows the C++ code to be compiled with the expectation that the function will be available when the code is run. When the Emscripten compiler sees the function signature, it'll create an import item for it in the WebAssembly module. When the module is instantiated, the WebAssembly framework will see the requested import and will expect the function to be provided.

The JavaScript function that you'll create will accept a `const char*` pointer for the parameter, which will hold the error message if there's an issue with the validation. The function won't return a value. To define your function signature, add the following line of code within the `extern "C"` block and before the `ValidateValueProvided` function in your validate.cpp file:

```
extern void UpdateHostAboutError(const char* error_message);
```

Because you're not going to pass a buffer to the module anymore, you'll need to remove the `char* return_error_message` parameters from the functions. Also, any location that's making a `strcpy` call to copy the error message into the buffer will now need to call the `UpdateHostAboutError` function instead.

Modify the `ValidateValueProvided` function to no longer have the `return_error_message` parameter and to now call the `UpdateHostAboutError` function rather than `strcpy`, as follows:

```
int ValidateValueProvided(const char* value,
    const char* error_message) {
```

> The return_error_message parameter has been removed.

```
  if ((value == NULL) || (value[0] == '\0')) {
    UpdateHostAboutError(error_message);
    return 0;
  }

  return 1;
}
```

strcpy is replaced with the call to UpdateHostAboutError.

As with the `ValidateValueProvided` function, modify the `ValidateName` function to no longer receive the `return_error_message` parameter and remove it from the `ValidateValueProvided` function call. Revise the code to now pass the error message to the `UpdateHostAboutError` function rather than use `strcpy`, as follows:

```
int ValidateName(char* name, int maximum_length) {
  if (ValidateValueProvided(name,
      "A Product Name must be provided.") == 0) {
    return 0;
  }

  if (strlen(name) > maximum_length) {
    UpdateHostAboutError("The Product Name is too long.");
    return 0;
  }

  return 1;
}
```

The return_error_message parameter has been removed.

strcpy is replaced with the call to UpdateHostAboutError.

No changes are needed for the `IsCategoryIdInArray` function.

Lastly, you need to make the same changes to the `ValidateCategory` function that you did with the `ValidateValueProvided` and `ValidateName` functions, as the following listing shows.

Listing 5.1 The modified `ValidateCategory` function in validate.cpp

```
int ValidateCategory(char* category_id, int* valid_category_ids,
    int array_length) {
  if (ValidateValueProvided(category_id,
      "A Product Category must be selected.") == 0) {
    return 0;
  }

  if ((valid_category_ids == NULL) || (array_length == 0)) {
    UpdateHostAboutError("There are no Product Categories available.");
    return 0;
  }

  if (IsCategoryIdInArray(category_id, valid_category_ids,
      array_length) == 0) {
    UpdateHostAboutError("The selected Product Category is not valid.");
    return 0;
  }

  return 1;
}
```

The return_error_message parameter has been removed.

5.1.2   Creating the JavaScript that you want included in Emscripten's generated JavaScript file

Now that you've revised the C++ code, the next step (figure 5.6) is to create the Java-Script code that you want included in Emscripten's generated JavaScript file.

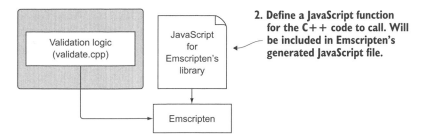

Figure 5.6   Step 2 is creating the JavaScript code to include in Emscripten's generated JavaScript file.

When creating JavaScript code that will be merged into Emscripten's generated Java-Script file, WebAssembly module creation is slightly different compared to how you've done it previously. In this case, you'll define your `UpdateHostAboutError` JavaScript function before you ask Emscripten to compile the C++ code, because you need the Emscripten compiler to merge your JavaScript code with the rest of the Emscripten JavaScript code that gets generated.

To have your JavaScript included in Emscripten's generated JavaScript file, you need to add your JavaScript to Emscripten's `LibraryManager.library` object; to do this, you can use Emscripten's `mergeInto` function, which takes two parameters:

- The object that you want to add properties to—in this case, the `LibraryManager` `.library` object
- An object whose properties will be copied into the first object—in this case, your code

You'll create a JavaScript object that will hold a property with the name `UpdateHost-AboutError`; the value will be a function that receives an error message pointer. The function will read the string from the module's memory using the Emscripten helper function `UTF8ToString` and will then call the JavaScript function `setErrorMessage` that's part of your web page's main JavaScript code.

In the WebAssembly\Chapter 5\5.1.1 EmJsLibrary\source\ folder, create a file called mergeinto.js, open it with your favorite editor, and add the following code snippet:

```
mergeInto(LibraryManager.library, {        ◁─────────
  UpdateHostAboutError: function(errorMessagePointer) {
    setErrorMessage(Module.UTF8ToString(errorMessagePointer));
  }
});
```

Copies the properties of the object into the LibraryManager.library object

5.1.3　*Compiling the code into a WebAssembly module*

Now that you've modified the C++ code and created the JavaScript function that you want included in Emscripten's generated JavaScript file, you can move to the next step. As figure 5.7 shows, this step is to have Emscripten compile the code into a WebAssembly module. Emscripten will also be instructed to include the code from your mergeinto.js file in the generated JavaScript file.

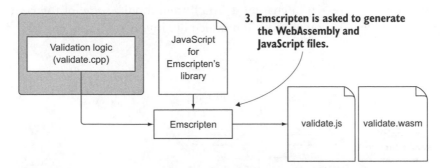

Figure 5.7　Step 3 is to ask Emscripten to generate both the WebAssembly and JavaScript files. In this case, you'll also ask Emscripten to include the mergeinto.js file.

To tell the Emscripten compiler to include your JavaScript code in the generated JavaScript file, you'll need to use the `--js-library` flag followed by the path of the file to include. To ensure that the Emscripten helper functions that your JavaScript code needs are included in the generated JavaScript file, you'll specify them when compiling the C++ code by including them in the EXTRA_EXPORTED_RUNTIME_METHODS command-line array. You'll include two Emscripten helper functions:

- `ccall`—Used by the web page's JavaScript code to call into the module
- `UTF8ToString`—Used by the JavaScript you wrote in the mergeinto.js file to read the strings from the module's memory

To compile the code into a WebAssembly module, open a command prompt, navigate to the folder where you saved your validate.cpp and mergeinto.js files, and run the following command:

```
emcc validate.cpp --js-library mergeinto.js
    -s EXTRA_EXPORTED_RUNTIME_METHODS=['ccall','UTF8ToString']
    -o validate.js
```

If you open the Emscripten-generated JavaScript file, validate.js, and search for the `UpdateHostAboutError` function, you should see that the function you defined now is part of the generated JavaScript file:

```
function _UpdateHostAboutError(errorMessagePointer) {
  setErrorMessage(Module.UTF8ToString(errorMessagePointer));
}
```

One nice thing about including functions in the generated JavaScript file is that, if you have several other functions along with `UpdateHostAboutError`, only the functions that are actually called by the module's code will be included.

5.1.4 Adjusting the web page's JavaScript code

Figure 5.8 shows the next step of the process, in which you'll copy the files generated by Emscripten to a folder along with a copy of the editproduct.html and editproduct.js files that you created in chapter 4. You'll then modify some of the code in the editproduct.js file based on how you'll now need to interact with the module.

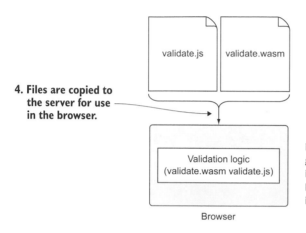

4. Files are copied to the server for use in the browser.

validate.js   validate.wasm

Validation logic
(validate.wasm validate.js)

Browser

Figure 5.8   Step 4 is to copy the generated files to where the HTML file is and update the JavaScript code based on the new way it needs to interact with the module.

In your WebAssembly\Chapter 5\5.1.1 EmJsLibrary\ folder, create a folder called frontend. Copy the following files into your new frontend folder:

- The validate.js and validate.wasm files from your Chapter 5\5.1.1 EmJsLibrary\ source\ folder
- The editproduct.html and editproduct.js files from your Chapter 4\4.1 js_plumbing\ frontend\ folder

Open the editproduct.js file with your editor.

Because the JavaScript no longer needs to create a string buffer and pass it to the module, you can simplify the `onClickSave` function in the editproduct.js file:

- The `errorMessage` and `errorMessagePointer` variables are no longer needed, so you can delete these two lines of code. In their place, you'll put a call to the `setErrorMessage` function and pass in an empty string so that, if there was a previous error displayed on the web page, the message will be hidden in the event that there are no issues with the current call to the save function.
- Remove the `errorMessagePointer` parameter from the call to the `validateName` and `validateCategory` functions.
- Remove the `Module.UTF8ToString` line of code within the `if` statement.

- Revise the if statement so that the or (||) condition between the two checks is now an and (&&) condition, and remove the inequality check (!) from before both function calls. Now, if both function calls indicate that there were no errors, then everything's valid, and the data can be passed to the server-side code.
- You can remove the rest of the code that follows the if statement in the function.

Your onClickSave function should now look like this:

```
function onClickSave() {          Clears any previous
  setErrorMessage("");      ←──── error message

  const name = document.getElementById("name").value;
  const categoryId = getSelectedCategoryId();      The second parameter of each
                                                   function call was removed.
  if (validateName(name) &&      ←──────────
      validateCategory(categoryId)) {  ←──┐ Inequality checks removed from
                                         │ before the function calls. The or
        ←──────┐                        │ condition is changed to and.
  }            There were no issues. The
}              data can be passed to the
               server-side code.
```

You'll also need to modify the validateName function:

- Remove the errorMessagePointer parameter.
- Because the ValidateName function in the WebAssembly module now expects only two parameters, remove the last array item ('number') in the ccall function's third parameter.
- Remove the errorMessagePointer array item from the ccall function's last parameter.

The validateName function should now look like the following code snippet:

```
function validateName(name) {  ←──────────
  const isValid = Module.ccall('ValidateName',      The second parameter
      'number',                                     (errorMessagePointer)
      ['string', 'number'],      ←──                has been removed.
      [name, MAXIMUM_NAME_LENGTH]);  ←──┐ The third array item
                                        │ (number) has been removed.
  return (isValid === 1);
}              The third array item
               (errorMessagePointer)
               has been removed.
```

You'll make the same changes to the validateCategory function that you did to the validateName function:

- Remove the errorMessagePointer parameter.
- Remove the last array item ('number') from the ccall function's third parameter.
- Remove the errorMessagePointer array item from the ccall function's last parameter.

The validateCategory function should now look like the code in the next listing.

Listing 5.2   The modified validateCategory function in editproduct.js

```
function validateCategory(categoryId) {
  const arrayLength = VALID_CATEGORY_IDS.length;
  const bytesPerElement = Module.HEAP32.BYTES_PER_ELEMENT;
  const arrayPointer = Module._malloc((arrayLength * bytesPerElement));
  Module.HEAP32.set(VALID_CATEGORY_IDS, (arrayPointer / bytesPerElement));

  const isValid = Module.ccall('ValidateCategory',
      'number',
      ['string', 'number', 'number'],
      [categoryId, arrayPointer, arrayLength]);

  Module._free(arrayPointer);

  return (isValid === 1);}
```

The second parameter (errorMessagePointer) has been removed.

The fourth array item (number) has been removed.

The fourth array item (errorMessagePointer) has been removed.

5.1.5   *Viewing the results*

Now that you've finished modifying the JavaScript code, you can open your browser and type `http://localhost:8080/editproduct.html` into the address box to see the web page. You can test the validation by removing all the text from the Name field and then clicking the Save button. An error should display on the web page (figure 5.9).

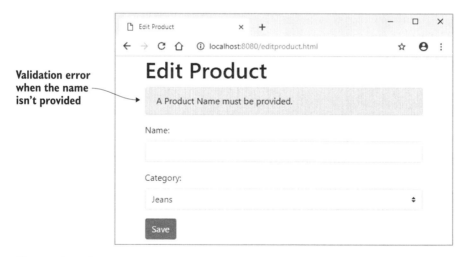

Validation error when the name isn't provided

Figure 5.9   Edit Product page's Name validation error

5.2 Using C or C++ to create a module without Emscripten plumbing

Suppose you want to have Emscripten compile the C++ code and not include any of the standard C library functions or generate the JavaScript plumbing file. Emscripten's plumbing code is convenient, but it also hides a lot of the details of working with a WebAssembly module. The approach you'll see here is quite helpful in learning because you'll be working with the module directly.

The process you saw in section 5.1, with Emscripten's plumbing code, is typically what's used for production code. Emscripten's generated JavaScript file is convenient because it handles loading and instantiating the module and includes helper functions to make interacting with the module easier.

In section 5.1, when you compiled your WebAssembly module and included the Emscripten plumbing code, your updateHostAboutError function was placed within Emscripten's generated JavaScript file, as figure 5.10 shows.

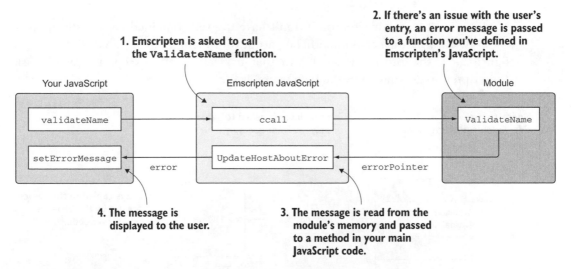

Figure 5.10   The module calling back to the JavaScript through a function you defined in the Emscripten-generated JavaScript file

When you're not using Emscripten's plumbing code, your C or C++ code won't have access to Emscripten macros or Emscripten's JavaScript file, but it's still possible to call into JavaScript directly. Because you won't have access to Emscripten's generated JavaScript file, the callback function will need to be placed in your website's JavaScript file, as figure 5.11 shows.

In section 5.1.1, I warned you that when including JavaScript in Emscripten's JavaScript code, the code needs to be self-contained if you plan to target Node.js. In chapter 10, you'll work with WebAssembly modules in Node.js and see this in more detail, but the warning is due to how the Emscripten-generated JavaScript files are loaded into Node.js.

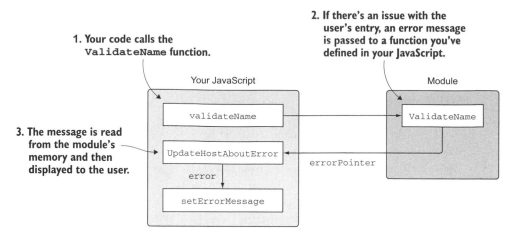

Figure 5.11   How the callback logic works without Emscripten plumbing code

Modules built using this approach don't have the self-contained code restrictions—the code your module calls into will be part of your main JavaScript. As you can see in figure 5.12, the process is similar to that in section 5.1, except that you'll ask Emscripten to generate only the WebAssembly file.

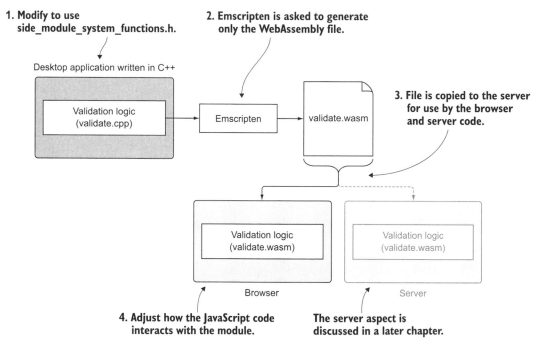

Figure 5.12   Steps in which existing C++ logic is turned into WebAssembly for use by a website and the server-side code but without any generated Emscripten JavaScript code. I discuss the server aspect, Node.js, in a future chapter.

5.2.1 Making the C++ modifications

The first step of the process (figure 5.13) is to modify the C++ code that you created in section 5.1 so that it uses the side_module_system_functions.h and .cpp files that you created in chapter 4. In your Chapter 5\ folder, create a 5.2.1 SideModuleCallingJS\ source\ folder for your files in this section. Copy the following files into your new source folder:

- The validate.cpp file from your 5.1.1 EmJsLibrary\source\ folder
- The side_module_system_functions.h and .cpp files from your Chapter 4\4.2 side_module\source\ folder

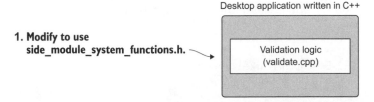

Figure 5.13   You need to modify the C++ code from section 5.1 to use the side_module_system_functions files that you created in chapter 4.

When it comes to calling into JavaScript directly, the C++ code is identical to what you created in section 5.1, in which the `extern` keyword is used to define the function signature of the JavaScript function:

```
extern void UpdateHostAboutError(const char* error_message);
```

The only difference between the C++ code here and the code you wrote in section 5.1 is that this code won't have access to the standard C library. You'll need to import the code you wrote in chapter 4 that gave you functions like `strcpy`, `strlen`, and `atoi`.

Open the validate.cpp file in your favorite editor, and then remove the includes for the standard system library cstdlib and cstring. Then, add the header for your version of the standard C library functions, side_module_system_functions.h, within the `extern "C"` block.

> **WARNING**   The include for the header file must be placed within the `extern "C"` block because you'll be asking the Emscripten compiler to compile two .cpp files. Although both files' functions are within `extern "C"` blocks, the Emscripten compiler still assumes that function calls in the validate.cpp file are being compiled to a C++ file, where the functions have been mangled. The compiler won't see the mangled function names in the generated module and will assume they need to be imported instead.

The following snippet shows the modifications to the validate.cpp file:

```
#ifdef __EMSCRIPTEN__
  #include <emscripten.h>
#endif

#ifdef __cplusplus
extern "C" {
#endif

#include "side_module_system_functions.h"
```
Important: place the header file within the extern "C" block.

5.2.2   Compiling the code into a WebAssembly module

Now that the C++ code is modified, the next step is to have Emscripten compile it into a WebAssembly module but without the JavaScript plumbing code, as figure 5.14 shows.

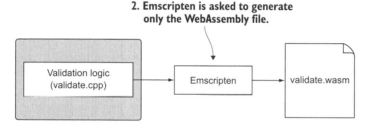

2. Emscripten is asked to generate only the WebAssembly file.

Figure 5.14   In this case, you need to ask Emscripten to generate only the WebAssembly file but not the JavaScript plumbing file.

To compile the C++ code into a WebAssembly module, open a command prompt, navigate to the folder where you saved the C++ files, and run the following command:

```
emcc side_module_system_functions.cpp validate.cpp
    -s SIDE_MODULE=2 -O1 -o validate.wasm
```

5.2.3   Adjusting the JavaScript that will interact with the module

Once you've generated the WebAssembly module, figure 5.15 shows the next step, in which you'll copy the generated Wasm file to where the HTML file is located. You'll then modify how the JavaScript code interacts with the module now that it's not passing a buffer to the module's functions.

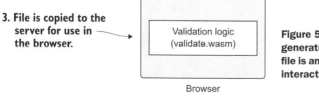

3. File is copied to the server for use in the browser.

Browser

Figure 5.15   You need to copy the generated Wasm file to where the HTML file is and modify how the JavaScript code interacts with the module.

In your Chapter 5\5.2.1 SideModuleCallingJS\ folder, create a frontend\ folder. Copy the following files into this folder:

- Your newly generated validate.wasm file from the 5.2.1 SideModuleCalling-JS\source\ folder
- The editproduct.html and editproduct.js files from the Chapter 4\4.2 side_module\frontend\ folder

In your C++ code, the `extern` keyword and function signature tell the Emscripten compiler that the module will be importing the `_UpdateHostAboutError` function (the Emscripten compiler adds an underscore before the function's name in the generated WebAssembly module). Because you don't have the Emscripten plumbing code, when your JavaScript instantiates the module, it's up to you to pass the `_Update-HostAboutError` function to the module.

THE INITIALIZEPAGE FUNCTION

Your first step is to open the editproduct.js file in your editor and then locate the `initializePage` function. Revise `importObject` by adding a new property to the end with the name `_UpdateHostAboutError` and a function that receives the `error-MessagePointer` parameter. Within the function's body, you'll call the `getString-FromMemory` function to read the string from the module's memory. You'll then pass the string to the `setErrorMessage` function.

The next listing shows what the `importObject` should now look like in the `initializePage` function of the editproduct.js file.

> **Listing 5.3 `_UpdateHostAboutError` added to the `importObject`**

```
function initializePage() {
  ...

  moduleMemory = new WebAssembly.Memory({initial: 256});

  const importObject = {
    env: {
      __memory_base: 0,                                    Function created to respond
      memory: moduleMemory,                                  to calls from the module
      _UpdateHostAboutError: function(errorMessagePointer) {  ◄
        setErrorMessage(getStringFromMemory(errorMessagePointer));  ◄
      },
    }                                                      Reads the string from the
  };                                                       module's memory and
                                                           displays it to the user
  ...
}
```

The rest of the changes to the editproduct.js file will be the same ones that you made in section 5.1, with the removal of the error buffer variable from the `onClickSave`, `validateName`, and `validateCategory` functions.

THE ONCLICKSAVE FUNCTION

Locate the onClickSave function, and do the following:

- Replace the errorMessage and errorMessagePointer lines of code with a call to setErrorMessage, passing in an empty string. If there are no validation issues, calling the setErrorMessage function with an empty string will remove any error message that might have been displayed the last time the user clicked the Save button.
- Modify the if statement to no longer pass in the errorMessagePointer parameter.
- Remove the inequality checks (!) from before the validateName and validate-Category function calls. Change the or (||) check to an and (&&) check.
- Remove the getStringFromMemory line of code from within the if statement's body. If everything is ok with the validation, the body of the if statement will be where you put the code to pass the information to the server side to be saved.
- Delete the rest of the code that follows the if statement in the onClickSave function.

The onClickSave function should now look like the following code snippet:

```
function onClickSave() {              Clears any previous
  setErrorMessage("");            ⊲──  error message

  const name = document.getElementById("name").value;
  const categoryId = getSelectedCategoryId();          The second parameter
                                                       of each function call
  if (validateName(name) &&          ⊲──               was removed.
      validateCategory(categoryId)) {  ⊲──
                                           Inequality checks removed.
          ⊲──  There were no issues. The    The or condition is
  }          data can be passed to the     changed to and.
}            server-side code.
```

THE VALIDATENAME AND VALIDATECATEGORY FUNCTIONS

Your next step is to modify the validateName and validateCategory functions to no longer receive an errorMessagePointer parameter or pass the value to the module's functions. The following listing shows the modified functions.

Listing 5.4   Modifications to the `validateName` and `validateCategory` functions

```
function validateName(name) {          ⊲──
  const namePointer = moduleExports._create_buffer((name.length + 1));
  copyStringToMemory(name, namePointer);
                                                    errorMessagePointer
  const isValid = moduleExports._ValidateName(namePointer,  removed as the
      MAXIMUM_NAME_LENGTH);          ⊲──            second parameter to
                                                     the function
  moduleExports._free_buffer(namePointer);

  return (isValid === 1);          errorMessagePointer no
}                                  longer passed to the
                                   module's function
```

```
function validateCategory(categoryId) {
  const categoryIdPointer = moduleExports._create_buffer(
  (categoryId.length + 1));
  copyStringToMemory(categoryId, categoryIdPointer);

  const arrayLength = VALID_CATEGORY_IDS.length;
  const bytesPerElement = Int32Array.BYTES_PER_ELEMENT;
  const arrayPointer = moduleExports._create_buffer((arrayLength *
  bytesPerElement));

  const bytesForArray = new Int32Array(moduleMemory.buffer);
  bytesForArray.set(VALID_CATEGORY_IDS, (arrayPointer / bytesPerElement));

  const isValid = moduleExports._ValidateCategory(categoryIdPointer,
      arrayPointer, arrayLength);

  moduleExports._free_buffer(arrayPointer);
  moduleExports._free_buffer(categoryIdPointer);

  return (isValid === 1);
}
```

errorMessagePointer removed as the second parameter to the function

errorMessagePointer no longer passed to the module's function

5.2.4   *Viewing the results*

Now that you have everything adjusted, you can type http://localhost:8080/editproduct.html into the address box of your browser to see the web page. You can test that the validation is working correctly by changing the selection of the Category drop-down so that nothing is selected and then clicking the Save button. The validation check should cause an error to be displayed on the web page, as figure 5.16 shows.

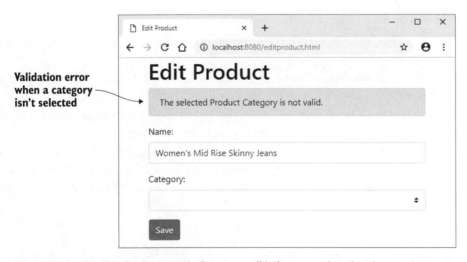

Validation error when a category isn't selected

Figure 5.16   The Edit Product page's Category validation error when there's no category selected

How can you use what you learned in this chapter in the real world?

Real-world use cases

With the ability to call into JavaScript, your module can now interact with the web page and the browser's Web APIs, opening up a lot of possibilities. Some options include:

- Creating a WebAssembly module that performs ray-tracing computations for 3D graphics. The graphics could then be used for an interactive web page or a game.
- Creating a file converter (take a photo and convert it to a PDF before including it in an email, for example).
- Taking an existing open source C++ library—cryptography, for example—and compiling it to WebAssembly for use by your website. This website lists a number of open source C++ libraries: https://en.cppreference.com/w/cpp/links/libs.

Exercises

You can find the solutions to these exercises in appendix D.

1 Which keyword do you need to use to define a signature in your C or C++ code so that the compiler knows the function will be available when the code is run?
2 Suppose you need to include a function in Emscripten's JavaScript code that your module will call to determine if the user's device is online or not. How would you include a function called `IsOnline` that returns 1 for true and 0 (zero) for false?

Summary

In this chapter, you learned the following:

- You can modify a WebAssembly module so it can talk to the JavaScript code directly.
- External functions can be defined in your C or C++ code using the `extern` keyword.
- You can add your own JavaScript code to Emscripten's generated JavaScript file by adding it to the `LibraryManager.library` object.
- When not using Emscripten's plumbing code, you can include a function for the module to import by placing it in the JavaScript object that you pass to the `WebAssembly.instantiate` or `WebAssembly.instantiateStreaming` functions.

Creating a WebAssembly module that talks to JavaScript using function pointers

This chapter covers

- Adjusting C or C++ code to work with function pointers
- Using Emscripten's helper functions to pass JavaScript functions to the WebAssembly module
- Calling function pointers in the WebAssembly module when not using Emscripten's plumbing code

In chapter 5, you modified your module so that it was no longer passing a validation error message back to the JavaScript through a parameter. Instead, you modified the module so that it called a JavaScript function directly, as figure 6.1 illustrates.

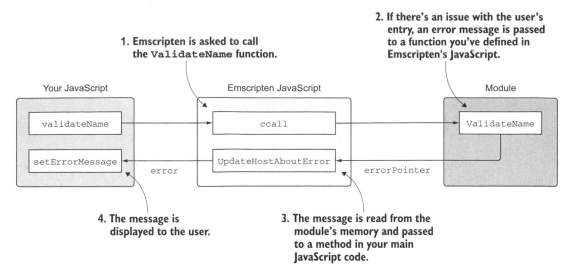

Figure 6.1   The module calling a function in the JavaScript code

Imagine being able to pass a JavaScript function to the module based on your Java-Script code's needs at the time. When the module finishes processing, it can then call the function that was specified, as figure 6.2 shows.

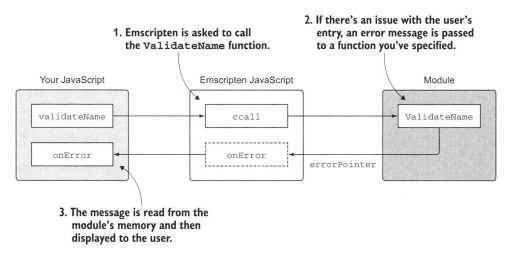

Figure 6.2   The module calling a JavaScript function pointer

6.1 Using C or C++ to create a module with Emscripten plumbing

In this section, you're going to build the C++ code for the validation logic. You'll include the standard C library and Emscripten helper functions, which is the recommended way to build a module for use in production. Later in this chapter, you'll learn the other approach to building a WebAssembly module, which doesn't include the standard C library or Emscripten helper functions.

6.1.1 Using a function pointer given to the module by JavaScript

As figure 6.3 shows, adjusting the module so that it uses function pointers requires the following steps:

1 Modify the C++ code so that the exported functions receive success and error function pointers.
2 Ask Emscripten to generate the WebAssembly file and JavaScript plumbing file.
3 Copy the generated files for use in the browser.
4 Revise the website's JavaScript code to interact with the WebAssembly module now that it expects function pointers to be specified.

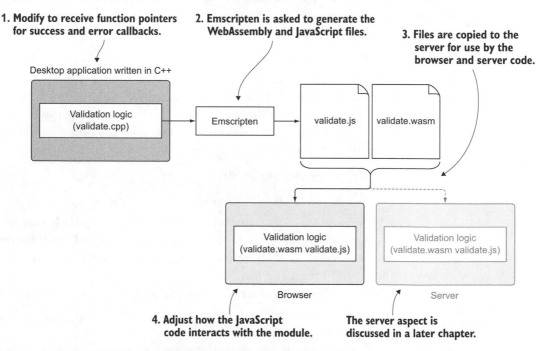

Figure 6.3 Steps showing existing C++ logic modified to accept function pointers and then turned into WebAssembly for use by a website and the server-side code. I discuss the server aspect, Node.js, in a future chapter.

6.1.2   *Adjusting the C++ code*

As figure 6.4 shows, the first step is to modify the C++ code to accept function pointers.

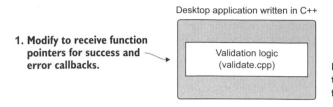

Figure 6.4   Step 1 is to modify the code so that it accepts function pointers.

Create the following folder to hold your files for this section: WebAssembly\Chapter 6\6.1.2 EmFunctionPointers\source\. Copy the validate.cpp file from the WebAssembly\Chapter 5\5.1.1 EmJsLibrary\ source\ folder to the source folder you just created. Then open it with your favorite editor to define the function signatures that your code will use to call the JavaScript code to indicate either success or that there's an issue with the user's data.

DEFINING THE FUNCTION SIGNATURES

In C or C++, functions can accept a parameter with a function pointer's signature. For example, the following parameter would be for a function pointer that doesn't receive any parameters or return a value:

```
void(*UpdateHostOnSuccess)(void)
```

You may run across code examples where the function pointer is being called by first dereferencing the pointer. This isn't needed because the dereferenced function pointer is immediately converted to a pointer, so you just get the same function pointer back. The C code can call the function pointer the same way it would call a normal function, as the following example shows:

```
void Test(void(*UpdateHostOnSuccess)(void)) {
  UpdateHostOnSuccess();
}
```

Although you can specify a function signature as the parameter in each function where it's needed, you can also create a definition of that signature and use it for the parameters instead. To create a definition of a function signature, you use the typedef keyword followed by the signature.

Using a predefined function signature rather than defining the function signature for each parameter has some advantages:

- It simplifies the functions.
- It improves maintainability. If you ever need to adjust a function signature, you don't need to modify every parameter where it's used. Instead, you need to update only one spot: the definition.

You'll be using the typedef approach to define the two function signatures the code needs in the validate.cpp file:

- One signature will be for a success callback function that will not have any parameters or return a value.
- The other signature will be for a validation error callback function. It will accept a const char* parameter and not return a value.

In the validate.cpp file, replace the extern void UpdateHostAboutError line of code with the following snippet of the two signatures:

```
typedef void(*OnSuccess)(void);
typedef void(*OnError)(const char*);
```

Now that the module won't be receiving a buffer parameter in order to return an error message, you'll need to remove that parameter from the module's functions, starting with the ValidateValueProvided function.

THE VALIDATEVALUEPROVIDED FUNCTION

Revise the ValidateValueProvided function to remove the error_message parameter. Then remove the UpdateHostAboutError call from the if statement.

The modified ValidateValueProvided function should now look like the following:

```
int ValidateValueProvided(const char* value) {        ◄─────────────┐  The error_message
  if ((value == NULL) || (value[0] == '\0')) {   ◄───┐              │  parameter has been
    return 0;                                         │              │  removed.
  }                       The code no longer calls    │
                          UpdateHostAboutError.       │
  return 1;
}
```

Next, you need to modify the ValidateName and ValidateCategory functions to receive success and error function pointers to call the appropriate function based on whether there's an issue with the user's data.

THE VALIDATENAME FUNCTION

You need to make several modifications to the ValidateName function. Start by changing the function's return type from int to void, and then add two function pointer parameters:

- OnSuccess UpdateHostOnSuccess
- OnError UpdateHostOnError

Because you removed the second parameter from the ValidateValueProvided function, you won't be able to pass the string to it, so remove the second parameter from the function call. Replace the return 0 line of code within that if statement with a call to the error function pointer:

```
UpdateHostOnError("A Product Name must be provided.");
```

Originally, the JavaScript function that the code was calling was called UpdateHost-AboutError. You've removed that function and now need to have the code in the string length (`strlen`) if statement call the error function pointer instead. Rename the `UpdateHostAboutError` function call as `UpdateHostOnError`, and then remove the `return 0` line of code.

Because the `ValidateName` function now returns `void`, you need to remove the `return 1` line of code from the end of the function and replace it with an `else` statement at the end of the `if` block. The `else` block is triggered when there are no issues with the user's entry, so you'll want to tell the JavaScript code that everything was successful; to do this, you'll call the success function pointer:

```
UpdateHostOnSuccess();
```

The `ValidateName` function in the validate.cpp file should now look like the code in the following listing.

Listing 6.1 `ValidateName` modified to use function pointers (validate.cpp)

```
...

#ifdef __EMSCRIPTEN__
  EMSCRIPTEN_KEEPALIVE
#endif
void ValidateName(char* name, int maximum_length,     ⟵——  The function now returns
    OnSuccess UpdateHostOnSuccess, OnError UpdateHostOnError) {   ⟵——   void. All return statements
  if (ValidateValueProvided(name) == 0) {                                          have been removed.
    UpdateHostOnError("A Product Name must be provided.");
  }                                                              OnSuccess and
  else if (strlen(name) > maximum_length) {                    OnError function
    UpdateHostOnError("The Product Name is too long.");         pointers have
  }                                                             been added.
  else {
    UpdateHostOnSuccess();
  }
}
...
```

No changes are needed for the `IsCategoryIdInArray` function.

You'll make the same changes to the `ValidateCategory` function that you made to the `ValidateName` function by adding the success and error function pointer parameters. You'll then modify the code to call the appropriate function pointer depending on whether there's an issue with the user's data.

THE VALIDATECATEGORY FUNCTION

Change the return type of the `ValidateCategory` function to now return `void` and then add the function pointer parameters for success and for if there's an issue with the user's entry:

- `OnSuccess UpdateHostOnSuccess`
- `OnError UpdateHostOnError`

Remove the second parameter from the call to the ValidateValueProvided function, and replace the return 0 line of code within that if statement with the following:

```
UpdateHostOnError("A Product Category must be selected.");
```

Because you're no longer calling the original JavaScript function, UpdateHostAbout-Error, you'll need to adjust the calls that were being made to that function to call the error function pointer. Replace the UpdateHostAboutError calls with UpdateHost-OnError, and remove the return statement line of code in the following spots:

- In the valid_category_ids == NULL if statement
- In the IsCategoryIdInArray if statement

Lastly, because the ValidateCategory function now returns void, remove the return 1 line of code from the end of the function, and add an else statement to the end of the if block. The else block will be triggered if there are no issues with the user's entry. At this point, you'll want to tell the JavaScript code that the user-selected category is valid, so you'll call the success function pointer:

```
UpdateHostOnSuccess();
```

The ValidateCategory function in the validate.cpp file should now look like the code in the next listing.

> **Listing 6.2 ValidateCategory modified to use function pointers (validate.cpp)**

```
...

#ifdef __EMSCRIPTEN__              The function now returns
  EMSCRIPTEN_KEEPALIVE             void. All return statements
#endif                             have been removed.
void ValidateCategory(char* category_id, int* valid_category_ids,   ◁
    int array_length, OnSuccess UpdateHostOnSuccess,
    OnError UpdateHostOnError) {   ◁
  if (ValidateValueProvided(category_id) == 0) {
    UpdateHostOnError("A Product Category must be selected.");
  }
  else if ((valid_category_ids == NULL) || (array_length == 0)) {
    UpdateHostOnError("There are no Product Categories available.");
  }
  else if (IsCategoryIdInArray(category_id, valid_category_ids,
      array_length) == 0) {
    UpdateHostOnError("The selected Product Category is not valid.");
  }
  else {                                    OnSuccess and
    UpdateHostOnSuccess();                  OnError parameters
  }                                         have been added.
}
...
```

Now that you've modified the C++ code to use function pointers, you can move on to the next step in the process (figure 6.5) and have Emscripten compile the code into a WebAssembly module.

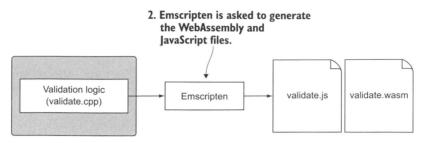

Figure 6.5   Step 2 is to ask Emscripten to generate both the WebAssembly and JavaScript files.

6.1.3   Compiling the code into a WebAssembly module

When the Emscripten compiler sees your C++ function pointer use, it will expect functions with those signatures to be imported during the module's instantiation. Once a module has been instantiated, you can only add exported WebAssembly functions from another module. This means the JavaScript code can't specify a function pointer later that hasn't already been imported.

If you can't import JavaScript functions after the module has been instantiated, how are you going to specify a JavaScript function dynamically? As it turns out, Emscripten provides the module with functions that have the necessary signatures during instantiation and then maintains a backing array in its JavaScript code. When the module calls the function pointer, Emscripten looks into the backing array to see if your JavaScript code has provided it with a function to call for that signature.

For the function pointers, the size of Emscripten's backing array needs to be explicitly set at compile-time by including the RESERVED_FUNCTION_POINTERS flag. The ValidateName and ValidateCategory functions are each expecting two function pointer parameters, and you'll be modifying your JavaScript to call both functions at the same time, so the backing array will need to be able to hold four items at once. As a result, you'll need to specify a value of 4 for this flag.

To add or remove function pointers from Emscripten's backing array, your JavaScript code will need access to Emscripten's addFunction and removeFunction helper functions. To make sure these functions are included in the generated JavaScript file, you'll include them in the EXTRA_EXPORTED_RUNTIME_METHODS command-line array.

To compile the code into a WebAssembly module, open a command prompt, navigate to the folder where you saved the validate.cpp file, and run the following command:

```
emcc validate.cpp -s RESERVED_FUNCTION_POINTERS=4
   -s EXTRA_EXPORTED_RUNTIME_METHODS=['ccall','UTF8ToString',
   'addFunction','removeFunction'] -o validate.js
```

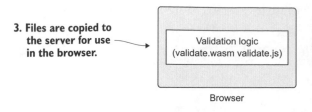

3. Files are copied to the server for use in the browser.

Validation logic (validate.wasm validate.js)

Browser

Figure 6.6   Step 3 is to copy the generated files to where your HTML and JavaScript files are located. You'll then update the JavaScript code to pass JavaScript functions to the module.

Now that you've generated the WebAssembly module and the Emscripten JavaScript file, the next step (figure 6.6) is to copy the generated files to a folder where you'll also copy the editproduct.html and editproduct.js files that you worked on in chapter 5. You'll then update the editproduct.js file to pass JavaScript functions to the module.

6.1.4 *Adjusting the web page's JavaScript code*

In your Chapter 6\6.1.2 EmFunctionPointers\ folder, create a frontend folder and then copy the following files into it:

- The validate.js and validate.wasm files from your Chapter 6\6.1.2 EmFunction-Pointers\source\ folder
- The editproduct.html and editproduct.js files from your Chapter 5\5.1.1 EmJs-Library\frontend\ folder

Open the editproduct.js file in your favorite editor so that you can modify the code to pass function pointers to the module.

THE ONCLICKSAVE FUNCTION

In the C++ code, you modified the module's validation functions to no longer have a return value but instead call the provided JavaScript function pointers to indicate success or an error when the validation logic is ready to call back. Because you don't know when the function pointers will be called, you'll modify the validateName and validateCategory JavaScript functions to return a Promise object.

Right now, the onClickSave function uses an if statement to call the validate-Name function first. If there are no issues with the user-entered name, the if statement then calls the validateCategory function. Because both functions will be modified to return a promise, you'll need to replace the if statement to work with promises.

You could call the validateName function, wait for it to succeed, and then call the validateCategory function. This would work, but the Promise.all method will call both validation functions at the same time and will simplify the code compared with doing one call at a time.

The Promise.all method is passed an array of promises and returns a single Promise object. If all the promises succeed, the then method is called. If any promise is rejected (there was an error), the rejected reason of the first promise to reject is the one that gets returned. You could use the second parameter of the then method to receive the rejected reason, but you'll use the promise's catch statement instead because that's the most common approach developers use to handle promise errors.

Modify the onClickSave function in the editproduct.js file to match the code in the next listing.

Listing 6.3   onClickSave modified to use Promise.all (editproduct.js)

```
...
function onClickSave() {
  setErrorMessage("");

  const name = document.getElementById("name").value;
  const categoryId = getSelectedCategoryId();

  Promise.all([                          ⟵          Calls both
    validateName(name),                             validation functions
    validateCategory(categoryId)
  ])                                                       Both validation
  .then(() => {              ⟵                            functions return success.

  })                ⟵                        There are no issues with the
  .catch((error) => {   ⟵                    validation. The data can be saved.
    setErrorMessage(error);
  });                                    If either validation function
}                                        returns an error, then this
...                                      block is triggered.
```

Displays the error message ⟶ (points to setErrorMessage(error);)

Before you move on to modify the validateName and validateCategory functions to pass a JavaScript function to the WebAssembly module, you'll need to learn how to pass a function to Emscripten's backing array.

CALLING EMSCRIPTEN'S ADDFUNCTION HELPER FUNCTION

For the JavaScript code to pass a function to the module, it needs to use the Emscripten helper function addFunction. The addFunction call will add the Java-Script function to a backing array and then return an index that you need to pass to the ccall function, as illustrated in figure 6.7. (You can find more information about ccall in appendix B.)

The addFunction function accepts two parameters:

- The JavaScript function that you want to pass to the module
- A string that represents the function's signature

The first character in the function signature string represents the return value's type, and the rest of the characters represent each parameter's value type. The following characters are available for the value types:

- v—Void
- i—32-bit integer
- j—64-bit integer
- f—32-bit float
- d—64-bit float

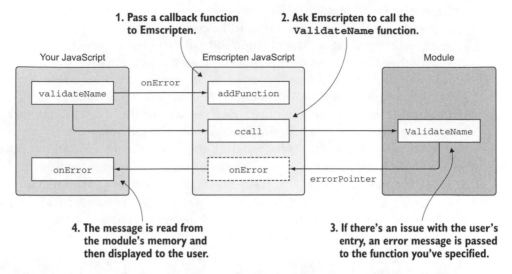

1. Pass a callback function to Emscripten.

2. Ask Emscripten to call the `ValidateName` function.

4. The message is read from the module's memory and then displayed to the user.

3. If there's an issue with the user's entry, an error message is passed to the function you've specified.

Figure 6.7 A JavaScript function being passed to Emscripten's backing array to be called later by the module

When your code finishes with the function pointer, you need to remove it from Emscripten's backing array. To do this, you pass the index you received from add-Function to removeFunction.

For each of your module's validation functions, you'll need to pass in two function pointers, one for a success callback and one for a validation error callback. To make things easier, you'll create a JavaScript helper function called createPointers that will help both JavaScript validation functions create the function pointers.

THE CREATEPOINTERS FUNCTION

The createPointers function will receive the following parameters:

- resolve—The resolve method of the promise belonging to the validateName or validateCategory function
- reject—The reject method of the promise belonging to the validateName or validateCategory function
- returnPointers—An object that will be returned to the calling function and will hold the index of each function that was added to Emscripten's backing array

You'll use *anonymous functions* for both function pointers that will be added to Emscripten's backing array.

INFO In JavaScript, anonymous functions are functions that are defined without including a name. For more information, you can visit this MDN Web Docs page: http://mng.bz/7zDV.

The success function pointer expected by the module has a `void` return type and no parameters, so the value that needs to be passed as the second parameter to `add-Function` is `'v'`. If called, this function will call first your `freePointers` helper function and then the `resolve` method that was passed into the `createPointers` function.

The error function pointer expected by the module has a `void` return type and a `const char*` parameter. In WebAssembly, pointers are represented by 32-bit integers. In this case, the function signature string needed for the second parameter of the `addFunction` is `'vi'`. If called, this function will first call your `freePointers` helper function, will read the error message from the module's memory, and will then call the `reject` method that was passed into the `createPointers` function.

At the end of the `createPointers` function, the index of each function that you added to Emscripten's backing array will be placed in the `returnPointers` object.

After the `onClickSave` function in your editproduct.js file, add the `createPointers` function shown in the next listing.

Listing 6.4   The new `createPointers` function in editproduct.js

Creates the function for a success call from the module

Calls the resolve (success) method of the promise

resolve and reject are from the promise. returnPointers holds the function indexes.

Removes both functions from Emscripten's backing array

```
...
function createPointers(resolve, reject, returnPointers) {
    const onSuccess = Module.addFunction(function() {
        freePointers(onSuccess, onError);
        resolve();
    }, 'v');

    const onError = Module.addFunction(function(errorMessage) {
        freePointers(onSuccess, onError);
        reject(Module.UTF8ToString(errorMessage));
    }, 'vi');

    returnPointers.onSuccess = onSuccess;
    returnPointers.onError = onError;
}
...
```

Function's signature: no return value and no parameters

Function signature: no return value and a 32-bit integer parameter (pointer)

Reads the error from the module's memory and then calls the promise's reject method

Adds the function indexes to the return object

Creates the function for an error call from the module

To help remove the function pointers from Emscripten's backing array once you're done with them, you'll create another helper function called `freePointers`.

THE FREEPOINTERS FUNCTION

Following the `createPointers` function, add the following snippet of code for the `freePointers` function to handle removing your functions from Emscripten's backing array:

```
function freePointers(onSuccess, onError){
  Module.removeFunction(onSuccess);
  Module.removeFunction(onError);
}
```

Removes the functions from Emscripten's backing array

Now that you've created the functions to help add functions to Emscripten's backing array and remove them when you're finished, you'll need to modify the `validateName` and `validateCategory` functions. You'll modify these functions to return a `Promise` object and, with help from your new `createPointers` function, pass JavaScript functions to the module.

THE VALIDATENAME FUNCTION

You'll modify the `validateName` function to return a `Promise` object, and you'll use an anonymous function within the `Promise` object. Within the anonymous function, the first thing you need to do is call the `createPointers` function to have your `Success` and `Error` functions created. The `createPointers` call will also return the indexes you need to pass to the module for the success and error function pointers. These indexes will be placed in the object, `pointers`, that's passed as the third parameter to the `createPointers` function.

Remove the `const  isValid =` code that's in front of `Module.ccall`, and then modify the `Module.ccall` function as follows:

- Set the second parameter to `null` to indicate that the `ValidateName` function's return value is `void`.
- Add two additional `'number'` types to the third parameter's array because the module's function now accepts two new parameters that are pointers. Pointers in WebAssembly are represented using 32-bit values, which is why the `number` type is used.
- Because two new parameters were added to the module's function, pass the indexes for the `Success` and `Error` functions to the `ccall` function's fourth parameter. The indexes are returned in the object `pointers` from the `createPointers` call.
- Remove the function's `return` statement.

The `validateName` function in the editproduct.js file should now look like the code in the following listing.

Listing 6.5 The modified `validateName` function in editproduct.js

```
...

function validateName(name) {
  return new Promise(function(resolve, reject) {
```

Returns a Promise object for the caller

```
        const pointers = { onSuccess: null, onError: null };
        createPointers(resolve, reject, pointers);

        Module.ccall('ValidateName',
            null,
            ['string', 'number', 'number', 'number'],
            [name, MAXIMUM_NAME_LENGTH, pointers.onSuccess,
                pointers.onError]);

    });
}
...
const isValid = removed
```

**Creates the function
pointers for the module**

**Success and Error
function indexes are
added to the array.**

**Two number types are added for
the two new pointer parameters.**

**Module's function
now returns void**

The same changes that were made to the validateName function now need to be made to the validateCategory function by returning a Promise object and using the create-Pointers function to create function pointers that can be passed to the module.

THE VALIDATECATEGORY FUNCTION

As you did for the validateName function, you'll modify the validateCategory function to return a Promise object. Call the createPointers function to have the Success and Error functions created.

Remove the const isValid = portion of code that's before the Module.ccall function, and then revise this function as follows:

- Change the second parameter to null, because the module's function now returns void.
- Add two new 'number' types to the array of the third parameter of ccall for the two pointer types.
- Add the Success and Error function indexes to the array of ccall's fourth parameter.
- Finally, remove the return statement from the end of the function.

Your validateCategory function should look like the code in the next listing.

> **Listing 6.6   The modified validateCategory function in editproduct.js**

```
...
function validateCategory(categoryId) {
    return new Promise(function(resolve, reject) {

        const pointers = { onSuccess: null, onError: null };
        createPointers(resolve, reject, pointers);

        const arrayLength = VALID_CATEGORY_IDS.length;
        const bytesPerElement = Module.HEAP32.BYTES_PER_ELEMENT;
        const arrayPointer = Module._malloc((arrayLength * bytesPerElement));
        Module.HEAP32.set(VALID_CATEGORY_IDS,
```

**Returns a Promise
object for the caller**

**Creates the function
pointers for the module**

```
                    (arrayPointer / bytesPerElement));
          Module.ccall('ValidateCategory',
          null,
          ['string', 'number', 'number', 'number', 'number'],
          [categoryId, arrayPointer, arrayLength,
               pointers.onSuccess, pointers.onError]);

          Module._free(arrayPointer);
      });
  }
```

const isValid = removed

Module's function now returns void

Two number types are added for the two new pointer parameters.

Success and Error function indexes are added to the array.

6.1.5   Viewing the results

Now that you've finished modifying the JavaScript code, you can open your browser and type `http://localhost:8080/editproduct.html` into the address box to see the web page. You can test the validation by adding more than 50 characters to the Name field and then pressing the Save button. An error should display on the page (figure 6.8).

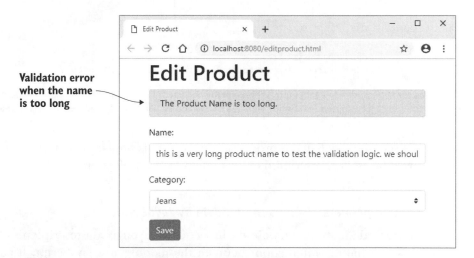

Validation error when the name is too long

Figure 6.8   The Edit Product page's validation error when the name is too long

6.2   Using C or C++ to create a module without Emscripten plumbing

Suppose that you want to have Emscripten compile the C++ code but not include any of the standard C library functions or generate the JavaScript plumbing file. Emscripten's plumbing code is convenient and is recommended for production use, but it also hides a lot of the details of working with WebAssembly modules. Not using Emscripten's plumbing allows you to work with the WebAssembly module directly.

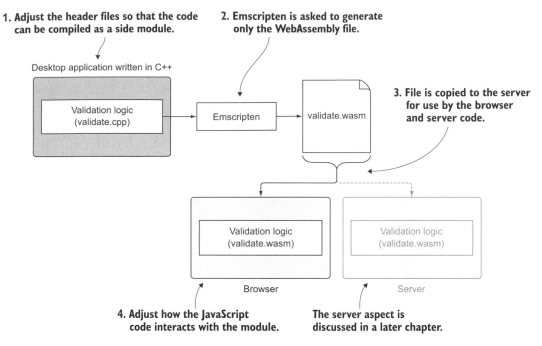

1. Adjust the header files so that the code can be compiled as a side module.

2. Emscripten is asked to generate only the WebAssembly file.

3. File is copied to the server for use by the browser and server code.

4. Adjust how the JavaScript code interacts with the module.

The server aspect is discussed in a later chapter.

Figure 6.9   Steps for turning the C++ logic into WebAssembly for use by a website and the server-side code but without any generated Emscripten JavaScript code. I discuss the server aspect, Node.js, in a later chapter.

As you can see in figure 6.9, the process in this section is similar to that in section 6.1, except you'll be asking Emscripten to generate only the WebAssembly file and not the JavaScript plumbing file.

6.2.1   *Using function pointers given to the module by JavaScript*

When you worked with function pointers in section 6.1, you used Emscripten's plumbing code, which hid the interactions between the module and JavaScript. It actually felt like the JavaScript code was passing a function pointer to the module.

When it comes to function pointers in WebAssembly, the C or C++ code is written as if it's calling the function pointers directly. When compiled into a WebAssembly module, however, the code is actually specifying an index of a function in the Table section of the module and asking the WebAssembly framework to call the function on its behalf.

> **INFO**   A module's Table section is optional, but, if present, it holds a typed array of references, like function pointers, that can't be stored in the module's memory as raw bytes. A module doesn't have direct access to the items in the Table section. Instead, the code asks the WebAssembly framework to access an item based on its index. The framework then accesses the memory and executes the item on the code's behalf. Chapter 2 goes into more detail about the sections of a module.

Function pointers can be functions within the module or can be imported. In your case, as figure 6.10 shows, you'll specify the functions for the OnSuccess and OnError calls so you can pass messages back to JavaScript. Similar to Emscripten's backing array, your JavaScript code will need to maintain an object that holds references to the callback functions that need to be called when the module calls the OnSuccess or OnError function.

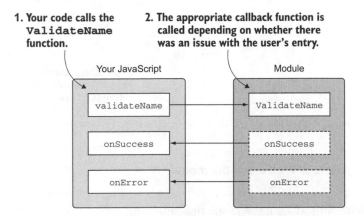

Figure 6.10   A module that has imported the onSuccess and onError JavaScript functions at instantiation. When the ValidateName module function calls either function, it's calling into the JavaScript code.

6.2.2   Making the C++ modifications

The first step of the process (figure 6.11) is to modify the C++ code that you created in section 6.1 so that it uses the side_module_system_functions.h and .cpp files.

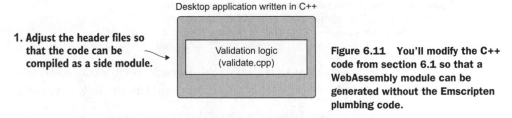

Figure 6.11   You'll modify the C++ code from section 6.1 so that a WebAssembly module can be generated without the Emscripten plumbing code.

In your Chapter 6\ folder, create a 6.2.2 SideModuleFunctionPointers\source\ folder for your files in this section. Copy the following files into your new source folder:

- The validate.cpp file from your 6.1.2 EmFunctionPointers\source\ folder
- The side_module_system_functions.h and .cpp files from your Chapter 4\4.2 side_module\source\ folder

Open the validate.cpp file in your favorite editor.

Because the WebAssembly module will be built as a side module, Emscripten won't include the standard C library, so you need to remove the includes for the cstdlib and cstring header files. To add in your own version of the standard C library functions for your code to use, add an include for the side_module_system_functions.h file in the extern "C" block.

The first part of your validate.cpp file should now look like the following snippet:

```
#ifdef __EMSCRIPTEN__
  #include <emscripten.h>
#endif

#ifdef __cplusplus
extern "C" {
#endif

#include "side_module_system_functions.h"
```

Important: place the header file within the extern "C" block.

That's all that needs to be modified in the validate.cpp file. The rest of the code is fine the way it is.

6.2.3   *Compiling the code into a WebAssembly module*

Now that the C++ code is modified, the next step is to have Emscripten compile it into a WebAssembly module but without the JavaScript plumbing code, as figure 6.12 shows.

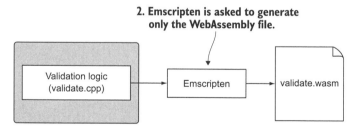

2. Emscripten is asked to generate only the WebAssembly file.

Validation logic (validate.cpp) → Emscripten → validate.wasm

Figure 6.12   Step 2 is to ask Emscripten to generate only the WebAssembly file. Emscripten won't generate the JavaScript plumbing file in this case.

To compile the C++ code into a WebAssembly module, open a command prompt, navigate to the folder where you saved the C++ files, and run the following command:

```
emcc side_module_system_functions.cpp validate.cpp
  -s SIDE_MODULE=2 -O1 -o validate.wasm
```

6.2.4   *Adjusting the JavaScript that will interact with the module*

Figure 6.13 shows the next step of the process, in which you'll copy the generated Wasm file to where the HTML file is located. You'll then modify how the JavaScript code interacts with the module now that you don't have access to Emscripten's plumbing code.

3. File is copied to the server for use in the browser. ⟶

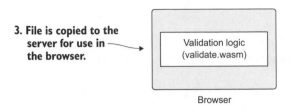

Browser

Figure 6.13 Step 3 is to copy the generated Wasm file to where the HTML file is and modify how the JavaScript code interacts with the module.

In your Chapter 6\6.2.2 SideModuleFunctionPointers\ folder, create a frontend\ folder. Copy the following files into this new folder:

- The validate.wasm file from your 6.2.2 SideModuleFunctionPointers\source\ folder
- The editproduct.html and editproduct.js files from the Chapter 5\5.2.1 SideModuleCallingJS\frontend\folder

Open the editproduct.js file in your favorite editor so that you can adjust the code to work with the WebAssembly module's function pointers.

NEW GLOBAL VARIABLES

You'll need to create some variables to hold the index locations of the success and error function pointers in the module's Table section. Place the following code snippet between the const VALID_CATEGORY_IDS = [100, 101]; line of code and the let moduleMemory = null; line of code in the editproduct.js file:

```
let validateOnSuccessNameIndex = -1;
let validateOnSuccessCategoryIndex = -1;
let validateOnErrorNameIndex = -1;
let validateOnErrorCategoryIndex = -1;
```

While waiting for the module to complete its processing, you'll also need some way of keeping track of the resolve and reject functions of the promises from the validateName and validateCategory functions. To do this, you'll create an object for each function, as shown in the following snippet, which you can place after the variables you just added in the editproduct.js file:

```
let validateNameCallbacks = { resolve: null, reject: null };
let validateCategoryCallbacks = { resolve: null, reject: null };
```

Even though your C++ code looks like it's calling a function pointer directly, it's not really. Under the hood, function pointer references are placed in the module's Table section. The code calls the desired function at a specific index using call_indirect, and WebAssembly calls the function at that index on the code's behalf. In JavaScript, the Table section is represented by the WebAssembly.Table object.

You'll also need a global variable to hold the module's `WebAssembly.Table` instance, which you'll pass to the module to hold its function pointer references. Place the following code after the `let moduleExports = null;` line in the editproduct.js file:

```
let moduleTable = null;
```

Now that the global variables have been created, the next step is to modify the `initializePage` function so that you can pass the module the objects and functions that it's expecting.

THE INITIALIZEPAGE FUNCTION

The first thing that you'll need to do is create a new instance of the `WebAssembly.Table` object for the module's function pointers. The `WebAssembly.Table` object expects a JavaScript object to the constructor.

The first property of the JavaScript object is called `initial`, and it indicates what the table's initial size should be. The second property is called `element`, and the only value that can be provided at the moment is the string `funcref`. There is a third optional property called `maximum`. If specified, the `maximum` property indicates the maximum size the table is allowed to grow.

The initial number of items needed for the table will depend on the Emscripten compiler. To determine what value to use, you can include the `-g` flag at the command line when you build your WebAssembly module. The flag will tell Emscripten to also create a WebAssembly text format file.

If you open the generated text format file (.wast), you can search for an `import` s-expression for the `table` object, which will look similar to the following:

```
(import "env" "table" (table $table 1 funcref))
```

The value you're looking for would be 1 in this case.

> **INFO**   The WebAssembly specification has been modified to use the word `funcref` rather than `anyfunc` for the table's element type. When Emscripten outputs a .wast file, it uses the new name, and the WebAssembly Binary Toolkit can now accept text format code that uses either name. At the time of this book's writing, developer tools in the browsers are still using the word `anyfunc` when you inspect a module. Firefox allows you to use either word when constructing a `WebAssembly.Table` object in your JavaScript, but, at the moment, other browsers allow only the old name, so the JavaScript used in this book will continue to use `anyfunc`.

In the `initializePage` function, after the `moduleMemory` line of code and just before the creation of the `importObject`, add the code in the following snippet:

```
moduleTable = new WebAssembly.Table({initial: 1, element: "anyfunc"});
```

Next, you'll need to add some properties to the `importObject`:

- After the `memory` property, add a `__table_base` property with a 0 (zero) value. Emscripten added this import because there will be a Table section in this module, and—because side modules are intended for dynamic linking—there could be multiple Table sections that need to be merged. Because you're not doing dynamic linking here, you can simply pass zero.

- After the __table_base property, you'll need to include a table object because this module is using function pointers, and function pointer references are kept in the module's Table section.
- The _UpdateHostAboutError function is no longer needed, so it can be removed.
- Emscripten added an import for an abort function to inform you if there's a problem preventing the module from loading. You'll provide a function for it that will throw an error indicating that abort was called.

Within the then function of the instantiateStreaming function, you'll need to add calls to an addToTable function (you'll build this in a moment) and pass in anonymous functions for the success and error function pointers that the module's ValidateName and ValidateCategory functions will call. The second parameter to the addToTable function will be a string representing the signature of the function you're adding. The first character of the string is the function's return value type, and each additional character indicates the parameter types. The characters Emscripten uses are

- v—Void
- i—32-bit integer
- j—64-bit integer
- f—32-bit float
- d—64-bit float

Modify the initializePage function to look like the code in the following listing.

Listing 6.7   Modifications to the `initializePage` function (editproduct.js)

```
...
let moduleMemory = null;
let moduleExports = null;
let moduleTable = null;

function initializePage() {
  ...
  moduleMemory = new WebAssembly.Memory({initial: 256});
  moduleTable = new WebAssembly.Table({initial: 1,
      element: "anyfunc"});         ⟵ anyfunc rather than funcref
                                      for older browsers
  const importObject = {
    env: {
      __memory_base: 0,
      memory: moduleMemory,
      __table_base: 0,
      table: moduleTable,
      abort: function(i) { throw new Error('abort'); },
    }
```

```
};

WebAssembly.instantiateStreaming(fetch("validate.wasm"),
    importObject).then(result => {
  moduleExports = result.instance.exports;

  validateOnSuccessNameIndex = addToTable(() => {
    onSuccessCallback(validateNameCallbacks);
  }, 'v');

  validateOnSuccessCategoryIndex = addToTable(() => {
    onSuccessCallback(validateCategoryCallbacks);
  }, 'v');

  validateOnErrorNameIndex = addToTable((errorMessagePointer) => {
    onErrorCallback(validateNameCallbacks, errorMessagePointer);
  }, 'vi');

  validateOnErrorCategoryIndex = addToTable((errorMessagePointer) => {
    onErrorCallback(validateCategoryCallbacks, errorMessagePointer);
  }, 'vi');
});
}
...
```

> **Anonymous functions added to the Table for the success and error function pointers**

You now need to create the `addToTable` function that will add the specified JavaScript function to the module's Table section.

THE ADDTOTABLE FUNCTION

The `addToTable` function first needs to determine the Table section's size, because that will be the index for where the JavaScript function needs to be inserted. The WebAssembly.`Table` object's `grow` method is used to increase the size of the Table section by the desired number of elements. You only need to add one function, so you'll tell the Table to grow by 1.

Next, you'll call the WebAssembly.`Table` object's `set` method to insert the function. Because JavaScript functions can't be passed to the WebAssembly.`Table` object but exports from another WebAssembly module can, you'll pass the JavaScript function to a special helper function (`convertJsFunctionToWasm`) that will convert the function into a WebAssembly function.

Add the following code after the `initializePage` function in your editproduct.js file:

```
function addToTable(jsFunction, signature) {
  const index = moduleTable.length;
  moduleTable.grow(1);
  moduleTable.set(index,
      convertJsFunctionToWasm(jsFunction, signature));

  return index;
}
```

> **The current size will be the new function's index.**

> **Returns the function's index in the Table to the caller**

> **Grows the Table to allow for the new function to be added**

> **Converts the JavaScript function into a Wasm function, and adds it to the Table**

Rather than create the `convertJsFunctionToWasm` function, you'll copy over the one used by the Emscripten-generated JavaScript file. The function creates a very small WebAssembly module that imports the JavaScript function you specify. The module exports the same function, but it's now a WebAssembly wrapped function that can be inserted into a `WebAssembly.Table` object.

Open the validate.js file in your Chapter 6\6.1.2 EmFunctionPointers\frontend\ folder, and search for the `convertJsFunctionToWasm` function. Copy the function, and paste it after your `addFunctionToTable` function in the editproduct.js file.

Your next task is to create a helper function for use when the module indicates that the validation was successful. This function will be called by both the `Validate-eName` and `ValidateCategory` module functions if there are no validation issues with the user's data.

THE ONSUCCESSCALLBACK FUNCTION

After the `initializePage` function in the editproduct.js file, define an `onSuccess-Callback` function that accepts the following object as a parameter: `validateCall-backs`. The `validateCallbacks` parameter will be a reference to either the `validate-NameCallbacks` or `validateCategoryCallbacks` global object, depending on whether this function is being called for the `validateName` or `validateCategory` function. Within the function, you'll call the callback object's `resolve` method and then remove the functions from that object.

Add the following code snippet after the `initializePage` function in the edit-product.js file:

```
function onSuccessCallback(validateCallbacks) {
  validateCallbacks.resolve();                    Calls the resolve
  validateCallbacks.resolve = null;               method of the promise
  validateCallbacks.reject = null;                Removes the functions
}                                                  from the object
```

Similar to the `onSuccessCallback` function that you just created, you'll need to create a helper function for use when the module indicates that there's a validation error with one of the user's entries. This function will be called by both the `ValidateName` and `ValidateCategory` module functions.

THE ONERRORCALLBACK FUNCTION

Following the `onSuccessCallback` function in the editproduct.js file, you'll create the `onErrorCallback` function that accepts two parameters:

- `validateCallbacks`—This parameter will be a reference to either the `validate-NameCallbacks` or `validateCategoryCallbacks` global object, depending on whether this function is being called for the `validateName` or `validate-Category` function.
- `errorMessagePointer`—A pointer to the location in the module's memory where the validation error message is located.

The first thing that the function will need to do is read the string from the module's memory by calling your `getStringFromMemory` helper function. You'll then call the callback object's `reject` method before removing the functions from that object.

Add the code in the following snippet after the `onSuccessCallback` function in the editproduct.js file:

```
function onErrorCallback(validateCallbacks, errorMessagePointer) {
  const errorMessage = getStringFromMemory(errorMessagePointer);

  validateCallbacks.reject(errorMessage);


  validateCallbacks.resolve = null;
  validateCallbacks.reject = null;
}
```

Calls the reject method of the promise

Reads in the error message from the module's memory

Removes the functions from the object

In a moment, you'll modify the `validateName` and `validateCategory` JavaScript functions to return a `Promise` object because you won't know when the module will call the Success and Error functions. Because the functions will return a `Promise` object, the `onClickSave` function will need to be modified to work with the promises.

THE ONCLICKSAVE FUNCTION

Modify the `onClickSave` function to replace the `if` statement with the `Promise.all` code that you saw in section 6.1. Revise the code in the `onClickSave` function of the editproduct.js file so that it matches the next listing.

Listing 6.8   The modified `onClickSave` function (editproduct.js)

```
...

function onClickSave() {
  setErrorMessage("");

  const name = document.getElementById("name").value;
  const categoryId = getSelectedCategoryId();

  Promise.all([
    validateName(name),
    validateCategory(categoryId)
  ])
  .then(() => {

  })
  .catch((error) => {
    setErrorMessage(error);
  });
}
...
```

Calls both validation functions

Both validation functions return success.

There were no issues with the validation. The data can be saved.

If either validation function had an error...

... displays the validation error to the user

Because both the `validateName` and `validateCategory` functions will need to have the `resolve` and `reject` methods of their `Promise` placed into the global variables, you'll create a helper function, `createPointers`, that both functions can use.

THE CREATEPOINTERS FUNCTION

Following the `onClickSave` function, add a `createPointers` function that accepts the following parameters:

- `isForName`—A flag indicating whether it's the `validateName` or `validate-Category` function calling
- `resolve`—The `resolve` method of the calling function's promise
- `reject`—The `reject` method of the calling function's promise
- `returnPointers`—An object that you'll use to return the index of the `_On-Success` and `_OnError` functions that the module's function should call

Based on the `isForName` value, you'll place the `resolve` and `reject` methods into the proper callback object.

The module's function will need to know which index in the module's Table section it needs to call for the `_OnSuccess` and `_OnError` function pointers. You'll place the proper index in the `returnPointers` object.

Place the code in the next listing after the `onClickSave` function in the editproduct .js file.

Listing 6.9 The `createPointers` function (editproduct.js)

Places the promise methods into validateName's callback object

The caller is the validateName function.

Returns the indexes for validateName's function pointers

The caller is the validateCategory function.

Places the promise methods into validateCategory's callback object

Returns the indexes for validateCategory's function pointers

```
    . . .
    function createPointers(isForName, resolve, reject, returnPointers) {
      if (isForName) {
        validateNameCallbacks.resolve = resolve;
        validateNameCallbacks.reject = reject;

        returnPointers.onSuccess = validateOnSuccessNameIndex;
        returnPointers.onError = validateOnErrorNameIndex;
      } else {
        validateCategoryCallbacks.resolve = resolve;
        validateCategoryCallbacks.reject = reject;

        returnPointers.onSuccess = validateOnSuccessCategoryIndex;
        returnPointers.onError = validateOnErrorCategoryIndex;
      }
    }
    . . .
```

You'll now need to modify the `validateName` and `validateCategory` functions to return a `Promise` object and, with the help of your new `createPointers` function, have the module's function call the appropriate function pointer.

THE VALIDATENAME FUNCTION

Modify the `validateName` function, which will now return a `Promise` object. The contents of the promise will be wrapped in an anonymous function.

You'll need to add a call to the `createPointers` function to have the promise's `resolve` and `reject` methods placed into the `validateNameCallbacks` global object. The call to the `createPointers` object will also return the proper indexes to pass to the module's `_ValidateName` function so that it will call the `_OnSuccessName` or `_OnErrorName` function pointer.

The module's `_ValidateName` function no longer returns a value, so you'll need to remove the `const isValid =` portion of code as well as the `return` statement at the end of the function. The call to the `_ValidateName` function also needs to be modified to receive the two function pointer indexes.

Revise the `validateName` function in the editproduct.js file to match the code in the next listing.

Listing 6.10   Modifications to the `validateName` function (editproduct.js)

```
...
                                        Returns a Promise
                                        object to the caller          Places the resolve and
function validateName(name) {                                         reject methods into
  return new Promise(function(resolve, reject) {  ◁──────┘            the global object and
                                                                      gets the function
    const pointers = { onSuccess: null, onError: null };             pointer indexes
    createPointers(true, resolve, reject, pointers);   ◁─────────┘

    const namePointer = moduleExports._create_buffer((name.length + 1));
    copyStringToMemory(name, namePointer);

    moduleExports._ValidateName(namePointer, MAXIMUM_NAME_LENGTH,
        pointers.onSuccess, pointers.onError);   ◁───── Passes in indexes for
                                                        the function pointers
    moduleExports._free_buffer(namePointer);            _OnSuccessName and
  });                                                   _OnErrorName
}
...
```

You'll need to make the same adjustments to the `validateCategory` function that you did for the `validateName` function.

THE VALIDATECATEGORY FUNCTION

The only difference in the changes here is that you'll specify `false` as the first parameter to the `createPointers` function so that it knows the `validateCategory` function is calling and not the `validateName` function.

Revise the `validateCategory` function in the editproduct.js file to match the code in the next listing.

Listing 6.11   Modifications to the `validateCategory` function (editproduct.js)

```
...
                                                         Returns a Promise
function validateCategory(categoryId) {                  object to the caller
  return new Promise(function(resolve, reject) {  ◁──────┘

    const pointers = { onSuccess: null, onError: null };
    createPointers(false, resolve, reject, pointers);   ◁──┐
                                                           │
                  Places the resolve and reject           │
                  methods into the global object and  ────┘
                  gets the function pointer indexes
```

```
const categoryIdPointer =
  moduleExports._create_buffer((categoryId.length + 1));
copyStringToMemory(categoryId, categoryIdPointer);

const arrayLength = VALID_CATEGORY_IDS.length;
const bytesPerElement = Int32Array.BYTES_PER_ELEMENT;
const arrayPointer = moduleExports._create_buffer((arrayLength *
  bytesPerElement));

const bytesForArray = new Int32Array(moduleMemory.buffer);
bytesForArray.set(VALID_CATEGORY_IDS,
    (arrayPointer / bytesPerElement));

moduleExports._ValidateCategory(categoryIdPointer, arrayPointer,
    arrayLength, pointers.onSuccess, pointers.onError);

moduleExports._free_buffer(arrayPointer);
moduleExports._free_buffer(categoryIdPointer);
});
}
```

Passes in indexes for the function pointers _OnSuccessCategory and _OnErrorCategory

6.2.5   *Viewing the results*

Now that you've adjusted the code, you can open a web browser and type `http://localhost:8080/editproduct.html` into the address box to see the web page. You can test the validation by changing the selection in the Category drop-down so that nothing is selected and then clicking the Save button. The validation should display an error on the web page as shown in figure 6.14.

Validation error when a category isn't selected

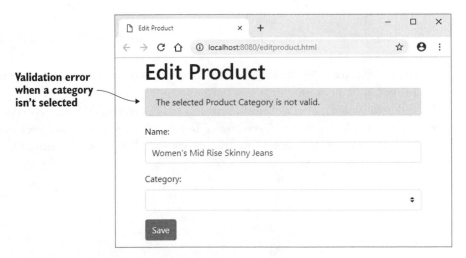

Figure 6.14   The Edit Product page's Category validation error

How can you use what you learned in this chapter in the real world?

Real-world use cases

The following are some possible use cases for what you've learned in this chapter:

- With function pointers, you can create JavaScript functions that return a promise, allowing your module to work the same as other JavaScript methods like `fetch`. By returning a `Promise` object, your function can even be chained together with other promises.
- As long as the function pointer specified has the same signature that the WebAssembly module is expecting, it can be called. For example, this allows the module's code to use one signature for `onSuccess` in each function. The JavaScript code can specify two or more functions that match that signature and, depending on what JavaScript code is calling, have the module call the desired `onSuccess` function that matches the current action.

Exercises

You can find the solutions to the exercises in appendix D.

1 Which two functions do you use to add and remove function pointers from Emscripten's backing array?
2 Which instruction does WebAssembly use to call a function defined in the Table section?

Summary

In this chapter, you learned the following:

- You can define a function pointer's signature directly in a function parameter in C or C++.
- It's possible to define the signature using the `typedef` keyword and then use the defined signature name in the function parameters.
- Under the hood, function pointers aren't really called directly by WebAssembly code. Instead, function references are held in the module's Table section, and the code asks the WebAssembly framework to call the desired function at the index specified.

Part 3

Advanced topics

Now that you know the basics of creating and working with WebAssembly modules, this part of the book looks at ways to help you reduce download sizes and improve reusability, take advantage of parallel processing, or even use your WebAssembly modules outside a web browser.

Chapter 7 introduces you to the basics of dynamic linking, in which two or more WebAssembly modules can be linked together at runtime to use each other's features.

Chapter 8 expands on what you learned in chapter 7, teaching you how to create multiple instances of the same WebAssembly module and have each instance dynamically link to another WebAssembly module on-demand.

In chapter 9, you'll learn how to prefetch WebAssembly modules as needed using web workers. You'll also learn how to perform parallel processing using pthreads in a WebAssembly module.

Chapter 10 demonstrates that WebAssembly isn't limited to a web browser. In this chapter, you'll learn how to use several of your WebAssembly modules in Node.js.

Dynamic linking: 7
The basics

This chapter covers

- How dynamic linking works for WebAssembly modules
- Why you might want to use dynamic linking and why you might not
- How to create WebAssembly modules as main or side modules
- What the different options are for dynamic linking and how to use each approach

When it comes to WebAssembly modules, *dynamic linking* is the process of joining two or more modules together at runtime, where the unresolved symbols from one module (functions, for example) resolve to symbols existing in another. You'll still have the original number of WebAssembly modules, but now they're linked together and able to access each other's functionality, as figure 7.1 shows.

You can implement dynamic linking for WebAssembly modules in several ways, making this a large topic. You'll learn how to build a website that uses dynamic linking in chapter 8, but first you'll need to learn what your options are.

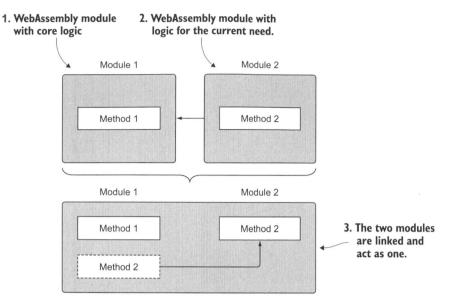

Figure 7.1   At runtime, the logic from one module (Module 2, in this case) is linked to another module (Module 1), allowing the two to communicate and act as one.

7.1   *Dynamic linking: Pros and cons*

Why would you want to use dynamic linking instead of just using the single WebAssembly module approach that you've used so far in this book? You might consider using dynamic linking for several reasons:

- To speed up development time. Rather than compiling one big module, you compile only the modules that changed.
- The core of your application can be separated out so that it can be shared more easily. Rather than having two or three big WebAssembly modules with the same logic in each, you can have a core module with several smaller modules that link to it. An example of this approach would be with game engines, in which the engine could be downloaded separately from the game. Multiple games could share the same engine.
- The smaller something is, the faster it downloads, so downloading only what you need initially will speed up load time. As the web page needs additional logic, a smaller module with logic specific to that area can be downloaded.
- If a portion of your logic is never used, it's never downloaded because logic is downloaded only as needed. The result is that you won't waste time downloading and processing something up front if it isn't nccdcd.

- The browser caches the module, similar to how it caches images or JavaScript files. Only the modules that change are downloaded again, making subsequent page views faster because only a portion of the logic needs to be redownloaded.

Although dynamic linking has a number of advantages, it isn't the best choice for every situation, so it's best to test to see if it's right for your needs.

Dynamic linking can have some performance impacts. According to Emscripten's documentation, the performance hit could be 5 to 10% or higher, depending on how your code is structured. Some areas where you could see a performance impact include the following:

- In development, the build configuration becomes more complicated because you now need to create two or more WebAssembly modules rather than one.
- Rather than having one WebAssembly module to download, you'll have at least two modules initially, which means you'll also have more network requests.
- The modules need to be linked together, so there's more processing involved during instantiation.
- Browser vendors are working on improving performance for various types of calls, but, according to Emscripten, function calls between linked modules can be slower than calls within the module. If you have a lot of calls between the linked modules, you may see performance issues.

Now that you know the pros and cons of dynamic linking, let's look at the different ways it can be implemented with WebAssembly modules.

7.2　Dynamic linking options

There are three options available for dynamic linking when using Emscripten:

- Your C or C++ code can manually link to a module by using the `dlopen` function.
- You can instruct Emscripten that there are WebAssembly modules to link to by specifying them in the `dynamicLibraries` array of Emscripten's generated JavaScript file. When Emscripten instantiates the WebAssembly module, it will automatically download and link modules that are specified in this array.
- In your JavaScript, you can manually take the exports of one module and pass them in as imports to another using the WebAssembly JavaScript API.

> **INFO** You can find a brief overview of the WebAssembly JavaScript API in chapter 3. The following MDN Web Docs page also has a good overview: http://mng.bz/vln1.

Before you learn how to use each dynamic linking technique, let's look at what the differences are between side modules and main modules.

7.2.1   *Side modules and main modules*

In the previous chapters of this book, you created WebAssembly modules as side modules so that the Emscripten JavaScript file wasn't generated. This let you manually download and instantiate the WebAssembly modules using the WebAssembly JavaScript API. Although creating a side module so that you can manually use the API is a useful side effect to aid in learning how things work under the hood, side modules are actually intended for dynamic linking.

With side modules, Emscripten omits the standard C library functions and the JavaScript file because the side modules will be linked to a main module at runtime (figure 7.2). The main module will have the Emscripten-generated JavaScript file and standard C library functions; when linked, the side module gains access to the main module's features.

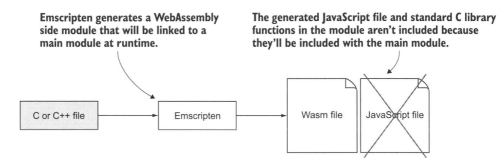

Figure 7.2   Using Emscripten to generate a WebAssembly module as a side module. No standard C library functions are included in the module, and the Emscripten JavaScript file isn't generated in this case.

Side modules are created by including the SIDE_MODULE flag as part of the command line to instruct Emscripten to not generate the JavaScript file or include any standard C library functions in the module.

Main modules are created similar to how you create a side module but using the MAIN_MODULE flag as part of the command line. This flag tells the Emscripten compiler to include system libraries and logic needed for dynamic linking. As figure 7.3 shows, the main module will have the Emscripten-generated JavaScript file as well as the standard C library functions.

> **NOTE**   One thing to be aware of with dynamic linking is that while multiple side modules can be linked to a main module, there can be only one main module. Also, being a main module has nothing to do with the main() function, which can actually be placed in any of the modules, including a side module.

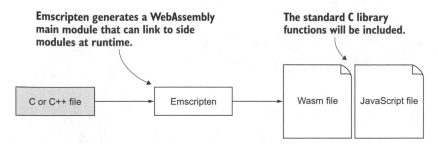

Figure 7.3 Using Emscripten to generate a WebAssembly module as a main module. The standard C library functions are included in the module, and the Emscripten JavaScript file is also generated in this case.

The first type of dynamic linking you'll learn is the `dlopen` approach.

7.2.2 *Dynamic linking: dlopen*

Suppose your boss has asked you to create a WebAssembly module, and one of the things it will need to do is determine the prime numbers that exist in a certain number range. Thinking back, you remember that you already built this logic in chapter 3 as a normal WebAssembly module (calculate_primes.c). You'd rather not just copy and paste the logic into this new WebAssembly module because you don't want to maintain two identical sets of code; if an issue was discovered in the code, you'd need to modify the same logic in two places, which could lead to one spot being missed if a developer isn't aware of the second spot or one of the locations is modified incorrectly.

Instead of duplicating the code, what you'd like to do is modify the existing calculate_primes code so that it can both be used as a normal WebAssembly module and also be callable from your new WebAssembly module. As figure 7.4 shows, the steps for this scenario are as follows:

1 Modify the calculate_primes.c file that you created in chapter 3 so that it can also be called by the main module. You'll rename the file calculate_primes.cpp.
2 Use Emscripten to generate the WebAssembly file from the calculate_primes .cpp file as a side module.
3 Create the logic (main.cpp) that will link to the side module using a call to the `dlopen` function.
4 Use Emscripten to generate the WebAssembly file from the main.cpp file as a main module and to generate the HTML template file.

For this scenario, you're going to call the `dlopen` function from your C++ code to link to the calculate_primes side module. To open the side module, however, `dlopen` needs the WebAssembly file to be in Emscripten's file system.

The trick with a file system, however, is that a WebAssembly module is running in a VM and doesn't have access to the device's actual file system. To get around this, Emscripten provides the WebAssembly module with one of several different types of

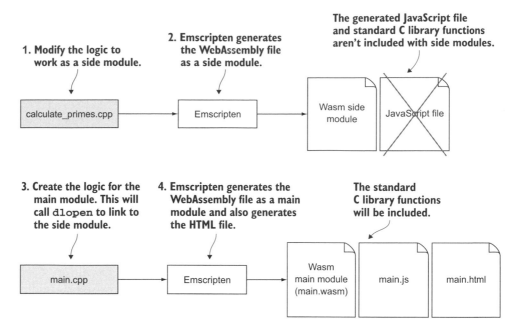

Figure 7.4   Steps for modifying calculate_primes.cpp so that it can be compiled into a WebAssembly side module, and steps for creating a WebAssembly main module that will link to the side module by calling the `dlopen` function.

file system depending on where the module is running (in a browser or in Node.js, for example) and how persistent the storage needs to be. By default, Emscripten's file system is in memory, and any data written to it will be lost when the web page is refreshed.

Emscripten's file system is accessed through the FS object in Emscripten's generated JavaScript file, but this object is included only if your WebAssembly module's code accesses files. (To learn more about Emscripten's file system, visit https://emscripten.org/docs/api_reference/Filesystem-API.html.) In this chapter, you'll only learn how to use the emscripten_async_wget function, which will allow you to download a WebAssembly module to Emscripten's file system so that you can open it with the dlopen function.

When using the dlopen approach to dynamic linking, your module will be able to call the main function in the calculate_primes module even if your module also has a main function. This might be useful if the module is from a third party and contains initialization logic. Being able to call a main function in another module is possible because dlopen returns a handle to the side module, and you then get a reference to the function you want to call based on that handle.

TIP This is one advantage of using the `dlopen` approach of dynamic linking compared with using the `dynamicLibraries` approach that you'll learn about in the next section. When it comes to using the latter approach, calling a function in another module when you already have a function with the same name in your module won't work. You'll end up just calling the function in your module, which could result in a recursive function call.

The first step of the process for implementing dynamic linking (figure 7.5) is to modify the calculate_primes.cpp file so that it can be compiled into a side module.

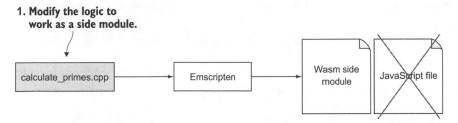

Figure 7.5 Step 1 in implementing dynamic linking using `dlopen` is to modify the calculate_primes.cpp file so that it can be compiled into a side module.

MODIFYING THE CALCULATE_PRIMES.CPP FILE

In your WebAssembly\ folder, create a folder named Chapter 7\7.2.2 dlopen\source\ for the files that you'll use in this section. Copy the calculate_primes.c file from your Chapter 3\3.5 js_plumbing\source\ folder to your newly created source\ folder, and change the file extension to .cpp. Open the calculate_primes.cpp file with your favorite editor.

Replace the stdlib.h header file with cstdlib and the stdio.h header file with cstdio; then add the `extern "C"` opening block between the emscripten.h header file and before the `IsPrime` function. The beginning of your calculate_primes.cpp file should now look like the code in the following snippet:

```
#include <cstdlib>        ◁——— Replaces the stdlib.h header
#include <cstdio>         ◁——— Replaces the stdio.h header
#include <emscripten.h>

#ifdef __cplusplus        ◁——— Adds the opening extern "C" block
extern "C" {
#endif
```

In the calculate_primes.cpp file, after the `IsPrime` function and before the `main` function, create a function called `FindPrimes` that returns `void` and accepts two integer parameters (`start` and `end`) for the start and end range of the prime number search.

Delete the start and end variable declaration lines of code from the `main` function and then move the remaining code—except for the `return 0` line—from the `main` function into the `FindPrimes` function.

Add the `EMSCRIPTEN_KEEPALIVE` declaration above the `FindPrimes` function so that the function is automatically added to the list of exported functions when you compile. Doing this simplifies things when you use Emscripten to generate the WebAssembly module because you don't have to explicitly specify the function at the command line.

Modify the `main` function to call the new `FindPrimes` function and pass in the original range of 3 and 100000. Finally, after the `main` function, add the closing bracket for the `extern "C"` block.

Your new `FindPrimes` function, the modified `main` function, and the closing bracket for the `extern "C"` block should now look like the code in the following listing.

Listing 7.1   The new `FindPrimes` function and the modified `main` function

```
...
EMSCRIPTEN_KEEPALIVE                          New function that's now exported
void FindPrimes(int start, int end) {         and callable by other modules
  printf("Prime numbers between %d and %d:\n", start, end);

  for (int i = start; i <= end; i += 2) {
    if (IsPrime(i)) {
      printf("%d ", i);
    }
  }
  printf("\n");
}

int main() {                     Displays the original
  FindPrimes(3, 100000);         range of prime numbers

  return 0;
}
                                 Adds the closing bracket
#ifdef __cplusplus               for the extern "C" block
}
#endif
```

Now that you've modified the code so that other modules can call it, it's time to move to step 2 (figure 7.6) and compile the code into a WebAssembly side module.

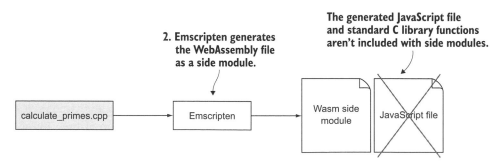

Figure 7.6   Use Emscripten to generate the WebAssembly file as a side module.

USING EMSCRIPTEN TO GENERATE THE WEBASSEMBLY FILE
AS A SIDE MODULE FROM CALCULATE_PRIMES.CPP

In previous chapters, when you created WebAssembly side modules, you replaced the standard C library functions with some replacement code that you built in chapter 4. You did this so the side module would still work, even though the standard C library functions weren't available. You don't need the replacement code in this case because the side module will be linked to the main module at runtime, and the main module will have the standard C library functions.

To compile the modified calculate_primes.cpp file as a WebAssembly side module, open a command prompt, navigate to the Chapter 7\7.2.2 dlopen\source\ folder, and run the following command:

```
emcc calculate_primes.cpp -s SIDE_MODULE=2 -O1
➥ -o calculate_primes.wasm
```

Now that you've created the side module, the next step (figure 7.7) is to create the main module.

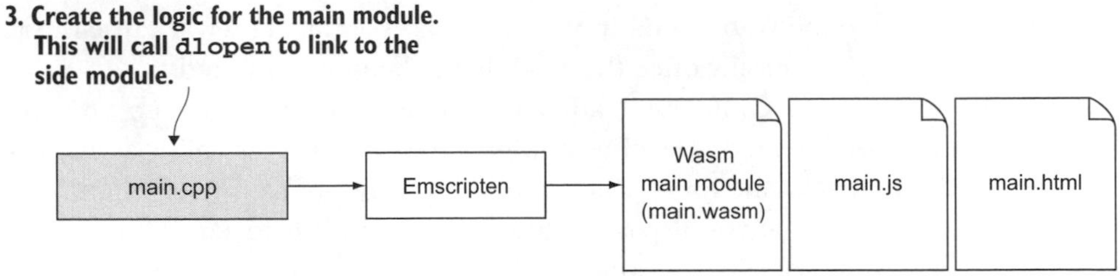

3. Create the logic for the main module. This will call `dlopen` to link to the side module.

main.cpp → Emscripten → Wasm main module (main.wasm) | main.js | main.html

Figure 7.7   Step 3 in implementing dynamic linking using `dlopen` is to create the logic that will use `dlopen` to link to the side module.

CREATING THE LOGIC THAT WILL LINK TO THE SIDE MODULE

In your Chapter 7\7.2.2 dlopen\source\ folder, create a file named main.cpp, and then open it in your favorite editor. The first things you need to add to the main.cpp file are the includes for the header files. In this case, you'll want to include the dlfcn.h header file—along with cstdlib and emscripten.h—because it has declarations related to dynamic linking when using dlopen. Then, you need to add the extern "C" block.

The code in your main.cpp file should now look like that in the next listing.

> **Listing 7.2   The main.cpp file with the header file includes an `extern "C"` block**

```
#include <cstdlib>

#ifdef __EMSCRIPTEN__          The header file needed for
  #include <dlfcn.h>      ◁─┐  dlopen-related logic
  #include <emscripten.h>
#endif

#ifdef __cplusplus
extern "C" {
```

```
#endif
```
| Your module's code will
be placed here.

```
#ifdef __cplusplus
}
#endif
```

In the code you're about to write, you'll be using the dlopen function to get a handle to a WebAssembly side module. Once you have that handle, you'll use the dlsym function to get a function pointer to the desired function in that module. To simplify the code when you call the dlsym function, the next thing you'll need to do is define the function signature for the FindPrimes function that you'll be calling in the side module.

The FindPrimes function returns void and has two integer parameters. The function pointer signature for the FindPrimes function is shown in the following snippet, which you need to include in the main.cpp file within the extern "C" block:

```
typedef void(*FindPrimes)(int,int);
```

You'll now add a main function to your file so that the Emscripten compiler will add the function to the WebAssembly module's Start section. This will cause the main function to run automatically once the module has been instantiated.

In your main function, you'll add a call to the emscripten_async_wget function to download the side module to Emscripten's file system. This call is asynchronous and will call a callback function—which you will specify—once the download is complete. The parameters that you'll pass to the emscripten_async_wget function, and their order, will be as follows:

1 The file to download: "calculate_primes.wasm".
2 The name to give the file when it gets added to Emscripten's file system. In this case, it will be given the same name it already has.
3 A callback function if the download is successful, CalculatePrimes.
4 You'll leave the fourth parameter NULL in this case because you won't specify a callback function. If you wanted to, you could specify a callback function in the event that there was an error downloading the file.

Following the FindPrimes function pointer signature in your main.cpp file, and within the extern "C" block, add the following code:

```
int main() {
  emscripten_async_wget("calculate_primes.wasm",      ⟵──────── File to download
      "calculate_primes.wasm",           ⟵──────── Name to give to the file in
      CalculatePrimes,       ⟵──────── Emscripten's file system
      NULL);    ⟵───  Callback function
                      on success
  return 0;         Callback function
}                   on error
```

The last thing that you'll need to add to the main.cpp file is a function that will hold the logic to open the side module, get a reference to the FindPrimes function, and then call that function.

When the emscripten_async_wget function finishes downloading the calculate_primes WebAssembly module, it will call the CalculatePrimes function that you specified and pass in a parameter indicating the file name that was loaded. To open the side module, you'll use the dlopen function, passing in two parameter values:

- The file name to open from the file name parameter the CalculatePrimes function receives
- An integer indicating the *mode*: RTLD_NOW

DEFINITION When an executable file is brought into a process's address space, it might have references to symbols that aren't known until the file is loaded. These references need to be relocated before the symbols can be accessed. The mode value is used to tell dlopen when the relocation should happen. The RTLD_NOW value is asking dlopen for the relocations to happen when the file is loaded. More information about dlopen and the mode flags can be found in the Open Group Base Specifications at http://mng.bz/4eDQ.

The dlopen function call will return a handle to the file, as the following code snippet shows:

```
void* handle = dlopen(file_name, RTLD_NOW);
```

Once you have a handle to the side module, you'll call the dlsym function, passing in the following parameter values to get a reference to the function you want to call:

- The handle of the side module
- The name of the function you want a reference to: "FindPrimes"

The dlsym function will return a function pointer to the requested function:

```
FindPrimes find_primes = (FindPrimes)dlsym(handle, "FindPrimes");
```

Once you have a function pointer, you can call it the same way you would call a normal function. When you've finished with a linked module, you can release it by passing the file's handle to the dlclose function.

Pulling everything together, your CalculatePrimes function should look like the code in listing 7.3. Add the code in this listing to your main.cpp file between the FindPrimes function pointer signature and the main function.

Listing 7.3   The `CalculatePrimes` function that calls a function in the side module

```
...
void CalculatePrimes(const char* file_name) {
  void* handle = dlopen(file_name, RTLD_NOW);    ◁——————— Opens the side module
  if (handle == NULL) { return; }

  FindPrimes find_primes =                             Gets a reference to the
      (FindPrimes)dlsym(handle, "FindPrimes");    ◁─┘  FindPrimes function
  if (find_primes == NULL) { return; }

  find_primes(3, 100000);    ◁─┐              Calls the function
                               │              in the side module
  dlclose(handle);    ◁─┐
}                        Closes the
...                      side module
```

Now that you've created the code for your main module, you can move on to the final step (figure 7.8) and compile it into a WebAssembly module. You'll also have Emscripten generate the HTML template file.

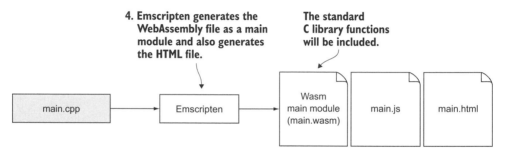

4. Emscripten generates the WebAssembly file as a main module and also generates the HTML file.

The standard C library functions will be included.

Figure 7.8   Step 4 in implementing dynamic linking using dlopen is to use Emscripten to generate the WebAssembly module as a main module from the main.cpp file. In this case, you'll also have Emscripten generate the HTML file.

USING EMSCRIPTEN TO GENERATE THE WEBASSEMBLY FILE AS A MAIN MODULE FROM MAIN.CPP

Rather than creating an HTML page to view the results, you'll use Emscripten's HTML template by specifying the output file with an .html extension. To compile your main.cpp file into a main module, you'll need to include the `-s MAIN_MODULE=1` flag. Unfortunately, if you were to view the generated HTML page using only the following command line, you would see the error shown in figure 7.9:

```
emcc main.cpp -s MAIN_MODULE=1 -o main.html
```

You can see that the WebAssembly module was loaded and `dlopen` linked to the side module without issue, because the text `"Prime numbers between 3 and 100000"` is written by the `FindPrimes` function in the side module. If there was an issue with the dynamic linking, your code wouldn't have reached this point. None of the prime numbers have been written to the screen, which suggests that the issue is in your side module's `FindPrimes` function but after the `printf` call to indicate the range.

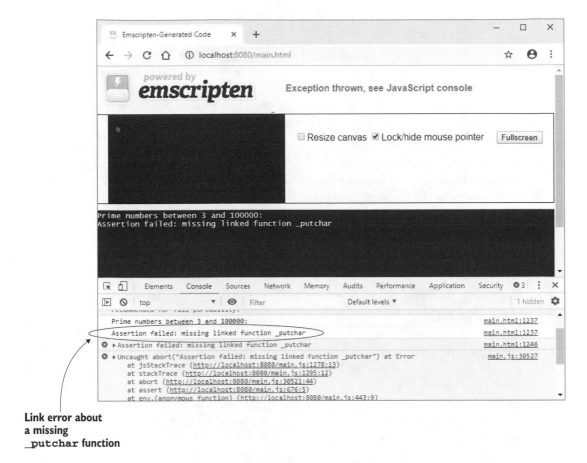

Link error about a missing `_putchar` function

Figure 7.9   When the web page is viewed, a link error is thrown about a missing `_putchar` function.

It turns out that the issue is with the calculate_primes.cpp file's use of the `printf` function when passing in only one character. In this case, the linefeed character (`\n`) at the end of the `FindPrimes` function is causing the error. The `printf` function uses a `putchar` function under the hood that isn't being included by default.

There are three options for correcting this error:

- Include the `_putchar` function in the `EXPORTED_FUNCTIONS` array as part of the command line when generating the WebAssembly module. When testing this as a possible fix, including this function alone would cause the error to go away, but, unfortunately, nothing would be displayed on the web page. If you use this approach, you'll need to include the `_main` function of the module in the array, too.

- You could modify the `printf` call in the calculate_primes.cpp file so that it outputs at least two characters to prevent the `printf` call from using the `putchar` function internally. The problem with this approach is that if a `printf` of one character is used anywhere else, the error will happen again. Consequently, this isn't a recommended fix.

- You could include the `s EXPORT_ALL=1` flag to force Emscripten to include all the symbols when it generates the WebAssembly module and JavaScript file. This will work, but using this approach isn't recommended unless there are no other workarounds because, in this case, it results in a doubling of the generated JavaScript file's size just to have one function exported.

Unfortunately, all three approaches feel like a hack. The first approach appears to be the best option available, so, to correct the error, you'll use the `EXPORTED_FUNCTIONS` command-line array to have the module export the `_putchar` and `_main` functions.

To compile the main.cpp file into a WebAssembly main module, open a command prompt, navigate to the Chapter 7\7.2.2 dlopen\source\ folder, and run the following command:

```
emcc main.cpp -s MAIN_MODULE=1
  -s EXPORTED_FUNCTIONS=['_putchar','_main'] -o main.html
```

Once your WebAssembly modules have been created, you can view the results.

VIEWING THE RESULTS

Open your browser and type `http://localhost:8080/main.html` into the address box to see the generated web page. As figure 7.10 shows, the web page should display the list of prime numbers in both the text box and in the console window of the browser's developer tools. The prime numbers are determined by the side module, which calls the `printf` function that's part of the main module.

Now that you've learned how to do dynamic linking using `dlopen`, you'll learn how to use the `dynamicLibraries` approach.

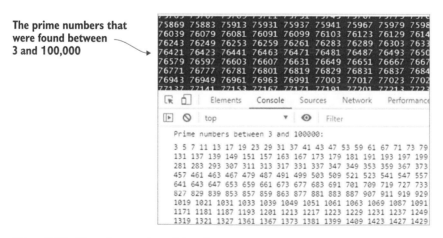

The prime numbers that were found between 3 and 100,000

Figure 7.10   The prime numbers determined by the side module and displayed to the web page using the `printf` function that's part of the main module

7.2.3 *Dynamic linking:* dynamicLibraries

Imagine that your coworkers and boss have had a chance to see your new WebAssembly modules in action. They're quite impressed with what you've done with dlopen, but your boss read up on dynamic linking while you were building the modules and discovered that you can also implement it using Emscripten's dynamicLibraries array. Your boss is curious to know how the dynamicLibraries approach compares with dlopen, so you've been asked to leave the calculate_primes side module as is but create a main module that links to it using dynamicLibraries.

As figure 7.11 shows, the steps for this scenario will be as follows:

1 Create the logic (main.cpp) that will talk to the side module.
2 Create a JavaScript file that will be included in Emscripten's generated JavaScript file to instruct Emscripten about the side module you'll want it to link to.
3 Use Emscripten to generate the WebAssembly file from the main.cpp file as a main module and to also generate the HTML template file.

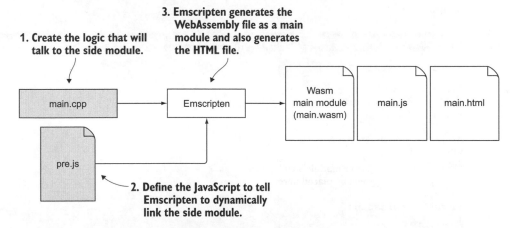

Figure 7.11 The steps for creating the WebAssembly main module that will instruct Emscripten's dynamicLibraries **array about which side module you want it to dynamically link to.**

CREATING THE LOGIC THAT WILL TALK TO THE SIDE MODULE

For this scenario, the first step of the process (figure 7.12) is to create the main.cpp file that will hold the logic that talks to the side module. In your Chapter 7\ folder, create a 7.2.3 dynamicLibraries\source\ folder. In this folder,

- Copy in the calculate_primes.wasm file from your 7.2.2 dlopen\source\ folder.
- Create a main.cpp file and then open it with your favorite editor.

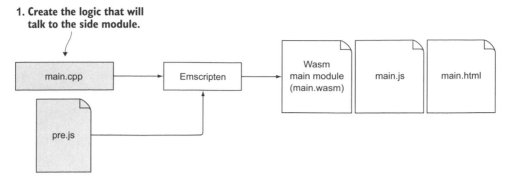

Figure 7.12   The first step toward implementing dynamic linking using `dynamicLibraries` is to create the main.cpp file.

Add the header files for the standard C library and Emscripten. Then add the `extern` `"C"` block. The code in your main.cpp file should now look like the code in the next listing.

Listing 7.4   The main.cpp file with the header file including an `extern` `"C"` block

```
#include <cstdlib>

#ifdef __EMSCRIPTEN__
  #include <emscripten.h>
#endif

#ifdef __cplusplus
extern "C" {
#endif
```

> Your module's code
> will be placed here.

```
#ifdef __cplusplus
}
#endif
```

In a moment, you'll write a `main` function that will call the `FindPrimes` function in the calculate_primes side module. Because the `FindPrimes` function is part of a different module, you need to include its function signature, prefixed with the `extern` keyword, so that the compiler knows that the function will be available when the code is run.

Add the following function signature within the `extern` `"C"` block in the main.cpp file:

```
extern void FindPrimes(int start, int end);
```

The last thing you need to do in the main.cpp file is add the `main` function so that the code is run automatically when the WebAssembly module is instantiated. In the `main` function, you'll simply call the `FindPrimes` function, passing in the number range of 3 to 99.

Add the following snippet to your main.cpp file within the extern "C" block but after the FindPrimes function signature:

```
int main() {
  FindPrimes(3, 99);

  return 0;
}
```

Your C++ code is now ready to be turned into a WebAssembly module. Before you use Emscripten to do that, you need to create the JavaScript code that will instruct Emscripten to link to your side module (figure 7.13).

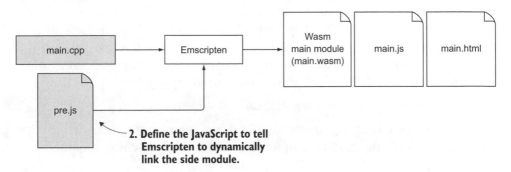

Figure 7.13 Step 2 when implementing dynamic linking using `dynamicLibraries` is to create the JavaScript code that will instruct Emscripten to link to your side module.

CREATING JAVASCRIPT TO INSTRUCT EMSCRIPTEN ABOUT THE SIDE MODULE YOU WANT IT TO LINK TO

Because your boss just wants to know what the differences are between the dlopen and dynamicLibraries approaches, you're going to create the WebAssembly module and have Emscripten generate the HTML template to run it for you, rather than creating an HTML web page of your own.

To link a side module to your main module using the dynamicLibraries approach, you need to write some JavaScript to specify the side module that Emscripten needs to link to. To do this, you specify the side module file names in Emscripten's dynamicLibraries array before Emscripten instantiates the module.

When using Emscripten's HTML template, you can include JavaScript near the beginning of the Emscripten-generated JavaScript file by specifying a JavaScript file in the command line using the --pre-js flag when creating the WebAssembly module. If you were building your own web page, you could specify settings, like the dynamicLibraries array, in a Module object before the HTML page's script tag for Emscripten's generated JavaScript file. When Emscripten's JavaScript file loads, it creates its own Module object; but, if there's an existing Module object, it will copy the values from that object into the new Module object.

MORE INFO   A number of settings can be adjusted to control the execution of Emscripten's generated JavaScript code. The following web page lists some of them: https://emscripten.org/docs/api_reference/module.html.

If you're using the Emscripten-generated HTML template, it specifies a `Module` object so that it can respond to certain things. For example, it handles the `printf` calls so that they're displayed in the text box on the web page and in the browser's console window, rather than just in the console window.

It's important not to specify your own `Module` object when using the HTML template because, if you do, you'll remove all of the template's settings. When using the HTML template, any values you want to set need to be set directly on the `Module` object rather than creating a new object.

In your Chapter 7\7.2.3 dynamicLibraries\source\ folder, create a file named pre.js and then open it with your favorite editor. You'll need to add an array, containing the name of the side module you want linked, to the `dynamicLibraries` property of the `Module` object. Add the following snippet to your pre.js file:

```
Module['dynamicLibraries'] = ['calculate_primes.wasm'];
```

Now that the JavaScript has been written, you can move to the final step of the process (figure 7.14) and have Emscripten generate the WebAssembly module.

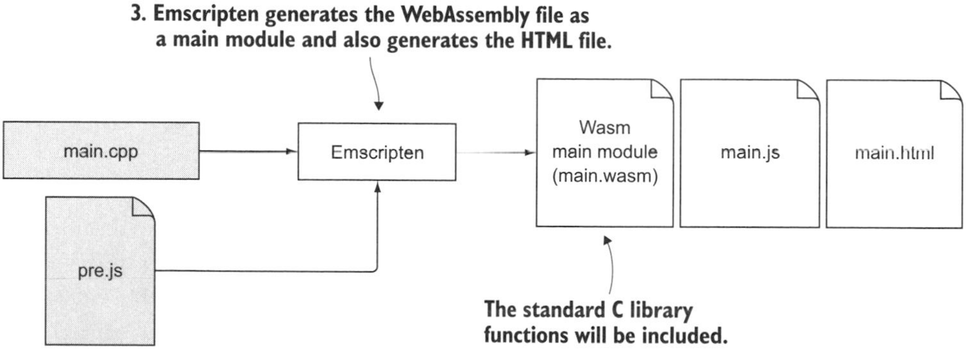

Figure 7.14   The last step of the process when implementing dynamic linking using `dynamicLibraries` is to have Emscripten generate the WebAssembly module.

USING EMSCRIPTEN TO GENERATE THE WEBASSEMBLY FILE AS A MAIN MODULE FROM MAIN.CPP

When you use Emscripten to generate your WebAssembly module, you'll want it to include the pre.js file's contents in the generated JavaScript file. To have Emscripten include the file, you'll need to specify it using the `--pre-js` command-line flag.

TIP   The pre.js file name is used here as a naming convention because it will be passed to the Emscripten compiler via the `--pre-js` flag. You don't have to use this naming convention, but it makes it easier to understand the file's purpose when you see it in your file system.

To generate your WebAssembly module as a main module, open a command prompt, navigate to the Chapter 7\7.2.3 dynamicLibraries\source\ folder, and run the following command:

```
emcc main.cpp -s MAIN_MODULE=1 --pre-js pre.js
    -s EXPORTED_FUNCTIONS=['_putchar','_main'] -o main.html
```

Once your WebAssembly main module has been created, you can view the results.

VIEWING THE RESULTS

To view your new WebAssembly module in action, open your browser and type `http://localhost:8080/main.html` into the address box to see the generated web page, shown in figure 7.15.

Figure 7.15   The prime numbers determined by the side module when both modules were linked together using Emscripten's `dynamicLibraries` array

Now, imagine that, as you were finishing up the WebAssembly module that was using the `dynamicLibraries` approach, you started to wonder if your boss might also want to see how manual dynamic linking might work.

7.2.4   *Dynamic linking: WebAssembly JavaScript API*

With `dlopen`, you need to download the side module, but, after that, the `dlopen` function handles linking it for you. With `dynamicLibraries`, Emscripten handles downloading and instantiating the modules for you. With this approach, you'll need to write the JavaScript code to download and instantiate the modules yourself using the WebAssembly JavaScript API.

For this scenario, you've decided to take the calculate_primes.c file from chapter 3 and split it in two, where one WebAssembly module will hold the `IsPrime` function and the other will have the `FindPrimes` function. Because you'll want to use the WebAssembly JavaScript API, both WebAssembly modules will need to be compiled as side modules, which means neither will have access to the standard C library functions. Without the standard C library available, you'll need to replace the `printf` calls with a call to your own JavaScript function to log the prime numbers to the browser's console window.

As figure 7.16 shows, the steps for this scenario will be as follows:

1 Split the logic in calculate_primes.c into two files: is_prime.c and find_primes.c.
2 Use Emscripten to generate the WebAssembly side modules from the is_prime.c and find_primes.c files.
3 Copy the generated WebAssembly files to the server for use by the browser.
4 Create the HTML and JavaScript files needed to download, link, and interact with the two WebAssembly modules using the WebAssembly JavaScript API.

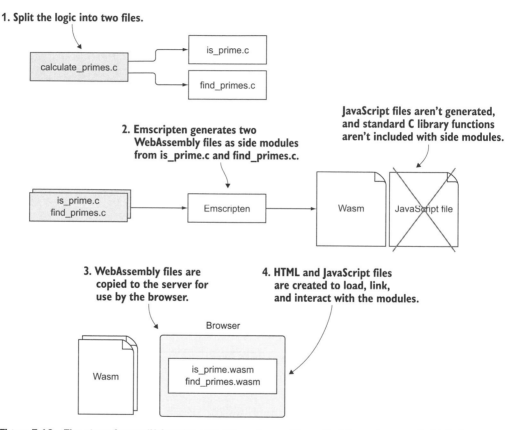

Figure 7.16 The steps for modifying the calculate_primes.c file so that it can be compiled into two WebAssembly side modules. The generated WebAssembly files are copied to the server, and then the HTML and JavaScript files are created to load, link, and interact with the two WebAssembly modules.

SPLITTING THE LOGIC IN THE CALCULATE_PRIMES.C FILE INTO TWO FILES

As figure 7.17 shows, the first thing you'll need to do is make a copy of the calculate_primes.c file so that you can adjust the logic and split the file in two. In your Chapter 7\ folder, create a 7.2.4 ManualLinking\source\ folder:

- Copy the calculate_primes.cpp file from your Chapter 7\7.2.2 dlopen\source\ folder to your new source\ folder. Rename the calculate_primes.cpp file that you just copied to is_prime.c.
- Make a copy of the is_prime.c file, and call it find_primes.c.

1. Split the logic into two files.

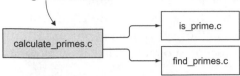

Figure 7.17   The first step toward implementing manual dynamic linking using the WebAssembly JavaScript API is to modify the calculate_primes.c file so that its logic is now part of two files.

Open the is_prime.c file with your favorite editor, and then delete the following items:

- The cstdlib and cstdio header files
- The opening `extern "C"` block and the closing curly brace at the end of the file
- The `FindPrimes` and `main` functions so that `IsPrime` is the only function left in the file

Add the `EMSCRIPTEN_KEEPALIVE` declaration above the `IsPrime` function so that the `IsPrime` function is included in the module's exported functions.

Open the find_primes.c file with your favorite editor, and delete the following items:

- The cstdlib and cstdio header files
- The opening `extern "C"` block and the closing curly brace at the end of the file
- The `IsPrime` and `main` functions so that `FindPrimes` is the only function left in the file

The `FindPrimes` function will be calling the `IsPrime` function that's in the is_prime module. Because the function exists in another module, you'll need to include the function signature for the `IsPrime` function, preceded by the `extern` keyword, so the Emscripten compiler knows that the function will be available when the code is run.

Add the following snippet before the `FindPrimes` function in your find_primes.c file:

```
extern int IsPrime(int value);
```

In a moment, you'll modify the `FindPrimes` function to call a function in your Java-Script code called `LogPrime`, rather than calling the `printf` function. Because this function is also external to the module, you'll need to include a function signature for

it, too. Add the next snippet before the `IsPrime` function signature in your find_
primes.c file:

```
extern void LogPrime(int prime);
```

Finally, the last thing that you need to modify in the find_primes.c file is the `Find-Primes` function so that it no longer calls the `printf` function. Delete the `printf` calls from the beginning and end of the function; replace the `printf` call that's within the `IsPrime` if statement with a call to the `LogPrime` function, but don't include the string. Pass in only the variable `i` to the `LogPrime` function.

The modified `FindPrimes` function should look like the following snippet in your find_primes.c file:

```
EMSCRIPTEN_KEEPALIVE
void FindPrimes(int start, int end) {
  for (int i = start; i <= end; i += 2) {
    if (IsPrime(i)) {
      LogPrime(i);        ◁──────    printf is replaced with
    }                                a call to LogPrime.
  }
}
```

Now that your C code has been created, you can move on to step 2 (figure 7.18), which is to use Emscripten to compile the code into WebAssembly side modules.

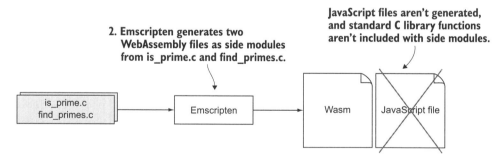

Figure 7.18   Step 2 is to use Emscripten to generate the WebAssembly side modules from your two files.

USING EMSCRIPTEN TO GENERATE THE WEBASSEMBLY SIDE MODULES

To generate your WebAssembly module from the is_prime.c file, open a command prompt, navigate to the 7.2.4 ManualLinking\source\ folder, and then run the following command:

```
emcc is_prime.c -s SIDE_MODULE=2 -O1 -o is_prime.wasm
```

To generate your WebAssembly module from the find_primes.c file, run the following command:

```
emcc find_primes.c -s SIDE_MODULE=2 -O1 -o find_primes.wasm
```

Once your two WebAssembly modules have been created, the next steps are to create the web page and JavaScript files that will load, link, and interact with the modules (figure 7.19).

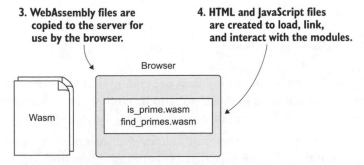

Figure 7.19 The final steps are to create the HTML and JavaScript files that will load, link, and interact with the WebAssembly modules.

CREATING THE HTML AND JAVASCRIPT FILES

In your Chapter 7\7.2.4 ManualLinking\ folder, create a frontend\ folder:

- Copy the is_prime.wasm and find_primes.wasm files from your 7.2.4 Manual-Linking\source\ folder to your new frontend\ folder.
- Create a main.html file in your frontend\ folder, and then open it with your favorite editor.

The HTML file will be a very basic web page. It will have some text so that you know the page has loaded and then a `script` tag to load in the JavaScript file (main.js) that will handle loading and linking the two side modules together.

Add the contents of the next listing to your main.html file.

Listing 7.5   The contents of the main.html file

```
<!DOCTYPE html>
<html>
  <head>
    <meta charset="utf-8"/>
  </head>
  <body>
    HTML page I created for my WebAssembly module.

    <script src="main.js"></script>
  </body>
</html>
```

Your next step is to create the JavaScript file that will handle downloading and linking the two WebAssembly modules together. In your 7.2.4 ManualLinking\frontend\ folder, create a main.js file, and then open it with your editor.

The find_primes WebAssembly module will be expecting a function that it can call to pass the prime number to the JavaScript code. You'll create a `logPrime` function to pass to the module during instantiation that will log the value received from the module to the console window of the browser's developer tools.

Add the following snippet to the main.js file:

```
function logPrime(prime) {
  console.log(prime.toString());
}
```

Because the find_primes WebAssembly module is dependent on the `IsPrime` function in the is_prime module, you'll need to download and instantiate the is_prime module first. In the `then` method of the `instantiateStreaming` call for the is_prime module,

- Create an `importObject` for the find_primes WebAssembly module. This `importObject` will be given the exported _IsPrime function from the is_prime module as well as the JavaScript `logPrime` function.
- Call the `instantiateStreaming` function for the find_primes WebAssembly module and return the `Promise`.

The next `then` method will be for the successful download and instantiation of the find_primes WebAssembly module. In this block, you'll call the _FindPrimes function, passing in a range of values to have the prime numbers within that range logged to the browser's console window.

Add the code in the following listing to the main.js file after the `logPrime` function.

Listing 7.6 Downloading and linking two WebAssembly modules

```
...
const isPrimeImportObject = {          ◁———————  The importObject for
  env: {                                          the is_prime module
    __memory_base: 0,
  }
};

WebAssembly.instantiateStreaming(fetch("is_prime.wasm"),   ◁———  Downloads and
    isPrimeImportObject)                                         instantiates the
.then(module => {   ◁———————  The is_prime module is ready.      is_prime module

  const findPrimesImportObject = {   ◁———  The importObject for
    env: {                                 the find_primes module
      __memory_base: 0,
      _IsPrime: module.instance.exports._IsPrime,   ◁———  The exported function
      _LogPrime: logPrime,   ◁———  The JavaScript function is passed   is passed to the
    }                               to the find_primes module.         find_primes module.
  };

  return WebAssembly.instantiateStreaming(fetch("find_primes.wasm"),   ◁———
      findPrimesImportObject);            Downloads and instantiates the
})                                        find_primes module. Returns
.then(module => {                         the instantiated module.
```

The find_primes module is ready.

```
    module.instance.exports._FindPrimes(3, 100);
});
```

Displays the prime numbers
between 3 and 100 to the
console window

VIEWING THE RESULTS

Once you've created the HTML and JavaScript code, you can open a web browser and
type `http://localhost:8080/main.html` into the address box to see the web page.
Press F12 to view the console window of the browser's developer tools. You should see
the prime numbers between 3 and 100 displayed, similar to figure 7.20.

Now that you've learned how to implement dynamic linking using all three
approaches, it's time to compare them.

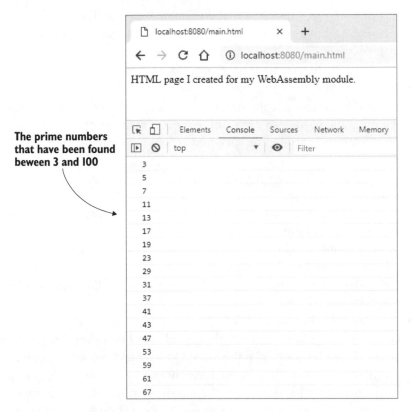

The prime numbers
that have been found
beween 3 and 100

Figure 7.20 The prime numbers between 3 and 100 logged by the find_primes
WebAssembly module

7.3   *Dynamic linking review*

You've learned about three approaches to dynamic linking in this chapter:

- `dlopen`
  - The side module needs to be downloaded to Emscripten's file system first.
  - Calling `dlopen` returns a handle to the side module file.
  - Passing the handle and the function name that you wish to call to the `dlsym` function will return a function pointer to the function in the side module.
  - At this point, calling the function pointer is the same as calling a normal function in your module.
  - Because you're requesting a function name based on the side module's handle, having a function with the same name in the main module won't cause any problems.
  - Linking to a side module is performed as needed.
- `dynamicLibraries`
  - You give Emscripten a list of side modules that you want it to link to by including them in the `dynamicLibraries` array property of the `Module` object. This list needs to be specified before Emscripten's JavaScript code is initialized.
  - Emscripten handles downloading and linking the side module to the main module for you.
  - Your module's code calls the functions in the side module the same way it calls its own functions.
  - It's not possible to call a function in another module if you already have a function with that name in the current module.
  - All the side modules specified are linked as soon as Emscripten's JavaScript code is initialized.
- The WebAssembly JavaScript API
  - You handle downloading the WebAssembly module using the `fetch` method and use the WebAssembly JavaScript API to have that module instantiated.
  - You then download the next WebAssembly module and pass the necessary exports from the first module as the imports for the current module.
  - Your module's code calls the functions in the side module the same way it calls its own functions.
  - As with the `dynamicLibraries` approach, it's not possible to call a function in another module if you already have a function with that name in the current module.

In summary, which approach to dynamic linking you want to use really depends on how much control you want over the process and if you want that control in the module or in JavaScript:

- `dlopen` gives the dynamic linking control to the backend code. This is also the only approach that's possible if you need to call a function in a side module when you already have a function with that name in your main module.
- `dynamicLibraries` gives the dynamic linking control to the tooling, where Emscripten does the work for you.
- The WebAssembly JavaScript API gives the dynamic linking control to the front-end code, where your JavaScript handles the linking.

How can you use what you learned in this chapter in the real world?

Real-world use cases

The following are some possible use cases for what you've learned in this chapter:

- A game engine is something that could benefit from dynamic linking. When you downloaded the first game, the engine would need to be downloaded for the first time, too, and then cached. The next time you went to play a game, the framework could check to see if the engine was already on the system and, if so, download only the requested game. This would save time and bandwidth.
- You could build an image-editing module so that the core logic was downloaded initially, but the things that might not be used as often (certain filters, perhaps) could be downloaded on-demand.
- You might have a web application with multiple subscription tiers. The free tier would have the fewest features, so only the basic module would be downloaded. For the Premium tier, additional logic could be included. For example, perhaps your web application's Premium tier adds the ability to track expenses. The add-on module could be used to parse the contents of an Excel file and format it the way your server expects.

Exercises

You can find the solutions to the exercises in appendix D.

1 Using one of the dynamic linking approaches you've learned in this chapter, create the following:
   a A side module containing an `Add` function that accepts two integer parameters and returns the sum as an integer
   b A main module that has a `main()` function that calls the side module's `Add` function and displays the result to the console window of the browser's developer tools
2 Which dynamic linking approach would you use if you needed to call a function in the side module but that function had the same name as a function in your main module?

Summary

In this chapter, you learned the following:

- As with most things, there are pros and cons to using dynamic linking. Before pursuing this approach, you should decide if the advantages outweigh the disadvantages for your application.
- Dynamic linking can be performed as needed by your WebAssembly's code using the `dlopen` function.
- It's possible to tell the Emscripten-generated JavaScript that you want certain side modules linked to your main module. Emscripten will automatically link the modules together during instantiation.
- Using the WebAssembly JavaScript API, it's possible to manually download, instantiate, and link multiple side modules together.
- You can control the execution of Emscripten's generated JavaScript by creating a `Module` object before Emscripten's JavaScript file is included. You can also adjust the `Module` object by including your own JavaScript in Emscripten's generated JavaScript file using the `--pre-js` command-line flag when compiling the WebAssembly module.

Dynamic linking: The implementation

This chapter covers

- Using dynamic linking in a single-page application
- Creating multiple instances of Emscripten's JavaScript `Module` object, with each instance dynamically linked to a different WebAssembly side module
- Reducing the size of the WebAssembly main module by enabling dead code elimination

In chapter 7, you learned about the different approaches available for dynamically linking WebAssembly modules:

- `dlopen`, in which your C or C++ code manually links to a module, obtaining function pointers to the specific functions as they're required
- `dynamicLibraries`, in which your JavaScript provides Emscripten with a list of modules to link to, and Emscripten automatically links to those modules during its initialization

- Manually linking, in which your JavaScript takes the exports of one module and passes them as the imports to another module using the WebAssembly JavaScript API

In this chapter, you're going to use the `dynamicLibraries` approach in which Emscripten handles the dynamic linking for you based on a list of modules that you specify.

Suppose the company that created the online version of its point-of-sale application's Edit Product page now wants to create the Place Order form shown in figure 8.1. Like the Edit Product page, the Place Order form will use a WebAssembly module for validating the user's entries.

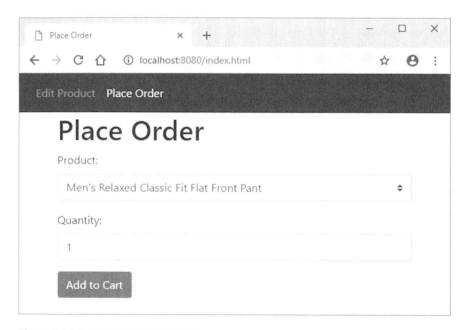

Figure 8.1   The new Place Order form

As the company is planning how the new web page will work, it notices that it will need validation similar to that of the existing Edit Product page:

- Both pages require that a valid item be selected from a drop-down list.
- Both pages need to ensure that a value was provided.

Rather than duplicate the logic listed in the WebAssembly module for each page, the company would like to take the common logic—the check for whether a value was provided and the check for whether the selected ID is in the array of valid IDs—and move it to its own module. Each page's validation module would then be dynamically linked at runtime to the module with the common logic to gain access to the core features that it needs, as figure 8.2 shows. Even though the two modules will remain

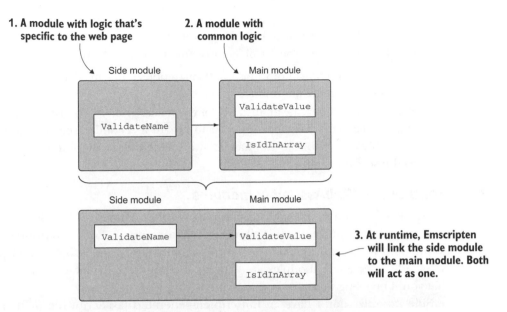

1. A module with logic that's specific to the web page

2. A module with common logic

Figure 8.2 At runtime, the logic that's specific to the page (the side module) will be linked to the common logic (the main module). As far as the code is concerned, the two modules will be acting as one.

separate and simply call into each other as needed, as far as the code is concerned, it feels like you're only working with one module.

For this scenario, the company would like to adjust the website so that it works as an *SPA* (single-page application).

DEFINITION What's an SPA? With a traditional website, you have one HTML file per web page. With SPAs, you have only one HTML page, and that page's content is modified by the code that's executing in the browser based on the user's interactions.

Adjusting the web page to work as an SPA adds some interesting twists when it comes to dynamic linking with the `dynamicLibraries` approach; you specify all the side modules that you want Emscripten to link to before Emscripten's JavaScript is initialized. Normally, Emscripten's generated JavaScript code exists as a global object called `Module` and is initialized the moment the browser loads the JavaScript file. When Emscripten's JavaScript is initialized, all the side modules that you specified are linked to the main module.

One advantage of dynamic linking is only loading and linking to a module as it's needed, to reduce the download and processing time when the page first loads. When working with the SPA, you'll want to specify only the side module for the page that's displayed initially. When the user navigates to the next page, how do you specify the side module for it in the SPA if Emscripten's `Module` object has already been initialized?

It turns out there's a flag you can specify when compiling the main module (-s MODULARIZE=1) that will tell the Emscripten compiler to wrap the Emscripten-generated JavaScript file's Module object in a function. This solves two problems:

- You're now in control of when the Module object gets initialized because you'll now need to create an instance of the object to use it.
- Because you can create an instance of the Module object, you're not limited to a single instance. This will allow you to create a second instance of your Web-Assembly main module and have that instance link to the side module specific to the second page.

8.1   *Creating the WebAssembly modules*

In chapters 3, 4 and 5, you created modules as side modules so that the Emscripten JavaScript file wasn't generated, allowing you to manually handle downloading the module and instantiating it with the WebAssembly JavaScript API. Although that's a useful side effect, side modules are actually intended for dynamic linking, which is what you'll be using them for in this chapter.

Side modules don't have an Emscripten-generated JavaScript file or standard C library functions because they are linked to a main module at runtime. The main module has these features, and, when linked, the side modules gain access to them.

REMINDER   With dynamic linking, there can be multiple side modules linked to a main module, but there can be only one main module.

Figure 8.3 shows the following steps for revising the C++ code and generating the WebAssembly modules:

1. Split the logic in the validate.cpp file into two files: one file for the common logic that will be shared (validate_core.cpp) and one for the logic that's specific to the Edit Product page (validate_product.cpp).
2. Create a new C++ file for the logic that will be specific to the new Place Order form (validate_order.cpp).
3. Use Emscripten to generate the WebAssembly side modules from validate_product.cpp and validate_order.cpp.
4. Define a JavaScript function for the C++ code to call if there's an issue with the validation. The function will be placed in a mergeinto.js file and included in Emscripten's generated JavaScript file during compilation of the main module.
5. Emscripten will be used to generate the WebAssembly file as a main module from validate_core.cpp.

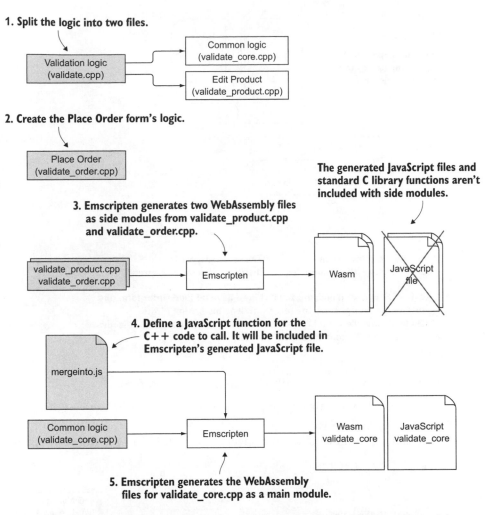

1. Split the logic into two files.

2. Create the Place Order form's logic.

3. Emscripten generates two WebAssembly files as side modules from validate_product.cpp and validate_order.cpp.

The generated JavaScript files and standard C library functions aren't included with side modules.

4. Define a JavaScript function for the C++ code to call. It will be included in Emscripten's generated JavaScript file.

5. Emscripten generates the WebAssembly files for validate_core.cpp as a main module.

Figure 8.3   The steps needed to revise the C++ logic and generate the WebAssembly modules

After the WebAssembly modules are created, the following steps remain for modifying the website (figure 8.4):

6 Adjust the web page to now have a navigation bar and the Place Order form's controls. You'll then modify the JavaScript to show the proper set of controls based on which navigation link is clicked.

7 Adjust your web page's JavaScript to link the proper side module to the common shared logic module. You'll also add the JavaScript code for validating the Place Order form.

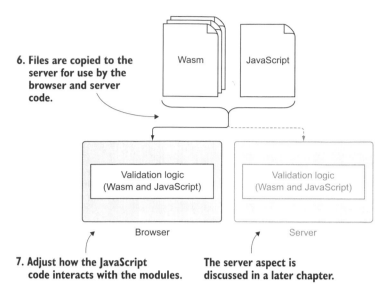

6. Files are copied to the server for use by the browser and server code.

7. Adjust how the JavaScript code interacts with the modules.

The server aspect is discussed in a later chapter.

Figure 8.4   Steps for modifying the HTML to have a Place Order form and revising the JavaScript code to implement dynamic linking of the WebAssembly modules in a browser and by the server-side code. I discuss the server aspect, Node.js, in a later chapter.

8.1.1   *Splitting the logic in the validate.cpp file into two files*

As figure 8.5 shows, your first step is to revise the C++ code that you wrote in chapter 5 so that the logic, which will be shared by both the Edit Product and Place Order forms, is in its own file. The logic specific to the Edit Product form will be moved to a new file.

1. Move edit-product-specific logic to its own file.

Figure 8.5   Step 1 of the process is to move the Edit Product page's specific logic to its own file.

In your WebAssembly folder, create a Chapter 8\8.1 EmDynamicLibraries\source\ folder for the files that you'll use in this section, and then complete the following:

- Copy the validate.cpp file from the Chapter 5\5.1.1 EmJsLibrary\source\ folder to your newly created source folder.
- Make a copy of the validate.cpp file, and rename it validate_product.cpp.
- Rename your other copy of the validate.cpp file to validate_core.cpp.

The first thing that you'll need to do is remove the edit-product-specific logic from the valiate_core.cpp file, because this file will be used to generate the common Web-Assembly module that will be used by both the Edit Product and Place Order forms.

ADJUSTING THE VALIDATE_CORE.CPP FILE

Open the validate_core.cpp file with your favorite editor, and then remove the Validate-Name and ValidateCategory functions. Remove the include for cstring because it's no longer needed by this file.

Because the ValidateValueProvided and IsCategoryIdInArray functions will now be called by other modules, these functions will need to be exported. Add the following code snippet above both the ValidateValueProvided and the IsCategoryId-InArray functions in the validate_core.cpp file:

```
#ifdef __EMSCRIPTEN__
  EMSCRIPTEN_KEEPALIVE
#endif
```

It's possible to use the IsCategoryIdInArray function to check and see if an ID is in any array specified, but the name the function uses indicates that it's only for a category ID. You'll want to modify this function so that its name is more generic, because it will be used by both side modules.

Adjust the IsCategoryIdInArray function in the validate_core.cpp file to no longer use the word category. The function should look like the code in the following listing.

Listing 8.1 The `IsCategoryIdInArray` function modified to now be called `IsIdInArray`

```
...
#ifdef __EMSCRIPTEN__            Automatically adds the IsIdInArray
  EMSCRIPTEN_KEEPALIVE    <----  function to the module's list of
#endif                          exported functions
int IsIdInArray(char* selected_id, int* valid_ids, int array_length) {
  int id = atoi(selected_id);
  for (int index = 0; index < array_length; index++) {
    if (valid_ids[index] == id) {
      return 1;
    }
  }

  return 0;
}
...
```

Now that you've removed the Edit Product page's logic from the validate_core.cpp file and modified the IsCategoryIdInArray function to be more generic, you'll need to revise the Edit Product page's logic.

ADJUSTING THE VALIDATE_PRODUCT.CPP FILE

Open the validate_product.cpp file in your favorite editor, and remove the Validate-ValueProvided and IsCategoryIdInArray functions because they're now part of the validate_core module. With the ValidateValueProvided and IsIdInArray functions now part of a different module, you'll have to include their function signatures, prefixed with the extern keyword, so that the compiler knows the functions will be available when the code is run.

Add the following function signatures within the extern "C" block and before the extern UpdateHostAboutError function signature in the validate_product.cpp file:

```
extern int ValidateValueProvided(const char* value,
    const char* error_message);

extern int IsIdInArray(char* selected_id, int* valid_ids,
    int array_length);
```

Because you renamed IsCategoryIdInArray to IsIdInArray in the core logic, you need to revise the ValidateCategory function to call IsIdInArray instead. The ValidateCategory function in the validate_product.cpp file should look like the code in the next listing.

Listing 8.2   The modified `ValidateCategory` function (validate_product.cpp)

```
...
int ValidateCategory(char* category_id, int* valid_category_ids,
    int array_length) {
  if (ValidateValueProvided(category_id,
    "A Product Category must be selected.") == 0) {
    return 0;
  }

  if ((valid_category_ids == NULL) || (array_length == 0)) {
    UpdateHostAboutError("There are no Product Categories available.");
    return 0;
  }
                                                              Function renamed
                                                              to IsIdInArray
  if (IsIdInArray(category_id, valid_category_ids,       ◁────┘
      array_length) == 0) {
    UpdateHostAboutError("The selected Product Category is not valid.");
    return 0;
  }

  return 1;
}
...
```

Once you've separated the Edit Product page's logic from the common logic, the next step (figure 8.6) is to create the Place Order form's logic.

2. Create the Place ⟍   ┌─────────────────────┐   Figure 8.6   Step 2 of the process is to
**   Order form's logic.** ─→ │   Place Order   │   create the logic for the Place Order form.
                              │ (validate_order.cpp)│
                              └─────────────────────┘

8.1.2 *Creating a new C++ file for the Place Order form's logic*

In your Chapter 8\8.1 EmDynamicLibraries\source\ folder, create a validate_order.cpp file and open it with your favorite editor. When creating a side module in the previous chapters, you didn't include the standard C library header files because the functions used wouldn't be available at runtime. In this case, because the side module will be linked to the main module (validate_core), and the main module will have access to the standard C library, the side module will be able to access those functions.

Add the includes for the standard C library and Emscripten header files, as well as the `extern "C"` block, to the validate_order.cpp file, as shown in the next listing.

Listing 8.3 The header files and `extern "C"` block added to the validate_order.cpp file

```
#include <cstdlib>

#ifdef __EMSCRIPTEN__
  #include <emscripten.h>
#endif

#ifdef __cplusplus
extern "C" {
#endif              Your WebAssembly functions
                    will be placed here.

#ifdef __cplusplus
}
#endif
```

You'll need to add the function signatures for the `ValidateValueProvided` and `IsId-InArray` functions that are in the validate_core module. You'll also add the function signature for the `UpdateHostAboutError` function that the module will import from the JavaScript code.

Add the function signatures, which are shown in the following code snippet, within the `extern "C"` block of the validate_order.cpp file:

```
extern int ValidateValueProvided(const char* value,
    const char* error_message);

extern int IsIdInArray(char* selected_id, int* valid_ids,
    int array_length);

extern void UpdateHostAboutError(const char* error_message);
```

The Place Order form that you'll be building will have a product drop-down list and a quantity field that you'll need to validate. Both field values will be passed to the module as strings, but the product ID will hold a numeric value.

To validate the user-selected product ID and the quantity that was entered, you'll create two functions: `ValidateProduct` and `ValidateQuantity`. The first function that you'll create is `ValidateProduct` to ensure a valid product ID was selected.

THE VALIDATEPRODUCT FUNCTION

The ValidateProduct function will receive the following parameters:

- The user-selected product ID
- A pointer to an array of integers holding the valid product IDs
- The number of items in the array of valid product IDs

The function will verify three things:

- Was a product ID provided?
- Was a pointer to the valid product IDs array provided?
- Is the user-selected product ID in the array of valid IDs?

If any of the validation checks fail, you'll pass an error message to the JavaScript code by calling the UpdateHostAboutError function. You'll then exit the ValidateProduct function by returning 0 to indicate that there was an error. If the code runs to the end of the function, there were no validation issues, so a 1 (success) message is returned.

Add the ValidateProduct function, shown in the following listing, below the UpdateHostAboutError function signature and within the extern "C" block in the validate_order.cpp file.

Listing 8.4   The ValidateProduct function

```
#ifdef __EMSCRIPTEN__
  EMSCRIPTEN_KEEPALIVE
#endif
int ValidateProduct(char* product_id, int* valid_product_ids,
    int array_length) {
  if (ValidateValueProvided(product_id,               If a value isn't received,
    "A Product must be selected.") == 0) {        ◁──  then returns an error
    return 0;
  }

  if ((valid_product_ids == NULL) || (array_length == 0)) {   ◁──
    UpdateHostAboutError("There are no Products available.");
    return 0;
  }                                                  If the array wasn't specified,
                                                          then returns an error

  if (IsIdInArray(product_id, valid_product_ids,
    array_length) == 0) {        ◁────────────────
    UpdateHostAboutError("The selected Product is not valid.");
    return 0;
  }                                               If the selected product ID
                                                  isn't found in the array,
  return 1;   ◁──── Tells the caller that everything was ok      then returns an error
}
```

The final function that you'll need to create is the ValidateQuantity function to verify that the quantity entered by the user is a valid value.

THE VALIDATEQUANTITY FUNCTION

The ValidateQuantity function will accept a single parameter, the user-entered quantity, and it will verify two things:

- Was a quantity specified?
- Is the quantity value 1 or greater?

If either validation check fails, you'll pass an error message to the JavaScript code by calling the `UpdateHostAboutError` function and then exit the function by returning 0 (zero) to indicate that there was an error. If the code runs to the end of the function, there were no validation issues, so a 1 (success) message is returned.

Add the `ValidateQuantity` function in the following listing below the `Validate-Product` function and within the `extern "C"` block in the validate_order.cpp file.

Listing 8.5   The `ValidateQuantity` function

```
#ifdef __EMSCRIPTEN__
  EMSCRIPTEN_KEEPALIVE
#endif
int ValidateQuantity(char* quantity) {
  if (ValidateValueProvided(quantity,                    If a value isn't received,
      "A quantity must be provided.") == 0) {            then returns an error
    return 0;
  }
                                                 If the value is less than
  if (atoi(quantity) <= 0) {                     1, then returns an error
    UpdateHostAboutError("Please enter a valid quantity.");
    return 0;
  }
                      Tells the caller that
  return 1;           everything was ok
}
```

Now that you've finished revising the C++ code, the next part of the process (figure 8.7) is to have Emscripten compile the C++ files into WebAssembly modules.

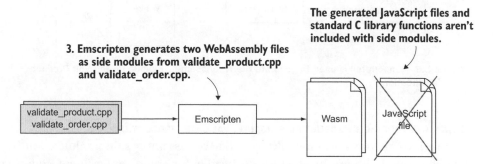

Figure 8.7   Step 3 is to use Emscripten to compile the C++ files into WebAssembly modules.

8.1.3   *Using Emscripten to generate the WebAssembly side modules*

When using dynamic linking with Emscripten, you can have at most one main module. The main module will include the standard C library functions and Emscripten's generated JavaScript file. The side modules won't include either of these features, but when they're linked to the main module, they gain access to this functionality. Your validate_core.cpp file will be built as a main module, and the other two C++ files, validate_product.cpp and validate_order.cpp, will be built as side modules.

By default, when you create a main module, Emscripten will include all the standard C library functions in the WebAssembly module because it doesn't know which ones the side modules will need. This makes the module much larger than it needs to be, especially if you use only a few standard C library functions.

To optimize the main module, there's a way to tell Emscripten to include only specific standard C library functions. You'll use this approach, but, before you can do this, you need to know which functions need to be included. To determine this, you could always read through the code line by line, but you could miss some that way. Another approach is commenting out the header files for the standard C library and then running the command line to generate the WebAssembly module. The Emscripten compiler will see that there are no function signatures defined for the standard C library functions that are being used and will display an error about them.

You'll use the second approach, so you'll need to compile the side modules before you compile the main module. As figure 8.8 shows, the first WebAssembly module that you'll generate will be the side module for the Edit Product page (validate_product.cpp).

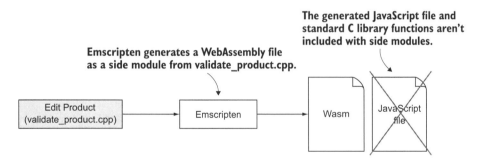

Figure 8.8 Emscripten is used to generate the WebAssembly module for the Edit Product page's validation.

GENERATING THE EDIT PRODUCT SIDE MODULE: VALIDATE_PRODUCT.CPP

In previous chapters, when you've created WebAssembly side modules, you replaced the standard C library headers with a header for some replacement code that you built in chapter 4. You don't need the replacement code in this case because the side module will be linked to the main module at runtime, and the main module will have the standard C library functions.

When you compile the main module in section 8.1.5, you're going to provide Emscripten with a list of the standard C library functions that your side modules are using. To determine which functions your code is using, you're going to comment out the standard C library header files and then try to compile the module. If there are any standard C library functions in use, the Emscripten compiler will throw errors about the missing function definitions.

Before you try to determine which standard C library functions are in use, however, you need to compile the module normally to make sure there aren't any issues. You want to know for sure that the errors you're seeing when you comment out the header files are related to the missing function definitions. To compile the module normally, open a command prompt, navigate to the Chapter 8\8.1 EmDynamicLibraries\source\ folder, and then run the following command:

```
emcc validate_product.cpp -s SIDE_MODULE=2 -O1
  -o validate_product.wasm
```

There shouldn't be any errors displayed in the console window, and there should be a new validate_product.wasm file in your source folder.

Next you need to determine which standard C library functions your code is using. In your Chapter 8\8.1 EmDynamicLibraries\source\ folder, open the validate_product .cpp file and then comment out the include statements for the cstdlib and cstring files. Save your file, but don't close it because you'll need to uncomment those lines of code in a moment.

At your command prompt, run the following command, which is the same one you ran a moment ago:

```
emcc validate_product.cpp -s SIDE_MODULE=2 -O1
  -o validate_product.wasm
```

This time, you should see an error message displayed in the console window, similar to figure 8.9, indicating that the strlen function isn't defined. This error message also indicates that NULL isn't defined, but you can ignore that because you don't need to

**A standard C library
function used by the code**

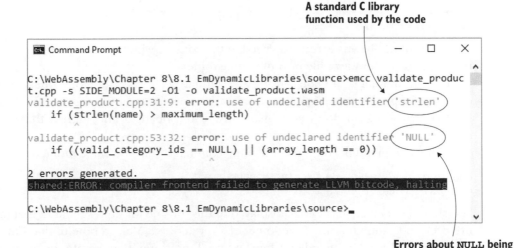

**Errors about NULL being
undefined can be ignored.**

Figure 8.9   Emscripten throws an error about the strlen function and NULL not being defined.

do anything to have that included. Make note of the `strlen` function because you'll need to include it when you use Emscripten to generate the main module.

In your validate_product.cpp file, remove the comments from in front of the cstdlib and cstring header files. Then save the file.

Now that you have your Edit Product page's WebAssembly module, you need to create the Place Order form's module. As figure 8.10 shows, you'll follow the same process as you did here.

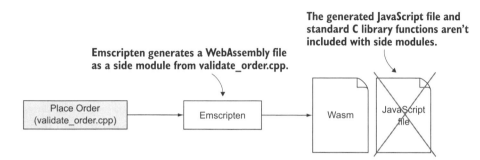

Figure 8.10   Emscripten used to generate the WebAssembly module for the Place Order form's validation

GENERATING THE PLACE ORDER SIDE MODULE: VALIDATE_ORDER.CPP

As with the Edit Product page's module, before you try to determine which standard C library functions this module is using, you need to make sure your code compiles without issue. Open a command prompt, navigate to the Chapter 8\8.1 EmDynamicLibraries\source\ folder, and then run the following command:

```
emcc validate_order.cpp -s SIDE_MODULE=2 -O1
  -o validate_order.wasm
```

There shouldn't be any errors displayed in the console window, and there should be a new validate_order.wasm file in your source folder.

To determine if your code is using any standard C library functions, open the validate_order.cpp file and comment out the `include` statement for the cstdlib header file. Save the file, but don't close it because you'll need to uncomment that line of code in a moment.

At the command prompt, run the same command that you ran a moment ago:

```
emcc validate_order.cpp -s SIDE_MODULE=2 -O1
  -o validate_order.wasm
```

You should see an error message displayed in the console window, similar to that in figure 8.11, indicating that the function `atoi` isn't defined. Make a note of that function because you'll need to include it when you use Emscripten to generate the main module. Again, you can safely ignore the error about NULL being an undeclared identifier.

Errors about NULL being
undefined can be ignored.

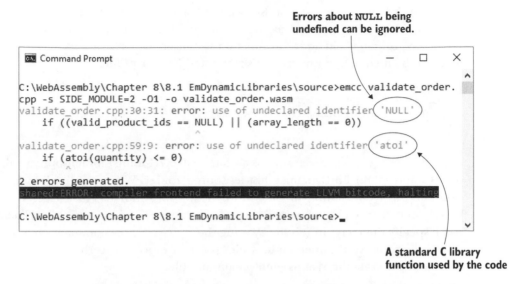

Figure 8.11   Emscripten throws an error about the atoi function and NULL not being defined.

In your validate_order.cpp file, remove the comment from in front of the cstdlib header file. Then save the file.

Now that you've created both side modules, it's time to create the JavaScript that the main module will use (figure 8.12).

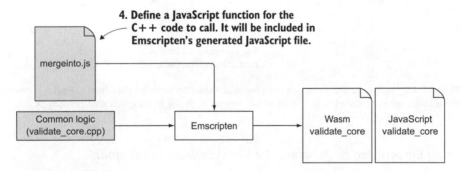

Figure 8.12   Define the JavaScript function that the C++ code will call if there's an issue with the validation. The code in this file will be included in Emscripten's generated JavaScript file.

8.1.4   Defining a JavaScript function to handle an issue with the validation

In chapter 5, you created a mergeinto.js file that holds the UpdateHostAboutError JavaScript function that the C++ functions will call into if there's an issue with the validation. The UpdateHostAboutError function will read the message from the module's memory and then pass the string to your web page's main JavaScript.

As the following code snippet shows, the `UpdateHostAboutError` function is part of a JavaScript object passed as the `mergeInto` function's second parameter. The `mergeInto` function will add your function to Emscripten's `LibraryManager.library` object to be included in Emscripten's generated JavaScript file:

```
mergeInto(LibraryManager.library, {
  UpdateHostAboutError: function(errorMessagePointer) {
    setErrorMessage(Module.UTF8ToString(errorMessagePointer));
  }
});
```

Copy the mergeinto.js file from your Chapter 5\5.1.1 EmJsLibrary\source\ folder to your Chapter 8\8.1 EmDynamicLibraries\source\ folder. When you use Emscripten to generate the WebAssembly module in the next step, you'll also instruct it to add the JavaScript contained in the mergeinto.js file in its generated JavaScript file. To do this, you'll specify the mergeinto.js file by using the `--js-library` command-line option.

Once you have the mergeinfo.js file, you can move on to the next step (figure 8.13) and generate the WebAssembly main module.

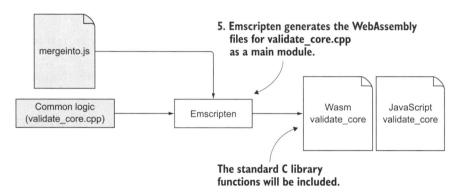

Figure 8.13 Use Emscripten to generate the WebAssembly main module from validate_core.cpp. Have Emscripten include the contents of the mergeinto.js file in its generated JavaScript file.

8.1.5 Using Emscripten to generate the WebAssembly main module

To have Emscripten generate a main module, you need to include the MAIN_MODULE flag. If you specify 1 for the value (`-s MAIN_MODULE=1`), Emscripten disables *dead code elimination*.

> **INFO** Dead code elimination prevents functions that aren't used by your code from being included in the resulting WebAssembly module.

Disabling dead code elimination is typically desired for a main module because it doesn't know what the side modules are going to need. As a result, it keeps all the functions that are defined in your code and all the standard C library functions. For a large application, this approach is desired because your code will likely use quite a few of the standard C library functions.

If your code is using only a small number of standard C library functions, as it is in this case, then all those extra functions that are being included just increase the module's size and slow down the download and instantiation. In this case, you'll want to enable dead code elimination for the main module; to do this, you specify 2 for the MAIN_MODULE value:

```
-s MAIN_MODULE=2
```

> **WARNING** Enabling dead code elimination for a main module means that it's up to you to make sure your side modules' necessary functions are kept alive.

When you created your validate_product and validate_order WebAssembly modules, you determined that they needed the following standard C library functions: strlen and atoi. To tell Emscripten to include these functions in the generated module, you'll include the functions in the command-line array EXPORTED_FUNCTIONS.

Your JavaScript code will be using the ccall, stringToUTF8, and UTF8ToString Emscripten helper functions, so you'll need to include them in the generated JavaScript file. To do this, you'll include them in the EXTRA_EXPORTED_RUNTIME_METHODS command-line array when you run the Emscripten compiler.

Normally when you create a WebAssembly module, Emscripten's generated JavaScript code exists as a global object called Module. This works when you have only one WebAssembly module per web page, but, for this chapter's scenario, you'll be creating a second WebAssembly module instance:

- One instance for the Edit Product form
- One instance for the Place Order form

You can allow for this to work by specifying the -s MODULARIZE=1 command-line flag, which will cause the Module object in Emscripten's generated JavaScript code to be wrapped in a function.

> **INFO** When you don't use the MODULARIZE flag, just including a link to Emscripten's JavaScript file in your web page will cause the WebAssembly module to be downloaded and instantiated when the page loads the file. When using the MODULARIZE flag, however, you're responsible for creating an instance of the Module object in your JavaScript code to trigger the download and instantiation of the WebAssembly module.

Open a command prompt, navigate to the Chapter 8\8.1 EmDynamicLibraries\source\ folder, and run the following command to create your validate_core WebAssembly module:

```
emcc validate_core.cpp --js-library mergeinto.js -s MAIN_MODULE=2
  -s MODULARIZE=1
  -s EXPORTED_FUNCTIONS=['_strlen','_atoi']
```

```
→ -s EXTRA_EXPORTED_RUNTIME_METHODS=['ccall','stringToUTF8',
→ 'UTF8ToString'] -o validate_core.js
```

Now that the WebAssembly modules have been created, you can move on to the next steps (figure 8.14), which are to copy the WebAssembly files and Emscripten's generated JavaScript file to the location where they'll be used by your website. You'll modify the web page's HTML to now also have a Place Order form section. You'll then update the JavaScript code to implement dynamic linking of the modules.

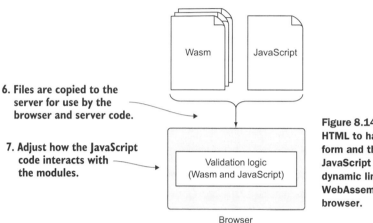

6. Files are copied to the server for use by the browser and server code.

7. Adjust how the JavaScript code interacts with the modules.

Figure 8.14 You'll adjust the HTML to have a Place Order form and then revise the JavaScript code to implement dynamic linking of the WebAssembly modules in a browser.

8.2   *Adjusting the web page*

In your Chapter 8\8.1 EmDynamicLibraries\ folder, create a frontend\ folder and then copy the following files into it:

- validate_core.js, validate_core.wasm, validate_product.wasm, and validate_order.wasm from your Chapter 8\8.1 EmDynamicLibraries\source\ folder
- editproduct.html and editproduct.js from your Chapter 5\5.1.1 EmJsLibrary\ frontend\ folder

Because the Place Order form will be added to the same web page as the Entry Product form, you'll rename the files to be more generic. Rename editproduct.html to index.html and editproduct.js to index.js.

Open the index.html file with your favorite editor so that you can add the new navigation bar and controls for the Place Order form, as shown in figure 8.15. To create a navigation section on your web page for things like menus, you'll use a Nav tag.

When creating menu systems, it's common practice to define the menu's items by using UL and LI tags and then using CSS to style them. The UL tag stands for *Unordered List*, which uses bullets. An OL tag, which stands for an *Ordered List* (a numbered list), can also be used but is a less common approach. Within the UL tag, you specify one or

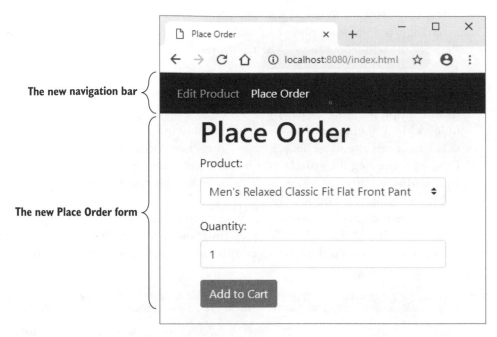

The new navigation bar

The new Place Order form

Figure 8.15   The new navigation bar and Place Order form controls that you will add to the web page

more LI (list item) tags for each menu item. If you'd like more information about building navigation bars, you can visit www.w3schools.com/css/css_navbar.asp.

Between the `<body onload="initializePage()">` tag and the first opening div tag (`<div class="container">`) in the index.html file, add the HTML from the following listing for the new navigation bar.

Listing 8.6   The HTML for the new navigation bar

```
...
<nav class="navbar navbar-expand-sm bg-dark navbar-dark">    ⟵──── The new
  <ul class="navbar-nav">                                            navigation bar
    <li class="nav-item">
      <a id="navEditProduct" class="nav-link" href="#Edit Product"
         onclick="switchForm(true)">Edit Product</a>    ⟵── Clicking this link will show
    </li>                                                    the Edit  Product form.
    <li class="nav-item">
      <a id="navPlaceOrder" class="nav-link" href="#PlaceOrder"
         onclick="switchForm(false)">Place Order</a>    ⟵──┐
    </li>                                  Clicking this link will show  │
  </ul>                                       the Place Order form.  │
</nav>
...
```

Add an `id` attribute to the H1 tag called `formTitle` so the JavaScript code will be able to change the value displayed to the user that indicates which form is displayed. Remove the text from the tag. The tag should look like this:

```
<h1 id="formTitle"></h1>
```

Because you'll need to hide the Edit Product form's controls when the Place Order form is displayed, you'll wrap them with a `div` that the JavaScript code can show or hide. Add an opening `div` tag—with an `id` value of `productForm`—before the `div` tag that surrounds the `Name` field. Because the Place Order form, rather than the Edit Product form, might be displayed when the web page first loads, you'll also include a style attribute on the `productForm` div to have it hidden by default. Add the closing `div` tag after the `save` button tag.

Change the `onclick` value of the Save button from `onClickSave` to `onClickSaveProduct` so it's obvious that the `save` function is for the Edit Product form. The HTML for the Edit Product form's controls in index.html should look like the HTML in the next listing.

Listing 8.7   The modified HTML for the Edit Product form section in index.html

```
...
<div id="productForm" style="display:none;">   ⟵——  New opening div tag surrounding
  <div class="form-group">                            the Edit Product form's controls
    <label for="name">Name:</label>
    <input type="text" class="form-control" id="name">
  </div>
  <div class="form-group">
    <label for="category">Category:</label>
    <select class="custom-select" id="category">
      <option value="0"></option>
      <option value="100">Jeans</option>
      <option value="101">Dress Pants</option>
    </select>
  </div>

  <button type="button" class="btn btn-primary"           ⟵——  onclick value changed to
      onclick="onClickSaveProduct()">Save</button>              onClickSaveProduct
</div>    ⟵——  Closing div tag for the productForm
...              tag that was added
```

You'll now need to add the Place Order form's controls to the HTML. As with the Edit Product controls, you'll surround the Place Order form's controls with a `div` having an `id` value of `orderForm`.

The Place Order form will have three controls:

- A drop-down list of products
- A Quantity text box
- An Add to Cart button

Add the HTML from the next listing following the closing div that you added for the productForm div in the index.html file.

Listing 8.8 The new HTML for the Place Order form

```
...
<div id="orderForm" style="display:none;">
  <div class="form-group">
    <label for="product">Product:</label>
    <select class="custom-select" id="product">
      <option value="0"></option>
      <option value="200">Women's Mid Rise Skinny Jeans</option>
      <option value="301">
        Men's Relaxed Classic Fit Flat Front Pant
      </option>
    </select>
  </div>
  <div class="form-group">
    <label for="quantity">Quantity:</label>
    <input type="text" class="form-control" id="quantity" value="0">
  </div>

  <button type="button" class="btn btn-primary"
      onclick="onClickAddToCart()">Add to Cart</button>
</div>
...
```

The final edits that you'll need to make will be the links to the JavaScript files at the end of the index.html file:

- Because you renamed the editproduct.js file to index.js, change the src attribute value of the first script tag to index.js.
- When you used Emscripten to create the main module, you gave it the name validate_core.js, so you'll need to change the src attribute value of the second script tag to validate_core.js.

The two script tags should look like this:

```
<script src="index.js"></script>
<script src="validate_core.js"></script>
```

Now that the HTML has been modified to contain a new navigation bar and the new Place Order form's controls, it's time to revise the JavaScript to work with the new WebAssembly modules.

8.2.1 Adjusting your web page's JavaScript

Open your index.js file in your favorite editor. This file will now handle the logic for two forms: Edit Product and Place Order. Because of this, the first thing you'll need to do is modify the name of the initialData object so it's clear that the object is for the Edit Product form. Change the name from initialData to initialProductData so that it looks like the following snippet:

```
const initialProductData = {
  name: "Women's Mid Rise Skinny Jeans",
  categoryId: "100",
};
```

The Place Order form's product drop-down list will need to be validated to ensure the user's selection is a valid ID. To do this, you'll pass an array to the Place Order form's WebAssembly module indicating what the valid IDs are. Add the following global array of valid IDs after the VALID_CATEGORY_IDS array in the index.js file:

```
const VALID_PRODUCT_IDS = [200, 301];
```

When you compiled the main module (validate_core.wasm), you instructed Emscripten to wrap its Module object in a function so that multiple instances of that object could be created. You did this because you'll be creating two WebAssembly module instances for this web page.

The Edit Product form will have a WebAssembly instance in which the main module is linked to the Edit Product side module: validate_product.wasm. The Place Order form will also have a WebAssembly instance, in which the main module is linked to the Place Order form's side module: validate_order.wasm.

To hold these two Emscripten Module instances, you need to add the global variables in the following code snippet after the VALID_PRODUCT_IDS array in the index.js file:

```
let productModule = null;   ⟵──  Will hold the validate_core and
                                 validate_product linked modules
let orderModule = null;     ⟵
                                 Will hold the validate_core and
                                 validate_order linked modules
```

That's it for the changes for the global objects. Now you'll need to make a few changes to the initializePage function.

THE INITIALIZEPAGE FUNCTION

The first change that's needed in the initializePage function is the name of the object used to populate the name field and category drop-down. The object's name needs to be changed from initialData to initialProductData.

This web page is being built as an SPA, so clicking the links in the navigation bar won't bring you to a new page. Instead, a *fragment identifier* is placed at the end of the address in the browser's address box, and the web page's contents are adjusted to show the desired view. If you were to give someone the address to the web page, and it included the fragment identifier, the web page should display that section as if the user had navigated to it by clicking that navigation link.

> **INFO** A fragment identifier is an optional portion at the end of a URL that starts with a hash (#) symbol, as figure 8.16 shows. It's typically used to identify a section of the web page. When you click a hyperlink that points to a fragment identifier, the web page jumps to that location, which is useful when navigating large documents.

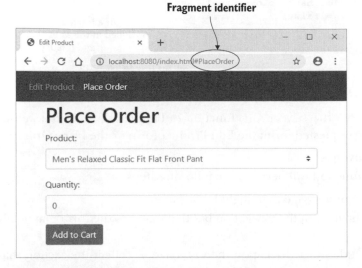

Figure 8.16 The URL of your web page with "PlaceOrder" as the fragment identifier

Because you'll want the web page to show the proper view based on whether a fragment identifier was specified in the page's address, you'll add some code to the end of the `initializePage` function to check and see if an identifier was included. By default, the web page will show the Edit Product form; but if the #PlaceOrder identifier is included in the address, you'll display the Place Order form instead. After the fragment identifier detection code, you'll add a call to a function that will cause the proper form to be displayed.

Revise the `initializePage` function in the index.js file so that it matches the code in the next listing.

Listing 8.9 The modified `initializePage` function

```
...
function initializePage() {
  document.getElementById("name").value = initialProductData.name;

  const category = document.getElementById("category");
  const count = category.length;
  for (let index = 0; index < count; index++) {
    if (category[index].value === initialProductData.categoryId) {
      category.selectedIndex = index;
      break;
    }
  }

  let showEditProduct = true;
  if ((window.location.hash) &&
```

initialData changed to initialProductData

initialData changed to initialProductData

Displays the Edit Product view by default

```
    (window.location.hash.toLowerCase() === "#placeorder")) {    ⟵
  showEditProduct = false;    ⟵
}

switchForm(showEditProduct);    ⟵
}
...
```

If a fragment identifier was included in the website's address, and it is #placeorder...

...the Place Order form is to be displayed.

Displays the proper form

You'll need to create the switchForm function to handle adjusting the web page so that it displays the requested form: the Edit Product form or the Place Order form.

THE SWITCHFORM FUNCTION

The switchForm function will perform the following steps:

- Clear any error message that might be displayed.
- Highlight the item in the navigation bar that matches the form that needs to be displayed.
- Modify the title in the H1 tag on the web page to reflect the section that's displayed.
- Show the requested form and hide the other.

Because the main module was compiled with the MODULARIZE flag, Emscripten doesn't automatically download and instantiate the WebAssembly module for you. It's up to you to create an instance of the Emscripten Module object.

If an instance of this object hasn't been created for the requested form yet, the switchForm function will also create one. The Emscripten Module object can accept a JavaScript object to control code execution, so your code will use it to pass in the name of the side module that it needs to link to via the dynamicLibraries array property.

Add the code in the next listing after the initializePage function in your index.js file.

Listing 8.10 The switchForm function

```
...
function switchForm(showEditProduct) {
  setErrorMessage("");
  setActiveNavLink(showEditProduct);    ⟵
  setFormTitle(showEditProduct);

  if (showEditProduct) {    ⟵
    if (productModule === null) {    ⟵
      productModule = new Module({
        dynamicLibraries: ['validate_product.wasm']    ⟵
      });
    }

    showElement("productForm", true);    ⟵
    showElement("orderForm", false);
  } else {
    if (orderModule === null) {
```

Highlights the navigation bar item for the view

The Edit Product view is to be displayed.

Modifies the title for the view

Only creates an instance if one hasn't been created yet

Creates a new WebAssembly instance of the main module

Tells Emscripten that it needs to link to the Product side module

The Order form is to be displayed.

Shows the Edit Product form and hides the Order form

```
    orderModule = new Module({
        dynamicLibraries: ['validate_order.wasm']
    });
    }

    showElement("productForm", false);
    showElement("orderForm", true);
    }
}
...
```

Creates a new WebAssembly instance of the main module

Tells Emscripten that it needs to link to the Order side module

Hides the Edit Product form and shows the Order form

The next function that you need to create is the setActiveNavLink function, which will highlight the displayed form's navigation bar.

THE SETACTIVENAVLINK FUNCTION

Because navigation bar items can have multiple CSS class names specified, you'll use the DOM element's classList object, which allows you to insert and delete individual class names. Your function will make sure both navigation bar items have the "active" class name removed and will then apply it to only the navigation bar item for the view that's being displayed.

Add the setActiveNavLink function shown in the next listing after the switch-Form function in the index.js file.

Listing 8.11 The setActiveNavLink function

```
...
function setActiveNavLink(Editproduct) {
  const navEditProduct = document.getElementById("navEditProduct");
  const navPlaceOrder = document.getElementById("navPlaceOrder");
  navEditProduct.classList.remove("active");
  navPlaceOrder.classList.remove("active");

  if (editProduct) { navEditProduct.classList.add("active"); }
  else { navPlaceOrder.classList.add("active"); }
}
...
```

Makes sure both elements have the "active" class name removed

Applies the "active" class name to the item for the form being displayed

The next function that you need to create is the setFormTitle function, which will adjust the text on the web page to indicate which form is displayed.

THE SETFORMTITLE FUNCTION

Following the setActiveNavLink function in the index.js file, add the setFormTitle function to display the form's title in the H1 tag on the web page:

```
function setFormTitle(editProduct) {
  const title = (editProduct ? "Edit Product" : "Place Order");
  document.getElementById("formTitle").innerText = title;
}
```

Originally, only the web page's error section needed to be shown or hidden, so the code to show or hide the element was part of the setErrorMessage function. Now that there are additional elements of the web page that need to be shown or hidden, you'll move that logic to its own function.

THE SHOWELEMENT FUNCTION

Add the showElement function following the setFormTitle function in your index.js file, as in the following snippet:

```
function showElement(elementId, show) {
  const element = document.getElementById(elementId);
  element.style.display = (show ? "" : "none");
}
```

The validation for the order form will need to get the user-selected product ID from the product drop-down list. The getSelectedCategoryId function already gets the user-selected ID from a drop-down list but is specific to the category drop-down of the Edit Product form. You'll now revise that function to be more generic so that it can also be used by the Place Order form.

THE GETSELECTEDCATEGORYID FUNCTION

Change the name of the getSelectedCategoryId function to getSelectedDropdownId, and add elementId as a parameter. Within the function, change the variable name from category to dropdown and replace the string "category" with elementId in the getElementById call.

The getSelectedDropdownId function should look like the code in the following snippet:

```
function getSelectedDropdownId(elementId) {          ◁——————  The function name
  const dropdown = document.getElementById(elementId); ◁——     is changed and the
  const index = dropdown.selectedIndex;                        elementId
  if (index !== -1) { return dropdown[index].value; }          parameter added.

  return "0";                    The variable name is changed, and
}                               elementId is passed to getElementById.
```

Now that you've created the showElement function to handle showing or hiding elements on the web page, you can revise the setErrorMessage function to call the new function rather than adjust the visibility of the element directly.

THE SETERRORMESSAGE FUNCTION

Modify the setErrorMessage function in your index.js file to call the showElement function rather than setting the element's style directly. Your function should look like this:

```
function setErrorMessage(error) {
  const errorMessage = document.getElementById("errorMessage");
  errorMessage.innerText = error;
  showElement("errorMessage", (error !== ""));   ◁——  Shows the errorMessage
}                                                     element if there's an error
                                                      and hides it if not
```

Because your web page will now have two sets of controls, having an onClickSave function would be confusing, so you'll rename the function so its name indicates that it's used by the Edit Product form.

THE ONCLICKSAVE FUNCTION

Rename the onClickSave function to now be onClickSaveProduct. Because you renamed the getSelectedCategoryId function to getSelectedDropdownId, you'll need to rename the function call. You'll also need to pass in the drop-down's ID ("category") as a parameter to the getSelectedDropdownId function.

Your onClickSaveProduct function should look like the code in the next listing.

Listing 8.12 The onClickSave function renamed to onClickSaveProduct

```
...

function onClickSaveProduct() {          ◁——— Name changed
  setErrorMessage("");                         from onClickSave

  const name = document.getElementById("name").value;        ◁——— Changes the function
  const categoryId = getSelectedDropdownId("category");       ◁——— name and specifies
                                                                   the drop-down's ID
  if (validateName(name) && validateCategory(categoryId)) {

  ◁
  }            There were no issues. The data can
}              be passed to the server-side code.
...
```

Because the main module was compiled with the MODULARIZE flag, you needed to create an instance of Emscripten's Module object. The validateName and validate-Category functions will need to be modified to call the Module instance that you created, productModule, rather than calling Emscripten's Module object.

THE VALIDATENAME AND VALIDATECATEGORY FUNCTIONS

You'll need to modify each spot in the validateName and validateCategory functions that calls Emscripten's Module object to now use the Module instance: product-Module. Your validateName and validateCategory functions in index.js should look like the code in the following listing.

Listing 8.13 The modified validateName and validateCategory functions

```
...

function validateName(name) {
  const isValid = productModule.ccall('ValidateName',    ◁——— Module replaced
      'number',                                               with productModule
      ['string', 'number'],
      [name, MAXIMUM_NAME_LENGTH]);

  return (isValid === 1);
}

function validateCategory(categoryId) {
  const arrayLength = VALID_CATEGORY_IDS.length;
```

```
const bytesPerElement = productModule.HEAP32.BYTES_PER_ELEMENT;    ◁──
const arrayPointer = productModule._malloc((arrayLength *    ◁────────
    bytesPerElement));
productModule.HEAP32.set(VALID_CATEGORY_IDS,    ◁────────
        (arrayPointer / bytesPerElement));

const isValid = productModule.ccall('ValidateCategory',    ◁──────────
    'number',
    ['string', 'number', 'number'],
    [categoryId, arrayPointer, arrayLength]);        Module replaced
                                                   with productModule
productModule._free(arrayPointer);    ◁──────────────

return (isValid === 1);
}
```

Now that you've finished modifying the existing Edit Product code, it's time to add the Place Order code. Your first step is to create the onClickAddToCart function.

THE onClickAddToCart FUNCTION

The onClickAddToCart function for the Place Order form will be very similar to the onClickSaveProduct function of the Edit Product form. Here, you'll get the selected ID from the product drop-down as well as the user-entered quantity value. You'll then call the validateProduct and validateQuantity JavaScript functions to call into the WebAssembly module and have the user-entered values validated. If there are no validation issues, the data can be saved.

Add the code in the following listing after the validateCategory function in your index.js file.

> **Listing 8.14   The onClickAddToCart function in index.js**

```
...

function onClickAddToCart() {            Gets the user-selected ID from
  setErrorMessage("");                       the product drop-down

  const productId = getSelectedDropdownId("product");    ◁──
  const quantity = document.getElementById("quantity").value;    ◁──
                                                              Gets the user-
  if (validateProduct(productId) &&    ◁──                    entered quantity
      validateQuantity(quantity)) {    ◁──    Validates the
                                             product ID
  }        ◁──────  There were no issues with
}                   the user-entered values.    Validates the
                    The data can be saved.      quantity
```

You'll now need to create the validateProduct function that will call into the WebAssembly module to verify that the user-selected product ID is valid.

THE validateProduct FUNCTION

The validateProduct function will call the module's ValidateProduct function. The ValidateProduct function has the following signature in C++:

```
int ValidateProduct(char* product_id,
```

```
int* valid_product_ids,
int array_length);
```

Your validateProduct JavaScript function will pass the following parameters to the module's function:

- The user-selected product ID
- An array of valid IDs
- The length of the array

You'll pass the user-selected product ID to the module as a string and let Emscripten's ccall function handle the string's memory management for you by indicating the parameter type as a 'string'.

Your array of valid IDs are integers (32-bit), but Emscripten's ccall function can handle the memory management of an array for you only if you're dealing with 8-bit integers. As a result, you'll need to manually allocate some of the module's memory to hold the array's values and then copy the values into the memory. You'll pass the memory location pointer for the valid IDs to the ValidateProduct function. In Web-Assembly, pointers are represented as 32-bit integers, so you'll indicate this parameter type as 'number'.

Add the validateProduct function shown in the next listing to the end of the index.js file.

Listing 8.15 The validateProduct function in index.js

```
...
function validateProduct(productId) {
  const arrayLength = VALID_PRODUCT_IDS.length;
  const bytesPerElement = orderModule.HEAP32.BYTES_PER_ELEMENT;
  const arrayPointer = orderModule._malloc((arrayLength *
      bytesPerElement));          ◁─────────────┐  Allocates enough memory
  orderModule.HEAP32.set(VALID_PRODUCT_IDS,       for each item of the array
      (arrayPointer / bytesPerElement));  ◁───────┐ Copies the array's
                                                    elements into the
  const isValid = orderModule.ccall('ValidateProduct', ◁ module's memory
      'number',
      ['string', 'number', 'number'],              Calls the ValidateProduct
      [productId, arrayPointer, arrayLength]);      function in the module

  orderModule._free(arrayPointer);  ◁──┐ Frees the memory that was
                                         allocated for the array
  return (isValid === 1);
}
```

The final JavaScript function that you'll need to create is the validateQuantity function that will call into the module to validate the user-entered quantity.

THE VALIDATEQUANTITY FUNCTION

The validateQuantity function will call the module's ValidateQuantity function, which has the following signature in C++:

```
int ValidateQuantity(char* quantity);
```

You'll pass the user-entered quantity value to the module as a string and let Emscripten's `ccall` function handle the string's memory management for you by indicating the parameter type as a `'string'`.

Add the `validateQuantity` function from the following code snippet to the end of the index.js file:

```
function validateQuantity(quantity) {
  const isValid = orderModule.ccall('ValidateQuantity',
      'number',
      ['string'],
      [quantity]);

  return (isValid === 1);
}
```

8.2.2   Viewing the results

Now that you've finished modifying the JavaScript code, open your browser and type `http://localhost:8080/index.html` into the address box to see the web page. You can test the navigation by clicking the navigation bar's links. As shown in figure 8.17, the displayed view should switch between the Edit Product and Place Order forms, and the address box should have a matching fragment identifier based on the last link you clicked.

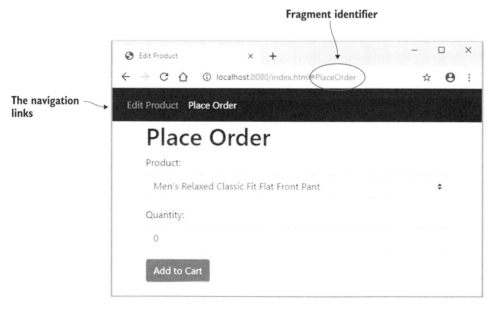

Figure 8.17   When you click the Place Order navigation link, the Place Order form's controls are displayed, and the fragment identifier is added to the address in the browser's address box.

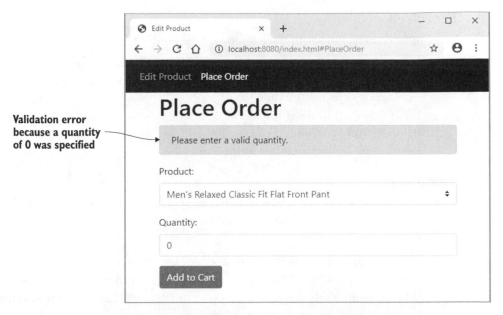

Figure 8.18 The new Place Order form's validation error message when a quantity of 0 is specified.

You can test the validation by selecting an item in the Product drop-down list, leaving the Quantity at 0, and then pressing the Add to Cart button. An error should display on the web page, as figure 8.18 shows.

Now, how can you use what you learned in this chapter in the real world?

Real-world use cases

The following are some possible use cases for what you've learned in this chapter:

- If your WebAssembly module doesn't need to be downloaded and instantiated until some point after the web page has loaded, you can include the -s MODULARIZE=1 flag when compiling the module. This will allow you to control when the module gets downloaded and instantiated, which will help speed up your website's initial load time.

- Another use case for the -s MODULARIZE=1 flag is that it allows you to create multiple instances of the WebAssembly module. A single-page application can potentially be long-running, and you might want to reduce memory use by creating an instance of the module when needed and destroying the instance when it's no longer needed (because the user navigated to another portion of the application, for example).

Exercises

You can find the solutions to the exercises in appendix D.

1   Suppose you have a side module called process_fulfillment.wasm. How would you create a new instance of Emscripten's `Module` object and tell it to dynamically link to this side module?

2   What flag do you need to pass to Emscripten when compiling a WebAssembly main module in order to have the `Module` object wrapped in a function in Emscripten's generated JavaScript file?

Summary

In this chapter, you learned how to create a simple SPA that uses a fragment identifier in the URL to indicate which form should be displayed.

You also learned the following:

- It's possible to create multiple instances of Emscripten's JavaScript `Module` object if you specify the `-s MODULARIZE=1` flag when compiling the main module.

- When a main module is compiled using the `MODULARIZE` flag, customizations for the `Module` object are passed as a JavaScript object to the `Module`'s constructor.

- Dead code elimination can be enabled for a main module by using the `-s MAIN_MODULE=2` flag. Doing so, however, requires you to explicitly indicate which functions to keep alive for the side modules by using the command-line array: `EXPORTED_FUNCTIONS`.

- You can test to see which standard C library functions are in use by a side module by commenting out the header files and trying to compile the module. Emscripten will throw errors at the command line indicating which functions are undefined.

Threading: Web workers and pthreads

In this chapter, you're going to learn about different options for using *threads* in a browser with relation to WebAssembly modules.

> **DEFINITION** A thread is a path of execution within a process, and a process can have multiple threads. A *pthread*, also known as a POSIX thread, is an API defined by the POSIX.1c standard for an execution module that's independent of programming language (see https://en.wikipedia.org/wiki/POSIX_Threads).

By default, a web page's UI and JavaScript all operate in a single thread. If your code does too much processing without periodically yielding to the UI, the UI can become unresponsive. Your animations will freeze, and the controls on the web page won't respond to a user's input, which can be frustrating for the user.

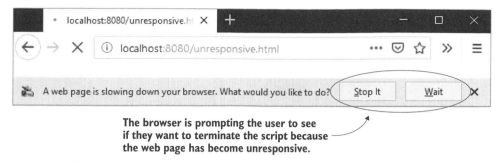

The browser is prompting the user to see
if they want to terminate the script because
the web page has become unresponsive.

Figure 9.1   A long-running process has caused Firefox to become unresponsive. The browser is prompting the user to see if they want to terminate the script.

If the web page remains unresponsive for long enough (typically around 10 seconds), a browser might even prompt the user to see if they want to stop the page, as figure 9.1 shows. If a user stops the script on your web page, the page may no longer function as expected unless the user refreshes it.

> **TIP**   To keep web pages as responsive as possible, whenever you interact with a Web API that has both synchronous and asynchronous functions, it's a best practice to use the asynchronous functions.

Being able to do some heavy processing without interfering with the UI is desirable, so browser makers created *web workers*.

9.1   Benefits of web workers

What do web workers do, and why would you want to use them? Web workers enable the creation of background threads in browsers. As figure 9.2 shows, they allow you to run JavaScript in a thread that's separate from the UI thread; communication between the two is accomplished by passing messages.

Unlike with the UI thread, using synchronous functions in a web worker is permitted, if desired, because doing so won't block the UI thread. Within a worker, you can

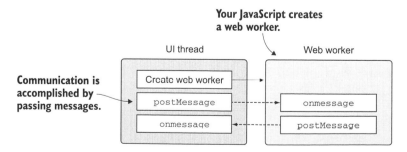

Figure 9.2   Your JavaScript creates a web worker and then communicates with it by passing messages.

spawn additional workers, and you have access to many of the same items that you have access to in the UI thread, such as fetch, WebSockets, and IndexedDB. For a complete list of APIs available to web workers, you can visit this MDN Web Docs page: http://mng.bz/gVBG.

Another advantage of web workers is that most devices now have multiple cores. If you're able to split up your processing across several threads, the length of time it takes to complete the processing should decrease. Web workers are also supported in nearly all web browsers, including mobile ones.

WebAssembly modules can use web workers in several ways:

- As you'll learn in section 9.3, a web worker can be used to prefetch a Web-Assembly module. The web worker can download and compile the module and then pass that compiled module to the main thread, which can then instantiate the compiled module and use it as per normal.
- Emscripten supports the ability to generate two WebAssembly modules, in which one sits in the main thread and the other in a web worker. The two modules communicate using Emscripten helper functions defined in Emscripten's *Worker API*. You won't learn about this approach in this chapter, but you'll see the JavaScript versions of many of Emscripten's functions. For more information about Emscripten's Worker API, you can visit this page in the documentation: http://mng.bz/eD1q.

  INFO   You would need to create two C or C++ files in order to compile one to run in the main thread and one to run in the web worker. The web worker file would need to be compiled with the `-s BUILD_AS_WORKER=1` flag set.

- A post-MVP feature is being developed that creates a special kind of web worker that allows a WebAssembly module to use pthreads (POSIX threads). At the moment, this approach is still considered experimental, and flags need to be enabled in some browsers to allow the code to run. You'll learn about this approach in section 9.4, where I'll also explain pthreads in greater detail.

9.2   *Considerations for using web workers*

You'll learn to use web workers shortly, but before you do, you should be aware of the following:

- Web workers have a high startup cost and a high memory cost, so they're not intended for use in large numbers, and they're expected to be long-lived.
- Because web workers run in a background thread, you have no direct access to the web page's UI features or the DOM.
- The only way to communicate with a web worker is by sending `postMessage` calls and responding to messages via an `onmessage` event handler.

- Even though the background thread's processing won't block the UI thread, you still need to be mindful of needless processing and memory usage because you're still using some of the device's resources. As an analogy, if a user is using a phone, a lot of network requests can use up their phone's data plan, and a lot of processing can use up the battery.

- Web workers are available only in browsers at the moment. If your WebAssembly module needs to also support Node.js, for example, this is something you'll need to keep in mind. As of version 10.5, Node.js has experimental support for *worker threads*, but they're not yet supported by Emscripten. More information about Node.js worker thread support can be found here: https://nodejs.org/api/worker_threads.html.

9.3   *Prefetching a WebAssembly module using a web worker*

Suppose you have a web page that will need a WebAssembly module at some point after the page has loaded. Rather than download and instantiate the module as the page is loading, you decide to defer the download until after it's loaded to keep the page load time as fast as possible. To keep your web page as responsive as possible, you also decide to use a web worker to handle downloading and compiling the WebAssembly module on a background thread.

As figure 9.3 illustrates, in this section, you'll learn how to

- Create a web worker
- Download and compile the WebAssembly module while in a web worker
- Pass and receive messages between the main UI thread and worker
- Override Emscripten's default behavior, in which it usually handles downloading and instantiating a WebAssembly module, and use the module that's already compiled

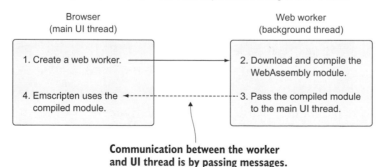

Figure 9.3   Your JavaScript creates a web worker. The worker will download and compile the WebAssembly module and then pass the compiled module to the main UI thread. Emscripten then uses the compiled module rather than downloading the module itself.

The following steps enumerate the solution for this scenario (figure 9.4):

1 Adjust the calculate_primes logic that you built in chapter 7 to determine how long it takes the calculations to complete.
2 Use Emscripten to generate the WebAssembly files from the calculate_primes logic.
3 Copy the generated WebAssembly files to the server for use by the browser.
4 Create the HTML and JavaScript for a web page that will create a web worker, and have Emscripten's JavaScript use the compiled WebAssembly module received from the worker.
5 Create the web worker's JavaScript file, which will download and compile the WebAssembly module.

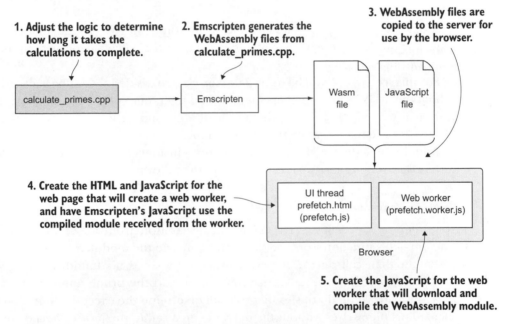

Figure 9.4   The steps for implementing the prefetch scenario. Modify calculate_primes.cpp to determine how long the computations take. Instruct Emscripten to generate the WebAssembly files and then create the HTML and JavaScript files. The JavaScript will create a web worker to download and compile the WebAssembly module. Finally, the compiled module will be passed back to the web page, where it will be instantiated by your code instead of Emscripten's JavaScript.

The first step, shown in figure 9.5, is to adjust the calculate_primes logic to determine how long it takes to do the calculations.

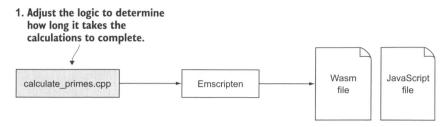

Figure 9.5   Modify the calculate_primes logic to determine how long the calculations take.

9.3.1   *Adjusting the calculate_primes logic*

Let's get started. In your WebAssembly\ folder create a Chapter 9\9.3 pre-fetch\source\ folder.

Copy the calculate_primes.cpp file from your Chapter 7\7.2.2 dlopen\source\ folder to your newly created source\ folder. Open the calculate_primes.cpp file with your favorite editor.

For this scenario, you'll be using a `vector` class that's defined in the `vector` header to hold the list of prime numbers found within the range specified. You'll also use the `high_resolution_clock` class, defined in the chrono header, to time how long it takes your code to determine the prime numbers.

Add the includes for the vector and chrono headers following the `cstdio` header in the calculate_primes.cpp file, as shown in the following code snippet:

```
#include <vector>
#include <chrono>
```

Now, remove the `EMSCRIPTEN_KEEPALIVE` declaration from above the `FindPrimes` function—this function won't be called from outside the module.

Rather than call `printf` for every prime number as it's found, you're going to modify the logic in the `FindPrimes` function to add the prime number to a `vector` object instead. You'll do this so that you can determine the execution duration of the calculations themselves without the delay due to a call to the JavaScript code on every loop. The `main` function will then be modified to handle sending the prime number information to the browser's console window.

> **DEFINITION**   A `vector` object is a sequence container for dynamic sized arrays in which the storage is automatically increased or decreased as needed. More information on the `vector` object can be found here: https://en.cppreference.com/w/cpp/container/vector.

You'll make the following modifications to the `FindPrimes` function:

- Add a parameter to the function that accepts an `std::vector<int>` reference.
- Remove all of the `printf` calls.
- Within the `IsPrime` if statement, add the value in i to the vector reference.

In your calculate_primes.cpp file, revise the FindPrimes function to match the code in the following snippet:

```cpp
void FindPrimes(int start, int end,
    std::vector<int>& primes_found) {     ◁——— A vector reference parameter has been added.
  for (int i = start; i <= end; i += 2) {
    if (IsPrime(i)) {
      primes_found.push_back(i);     ◁——— The prime number is added to the list.
    }
  }
}
```

A vector reference parameter has been added.

The prime number is added to the list.

Your next step is to modify the main function to

- Update the browser's console window with the range of numbers that will be checked for prime numbers.
- Determine how long the FindPrimes function takes to execute by getting the value of the clock before and after the call to the FindPrimes function and subtracting the difference.
- Create a vector object to hold the prime numbers found, and pass it to the FindPrimes function.
- Update the browser's console to indicate how long it took for the FindPrimes function to execute.
- Output each of the prime numbers that were found by looping through the vector object's values.

Your main function in your calculate_primes.cpp file should now look like the code in the following listing.

Listing 9.1 The main function in calculate_primes.cpp

```cpp
...
int main() {
  int start = 3, end = 1000000;
  printf("Prime numbers between %d and %d:\n", start, end);

  std::chrono::high_resolution_clock::time_point duration_start =
      std::chrono::high_resolution_clock::now();     ◁——— Gets the current time to mark the start of the FindPrimes execution

  std::vector<int> primes_found;
  FindPrimes(start, end, primes_found);     ◁——— Creates a vector object that will hold integers, and passes it to the FindPrimes function

  std::chrono::high_resolution_clock::time_point duration_end =
  ▷ std::chrono::high_resolution_clock::now();

  std::chrono::duration<double, std::milli> duration =
      (duration_end - duration_start);     ◁———
```

Gets the current time to mark the start of the FindPrimes execution

Creates a vector object that will hold integers, and passes it to the FindPrimes function

Gets the current time to mark the end of the FindPrimes execution

Determines the amount of time, in milliseconds, that it took FindPrimes to execute

```
printf("FindPrimes took %f milliseconds to execute\n", duration.count());

printf("The values found:\n");
for(int n : primes found) {          ⊲──┐  Loops through each value in
  printf("%d ", n);                        the vector object and outputs
}                                          the value to the console
printf("\n");

return 0;
}
```

Now that the calculate_primes.cpp file has been modified, the second step (figure 9.6) is where you'll have Emscripten generate the WebAssembly files.

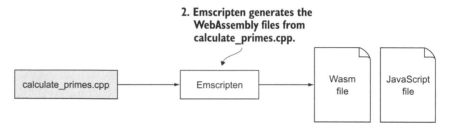

2. Emscripten generates the WebAssembly files from calculate_primes.cpp.

Figure 9.6   Use Emscripten to generate the WebAssembly files from calculate_primes.cpp.

9.3.2   *Using Emscripten to generate the WebAssembly files*

Because the C++ code in calculate_primes.cpp is now using chrono, which was introduced as one of the features in the ISO C++ 2011 standard, you'll need to tell Clang, Emscripten's frontend compiler, to use that standard by specifying the -std=c++11 flag.

> **INFO**   Emscripten uses Clang as the frontend compiler that takes your C++ code and compiles it to LLVM IR. By default, Clang uses the C++98 standard, but other standards can be enabled using the -std flag. Clang supports the C++98/C++03, C++11, C++14, and C++17 standards. If you're interested, the following web page gives more details on the C++ standards Clang supports: https://clang.llvm.org/cxx_status.html.

Also, because you'll be initializing Emscripten's Module object after the web page has loaded, you'll specify the -s MODULARIZE=1 flag as well. This flag will tell Emscripten to wrap the generated JavaScript file's Module object in a function. Being wrapped in a function prevents the Module object from being initialized until you create an instance of it, allowing you to control when initialization happens.

To compile calculate_primes.cpp into a WebAssembly module, open a command prompt, navigate to the Chapter 9\9.3 pre-fetch\source\ folder, and then run the following command:

```
emcc calculate_primes.cpp -O1 -std=c++11 -s MODULARIZE=1
➥ -o calculate_primes.js
```

9.3.3 Copying files to the correct location

Now that you've created your WebAssembly files, your next steps are to copy those files to a location where your website can use them (figure 9.7). You'll then create the HTML and JavaScript files for the web page that will create a web worker. When the web page receives the compiled WebAssembly module from the worker, it will have Emscripten's JavaScript use the compiled module rather than download it itself.

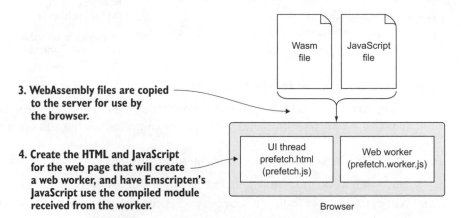

3. WebAssembly files are copied to the server for use by the browser.

4. Create the HTML and JavaScript for the web page that will create a web worker, and have Emscripten's JavaScript use the compiled module received from the worker.

Figure 9.7   Copy the WebAssembly files to the server for use by the browser. Then create the HTML and JavaScript for the web page. The JavaScript will create a web worker and will then have Emscripten's JavaScript use the compiled module received from the worker.

In your Chapter 9\9.3 pre-fetch\ folder, create a frontend\ folder and then copy the following into your new folder:

- The calculate_primes.wasm and calculate_primes.js files from your source\ folder.
- The main.html file from your Chapter 7\7.2.4 ManualLinking\frontend\ folder; rename the file to prefetch.html.

9.3.4 Creating the HTML file for the web page

In your Chapter 9\9.3 pre-fetch\frontend\ folder, open the prefetch.html file in your editor. Add a new `script` tag before the current `script` tag, and give its `src` attribute a value of `prefetch.js` for the JavaScript file of this web page, which you'll create in a moment.

You'll also need to modify the other `script` tag's `src` value to be `calculate_primes.js` to load in the Emscripten-generated JavaScript file. Your prefetch.html file's code should now match the code in the following listing.

Listing 9.2   The HTML in prefetch.html

```
<!DOCTYPE html>
<html>
  <head>
    <meta charset="utf-8"/>
  </head>
  <body>
    HTML page I created for my WebAssembly module.

    <script src="prefetch.js"></script>
    <script src="calculate_primes.js"></script>
  </body>
</html>
```

Adds a new script tag for prefetch.js

Changes the src value to calculate_primes.js

9.3.5   *Creating the JavaScript file for the web page*

Now that you've created the HTML, you need to create the JavaScript file for the web page. In your Chapter 9\9.3 pre-fetch\frontend\ folder, create a prefetch.js file and open it with your favorite editor.

Your JavaScript will need to perform the following tasks:

1 Create a web worker and attach an `onmessage` event listener:
   a When the worker calls the `onmessage` event listener, place the compiled module that's received into a global variable.
   b Then create an instance of the Emscripten `Module` object and specify a callback function for Emscripten's `instantiateWasm` function.
2 Define your callback function for Emscripten's `instantiateWasm` function. When called, your function will instantiate the compiled module that's held by your global variable and pass the instantiated WebAssembly module to Emscripten's code.

INFO   The `instantiateWasm` function is called by Emscripten's JavaScript code to instantiate the WebAssembly module. By default, Emscripten's JavaScript will download and instantiate a WebAssembly module automatically for you, but this function allows you to handle the process yourself.

The first thing that your JavaScript code will need is a couple of global variables:

- One variable will hold the compiled module that you'll receive from the web worker.
- The other variable will hold an instance of Emscripten's JavaScript `Module` object.

Add the variables in the following code snippet to your prefetch.js file:

```
let compiledModule = null;
let emscriptenModule = null;
```

You'll now need to create a web worker and attach an `onmessage` event listener so that you can receive messages from that worker.

CREATING A WEB WORKER AND ATTACH AN ONMESSAGE EVENT LISTENER

You can create a web worker by creating an instance of a `Worker` object. The `Worker` object's constructor expects a path to a JavaScript file that will be the worker's code. In this case, that file will be prefetch.worker.js.

Once you have an instance of a `Worker` object, you can pass the worker messages by calling the `postMessage` method of the instance. You can also receive messages by attaching to the `onmessage` event of the instance.

When you create your web worker, you'll set up an `onmessage` event handler to listen for a message from the worker. When the event is called, your code will place the compiled WebAssembly module that it receives in the global `compiledModule` variable.

> **INFO** The `onmessage` event handler will receive a `MessageEvent` object that has the data sent by the caller in the `data` property. The `MessageEvent` object is derived from an `Event` object to represent a message received by a target object. More information about the `MessageEvent` object can be found on the MDN Web Docs page at http://mng.bz/pyPw.

Your `onmessage` event handler will then create an instance of Emscripten's JavaScript `Module` object and will specify a callback function for Emscripten's `instantiateWasm` function. You'll be specifying this callback function in order to override the normal Emscripten behavior and instantiate the WebAssembly module from the compiled module that you have in the global variable.

Add the code in the following snippet to your prefetch.js file:

Creates a web worker

Adds an event listener for messages from the worker

Places the compiled module into the global variable

Creates a new instance of Emscripten's Module object

Specifies a callback function for instantiateWasm

```
const worker = new Worker("prefetch.worker.js");
worker.onmessage = function(e) {
  compiledModule = e.data;

  emscriptenModule = new Module({
    instantiateWasm: onInstantiateWasm
  });
}
```

Now you'll need to implement the `onInstantiateWasm` callback function that you've specified for Emscripten's `instantiateWasm` function.

DEFINING YOUR CALLBACK FUNCTION FOR EMSCRIPTEN'S INSTANTIATEWASM FUNCTION

The `instantiateWasm` callback function accepts two parameters:

- `imports`
  - This parameter is the `importObject` that you'll need to pass to the instantiate function of the WebAssembly JavaScript API.
- `successCallback`
  - Once the WebAssembly module has been instantiated, you need to pass the instantiated module back to Emscripten using this function.

The return value of the `instantiateWasm` function depends on whether you instantiate the WebAssembly module asynchronously or synchronously:

- If you choose to use an asynchronous function, as you will in this case, the return value needs to be an empty JavaScript object (`{}`).
- Synchronous WebAssembly JavaScript API calls aren't recommended if your code is running in the browser's main thread and may even be blocked by some browsers. If a synchronous function is used, then the return value needs to be the module instance's `exports` object.

You won't be able to use the `WebAssembly.instantiateStreaming` function to instantiate the WebAssembly module in this case because the `instantiateStreaming` function doesn't accept a compiled module. Instead, you'll need to use the overloaded `WebAssembly.instantiate` function:

- The main overloaded `WebAssembly.instantiate` function accepts the WebAssembly binary's bytecode, in the form of an ArrayBuffer, and then compiles and instantiates the module. When the promise resolves, you're given an object that has both a `WebAssembly.Module` (the compiled module) and a `WebAssembly.Instance` object.
- The other overloaded `WebAssembly.instantiate` function is the one that you'll be using here. The overloaded function accepts a `WebAssembly.Module` object and instantiates it. When the promise resolves in this case, you're given only the `WebAssembly.Instance` object.

Add the code in the following snippet after your `onmessage` event handler in the prefetch.js file:

```
function onInstantiateWasm(importObject, successCallback) {    ◁──── Callback for
  WebAssembly.instantiate(compiledModule,                              Emscripten's
      importObject).then(instance =>   ◁──────── Instantiates the      instantiateWasm
    successCallback(instance)   ◁───────         compiled module       function
  );
                                      Passes the instantiated
  return {};   ◁─────────────         module to Emscripten's
}                                     callback function
      Because this was handled
      asynchronously, returns an
      empty JavaScript object
```

Now that you've created the web page's main JavaScript, your final step is to create the web worker's JavaScript (figure 9.8). The JavaScript will fetch and compile the WebAssembly module and will then pass the compiled module to the UI thread.

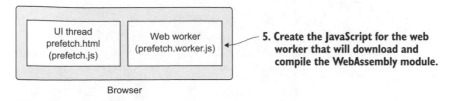

Figure 9.8   The final step is to create the JavaScript file for the web worker that will download and compile the WebAssembly module. Once compiled, the WebAssembly module will be passed to the UI thread.

9.3.6   Creating the web worker's JavaScript file

In your Chapter 9\9.3 pre-fetch\frontend\ folder, create a prefetch.worker.js file and open it with your favorite editor.

> **TIP**   The name of the JavaScript file doesn't matter, but this naming convention ([file name of the JavaScript that will create the worker].worker.js) makes it easier to distinguish between normal JavaScript files and those that are used in web workers when you're browsing your file system. It also makes it easier to determine the relationship between the files, which will help if you need to debug or maintain the code.

The first thing your web worker's code will do is fetch and compile the calculate_primes.wasm WebAssembly module. To compile the module, you'll use the `WebAssembly.compileStreaming` function. Once compiled, your code will pass the module to the UI thread by calling `postMessage` on its global object, `self`.

> **INFO**   In a web browser's UI thread, the global object is the `window` object. In a web worker, the global object is `self`.

Add the code in the following snippet to your prefetch.worker.js file:

```
WebAssembly.compileStreaming(fetch("calculate_primes.wasm"))   ⟵  Downloads and
.then(module => {                                                   compiles the
  self.postMessage(module);  ⟵  Passes the compiled                 WebAssembly
});                               module to the main thread         module
```

Now that everything has been created, you can view the results.

9.3.7   Viewing the results

You can open your browser and type `http://localhost:8080/prefetch.html` into the address box to see the generated web page. If you press the F12 key to display the browser's developer tools (figure 9.9), the console window should show you the list of prime numbers that were found. You should also see the duration of how long the calculations took to execute.

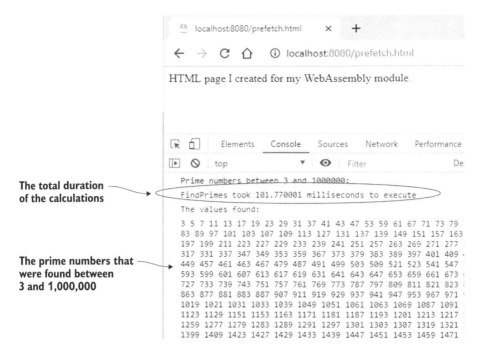

The total duration of the calculations

The prime numbers that were found between 3 and 1,000,000

Figure 9.9   The prime numbers found by the WebAssembly module with the total duration for the calculations indicated

Suppose you want to speed up the execution time needed to determine the prime numbers between 3 and 1,000,000. To do this, you decide that it will help to create several pthreads that will each process a smaller block of numbers in parallel.

9.4   *Using pthreads*

WebAssembly supports pthreads by using web workers and a *SharedArrayBuffer*.

> **REMINDER**   A thread is a path of execution within a process, and a process can have multiple threads. A *pthread*, also known as a POSIX thread, is an API defined by the POSIX.1c standard for an execution module that's independent of programming language (see https://en.wikipedia.org/wiki/POSIX_Threads).

A SharedArrayBuffer is similar to an ArrayBuffer, which is usually used for a WebAssembly module's memory. The difference is that a SharedArrayBuffer allows the module's memory to be shared between the main module and each of its web workers. It also allows for *atomic* operations for memory synchronization.

Because the memory is shared between a module and its web workers, each area can read and write to that same data in memory. Atomic memory access operations ensure the following:

- Predictable values are written and read.
- The current operation is finished before the next one starts.
- Operations aren't interrupted.

For more information about WebAssembly's threads proposal, including detailed information about the various atomic memory access instructions available, you can visit this GitHub page: http://mng.bz/O9xa.

> **WARNING** The WebAssembly threading proposal for pthreads was put on hold in January 2018 because browser makers disabled support for the Shared-ArrayBuffer in order to prevent Spectre/Meltdown vulnerabilities from being exploited. Browser makers are working on solutions to prevent the Shared-ArrayBuffer from being exploited, but, for the moment, pthreads are available only in the desktop version of the Chrome browser or if you turn on a flag in the Firefox browser. You'll learn how to do the latter in section 9.4.3.

For more information about Emscripten's support of pthreads, you can visit https://emscripten.org/docs/porting/pthreads.html.

The steps to the solution for this scenario (figure 9.10) are as follows:

1. Revise the calculate_primes logic from section 9.3 to create four pthreads. Each pthread will be given a block of numbers to process, looking for prime numbers.
2. Use Emscripten to generate the WebAssembly files with pthread support enabled. In this case, you'll use Emscripten's HTML template to view the results.

Your first step is to modify the calculate_primes logic to create four pthreads and instruct each thread to look for prime numbers within a specific block of numbers.

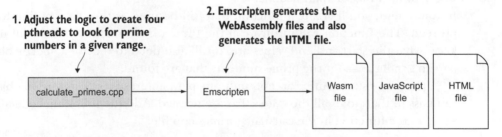

Figure 9.10 The steps for this scenario modify the calculate_primes.cpp logic to create four pthreads, each of which will look for prime numbers in a given range. Then Emscripten will be used to generate the WebAssembly files along with the HTML template.

9.4.1 *Adjusting the calculate_primes logic to create and use four pthreads*

In your Chapter9\ folder, create a 9.4 pthreads\source\ folder. Copy the calculate_primes.cpp file from your 9.3 pre-fetch\source\ folder to your newly created source\ folder, and open the file in your favorite editor.

Because you'll be using pthreads, you'll need to add the pthread.h header file to the calculate_primes.cpp file, as shown in this snippet:

```
#include <pthread.h>
```

The first function that you'll need to modify is the `FindPrimes` function.

MODIFYING THE FINDPRIMES FUNCTION

The `FindPrimes` function needs a line of code to check and see if the start value specified is an odd number or not. If the number is even, you'll increment the value so that the loop starts with an odd number.

In the calculate_primes.cpp file, your `FindPrimes` function should look like the following snippet:

```
void FindPrimes(int start, int end,
    std::vector<int>& primes_found) {
  if (start % 2 == 0) { start++; }     ◁——————  If the value is even,
                                                 increment it so that it's odd.
  for (int i – start; i <= end; i += 2) {
    if (IsPrime(i)) {
      primes_found.push_back(i);
    }
  }
}
```

Your next step is to create a function to serve as a start routine for your pthreads.

CREATING THE PTHREAD START ROUTINE

In a moment, you'll create a function that will be used as the start routine for each pthread. The function will in turn call the `FindPrimes` function, but it will need to know what the start and end values are. It will also need to receive a `vector` object to pass to `FindPrimes` for the prime numbers that are found.

A pthread's start routine accepts only one parameter, so you'll define an object you can pass in that holds all the values that are needed. Add the following code after the `FindPrimes` function in the calculate_primes.cpp file:

```
struct thread_args {
  int start;
  int end;
  std::vector<int> primes_found;
};
```

Now you'll create the start routine for your pthreads. The start routine needs to return a `void*` and accepts a single `void*` parameter for the arguments that are passed in. When you create the pthreads, you'll pass in a `thread_args` object containing the values that need to be passed along to the `FindPrimes` function.

Add the code in the next snippet after the `thread_args` struct in your calculate_primes.cpp file:

```
void* thread_func(void* arg) {          ← The start routine that
                                           will be called when you
                                           create the pthreads
    struct thread_args* args = (struct thread_args*)arg;   ← Casts the arg value to
                                                              a thread_args pointer

    FindPrimes(args->start, args->end, args->primes_found);   ←

    return arg;          Calls the FindPrimes function, passing in
}                          the values received in the args pointer
```

The last area that you'll need to modify is the `main` function.

MODIFYING THE MAIN FUNCTION

You'll now modify the `main` function to create four pthreads and tell each one which range of 200,000 numbers you want it to search through. To create a pthread, you call the `pthread_create` function, passing in the following parameters:

- A reference to a `pthread_t` variable that will hold the thread's ID if the thread is created successfully.
- The *attributes* for the thread being created. In this case, you'll pass `NULL` to use the default attributes.
- The start routine for the thread.
- The value to pass to the start routine's parameter.

> **INFO**   The attributes object is created by calling the `pthread_attr_init` function, which will return a `pthread_attr_t` variable holding default attributes. Once you have the object, the attributes can be adjusted by calling various `pthread_attr` functions. When you're finished with the attributes object, you need to call the `pthread_attr_destroy` function. The following web page has more information about the pthread attributes object: https://linux.die.net/man/3/pthread_attr_init.

Once you've created the pthreads, you'll have the main thread also call the `FindPrimes` function to check for the prime numbers between 3 and 199,999.

When the `FindPrimes` call completes on the main thread, you'll want to make sure that each pthread has finished its computations before moving on to print out the values found. To have the main thread wait for each pthread to complete, you call the `pthread_join` function, passing in the thread ID of the thread you want to wait for as the first parameter. The second parameter can be used to get the exit status of the joined thread, but you don't need that in this case, so you'll pass in `NULL`. Both the `pthread_create` and `pthread_join` functions will return 0 (zero) if the call is successful.

In your calculate_primes.cpp file, modify your `main` function so that it matches the code in the next listing.

Listing 9.3   The `main` function in calculate_primes.cpp

```
...
int main() {
  int start = 3, end = 1000000;
  printf("Prime numbers between %d and %d:\n", start, end);

  std::chrono::high_resolution_clock::time_point duration_start =
      std::chrono::high_resolution_clock::now();

  pthread_t thread_ids[4];
  struct thread_args args[5];

  int args_index = 1;
  int args_start = 200000;

  for (int i = 0; i < 4; i++) {
    args[args_index].start = args_start;
    args[args_index].end = (args_start + 199999);
    if (pthread_create(&thread_ids[i],
      NULL,
      thread_func,
      &args[args_index])) {
    perror("Thread create failed");
    return 1;
    }
    args_index += 1;
    args_start += 200000;
  }
  FindPrimes(3, 199999, args[0].primes_found);

  for (int j = 0; j < 4; j++) {
    pthread_join(thread_ids[j], NULL);
  }

  std::chrono::high_resolution_clock::time_point duration_end =
      std::chrono::high_resolution_clock::now();

  std::chrono::duration<double, std::milli> duration =
      (duration_end - duration_start);

  printf("FindPrimes took %f milliseconds to execute\n", duration.count());

  printf("The values found:\n");
  for (int k = 0; k < 5; k++) {
    for(int n : args[k].primes_found) {
      printf("%d ", n);
    }
  }
  printf("\n");

  rcturn 0;
}
```

Annotations:

- The ID of each thread created → `pthread_t thread_ids[4];`
- The arguments for each thread, including the main thread that will do processing → `struct thread_args args[5];`
- Skips zero so that the main thread can put its prime numbers in the first args index → `int args_index = 1;`
- The first background thread will start computations at 200,000. → `int args_start = 200000;`
- Sets the start and end range for the current thread's computations → `args[args_index].start = args_start;`
- Uses the thread's default attributes → `NULL`
- The start routine for the thread → `thread_func,`
- Creates the pthread. If successful, the thread ID will be placed at this array index. → `if (pthread_create(&thread_ids[i],`
- Arguments for the current thread → `&args[args_index]))`
- Increments the values for the next loop → `args_index += 1; args_start += 200000;`
- Uses the main thread to also find prime numbers, and places them in the first index of args → `FindPrimes(3, 199999, args[0].primes_found);`
- Indicates that the main thread is to wait until all pthreads are finished → `pthread_join(thread_ids[j], NULL);`
- Loops through the args array → `for (int k = 0; k < 5; k++) {`
- Loops through the list of prime numbers in the current args array item → `for(int n : args[k].primes_found) {`

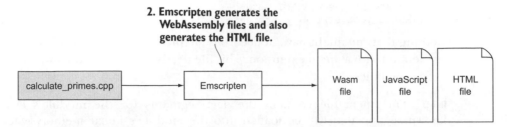

2. Emscripten generates the WebAssembly files and also generates the HTML file.

Figure 9.11 **The next step is to use Emscripten to generate the WebAssembly files and HTML file from calculate_primes.cpp.**

Now that the calculate_primes.cpp file has been modified, the next step is shown in figure 9.11, where you'll have Emscripten generate the WebAssembly files and HTML file.

9.4.2 *Using Emscripten to generate the WebAssembly files*

To enable pthreads in your WebAssembly module, you'll specify the -s USE_PTHREADS=1 flag at the command line when you compile the module. You'll also need to indicate how many threads you plan to use at once by using the following flag: -s PTHREAD_POOL_SIZE=4.

> **WARNING** When you specify a value greater than 0 (zero) for the PTHREAD_POOL_SIZE flag, all the web workers for the thread pool will be created when your module is instantiated rather than when your code calls pthread_create. If you request more threads than you actually need, you'll waste processing time at startup as well as some of the browser's memory for threads that aren't doing anything. It's also recommended that you test your WebAssembly module in all browsers that you intend to support. Firefox has indicated that it supports up to 512 concurrent web worker instances, but this number may vary by browser.

If you don't specify a PTHREAD_POOL_SIZE flag, it's the same as specifying the flag with a value of 0 (zero). This approach can be used in order to have the web workers created when pthread_create is called rather than during the module's instantiation. With this technique, however, thread execution won't start immediately. Instead, the thread must yield execution back to the browser first. One approach for this function would be as follows:

- Define two functions in your module—one that calls pthread_create and another that calls pthread_join.
- Your JavaScript first needs to call the function to trigger the pthread_create code.
- Your JavaScript then calls the pthread_join function to get the results.

To compile the module, open a command prompt, navigate to the Chapter 9\9.4 pthreads\source\ folder, and run the following command:

```
emcc calculate_primes.cpp -O1 -std=c++11 -s USE_PTHREADS=1
⇒ -s PTHREAD_POOL_SIZE=4 -o pthreads.html
```

Something that you might have noticed (also depicted in figure 9.12) is that there's a file generated with a .mem extension. This file needs to be distributed with the rest of the generated files.

> **INFO**   The .mem file contains the data segments for the module's Data known section that will be loaded into the module's linear memory when instantiated. Having the data segments in their own file allows a WebAssembly module to be instantiated multiple times but to only load that data into memory once. The way pthreads are set up, each thread has its own instance of the module to communicate with, but all modules share the same memory.

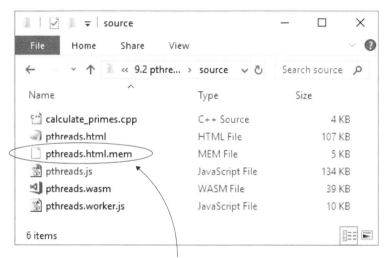

This generated file holds the data segments for the module's Data known section. The contents of this file will be loaded into the module's linear memory during instantiation.

Figure 9.12   The calculate_primes.cpp source file and the Emscripten-generated files. In this case, Emscripten has placed the data segments for the module's Data known section in their own file.

Once the WebAssembly files have been generated, you can view the results.

9.4.3   *Viewing the results*

At the time of this book's writing, WebAssembly threading support is available only in the desktop version of Chrome or if you turn on a flag in Firefox. Before you can view the pthreads.html file that was generated in the Firefox browser, you'll need to enable the flag.

Open your Firefox browser, and type about:config into the address box. You should see a screen similar to that in figure 9.13. Click the "I accept the risk!" button to enter the configuration view.

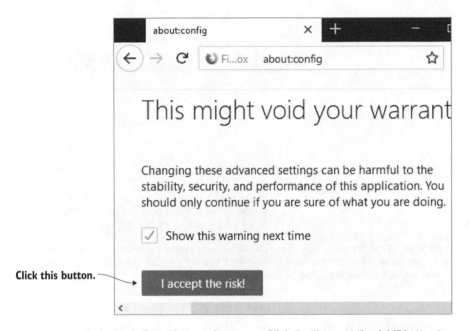

Figure 9.13   Firefox's configuration warning screen. Click the "I accept the risk!" button to enter the configuration view.

You should now see a page with a long list of items. Just above the list is a search box. Type javascript.options.shared_memory into the search box, and the list should now look like figure 9.14. You can either *double-click* the list item, or *right-click* the list item and select Toggle from the context menu, to change the flag to true.

> **WARNING**   This option is currently disabled in Firefox due to security concerns. Once you've finished testing, you should turn this flag back to false.

> **NOTE**   There have been some reports of Python's SimpleHTTPServer not indicating the proper Media Type for JavaScript files used by web workers. It should use application/javascript but, for some people, it uses text/plain instead. If you encounter errors in Chrome, try viewing your web page in Firefox.

To view the results, you can open your browser and type http://localhost:8080/pthreads.html into the address box to see the generated web page. As figure 9.15 shows, if you press the F12 key to display the browser's developer tools, the console window should show you how much time the computations took to execute and the list of prime numbers that were found.

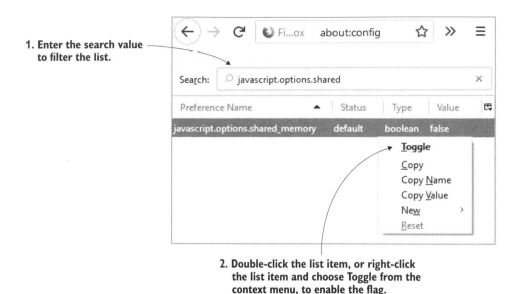

1. Enter the search value to filter the list.

2. Double-click the list item, or right-click the list item and choose Toggle from the context menu, to enable the flag.

Figure 9.14 Type `javascript.options.shared_memory` into the search box to filter the list. Either double-click the list item, or right-click the list item and choose Toggle from the context menu, to change the flag to `true`.

In section 9.3.7, the duration for the single threaded WebAssembly module to find the prime numbers between 3 and 1,000,000 was about 101 milliseconds. Here, using four pthreads and the main thread to do the calculations has almost tripled the execution speed.

How can you use what you learned in this chapter in the real world?

Real-world use cases

The ability to use web workers and pthreads opens the door to a number of possibilities, ranging from prefetching WebAssembly modules to parallel processing. Some of the options are as follows:

- Although not quite the same as pthreads in WebAssembly, web workers can be used as a polyfill for parallel processing in browsers that don't yet support pthreads.
- Web workers can be used to prefetch and compile WebAssembly modules in anticipation of their need. This improves load time because less is downloaded and instantiated when the web page first loads, making the web page more responsive because it's ready for the user's interactions.
- The article "WebAssembly at eBay: A Real-World Use Case," by Pranav Jha and Senthil Padmanabhan, details how eBay used WebAssembly, in conjunction with web workers and a JavaScript library, to improve its barcode scanner: http://mng.bz/Ye1a.

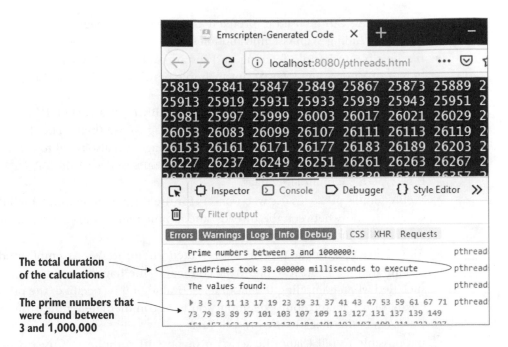

The total duration of the calculations

The prime numbers that were found between 3 and 1,000,000

Figure 9.15 Emscripten included a message indicating how many web workers it was creating for the pthreads. The total execution time to find the prime numbers between 3 and 1,000,000 was 38 milliseconds.

Exercises

You can find the solutions to the exercises in appendix D.

1 If you wanted to use a C++17 feature, what flag would you use when compiling your WebAssembly module to tell Clang to use that standard?

2 Test adjusting the calculate_primes logic from section 9.4 to use three threads rather than four to see how the calculation duration is impacted. Test using five threads, and place the main thread's calculation into a pthread to see if moving all the calculations off the main thread impacts the calculation duration.

Summary

In this chapter, you learned the following:

- If too much processing happens on a browser's main UI thread without yielding periodically, the UI may become unresponsive. If a browser's main UI thread is unresponsive for long enough, the browser might prompt the user to see if they want to terminate the script.
- Browsers have a means of creating background threads called web workers, and communication with workers is performed by passing messages. Web workers have no access to the DOM or other UI aspects of the browser.

- Web workers can be used to prefetch assets that a web page might need in the future, including WebAssembly modules.
- It's possible to handle fetching and instantiating a WebAssembly module on behalf of Emscripten's JavaScript by implementing the `instantiateWasm` callback function.
- There is experimental support for WebAssembly pthreads (POSIX threads) in Firefox, but you currently need to enable a flag to use them. The desktop version of Chrome supports pthreads without a flag. You also need to compile the WebAssembly module using the `-s USE_PTHREADS` and `-s PTHREAD_POOL_SIZE` Emscripten command-line flags.
- WebAssembly pthreads use web workers for the threads, a SharedArrayBuffer as shared memory between the threads, and atomic memory access instructions to synchronize interactions with the memory.
- All web workers for the pthreads are created when the WebAssembly module is instantiated if a `PTHREAD_POOL_SIZE` command-line flag value of 1 or greater is specified when compiling the module. If a value of 0 is specified, the pthread is created on demand, but execution won't start immediately unless the thread yields execution back to the browser first.
- It's possible to tell Clang, Emscripten's frontend compiler, to use a C++ standard other than the default C++98 standard by specifying the `-std` command-line flag.

WebAssembly modules in Node.js

In this chapter, you'll learn how to use WebAssembly modules in *Node.js*. Node.js has some differences compared with a browser—for example, having no GUI—but, when working with WebAssembly modules, there are a lot of similarities between the JavaScript needed in a browser and in Node.js. Even with these similarities, however, it's recommended that you test your WebAssembly module in Node.js to verify that it works as expected on the versions that you want to support.

DEFINITION Node.js is a JavaScript runtime built on the V8 engine—the same engine that powers the Chrome web browser. Node.js allows for JavaScript to be used as server-side code. It also has a large number of open source packages available to help with many programming needs. For a book dedicated to teaching you about Node.js, see *Node.js in Action, Second Edition* (Manning): www.manning.com/books/node-js-in-action-second-edition.

This chapter aims to demonstrate that WebAssembly can be used outside the web browser. The desire to use WebAssembly outside the browser has led to the creation of the WebAssembly Standard Interface, or WASI, to ensure that there's consistency in how hosts implement their interfaces. The idea is that a WebAssembly module will work on any host that supports WASI, which could include edge computing, serverless, and IoT (Internet of Things) hosts, to name a few. For more information about WASI, the following article has a good explanation: Simon Bisson, "Mozilla Extends WebAssembly Beyond the Browser with WASI," The New Stack, http://mng.bz/E19R.

10.1 Revisiting what you know

Let's briefly revisit what you know. In chapters 4 through 6, you learned about the code-reuse advantages that WebAssembly brings by exploring a scenario in which a company had an existing desktop point-of-sale application written in C++ that it wanted to port to an online solution. Being able to reuse code in multiple environments reduces the chances of bugs being introduced accidently when compared with having to maintain two or more versions of the same code. Code reuse also leads to consistency, where the logic behaves exactly the same across all systems. In addition, because there's only one code source for the logic, fewer developers need to maintain it, freeing them up to work on other aspects of systems, which brings higher productivity.

As figure 10.1 shows, you learned how to adjust the C++ code so that it could be compiled into a WebAssembly module using Emscripten's compiler. This allowed you to use the same code for both the desktop application and in a web browser. You then learned how to interact with the WebAssembly module in a web browser, but the discussion about server-side code was left until now.

In this chapter, you'll learn how to load a WebAssembly module in Node.js. You'll also learn how the module can call into JavaScript directly or by using function pointers.

10.2 Server-side validation

Suppose the company that created the online version of its point-of-sale application's Edit Product page now wants to pass the validated data to the server. Because it's not difficult to get around client-side (browser) validation, it's critical that the server-side code validate the data it receives from the website before it's used, as figure 10.2 shows.

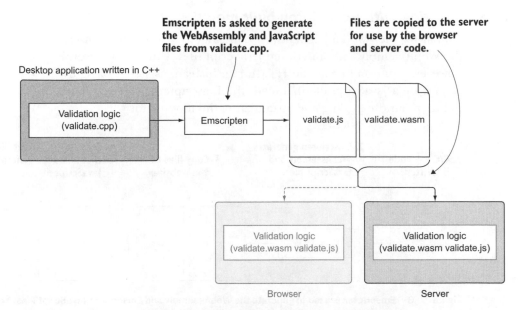

Figure 10.1 The steps for turning the existing C++ logic into a WebAssembly module for use by a browser and the server-side code. I discuss the server aspect in this chapter.

The web page's server-side logic will use Node.js and, because Node.js supports Web-Assembly, you won't need to re-create the validation logic. In this chapter, you'll use the exact same WebAssembly modules that you created for use in the browser in the previous chapters. This allows the company to use the same C++ code in three locations: the desktop application, a web browser, and Node.js.

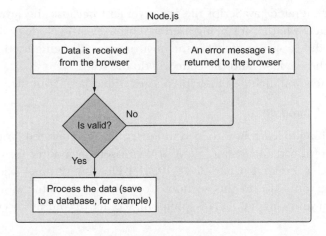

Figure 10.2 How validation works in Node.js

10.3   Working with Emscripten-built modules

Similar to when working in a browser, in Node.js, you still use Emscripten to generate the WebAssembly and Emscripten JavaScript files. Unlike when working in a browser, however, you don't create an HTML file. Instead, as step 4 of figure 10.3 illustrates, you create a JavaScript file that loads the Emscripten-generated JavaScript file, which will then handle loading and instantiating the module for you.

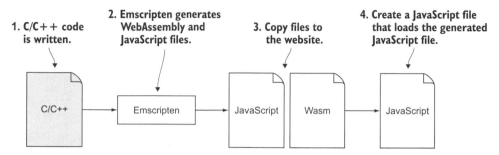

Figure 10.3   Emscripten is used to generate the WebAssembly and Emscripten JavaScript files. You then create a JavaScript file that loads the Emscripten-generated JavaScript file, which will in turn handle loading and instantiating the module for you.

The way you let the Emscripten-generated JavaScript wire itself up is different in Node.js compared to in a browser:

- *In a browser,* the Emscripten JavaScript code is wired up by including a reference to the JavaScript file as a `script` tag in the HTML file.
- *In Node.js,* to load JavaScript files, you use the `require` function, passing in the path to the file that you want to load.

Using the Emscripten-generated JavaScript file is convenient because the JavaScript code has checks that detect whether it's being used in a browser or in Node.js; it loads and instantiates the module appropriately for the environment it's being used in. All you need to do is have the file load, and the code will do the rest.

Let's take a look at how you include Emscripten's generated JavaScript file.

10.3.1   Loading a WebAssembly module

In this section, you're going to learn how to load in Emscripten's generated JavaScript file so that it can then download and instantiate your WebAssembly module for you. In your WebAssembly\ folder, create a Chapter 10\10.3.1 JsPlumbingPrimes\ backend\ folder for the files that you'll use in this section. Copy the js_plumbing.wasm and js_plumbing.js files from your Chapter 3\3.4 js_plumbing\ folder to your newly created backend\ folder.

In your backend\ folder, create a js_plumbing_nodejs.js file, and open it with your favorite editor. In your js_plumbing_nodejs.js file, you'll add a call to Node.js's require function, passing in the path to the Emscripten-generated JavaScript file js_plumbing.js. When loaded by Node.js, the Emscripten JavaScript code will detect that it's being used in Node.js and will automatically load and instantiate the js_plumbing.wasm WebAssembly module for you.

Add the code from the following snippet to your js_plumbing_nodejs.js file:

```
require('./js_plumbing.js');   ⟵——— Has the Emscripten plumbing code wire itself up
```

VIEWING THE RESULTS

To instruct Node.js to run JavaScript, you need to use the console window to run the node command, followed by the JavaScript file that you want it to execute. To run the js_plumbing_nodejs.js file that you just created, open a command prompt, navigate to the Chapter 10\10.3.1 JsPlumbingPrimes\backend\ folder, and then run the following command:

```
node js_plumbing_nodejs.js
```

As figure 10.4 shows, you can see that the module was loaded and run because the console window displays the output from the module: "Prime numbers between 3 and 100,000," followed by the prime numbers that were found within that range.

The output from the module ⟶

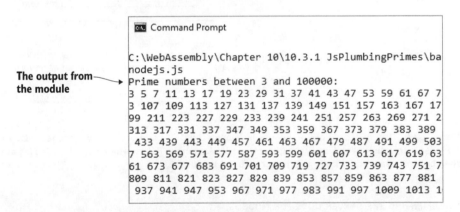

Figure 10.4   The console output from the WebAssembly module in Node.js

Now that you know how to load Emscripten's generated JavaScript file in Node.js, let's look into how you call the functions in the WebAssembly module when using Node.js.

10.3.2 *Calling functions in the WebAssembly module*

In chapter 4, you went through a series of steps (figure 10.5) to extend a desktop point-of-sale system to the web. Once the web page has verified that the data the user entered is valid, the data is sent to the server-side code so that it can be saved to a database or processed in some way. Before the server-side code does anything with the data received, it needs to make sure the data is valid, because there are ways to get around browser validation. In this case, your server is Node.js, and you'll use the same WebAssembly module that you were using in the browser to handle validating the data received.

You're now going to implement the final step of the process for extending the desktop point-of-sale system to the web by implementing the server-side aspect of it. You'll copy the generated WebAssembly files to where your Node.js files are and then create a JavaScript file to interact with the module.

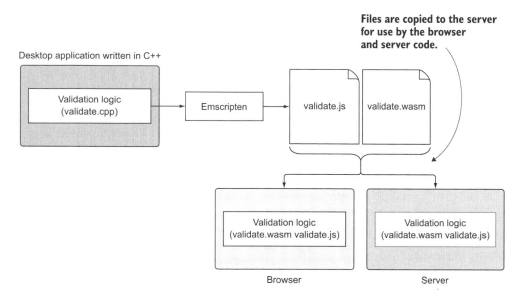

Figure 10.5   The final step of the process in reusing the C++ code is the server aspect, which is Node.js, in this case. You'll copy the generated WebAssembly files to where your Node.js files are and then build the JavaScript code to interact with the module.

IMPLEMENTING THE SERVER CODE FOR NODE.JS

In your WebAssembly\ folder, create a Chapter 10\10.3.2 JsPlumbing\backend\ folder to hold the files that you'll use in this section, and then complete the following:

- Copy the validate.js, validate.wasm, and editproduct.js files from your Chapter 4\4.1 js_plumbing\frontend\ folder to your newly created backend\ folder.
- Rename the editproduct.js file to nodejs_validate.js, and then open it with your favorite editor.

Rather than receive data from the web page, you'll simulate having received the data by using the InitialData object, but you'll rename the object to clientData. In your nodejs_validate.js file, rename the InitialData object to clientData as follows:

```
const clientData = {                    ◁          An object to simulate
  name: "Women's Mid Rise Skinny Jeans",            having received data
                                                     from a browser
```

```
    categoryId: "100",
};
```

Overall, the JavaScript that Node.js needs is similar to what you had in the browser. The main difference with the Node.js code is that there's no UI, so there are no input controls that need to be interacted with. Consequently, some of the helper functions aren't needed. Delete the following functions from the nodejs_validate.js file:

- `initializePage`
- `getSelectedCategoryId`

Because there's no UI, there's no element to display error messages received from the module. Instead, you output the error messages to the console. Adjust the setError-Message function to call `console.log`, as shown in the following snippet:

```
function setErrorMessage(error) { console.log(error); }
```
> Node.js has no UI, so you'll output any error messages to the console instead.

One difference between working with Emscripten's generated JavaScript file in Node.js compared to working in the browser is that, in the browser, your JavaScript code has access to a global `Module` object, but many of the helper functions are also in the global scope. In the browser, functions like `_malloc`, `_free`, and `UTF8ToString` are in the global scope and can be called directly without prefixing them with `Module`, like `Module._malloc`. In Node.js, however, the return object from the `require` call is the `Module` object, and all the Emscripten helper methods are available only through this object.

> **TIP** You can name the object that gets returned by the `require` function call anything you want. Because you're using the same JavaScript code here that you had in the browser, it's easier to use the name `Module` so that you don't have to modify as much of the JavaScript. If you do choose to use a different name, you'll need to modify the spots that do `Module.ccall`, for example, to use your object name instead of `Module`.

In the nodejs_validate.js file, after the `setErrorMessage` function, add a call to the `require` Node.js function to load Emscripten's generated JavaScript file (validate.js). Name the object received from the require function `Module`. Your line of code should look like this:

```
const Module = require('./validate.js');
```
> Loads Emscripten's generated JavaScript and names the return object Module

The instantiation of the WebAssembly module happens asynchronously, both in the browser and in Node.js. To be notified when Emscripten's JavaScript code is ready for interaction, define an `onRuntimeInitialized` function.

In your nodejs_validate.js file, convert the `onClickSave` function to be a function on the `Module` object's `onRuntimeInitialized` property. Also, revise the code in the function to no longer try to pull the `name` and `categoryId` from the controls but rather use the `clientData` object. Your `onClickSave` function in your nodejs_ validate.js file should now look like the code in the following listing.

> **Listing 10.1   onClickSave adjusted to now be onRuntimeInitialized**

```
...
Module['onRuntimeInitialized'] = function() {          ◁——— Adjusts onClickSave to now
  let errorMessage = "";                                       be onRuntimeInitialized
  const errorMessagePointer = Module._malloc(256);

  if (!validateName(clientData.name, errorMessagePointer) ||  ◁—
      !validateCategory(clientData.categoryId,  ◁——
        errorMessagePointer)) {
    errorMessage = Module.UTF8ToString(errorMessagePointer);
  }
  Module._free(errorMessagePointer);

  setErrorMessage(errorMessage);
  if (errorMessage === "") {

  }
}
...
```

Validates the name in the clientData object

Validates the categoryId in the clientData object

There were no issues. The data can be saved.

No other changes are needed in the nodejs_validate.js file.

VIEWING THE RESULTS

If you run the code right now, there are no validation issues reported because all the data in your `clientData` object is valid. To test the validation logic, you can modify the data in the `clientData` object by clearing the value from the `name` property (`name: ""`), saving the file, and running the code.

To run your JavaScript file in Node.js, open a command prompt, navigate to your Chapter 10\10.3.2 JsPlumbing\backend\ folder, and then run the following command:

```
node nodejs_validate.js
```

You should see the validation message shown in figure 10.6.

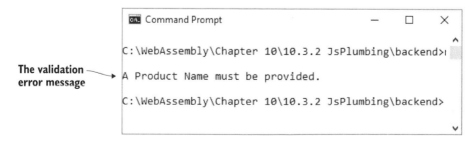

The validation error message

Figure 10.6   The product name validation error in Node.js

Now that you know how to load Emscripten's generated JavaScript file in Node.js and call functions in the WebAssembly module, let's look into how the module can call into the JavaScript file when running in Node.js.

10.3.3 *Calling into the JavaScript*

As you saw in the previous section, a function can call into the module and wait for a response. While this approach works, there are times when a module might want to call the JavaScript directly once it finishes doing some work—perhaps to obtain more information or to provide an update.

The WebAssembly module that you'll be using in this section included a function in Emscripten's generated JavaScript file. The module will call that function if there was an error passing a pointer to the error message. The function will read the error message from the module's memory and then pass the string to the setErrorMessage function in your main JavaScript.

IMPLEMENTING THE SERVER CODE FOR NODE.JS

In your WebAssembly\ folder, create a Chapter 10\10.3.3 EmJsLibrary\backend\ folder to hold the files that you'll use in this section, and then complete the following:

- Copy the validate.js, validate.wasm, and editproduct.js files from your Chapter 5\5.1.1 EmJsLibrary\frontend\ folder to your newly created backend\ folder.
- Rename the editproduct.js file to nodejs_validate.js, and then open it with your favorite editor.

In your nodejs_validate.js file, rename the InitialData object to clientData, as shown in the following code snippet:

```
const clientData = {        ◁──────────────────┐  Renamed from
  name: "Women's Mid Rise Skinny Jeans",       │  InitialData
  categoryId: "100",
};
```

Delete the following functions from the nodejs_validate.js file:

- initializePage
- getSelectedCategoryId

As it turns out, this particular use case for including your own JavaScript in Emscripten's generated JavaScript file isn't ideal when using Node.js. This is because the require function that's used to load a JavaScript file puts the code within that file into its own scope, meaning the code in Emscripten's generated JavaScript file can't access any of the functions in the scope of the parent (the code that loaded it). JavaScript code loaded by the require function is expected to be self-contained and to not call into the scope of the parent.

If the module needs to call into the scope of the parent, a better approach is to use a function pointer that the parent passes in, which you'll see in an upcoming section. But in this case, to get around the issue of the validate.js-generated code being unable to access the `setErrorMessage` function that it needs to call, you'll need to create the `setErrorMessage` function on the `global` object rather than as a normal function.

> **MORE INFO**   In browsers, the top-level scope is the global scope (the `window` object). In Node.js, however, the top-level scope isn't the global scope but is rather the module itself. By default, all variables and objects are local to the module in Node.js. The `global` object represents the global scope in Node.js.

To make the `setErrorMessage` function accessible to the Emscripten-generated Java-Script, you need to adjust the function to be part of the `global` object, as the following code snippet shows. To output the error message to the console, replace the function's contents with a call to `console.log`:

```
global.setErrorMessage = function(error) {      ◁───────────  Creates the function
    console.log(error);      ◁──────── Outputs the error                on the global object
}                                      messages to the console
```

After the `setErrorMessage` function, add a call to the `require` Node.js function to load Emscripten's generated JavaScript file (validate.js). Your line of code should look like this:

```
const Module = require('./validate.js');      ◁──── Loads Emscripten's generated
                                                     JavaScript, and names the
                                                     return object Module
```

In your nodejs_validate.js file, convert the `onClickSave` function to be a function on the `Module` object's `onRuntimeInitialized` property. Then, revise the code in the function to no longer call the `setErrorMessage` function or try to pull the `name` and `categoryId` from the controls. Finally, use the `clientData` object to pass the `name` and `categoryId` to the validation functions.

Your modified `onRuntimeInitialized` function should look like the following snippet:

```
                                                        Adjusts onClickSave to now be
                                                        onRuntimeInitialized
Module['onRuntimeInitialized'] = function() {    ◁──┘
    if (validateName(clientData.name) &&      ◁───────────  Validates the
        validateCategory(clientData.categoryId)){  ◁───      name in the
                                                             clientData object
    }      ◁────────────  There were no
}                         issues. The data          Validates the categoryId in
                          can be saved.             the clientData object
```

No other changes are needed for the nodejs_validate.js file.

VIEWING THE RESULTS

To test the validation logic, you can adjust the data in the `clientData` object by changing the `name` or `categoryId` property to a value that's invalid. For example, you could change the `categoryId` to hold a value that isn't in the `VALID_CATEGORY_IDS` array (`categoryId: "1001"`) and save the file.

To run your JavaScript file in Node.js, open a command prompt, navigate to your Chapter 10\10.3.3 EmJsLibrary\backend\ folder, and run the following command:

```
node nodejs_validate.js
```

You should see the validation message shown in figure 10.7.

The validation error message →

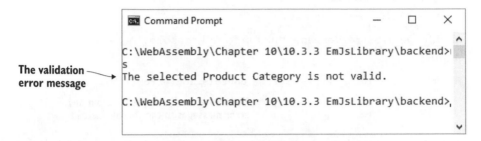

Figure 10.7   The product category validation error in Node.js

Using the Emscripten JavaScript library with code that calls into an application's main JavaScript isn't ideal if you plan on using Node.js, owing to scope issues with the `require` function. If you add custom JavaScript to Emscripten's generated JavaScript file that will be used in Node.js, the best approach is for the code to be self-contained and not call into the parent code.

  If a WebAssembly module needs to call into the application's main JavaScript, and you want to support Node.js, function pointers are the recommended approach, and you'll learn about them next.

10.3.4 *Calling JavaScript function pointers*

Being able to call into the JavaScript directly is useful, but your JavaScript needs to provide the function during the module's instantiation. Once a function has been passed to the module, you can't swap it out. This is fine in most cases, but there are times when being able to pass a module the function to call on an as-needed basis is useful.

IMPLEMENTING THE SERVER CODE FOR NODE.JS

In your WebAssembly\ folder, create a Chapter 10\10.3.4 EmFunctionPointers\backend\ folder to hold the files that you'll use in this section, and then do the following:

- Copy the validate.js, validate.wasm, and editproduct.js files from your Chapter 6\6.1.2 EmFunctionPointers\frontend\ folder to your newly created backend\ folder.
- Rename the editproduct.js file to nodejs_validate.js, and then open it with your favorite editor.

In your nodejs_validate.js file, rename the `InitialData` object to `clientData`, as the following code snippet shows:

```
const clientData = {          ◁──────────────
  name: "Women's Mid Rise Skinny Jeans",      An object to simulate having
  categoryId: "100",                          received data from a browser
};
```

Delete the following functions from the nodejs_validate.js file:

- initializePage
- getSelectedCategoryId

Modify the setErrorMessage function to call console.log, as shown in the following snippet:

```
function setErrorMessage(error) { console.log(error); }    ◁──────
```
Node.js has no UI, so you'll output any
error messages to the console instead.

After the setErrorMessage function, add a call to the require Node.js function to load the validate.js file. Your line of code should look like the following snippet:

```
const Module = require('./validate.js');    ◁──────
```
**Loads Emscripten's generated JavaScript
and names the return object Module**

In your nodejs_validate.js file, convert the onClickSave function to be a function on the Module object's onRuntimeInitialized property. Revise the code in the function to no longer call the setErrorMessage function or to try and pull the name and categoryId from the controls. Then, use the clientData object to pass the name and categoryId to the validation functions.

Your modified onClickSave function should now look like the code in the following listing.

Listing 10.2   onClickSave adjusted to now be onRuntimeInitialized

```
...

Module['onRuntimeInitialized'] = function() {    ◁──────  Adjusts onClickSave to
  Promise.all([                                           now be
      validateName(clientData.name),      ◁──            onRuntimeInitialized
      validateCategory(clientData.categoryId) ◁──┐
  ])                                             │   Validates the name in
  .then(() => {                                  │   the clientData object
                                                 │
  })             ◁──  There were no issues.     Validates the categoryId
  .catch((error) => {   The data can be saved.   in the clientData object
    setErrorMessage(error);
  });
}
```

No other changes are needed in the nodejs_validate.js file.

VIEWING THE RESULTS

To test the validation logic, you can adjust the data in the `clientData` object by changing the `name` property to a value that exceeds the `MAXIMUM_NAME_LENGTH` value of 50 characters (`name: "This is a very long product name to test the validation logic."`) and saving the file.

To run your JavaScript file in Node.js, open a command prompt, navigate to your Chapter 10\10.3.4 EmFunctionPointers\backend\ folder, and run the following command:

```
node nodejs_validate.js
```

You should see the validation message shown in figure 10.8.

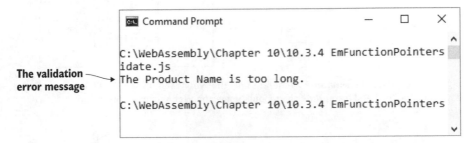

The validation error message

Figure 10.8　Validation message about the product name's length in Node.js

By this point in the chapter, you've learned how to work with WebAssembly modules in Node.js when those modules were built with Emscripten's generated JavaScript code. In the rest of this chapter, you'll learn how to use WebAssembly modules in Node.js when the modules have been built without generating Emscripten's JavaScript file.

10.4　*Using the WebAssembly JavaScript API*

When using the Emscripten compiler, production code typically includes the generated Emscripten JavaScript file. This file handles downloading the WebAssembly module and interacting with the WebAssembly JavaScript API for you. It also contains a number of helper functions to make interacting with the module easier.

Not generating the JavaScript file is useful for learning because it gives you a chance to download the .wasm file and work with the WebAssembly JavaScript API directly. You create a JavaScript object holding the values and functions that the module is expecting to import, and then you use the API to compile and instantiate the module. Once it's instantiated, you have access to the module's exports, allowing you to interact with the module.

As WebAssembly's use increases, it's likely that many third-party modules will be created to extend a browser's abilities. Knowing how to work with modules that don't use the Emscripten JavaScript code will also be useful if you ever need to use a third-party module that's been built using a compiler other than Emscripten.

In chapters 3 through 6, you used Emscripten to generate only the .wasm file by using the SIDE_MODULE flag. This created a module that didn't include any standard C library functions and didn't generate Emscripten's JavaScript file. Because the JavaScript file wasn't generated, it's now up to you to create the JavaScript needed to load and instantiate the module by using the WebAssembly JavaScript API, as step 4 of figure 10.9 shows.

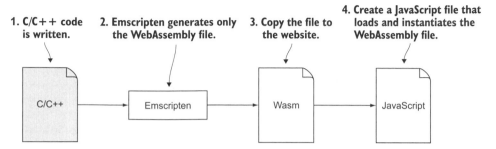

Figure 10.9   Using Emscripten to generate only the WebAssembly file. You'll then create the JavaScript to load and instantiate the module using the WebAssembly JavaScript API.

10.4.1   *Loading and instantiating a WebAssembly module*

To load and run your side_module.wasm file from chapter 3 in Node.js, you'll need to load and instantiate the module using the WebAssembly JavaScript API.

IMPLEMENTING THE SERVER CODE FOR NODE.JS

The first thing that you need to do is create a folder for the files you'll use in this section. In your WebAssembly\ folder, create a Chapter 10\10.4.1 SideModuleIncrement\ backend\ folder, and then do the following:

- Copy the side_module.wasm file from your Chapter 3\3.5.1 side_module\ folder to your newly created backend\ folder.
- Create a side_module_nodejs.js file in your backend\ folder, and then open it with your favorite editor.

Because Node.js is already running on the server, you don't need to fetch the .wasm file because it's sitting on the hard drive in the same folders as the JavaScript files. Instead, you'll use the File System module in Node.js to read in the WebAssembly file's bytes. Then, once you have the bytes, the process of calling WebAssembly .instantiate and working with the module is the same as in a browser.

You include the File System module by using the require function, passing in the string 'fs'. The require function returns an object that gives you access to various File System functions, such as readFile and writeFile. In this chapter, you'll use only the readFile function, but if you're interested in learning more about the Node.js File System object and the functions that are available, you can visit https://nodejs.org/api/fs.html.

You're going to use File System's readFile function to read in the contents of the side_module.wasm file asynchronously. The readFile function accepts three parameters. The first parameter is the path of the file to read. The second is optional and allows you to specify options like the file's encoding. You won't use the second parameter in this chapter. The third parameter is a callback function that will receive either an error object—if there was an issue reading in the file's contents—or, if the read was successful, the file's bytes.

MORE INFO If you'd like to read more about the File System module's readFile function and the optional second parameter, you can visit http://mng.bz/rPjy.

Add the following code snippet to your side_module_nodejs.js file to load the File System object ('fs') and then call the readFile function. If an error is passed to the callback function, then throw the error. Otherwise, pass the bytes that were received to the instantiateWebAssembly function that you'll create next:

```
const fs = require('fs');   ⟵————— Loads the File System object
fs.readFile('side_module.wasm', function(error, bytes) {   ⟵— Reads in the file asynchronously
  if (error) { throw error; }   ⟵————— If there was an error reading the file, then just rethrows the error

  instantiateWebAssembly(bytes);   ⟵—
});
```
Passes the file's bytes to the instantiateWebAssembly function

Create an instantiateWebAssembly function that accepts a parameter called bytes. Within the function, create a JavaScript object called importObject with an env object holding the __memory_base property of 0 (zero). You then need to call the WebAssembly .instantiate function, passing in the bytes received as well as the importObject. Finally, within the then method, call the exported _Increment function from the WebAssembly module, passing in a value of 2. Output the result to the console.

The instantiateWebAssembly function in your side_module_nodejs.js file should look like the code in the next listing.

Listing 10.3 The instantiateWebAssembly function

```
function instantiateWebAssembly(bytes) {
  const importObject = {
    env: {
      __memory_base: 0,
    }
  };

  WebAssembly.instantiate(bytes, importObject).then(result => {
    const value = result.instance.exports._Increment(2);
    console.log(value.toString());   ⟵——— Logs the result to the console window
  });
}
```

VIEWING THE RESULTS

To run your JavaScript file in Node.js, open a command prompt, navigate to your Chapter 10\10.4.1 SideModuleIncrement\backend\ folder, and run the following command:

```
node side_module_nodejs.js
```

You should see the result of the _Increment function call, as shown in figure 10.10.

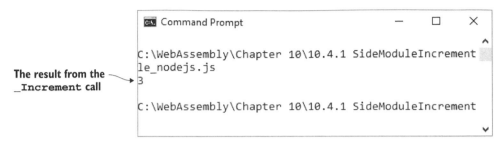

The result from the
_Increment call

Figure 10.10   The console output from your call to the module's _Increment function in Node.js

10.4.2 Calling functions in the WebAssembly module

The final step of the process, shown in figure 10.11, is to copy the WebAssembly file, validate.wasm (generated in chapter 4, section 4.2.2) to a folder where you'll host your Node.js files. You'll then create a JavaScript file that will bridge the gap between interacting with the data received from the browser and interacting with the module.

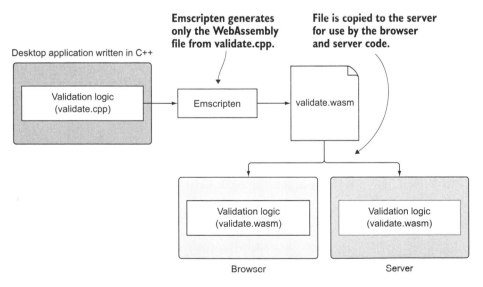

Figure 10.11   The final step of the process is to copy the generated WebAssembly file to where your Node.js files are and build the JavaScript code to interact with the module.

IMPLEMENTING THE SERVER CODE FOR NODE.JS

In your WebAssembly\ folder, create a Chapter 10\10.4.2 SideModule\backend\ folder, and then do the following:

- Copy the editproduct.js and validate.wasm files from your Chapter 4\4.2 side_module\frontend\ folder to your newly created backend\ folder.
- Rename the editproduct.js file to nodejs_validate.js, and open it with your favorite editor.

The JavaScript in the nodejs_validate.js file was written to work in a web browser, so you'll need to make a few modifications for it to work in Node.js.

Your JavaScript uses the JavaScript `TextEncoder` object to copy strings to the module's memory. In Node.js, the `TextEncoder` object is part of the `util` package. The first thing that you'll need to do in your JavaScript file is add a `require` function for the `util` package at the beginning of the file, as the following snippet shows:

```
const util = require('util');    ◁———  Loads the util package in
                                        order to have access to
                                        the TextEncoder object
```

Next, rename the `initialData` object to `clientData`:

```
const clientData = {        ◁——————————  Renamed from initialData
  name: "Women's Mid Rise Skinny Jeans",
  categoryId: "100",
};
```

In your nodejs_validate.js file, just before the `initializePage` function, add the following code to have the bytes from the validate.wasm file read in and passed to the `instantiateWebAssembly` function:

```
const fs = require('fs');
fs.readFile('validate.wasm', function(error, bytes) {   ◁——┐  Reads in the
  if (error) { throw error; }                                validate.wasm
                                                             file's bytes
  instantiateWebAssembly(bytes);   ◁——┐  Passes the bytes
});                                      to this function
```

Your next steps are to make the following modifications to the `initializePage` function:

- Rename the function to `instantiateWebAssembly`, and give it a parameter called `bytes`.
- Remove the line of code setting the `name`, as well as the `category` code that follows, so that the first thing in the `instantiateWebAssembly` function is the `moduleMemory` line of code.
- Replace `WebAssembly.instantiateStreaming` with `WebAssembly.instantiate`, and replace the `fetch("validate.wasm")` parameter with `bytes`.
- Last, within the `then` method of the `WebAssembly.instantiate` call, and following the `moduleExports` line of code, add a call to the `validateData` function, which you'll create in a moment.

The modified `initializePage` function in your nodejs_validate.js file should now look like the code in the next listing.

Listing 10.4   `initializePage` renamed to `instantiateWebAssembly`

```
...

function instantiateWebAssembly(bytes) {        ◁——————   Renamed from
  moduleMemory = new WebAssembly.Memory({initial: 256});    initializePage, and
                                                            bytes added as
  const importObject = {                                    the parameter
    env: {
      __memory_base: 0,
      memory: moduleMemory,                      Uses instantiate instead of
    }                                          instantiateStreaming and bytes
  };                                            passed in instead of the fetch call

  WebAssembly.instantiate(bytes, importObject).then(result => {     ◁——————
    moduleExports = result.instance.exports;
    validateData();      ◁————————   Calls validateData once
  });                               the module has been
}                                   instantiated
...
```

In your nodejs_validate.js file, delete the `getSelectedCategoryId` function. Then replace the content of the `setErrorMessage` function with a `console.log` call for the error parameter, as in the following snippet:

```
                                              Outputs any
function setErrorMessage(error) { console.log(error); }  ◁——  error messages
                                              to the console
```

The next adjustment that you need to make to the nodejs_validate.js file is to rename the `onClickSave` function to `validateData` so that it will be called once the module has been instantiated. Within the `validateData` function, remove the two lines of code above the `if` statement that get the `name` and `categoryId`. In the `if` statement, prefix the `name` and `categoryId` variables with your `clientData` object.

The `validateData` function in your nodejs_valdiate.js file should now look like the code in the following listing.

Listing 10.5   `onClickSave` renamed to `validateData`

```
...

function validateData() {        ◁————————   Renamed from onClickSave
  let errorMessage = "";
  const errorMessagePointer = moduleExports._create_buffer(256);

  if (!validateName(clientData.name, errorMessagePointer) ||
      !validateCategory(clientData.categoryId,    ◁
      errorMessagePointer)) {
    errorMessage = getStringFromMemory(errorMessagePointer);
  }
```

The clientData object's name value is passed to validateName.

The clientData object's categoryId is passed to validateCategory.

```
moduleExports._free_buffer(errorMessagePointer);

setErrorMessage(errorMessage);
if (errorMessage === "") {

}
}
...
```

> There were no issues with the
> validation. The data can be saved.

The final area that you need to modify is the `copyStringToMemory` function. In a browser, the `TextEncoder` object is global; but in Node.js, the object is found in the `util` package. In your nodejs_validate.js file, you need to prefix the `TextEncoder` object with the `util` object that you loaded earlier, as the following code snippet shows:

```
function copyStringToMemory(value, memoryOffset) {
  const bytes = new Uint8Array(moduleMemory.buffer);
  bytes.set(new util.TextEncoder().encode((value + "\0")),
    memoryOffset);
}
```

> The TextEncoder
> object is part of
> the util package
> in Node.js.

No other changes are needed to the JavaScript in the nodejs_validate.js file.

VIEWING THE RESULTS

To test the logic, you can adjust the data by changing the value for the `categoryId` property to a value that isn't in the `VALID_CATEGORY_IDS` array (`categoryId: "1001"`). To run your JavaScript file in Node.js, open a command prompt, navigate to your Chapter 10\10.4.2 SideModule\backend\ folder, and run the following command:

```
node nodejs_validate.js
```

You should see the validation message shown in figure 10.12.

In this section, you learned how to modify the JavaScript to load and instantiate a WebAssembly module that your code calls into. In the next section, you'll learn how to work with a module that makes calls into your JavaScript.

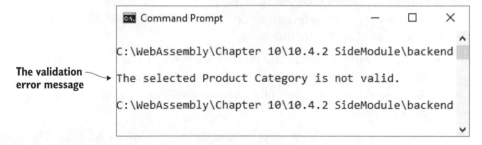

The validation error message →

Figure 10.12   The product category validation error in Node.js

10.4.3 The WebAssembly module calling into JavaScript

As an example, a module calling into JavaScript directly would be useful if your module needs to perform a long-running operation. Rather than the JavaScript making a function call and waiting for the results, a module could periodically call into the JavaScript to get more information or provide an update on its own.

When not using Emscripten's generated JavaScript, which you won't be doing here, things are a bit different because all the JavaScript code is in the same scope. As a result, a module can call into the JavaScript and have access to the main code, as figure 10.13 shows.

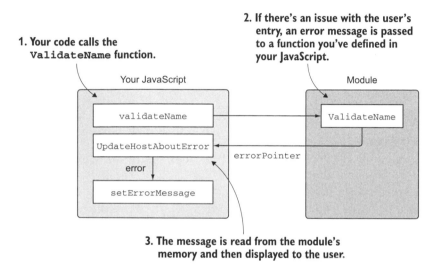

Figure 10.13   How the callback logic will work when not using Emscripten's generated JavaScript code

IMPLEMENTING THE SERVER CODE FOR NODE.JS

In your WebAssembly\ folder, create a Chapter 10\10.4.3 SideModuleCallingJS\backend\ folder, and then do the following:

- Copy the editproduct.js and validate.wasm files from your Chapter 5\5.2.1 SideModuleCallingJS\frontend\ folder to your newly created backend\ folder.
- Rename the editproduct.js file to nodejs_validate.js, and then open it with your favorite editor.

You're going to modify the nodejs_validate.js file to work in Node.js. The code uses the `TextEncoder` JavaScript object in the `copyStringToMemory` function; in Node.js, the `TextEncoder` object is part of the `util` package. You'll need to include a reference to the package so that your code can use the object. Add this code at the beginning of your nodejs_validate.js file:

```
const util = require('util');
```
← Loads the util package so that you'll have access to the TextEncoder object

Rename the initialData object to clientData. Then, in your nodejs_validate.js file, before the initializePage function, add the code from the following snippet to read in the bytes from the validate.wasm file and pass them to the instantiateWeb-Assembly function:

```
const fs = require('fs');
fs.readFile('validate.wasm', function(error, bytes) {      ◁─── Reads in the
  if (error) { throw error; }                                   validate.wasm
                                                                file's bytes
  instantiateWebAssembly(bytes);      ◁─── Passes the bytes
});                                        to this function
```

Next, you need to modify the initializePage function by doing the following:

- Rename the function to instantiateWebAssembly, and add a bytes parameter.
- Remove the lines of code that appear before the moduleMemory line of code.
- Change WebAssembly.instantiateStreaming to WebAssembly.instantiate, and replace the fetch("validate.wasm") parameter value with bytes.
- Add a call to the validateData function after the moduleExports line of code in the then method of the WebAssembly.instantiate call.

The modified initializePage function in your nodejs_validate.js file should now look like the code in the next listing.

Listing 10.6 `initializePage` renamed to `instantiateWebAssembly`

```
...                                         Renamed from initializePage, and
                                            bytes added as the parameter
function instantiateWebAssembly(bytes) {  ◁───┘
  moduleMemory = new WebAssembly.Memory({initial: 256});

  const importObject = {
    env: {
      __memory_base: 0,
      memory: moduleMemory,
      _UpdateHostAboutError: function(errorMessagePointer) {
        setErrorMessage(getStringFromMemory(errorMessagePointer));
      },                                    Uses instantiate instead of
    }                                       instantiateStreaming and bytes
  };                                        passed in instead of the fetch call

  WebAssembly.instantiate(bytes, importObject).then(result => {  ◁───┘
    moduleExports = result.instance.exports;
    validateData();      ◁─── Calls validateData once
  });                         the module has been
}                             instantiated
...
```

In your nodejs_validate.js file, delete the getSelectedCategoryId function. Then, replace the contents of the setErrorMessage function with a console.log call for the error parameter, as shown in the following snippet:

```
                                            Outputs any
function setErrorMessage(error) { console.log(error); }  ◁─── error messages
                                            to the console
```

Revise the `onClickSave` function by completing the following steps:

- Rename the function to `validateData`.
- Remove the `setErrorMessage()`, `const name`, and `const categoryId` lines of code.
- Add the `clientData` object prefix to the `name` and `categoryId` values in the `if` statements.

The modified `onClickSave` function in your nodejs_validate.js file should now look like this:

```
function validateData() {
    if (validateName(clientData.name) &&
        validateCategory(clientData.categoryId)) {

    }
}
```

Renamed from onClickSave

The clientData object's name value is passed to validateName.

There were no issues with the validation. The data can be saved.

The clientData object's categoryId is passed to validateCategory.

The last item that you need to adjust is the `copyStringToMemory` function. You need to prefix the `TextEncoder` object with the `util` object that you loaded earlier.

Your `copyStringToMemory` function in your nodejs_validate.js file should look like the code in the following snippet:

```
function copyStringToMemory(value, memoryOffset) {
    const bytes = new Uint8Array(moduleMemory.buffer);
    bytes.set(new util.TextEncoder().encode((value + "\0")),
        memoryOffset);
}
```

The TextEncoder object is part of the util package in Node.js.

No other changes are needed in the nodejs_validate.js file.

VIEWING THE RESULTS

To test the validation logic, you can adjust the data in `clientData` by changing the `name` property to a value that exceeds the `MAXIMUM_NAME_LENGTH` value of 50 characters (`name: "This is a very long product name to test the validation logic."`).

Open a command prompt, navigate to your Chapter 10\10.4.3 SideModule-CallingJS\backend\ folder, and run the following command:

```
node nodejs_validate.js
```

You should see the validation message shown in figure 10.14.

In this section, you learned how to load and work with a WebAssembly module that calls into your JavaScript code directly. In the next section, you'll learn how to work with a module that calls JavaScript function pointers.

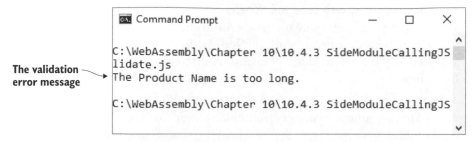

The validation error message

Figure 10.14   Validation message about the product name's length from Node.js

10.4.4 *The WebAssembly module calling JavaScript function pointers*

Being able to pass a module a JavaScript function pointer adds flexibility to your code compared to calling into JavaScript directly, because you're not dependent on a single specific function. Instead, the module can be passed a function as needed, as long as the function signature matches what's expected.

Also, depending on how the JavaScript is set up, calling a function may require multiple function calls to reach your JavaScript. With a function pointer, the module is calling your function directly.

WebAssembly modules can use function pointers that point to functions that are within the module, or the functions can be imported. In this case, you'll be using the WebAssembly module that you built in section 6.2 of chapter 6, which is expecting the OnSuccess and OnError functions to be specified, as figure 10.15 shows. When the module calls either function, it's calling into the JavaScript code.

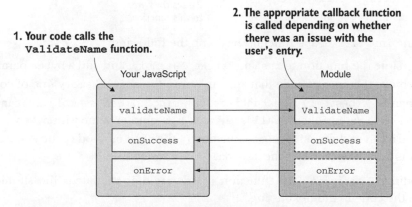

1. Your code calls the `ValidateName` function.

2. The appropriate callback function is called depending on whether there was an issue with the user's entry.

Figure 10.15   A module that has imported the `onSuccess` and `onError` JavaScript functions at instantiation. When the `ValidateName` module function calls either function, it's calling into the JavaScript code.

IMPLEMENTING THE SERVER CODE FOR NODE.JS

You're now going to modify the JavaScript code that you wrote for use in the browser in chapter 6 so that it can work in Node.js. In your WebAssembly\ folder, create a Chapter 10\10.4.4 SideModuleFunctionPointers\backend\ folder, and then do the following:

- Copy the editproduct.js and validate.wasm files from your Chapter 6\6.2.2 Side-ModuleFunctionPointers\frontend\ folder to your newly created backend\ folder.
- Rename the editproduct.js file to nodejs_validate.js, and then open it with your favorite editor.

Your JavaScript code uses the `TextEncoder` JavaScript object. Because the object is part of the `util` package in Node.js, the first thing that you'll need to do is include a reference to the package. Add the code in the following snippet at the beginning of your nodejs_validate.js file:

```
const util = require('util');     ⟵── Loads the util package so
                                       that you'll have access to
                                       the TextEncoder object
```

Rename the `initialData` object to `clientData`.

In your nodejs_validate.js file, before the `initializePage` function, add the following code to read in the bytes from the validate.wasm file and pass them to the `instantiateWebAssembly` function:

```
const fs = require('fs');
fs.readFile('validate.wasm', function(error, bytes) {     ⟵── Reads in the
  if (error) { throw error; }                                  validate.wasm
                                                               file's bytes
  instantiateWebAssembly(bytes);     ⟵── Passes the bytes
});                                       to this function
```

Modify the `initializePage` function by doing the following:

- Rename the function to `instantiateWebAssembly`, and add a `bytes` parameter.
- Remove the lines of code that appear before the `moduleMemory` line of code.
- Change `WebAssembly.instantiateStreaming` to `WebAssembly.instantiate`, and replace the `fetch("validate.wasm")` parameter value with `bytes`.
- Add a call to the `validateData` function in the `then` method of the `WebAssembly.instantiate` call after the last `addToTable` function call.

The modified `initializePage` function in your nodejs_validate.js file should now look like the code in the next listing.

Listing 10.7   `initializePage` renamed to `instantiateWebAssembly`

```
...
                                                 Renamed from initializePage, and
                                                 bytes added as the parameter
function instantiateWebAssembly(bytes) {     ⟵──

  moduleMemory = new WebAssembly.Memory({initial: 256});
```

```
moduleTable = new WebAssembly.Table({initial: 1, element: "anyfunc"});
  const importObject = {
    env: {
      __memory_base: 0,
      memory: moduleMemory,
      __table_base: 0,
      table: moduleTable,
      abort: function(i) { throw new Error('abort'); },
    }
  };

  WebAssembly.instantiate(bytes, importObject).then(result => {      ◁─────────┐
    moduleExports = result.instance.exports;                      **Uses instantiate instead of**
  validateOnSuccessNameIndex = addToTable(() => {                 **instantiateStreaming, and**
    onSuccessCallback(validateNameCallbacks);                     **bytes passed in instead of**
  }, 'v');                                                             **the fetch call**

    validateOnSuccessCategoryIndex = addToTable(() => {
      onSuccessCallback(validateCategoryCallbacks);
    }, 'v');

    validateOnErrorNameIndex = addToTable((errorMessagePointer) => {
      onErrorCallback(validateNameCallbacks, errorMessagePointer);
    }, 'vi');

    validateOnErrorCategoryIndex = addToTable((errorMessagePointer) => {
      onErrorCallback(validateCategoryCallbacks, errorMessagePointer);
  }, 'vi');    validateData();   ◁─┐ **Calls validateData**
  });                              **once the module has**
}                                  **been instantiated**
...
```

The next change you need to make in your nodejs_validate.js file is to delete the get-SelectedCategoryId function. Then replace the contents of the setErrorMessage function with a console.log call for the error parameter:

```
function setErrorMessage(error) { console.log(error); }    ◁──── **Outputs any**
                                                                 **error messages**
                                                                 **to the console**
```

Modify the onClickSave function by completing the following steps:

- Rename the function to validateData.
- Remove the setErrorMessage(), const name, and const categoryId lines of code.
- Add the clientData object prefix to the name and categoryId values that are passed to the validateName and validateCategory functions.

The modified onClickSave function in your nodejs_validate.js file should now look like the code in the following listing.

Listing 10.8 onClickSave renamed to validateData

```
...
function validateData() {            ◁———————— Renamed from onClickSave
  Promise.all([
    validateName(clientData.name),        ◁——————  The clientData object's
    validateCategory(clientData.categoryId)  ◁——┐   name value is passed to
  ])                                             validateName.
  .then(() => {
          ◁—————————————————————————————┐   The clientData object's
  })                                         categoryId is passed to
  .catch((error) => {                        validateCategory.
    setErrorMessage(error);
  });                                 There were no issues with the
}                                     validation. The data can be saved.
...
```

Finally, you need to modify the copyStringToMemory function to prefix the Text-Encoder object with the util object. Your copyStringToMemory function in the nodejs_validate.js file should look like this:

```
function copyStringToMemory(value, memoryOffset) {        The TextEncoder
  const bytes = new Uint8Array(moduleMemory.buffer);      object is part of
  bytes.set(new util.TextEncoder().encode((value + "\0")),  ◁—— the util package
    memoryOffset);                                         in Node.js.
}
```

No other changes are needed in the nodejs_validate.js file.

VIEWING THE RESULTS

To test the validation logic, you can adjust the data in the clientData object by clearing the value from the name property (name: "") and saving the file. Open a command prompt, navigate to your Chapter 10\10.4.4 SideModuleFunctionPointers\backend\ folder, and run the following command:

```
node nodejs_validate.js
```

You should see the validation message shown in figure 10.16.

Now: how can you use what you learned in this chapter in the real world?

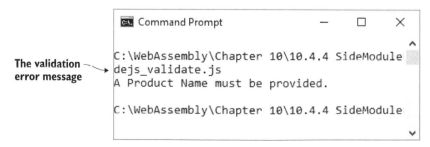

The validation error message →

Figure 10.16 The product name validation error in Node.js

Real-world use cases

The following are some possible use cases for what you've learned in this chapter:

- As you saw in this chapter, Node.js can be run from the command line, which means you can use your WebAssembly logic locally on your development machine to help you with your day-to-day tasks.
- With web sockets, Node.js can help implement real-time collaboration in your web application.
- You could use Node.js to add a chat component to your game.

Exercises

You can find the solutions to the exercises in appendix D.

1 Which Node.js function do you need to call in order to load Emscripten's generated JavaScript file?
2 What Emscripten `Module` property do you need to implement in order to be informed of when the WebAssembly module is ready to be interacted with?
3 How would you modify the index.js file from chapter 8 so that the dynamic linking logic works in Node.js?

Summary

- WebAssembly modules in Node.js are possible, and the JavaScript needed is quite similar to what you used when working in a web browser.
- Modules that include the Emscripten JavaScript code can load and instantiate themselves when you load the JavaScript using the `require` function. Unlike in the browser, however, there are no global Emscripten helper functions available. All functions within the Emscripten-generated JavaScript file need to be accessed through the return object from the `require` function.
- Node.js doesn't support the `WebAssembly.instantiateStreaming` function. Instead, you need to use the `WebAssembly.instantiate` function. If you're writing a single JavaScript file to use a WebAssembly module in both a web browser and Node.js, then you'll need the feature detection you learned about in chapter 3, section 3.6.
- When loading a WebAssembly file manually in Node.js, you don't use the `fetch` method because the WebAssembly file is on the same machine as the JavaScript code that's being executed. Instead, you read in the WebAssembly file's bytes from the `File System`, and then pass the bytes to the `WebAssembly.instantiate` function.
- Due to scope issues between the code that calls the `require` function and the generated Emscripten JavaScript, if you add custom JavaScript to Emscripten's JavaScript file, it should be self-contained and not try to call into the parent code.

Part 4

Debugging and testing

With most development, there comes a time when we run into an issue that needs to be tracked down. This could be as simple as reading over the code, but sometimes you need to dig deeper. In this part of the book, you'll learn about the options available for debugging and testing a WebAssembly module.

Chapter 11 teaches you about the WebAssembly text format by building a card-matching game. In chapter 12, you'll extend the card-matching game to learn about the various options available to debug a WebAssembly module. And chapter 13 rounds out your WebAssembly development skills by teaching you how to write integration tests for your modules.

WebAssembly text format

This chapter covers

- Creating a WebAssembly text format version of a module
- Compiling the text format code into a binary module using the WebAssembly Binary Toolkit's online tool
- Linking the Binary Toolkit's generated module to an Emscripten-generated module
- Building the HTML and JavaScript for the UI aspect of a game

WebAssembly is designed with a binary file format so that the WebAssembly files are as small as possible, allowing for fast transmissions and downloads; this doesn't mean it's a way for developers to hide their code. In fact, quite the opposite is true. WebAssembly is designed with the web's openness in mind. As a result, a text format equivalent of the binary format also exists.

The text format allows browser users to inspect a web page's WebAssembly in much the same way that they'd inspect JavaScript. The binary format's text format equivalent is also presented for debugging in the browser if the WebAssembly module doesn't include source maps, as highlighted in figure 11.1.

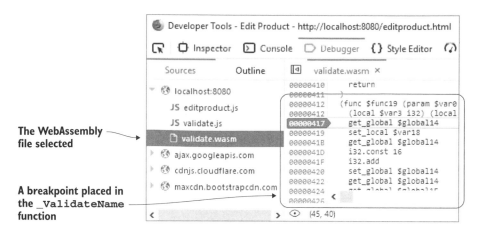

The WebAssembly file selected

A breakpoint placed in the _ValidateName function

Figure 11.1   Developer tools in Firefox, with a breakpoint placed in the `_ValidateName` function of the WebAssembly module you built in chapter 4, section 4.1

Suppose that you're going to build the card-matching game figure 11.2 shows. Level 1 will start with two rows of two cards, all facedown. The player will click two of the cards, and they'll turn faceup as they're clicked. If the cards are a match, they'll disappear. If the two cards don't match, they'll turn facedown again.

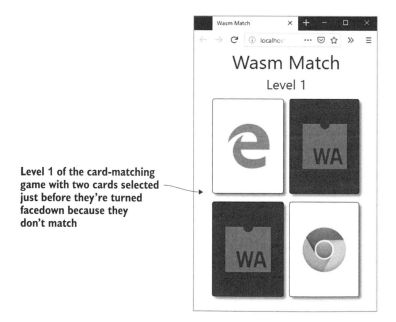

Level 1 of the card-matching game with two cards selected just before they're turned facedown because they don't match

Figure 11.2   Level 1 of the card-matching game, showing two cards clicked before they turn facedown because they're not a match

The summary screen when the player wins. They're given the opportunity to replay the current level or play the next level.

Figure 11.3 When the player wins, they can replay the current level or play the next level.

The player will win the level by causing all cards to disappear. As figure 11.3 illustrates, when the player wins, the game shows a message giving them the opportunity to replay the current level or play the next level.

We'll look at debugging a WebAssembly module in the next chapter, but before that, you need to have an understanding of the text format and how it works. In this chapter, you'll build the core logic for the card-playing game using the WebAssembly text format to see how it works in more detail. You'll then compile it into a WebAssembly module using the WebAssembly Binary Toolkit's online tool. HTML, CSS, and images will be used for the game's UI aspect.

When building a module using only the text format, you won't have access to the standard C library functions like `malloc` and `free`. As a workaround, you'll build a simple Emscripten-generated module that will export the additional functions that your text format module needs.

Figure 11.4 shows the following steps for creating this chapter's game:

1 Create the game's core logic using the WebAssembly text format.
2 Use the WebAssembly Binary Toolkit to generate a WebAssembly module from the text format (cards.wasm).
3 Create a C++ file that will allow the cards.wasm module to access certain standard C library functions.
4 Use Emscripten to generate a WebAssembly module from the C++ file.
5 Copy the generated WebAssembly files to the server for use by the browser. Then create the HTML and JavaScript that will load and link the two WebAssembly modules together. Also, create the JavaScript that will pass the information about the player's interactions to the module.

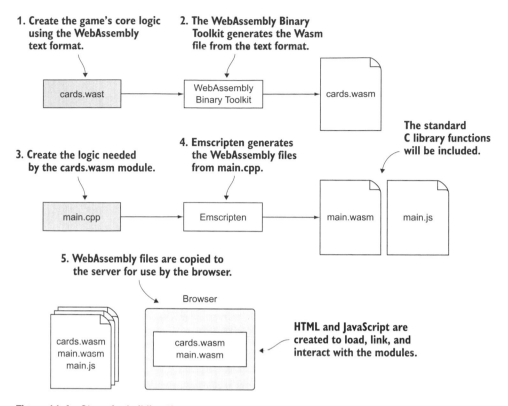

Figure 11.4   Steps for building the game

11.1   Creating the game's core logic using WebAssembly text format

WebAssembly text format uses *s-expression nodes*, which let you represent the module's elements in a simple way.

> **REMINDER**   The s-expression (shorthand for symbolic expression) was invented for the Lisp programming language. An s-expression can be either an atom or an ordered pair of s-expressions, allowing you to nest s-expressions. An atom is a symbol that's not a list: foo or 23, for example. A list is represented by parentheses and can be empty, or can hold atoms or even other lists. Each item is space-delimited: () or (foo) or (foo (bar 132)), for example.

In WebAssembly text format, each s-expression is surrounded by parentheses, and the first item within the parentheses is the label indicating the type of node it is. Following the label, the node can have a whitespace-separated list of attributes or even other nodes. Because the text format is meant for humans to read, child nodes are typically separated by a linefeed and indented to help show the parent/child relationship.

With the text format, you can refer to most items, like a function or a parameter, by the item's index. If you have a number of functions or variables, however, referring to everything by an index can sometimes get confusing. You can optionally include a variable name for an item when defining it, which is what you'll do for all variables and functions in this chapter.

Variable names in the text format start with a $ character, followed by alphanumeric characters indicating what the variable represents. Typically, the variable name represents the type of data it's for, like $func for function, but you could also use a variable name like $add for an add function. Sometimes, you'll even see the name of the variable end with a number indicating its index, like $func0.

WebAssembly supports four value types (32-bit integers, 64-bit integers, 32-bit floats, and 64-bit floats). Booleans are represented using a 32-bit integer. All other value types, like strings, need to be represented in the module's linear memory. The four value types represented in the text format are

- i32 for a 32-bit integer
- i64 for a 64-bit integer
- f32 for a 32-bit float
- f64 for a 64-bit float

To make working with the four types of data easier, the text format has an object for each type with that type's name. For example, to add two i32 values together, you would use i32.add. As another example, if you needed to use a float value of 10.5, you would use f32.const 10.5. A list of the memory and numeric instructions for the object types can be found here: http://webassembly.github.io/spec/core/text/instructions.html.

11.1.1 *The module's sections*

In chapter 2, you learned about the known and custom sections of a module. Known sections each have a specific purpose, are well-defined, and are validated when the WebAssembly module is instantiated. Custom sections are used for data that doesn't apply to the known sections, and they won't trigger a validation error if the data isn't laid out correctly.

Figure 11.5 represents the binary bytecode's basic structure. Each known section is optional but, if included, can be specified only once. Custom sections are also optional but, if included, can be placed before, after, or in between known sections.

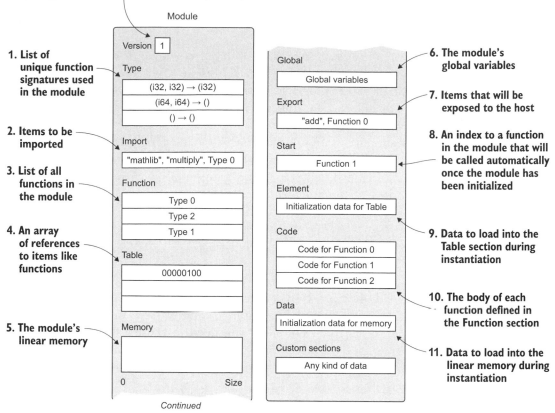

The preamble: this is a WebAssembly module and is built according to version 1 of the WebAssembly binary format.

1. List of unique function signatures used in the module

2. Items to be imported

3. List of all functions in the module

4. An array of references to items like functions

5. The module's linear memory

6. The module's global variables

7. Items that will be exposed to the host

8. An index to a function in the module that will be called automatically once the module has been initialized

9. Data to load into the Table section during instantiation

10. The body of each function defined in the Function section

11. Data to load into the linear memory during instantiation

Figure 11.5   Basic structure of the WebAssembly binary bytecode, highlighting the known and custom sections

As table 11.1 shows, the text format uses s-expression labels that correspond to the binary format's known sections.

Table 11.1   Known sections and their corresponding s-expression labels

Binary format	Text format	Binary format	Text format
preamble	`module`	Global	`global`
Type	`type`	Export	`export`
Import	`import`	Start	`start`
Function	`func`	Flement	`elem`
Table	`table`	Code	
Memory	`memory`	Data	`data`

You might have noticed in the table that the text format equivalent of the binary format's Code section wasn't specified. In the binary format, the function signature and the function's body are in separate sections. With the text format, the body of the function is included with the function as part of the `func` s-expression.

In the binary format, each known section is optional but, if included, can be included only once and must appear in the order shown in table 11.1. On the other hand, with the text format, the only node whose position matters is the `import` s-expression. If included, this s-expression must appear before the `table`, `memory`, `global`, and `func` s-expressions.

> **TIP** For code maintainability, it's recommended that all related nodes be kept together and that the sections be placed in the same order as you would expect to see those sections in the binary file.

11.1.2 *Comments*

If you wish to include a comment in the text format code, there are two ways to write one. A double semicolon is used for a single-line comment, and everything to the right of the semicolons is commented out, as in the following example:

```
;; this is a single-line comment
```

If you wish to comment out a section of code—either a portion of an element or several elements at once—you can begin the comment with an opening parenthesis and semicolon, and then close the comment later with a semicolon and closing parenthesis. Some tools include these types of comments within the elements to indicate which index something has, as in the following example:

```
(; 0 ;)
```

In some of the known sections that you'll define for this game, you'll need to include a function signature. Because function signatures are used by multiple sections, you'll learn about them next.

11.1.3 *Function signatures*

A function signature is a function definition without a body. The s-expression for the function signature starts with a label using the word `func`, optionally followed by a variable name.

If the function has parameters, a `param` s-expression is included that indicates the parameter's value type. For example, the following function signature has a single 32-bit integer parameter and doesn't return a value:

```
(func (param i32))
```

If a function has multiple parameters, you can include an additional `param` node for each parameter. For example, the following signature would be for a function with two `i32` parameters:

```
(func (param i32) (param i32))
```

You can also define parameters with a shorthand method that uses one `param` node but a space-separated list of each parameter's type, as in the following example, which is the same as the example shown previously with the two `param` nodes:

```
(func (param i32 i32))
```

If the function has a return value, a `result` s-expression is included, indicating the return value's type. The following is an example of a signature that has two 32-bit parameters and returns a 32-bit value:

```
(func (param i32 i32) (result i32))
```

If a function doesn't have parameters or a return value, you don't include `param` or `result` nodes:

```
(func)
```

Now that you understand some of the basics of the text format, your next step is to start building the game's logic (figure 11.6).

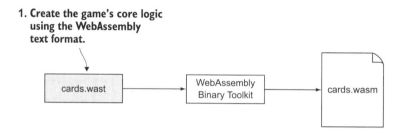

Figure 11.6   Creating the game's core logic using the WebAssembly text format

11.1.4 *The module node*

In your WebAssembly\ folder, create a Chapter 11\source\ folder for the files that you'll use in this section. Create a cards.wast file for your text format code, and then open it with your favorite editor.

The root s-expression node used for the WebAssembly text format is `module`, and all elements of a module are represented as child nodes of this node. Because all sections of a module are optional, it's possible to have an empty module, which is represented in the text format as `(module)`.

As figure 11.7 shows, the `module` node is the equivalent of the binary format's preamble section. The version of the binary format used will be included by the tool that's used to convert the text format into the binary format file.

Your first step in building the core logic for this game is to add the `module` node to the cards.wast file, as shown in the following snippet:

```
(module      ◁——— The root module node

)
```
            All elements of the module will
            be children of the module node.

The preamble: this is a WebAssembly module and is built
according to version 1 of the WebAssembly binary format.

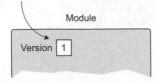

Figure 11.7 The module node is the
equivalent of the binary format's preamble
section. The version will be specified by the
tool used to create the binary format file.

With the `module` node created, you can now move on and add the known sections as
children of the `module` node. The `type` nodes will appear as the first children of the
`module` node, but you won't know what function signatures your module needs until
you've imported or built the necessary functions for your module's logic. Because of
this, you'll skip the `type` nodes for now, but will come back and add them once you've
written the module's functions.

The first section to add to the `module` node are the `import` nodes.

11.1.5 *The import nodes*

The Import known section (figure 11.8) declares all the items to be imported into the
module, which can include Function, Table, Memory, or Global imports. For the module
you're building, you'll import the memory needed as well as several functions.

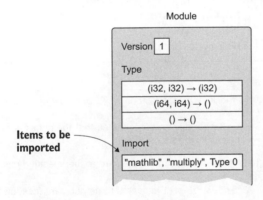

Figure 11.8 The Import known section
declares all the items to be imported
into the module.

An import is defined using an s-expression that has the label `import`, followed by a
namespace name, followed by the name of the item that will be imported, and then
followed by an s-expression representing the data being imported. To match what you
usually see with Emscripten-generated modules, the namespace name used will be
`"env"`. Emscripten puts an underscore character in front of the name of the item
being imported, so you'll do the same here to make your JavaScript code consistent.

The following is an example of an `import` node defined for a function that has two
`i32` parameters and an `i32` return value:

```
(import "env" "_Add"                                        "env" is the namespace name.
  (func $add (param i32 i32) (result i32))                  "_Add" is the name of the item
)                                                           being imported.
              The import is for a function that has two i32
              parameters and returns an i32 result.
```

When the WebAssembly module is instantiated, a JavaScript object needs to be passed to the `WebAssembly.instantiateStreaming` function that's providing the imports that the module expects. The following is an example of a JavaScript object for a module expecting the _Add function defined earlier:

```
const importObject = {
  env: {                                        The object's name must
    _Add: function(value1, value2) {            match the namespace
      return value1 + value2;                   name (env in this case).
    }
  }                  The name of the item is left of the colon,
};                   with the item being imported on the right.
```

Now that you understand how `import` nodes are defined, it's time to add them to the game.

ADDING THE IMPORT NODES TO THE GAME

The logic in this game will need to import some functions from the JavaScript so that the module can call into the JavaScript to update it at various stages of the game. The functions listed in table 11.2 will be imported from the JavaScript code.

Table 11.2   JavaScript functions that need to be imported

Item name	Parameters	Purpose
_GenerateCards	rows, columns, level	Tells the JavaScript how many rows and columns of cards to create. level is for display purposes so that the player knows which level they're playing.
_FlipCard	row, column, cardValue	Tells the JavaScript to flip the card at the specified row, column index. A cardValue of -1 indicates to flip the card facedown (the cards aren't a match). Otherwise, flip the card faceup because the player just clicked on.
_RemoveCards	row1, column1, row2, column2	Tells the JavaScript to remove two cards, based on their row and column indexes, because they're a match.
_LevelComplete	level, anotherLevel	Tells the JavaScript that the player completed the level and whether there's another level. The JavaScript will show a summary screen and allow the player to replay the current level. If there's another level, the player will also be given the option to play it.

Table 11.2   JavaScript functions that need to be imported *(continued)*

Item name	Parameters	Purpose
_Pause	namePointer, milliseconds	Called to pause the module's logic to allow the two cards to remain visible briefly before being flipped back facedown or removed, depending on whether they were a match. namePointer is an index in the module's memory where the string for the function name to call is located. milliseconds indicates how long to wait before calling the function.

The JavaScript code uses the item's name (_GenerateCards, for example) to specify the requested item. Your code here in the module, however, refers to the imported item by index or by a variable name (if you specify one). Rather than working with indexes, which can get confusing, you'll include a variable name for each of your import items.

Within your module s-expression in your cards.wast file, add the import s-expressions in the following listing for the functions specified in table 11.2.

Listing 11.1   The import s-expressions for items from the JavaScript code

```
. . .
(import "env" "_GenerateCards"
  (func $GenerateCards (param i32 i32 i32))     ◁──  Tells the JavaScript how many
)                                                      rows and columns to display
(import "env" "_FlipCard"                              as well as which level it is
  (func $FlipCard (param i32 i32 i32))   ◁──  Tells the JavaScript which
)                                                card to flip and its value
(import "env" "_RemoveCards"
  (func $RemoveCards (param i32 i32 i32 i32))  ◁──  Tells the JavaScript to remove
)                                                     the two cards based on their
(import "env" "_LevelComplete"                         row and column positions
  (func $LevelComplete (param i32 i32))     ◁─────
)                                                      Tells the JavaScript that
(import "env" "_Pause" (func $Pause (param i32 i32)))  ◁─  the level is complete
. . .                                                      and whether there's
                                                           another level
          Tells the JavaScript to call the
          function specified after the
          specified number of milliseconds
```

Later in this chapter, you're going to build an Emscripten-generated module that will be manually linked to this one at runtime. The Emscripten-generated module will provide access to functions like malloc and free to help with memory management. The module will also provide functions to help with generating random numbers.

The items listed in table 11.3 will be imported from the Emscripten-generated module.

Table 11.3   Items that need to be imported from the Emscripten-generated module

Item name	Type	Parameters	Purpose
`memory`	Memory		The Emscripten-generated module's linear memory that this module will share
`_SeedRandomNumberGenerator`	Function		Seeds the random number generator
`_GetRandomNumber`	Function	Range	Returns a random number within the range specified
`_malloc`	Function	Size	Allocates memory for the number of bytes specified
`_free`	Function	Pointer	Deallocates the memory that was allocated for the specified pointer

The function imports will be defined the same way here that you did for the JavaScript imports. The one thing that's different with this set of imports is the memory import.

Regardless of what you import, the first part of the import node is the same: the s-expression's label `import`, the namespace, and the item's name. The only thing that changes is the s-expression for the item being imported.

The s-expression for memory starts with the label `memory`, followed by an optional variable name, the initial number of memory pages desired, and, optionally, the maximum number of memory pages desired. Each page of memory is 64 KB (1 KB is 1,024 bytes, so 1 page holds 65,536 bytes). The following example would define a module's memory with 1 page of memory initially and a maximum of 10 pages:

```
(memory 1 10)
```

Within your `module` s-expression in your cards.wast file, add the `import` s-expressions in the next listing for the items specified in table 11.3. Place these `import` nodes after the _Pause import node.

Listing 11.2   The `import` s-expressions for items from the Emscripten-generated module

```
...

(import "env" "memory" (memory $memory 256))   ◁——— The module's memory
(import "env" "_SeedRandomNumberGenerator"
  (func $SeedRandomNumberGenerator)   ◁——— Seeds the random number generator
)
(import "env" "_GetRandomNumber"
  (func $GetRandomNumber (param i32) (result i32))   ◁——┐
)                                                        │
(import "env" "_malloc" (func $malloc (param i32) (result i32)))  │
(import "env" "_free" (func $free (param i32)))          │
...                                      Gets a random number
                                         from a range specified
```

Now that the imports have been specified, your next step is to define some global variables to help with the game's logic.

11.1.6 *The global nodes*

The Global known section (figure 11.9) defines all the global variables that are built into the module. Global variables can also be imported.

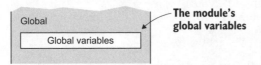

Figure 11.9　The Global known section declares the module's built-in global variables.

Global variables are declared at the module level for use by all functions and can be either *immutable* (a constant) or *mutable*. They are defined with an s-expression node that starts with the label `global`, followed by an optional variable name, the variable's type, and then an s-expression holding the variable's default value. For example, the following `global` node defines an immutable (constant) variable with the name `$MAX` that's a 32-bit integer and has a default value of 25:

```
(global $MAX i32 (i32.const 25))
```

If you need a mutable global variable, the global's type is wrapped in an s-expression with the label `mut`. For example, the following global variable with the name `$total` is a mutable 32-bit float with a default value of 1.5:

```
(global $total (mut f32) (f32.const 1.5))
```

Now that you understand how `global` nodes are defined, it's time to add them to the game.

ADDING THE GLOBAL NODES TO THE GAME

All the global variables the game needs will be 32-bit integers with a default value of zero. Following the `import` s-expressions, and within the `module` s-expression, add the following immutable global variable to your cards.wast file to indicate that the game will support a maximum of three levels:

```
(global $MAX_LEVEL i32 (i32.const 3))
```

The rest of the global variables that you'll create will be mutable, including the next one that you need to add, called `$cards`. This will be a pointer to the location in the module's memory where the array of card values is held. Add the code in the following snippet after the `$MAX_LEVEL` variable in your cards.wast file:

```
(global $cards (mut i32) (i32.const 0))
```

You now need some variables to keep track of the game's current level ($current_level) and how many matches remain before the player beats the level ($matches_remaining). You also need $rows and $columns variables to hold the number of rows and columns displayed for the current level.

Add the code in the following snippet after the $cards variable, and within the module s-expression, in your cards.wast file:

```
(global $current_level (mut i32) (i32.const 0))
(global $rows (mut i32) (i32.const 0))
(global $columns (mut i32) (i32.const 0))
(global $matches_remaining (mut i32) (i32.const 0))
```

When the player clicks the first card, you need to remember what the card's row and column positions are so that you can either flip it facedown if the second card isn't a match or remove the card if it is. You also need to keep track of the card's value so that you can compare the second card's value to see if they're a match or not.

When the player clicks the second card, execution will be handed off to the Java-Script. This pauses the game briefly so that the second card remains visible long enough for the player to see it before it gets flipped facedown or removed. Because the executing function will exit, you also need to remember the second card's row and column positions as well as the card value.

In your cards.wast file, add the following code after the $matches_ remaining variable and within the module s-expression:

```
(global $first_card_row (mut i32) (i32.const 0))
(global $first_card_column (mut i32) (i32.const 0))
(global $first_card_value (mut i32) (i32.const 0))
(global $second_card_row (mut i32) (i32.const 0))
(global $second_card_column (mut i32) (i32.const 0))
(global $second_card_value (mut i32) (i32.const 0))
```

When the module's execution is handed off to the JavaScript to pause the logic before the cards are flipped facedown or removed, you don't want the user continuing to trigger clicks by clicking the cards. The following global variable will be a flag for the logic to know that things are currently paused until the JavaScript calls back into the module. In your cards.wast file, add the code in the following snippet after the $second_card_value variable and within the module s-expression:

```
(global $execution_paused (mut i32) (i32.const 0))
```

With the global variables defined, the next area that you need to implement are the exports.

11.1.7 *The export nodes*

As figure 11.10 shows, the Export known section holds a list of all items that will get returned to the host environment once the module is instantiated. These are the portions of the module that the host environment can access. Exports can include Function, Table, Memory, or Global items. For this module's logic, you only need to export functions.

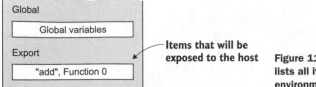

Figure 11.10   The Export known section lists all items in the module that the host environment can access.

To export an item, you need an s-expression that has the label `export`, followed by the name that you want the caller to use, and then by an s-expression that specifies the item being exported.

To export a function, the s-expression at the end of the `export` node is a `func` with either the zero-based index or the variable name of the function that the export is pointing to in the module. For example, the following would export a function that the host will see as `_Add` that points to a function in the module with the variable name `$add`:

```
(export "_Add" (func $add))
```

Now that you understand how `export` nodes are defined, it's time to add them to the game.

ADDING THE EXPORT NODES TO THE GAME

In a moment, you'll create the functions for the game's logic. Of the functions that you create, you need to export the following:

- `$CardSelected`—This function is called by the JavaScript code whenever the player clicks a card. The logic calls the imported `$Pause` JavaScript function if this function call was for a second card. The `$Pause` function is also told to call the `$SecondCardSelectedCallback` function after a brief delay.
- `$SecondCardSelectedCallback`—Called by the JavaScript code from the `$Pause` function, this function checks to see if the two cards are a match or not and flips them facedown if they're not a match or removes them if they are. If the number of matches remaining reaches zero, this function calls the `$Level-Complete` JavaScript function.
- `$ReplayLevel`—This function is called by the JavaScript code when the player clicks the Replay button on the summary screen after completing the current level.
- `$PlayNextLevel`—A Next Level button is displayed on the summary screen if the player hasn't reached the final level of the game. This function is called by the JavaScript code when the player clicks the Next Level button.

After the `global` s-expressions, and within the `module` s-expression, add the following export s-expressions to your cards.wast file:

```
(export "_CardSelected" (func $CardSelected))
(export "_SecondCardSelectedCallback"
```

Called to tell the module which card was clicked

```
    (func $SecondCardSelectedCallback)
)
(export "_ReplayLevel" (func $ReplayLevel))
(export "_PlayNextLevel" (func $PlayNextLevel))
```

Callback function when the Pause function's timeout completes

Called to reset the current level

Called to set up the next level

With the exports defined, the next area to implement is the Start section.

11.1.8   The start node

As figure 11.11 shows, the Start known section specifies a function that's to be called after the module is instantiated but before the exported items are callable. If specified, the function can't be imported and must exist within the module.

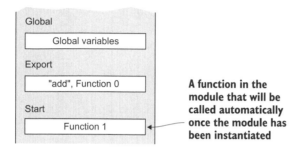

A function in the module that will be called automatically once the module has been instantiated

Figure 11.11   The Start known section specifies the function that's to be called after the module is instantiated.

For this game, the start function is used to initialize the global variables and memory. It also starts the game's first level.

To define the start section, you use an s-expression with the label start, followed by either the function's index or the variable name. Add the code in the following snippet to your cards.wast file after the export s-expressions and within the module s-expression to have the $main function called automatically once the module is instantiated:

```
(start $main)
```

The next step is to define this module's functions and their code.

11.1.9   The code nodes

As figure 11.12 shows, in the binary format, the Function (definition) and Code (body) known sections are separate. In the text format, the function definition and body are together in one func s-expression. When looking at Emscripten's generated text format or the browser's code, functions are usually shown in the Code known section's position, so you'll do that here, too, for consistency.

The code execution in WebAssembly is defined in terms of a stack machine, in which instructions push or pop a certain number of values onto and off the stack. When a function is first called, the stack for that function is empty. The WebAssembly framework validates the stack when the function ends to ensure that, if the function is

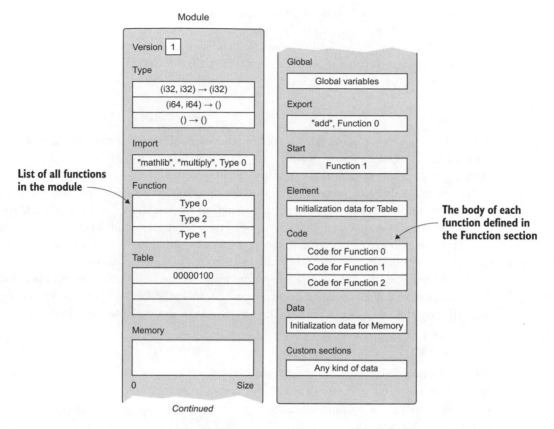

Figure 11.12   The Function and Code known sections in the binary format

returning an i32 value, for example, the last item on the stack when the function returns is an i32 value. If the function doesn't return anything, then the stack must be empty when the function returns.

> **MORE INFO**   Within the body of a function, the text format supports s-expression style, stack machine style, or a combination of the two. In this chapter, you'll use the stack machine style because that's the style that browsers use. For s-expression examples, see appendix E for alternative ways that you can write if statements and loops.

Before you start building the game's functions, let's look at how you interact with variables.

WORKING WITH VARIABLES

WebAssembly has two types of variables: globals and locals. Globals are accessible by all functions, whereas local variables are accessible only within the function that defined them.

Local variables need to be defined before anything else in the function and are defined as an s-expression with the label `local`, followed by an optional variable name, and then by the variable's type. The following is an example of an f32 local variable declaration with the variable name `$float` followed by an i32 local variable declaration without a variable name:

```
(local $float f32)
(local i32)
```

If you don't specify a name for a variable, you can reference it using its zero-based index. One thing to be aware of with local variables is that a function's parameters are considered locals as well, and are first in the index order.

To assign a value to a variable, the value needs to be on the stack first. You can then use either the `set_local` or `tee_local` instruction to pop the value off the stack and set the local variable's value. The difference between `set_local` and `tee_local` is that `tee_local` also returns the value that was set. For a global variable, you use the `set_global` instruction in the same way you use the `set_local` instruction.

As an example, the following code snippet places the value `10.3` on the stack and then calls the `set_local` instruction for the `$float` variable. The `set_local` instruction will pop the top value off the stack and place it in the variable specified:

```
f32.const 10.3
set_local $float
```

To get a value from a variable and push it onto the stack, you use the `get_local` instruction for local variables and `get_global` for global variables. For example, if your function had a parameter called $param0, the following code would place its value on the stack:

```
get_local $param0
```

> **INFO** The `set_local`, `tee_local`, `get_local`, `set_global`, and `get_global` instructions are used in this chapter because web browsers are still using this format. However, the WebAssembly specification has been adjusted to use `local.set`, `local.tee`, `local.get`, `global.set`, and `global.get`. The new format is called the exact same way as the old format. When Emscripten outputs a .wast file, it now uses the new format, and the WebAssembly Binary Toolkit can now accept text format code that uses either format. The new variable instructions can be found at http://mng.bz/xljX.

Now that you understand how variables work, the first `func` node that you'll build for the game's logic will be the `$InitializeRowsAndColumns` function.

THE $INITIALIZEROWSANDCOLUMNS FUNCTION

The `$InitializeRowsAndColumns` function has a single i32 parameter with the name $level and doesn't have a return value. This function is called to set the global $rows and $columns variables to their appropriate values based on the level parameter received.

Because each level has a different combination of rows and columns for the cards, the function needs to determine which level has been requested. To check and see if the parameter value is 1 (one), you place the parameter value onto the stack and then place i32.const 1 onto the stack. To determine if the two values on the stack are equal, you call the i32.eq instruction, which pops the top two items off the stack, checks to see if they're equal, and then pushes the result onto the stack (1 for true, 0 for false), as shown in the following snippet:

```
get_local $level        1 will be placed on the stack if
i32.const 1             $level holds the value 1. Otherwise,
i32.eq        ⟵_____  0 is placed on the stack.
```

Once you have the Boolean value on the stack, you'll use an if statement to check if the Boolean value is true and, if so, to set the $rows and $column values each to an i32.const 2. An if statement will pop the top item off the stack to do its evaluation. An if statement considers a zero value as false and any nonzero value as true. The following snippet extends the logic of the previous snippet to include an if statement:

```
get_local $level
i32.const 1
i32.eq                  If the top value on the stack is
if                      nonzero, then the code in this
      ⟵_____  block will run.
end
```

The code shown in the previous snippet will be repeated three times, once for each level being checked. The i32.const value will be changed to 2 when checking if the level specified is two and will be changed to 3 when checking if the level specified is three.

Set the global $rows and $columns values to the following based on the level specified:

- Level 1: both are i32.const 2
- Level 2: $rows is i32.const 2, $columns is i32.const 3
- Level 3: $rows is i32.const 2, $columns is i32.const 4

The game is capable of six levels, but only the first three are defined in this function to simplify the code. Add the code in the next listing after the start node in your cards.wast file.

Listing 11.3   The $InitializeRowsAndColumns function for your cards.wast file

```
...

(func $InitializeRowsAndColumns (param $level i32)    Pushes the parameter
  get_local $level        ⟵_____  value onto the stack
    i32.const 1  ⟵—— Pushes 1 onto the stack
    i32.eq   ⟵_____  Pops the top two values, checks to
                                see if they're equal, and pushes
                                the result onto the stack
```

```
if
  i32.const 2
  set_global $rows
  i32.const 2
  set_global $columns
end

get_local $level
i32.const 2
i32.eq
if
  i32.const 2
  set_global $rows

  i32.const 3
  set_global $columns
end

get_local $level
i32.const 3
i32.eq
if
  i32.const 2
  set_global $rows

  i32.const 4
  set_global $columns
end
)
```

Pushes 2 onto the stack

Pops the top item off the stack; if true, then sets the global variables

Pops the top item off the stack and puts it into the global variable $rows

Pops the top item off the stack and puts it into the global variable $columns

If level 2 was requested, sets the global variable $rows to 2

If level 2 was requested, sets the global variable $columns to 3

If level 3 was requested, sets the global variable $rows to 2

If level 3 was requested, sets the global variable $columns to 4

The next `func` node that you'll need to define is the `$ResetSelectedCardValues` function.

THE $RESETSELECTEDCARDVALUES FUNCTION

The `$ResetSelectedCardValues` function has no parameters or return value. This function is called to set the global variables for the first and second cards that are clicked to -1. Setting these card values to -1 indicates to the rest of the game's logic that all cards are currently facedown.

Add the code in the following listing after the `$InitializeRowsAndColumns` node in your cards.wast file.

> **Listing 11.4   The $ResetSelectedCardValues function for your cards.wast file**

```
...

(func $ResetSelectedCardValues
  i32.const -1
  set_global $first_card_row

  i32.const -1
  set_global $first_card_column

  i32.const -1
  set_global $first_card_value

  i32.const -1
```

```
    set_global $second_card_row

    i32.const -1
    set_global $second_card_column

    i32.const -1
    set_global $second_card_value
)
```

The next func node that you'll need to define is the $InitializeCards function.

THE $INITIALIZECARDS FUNCTION

The $InitializeCards function has an i32 parameter with the name $level and doesn't return a value. This function is called to set the global variables to their appropriate values based on the $level parameter received, create and populate the $cards array, and then shuffle the array.

Local variables need to be defined in a function before any other code, so the first thing that's needed in the function is an i32 local variable called $count that will be populated later in the function. The following snippet shows the local variable's definition:

```
(local $count i32)
```

The next thing the function does is push the $level parameter received onto the stack and then call set_global to pop the value off the stack and place it into the global variable $current_level:

```
get_local $level
set_global $current_level
```

Next, the $level parameter value is pushed onto the stack again, and the $Initialize-RowsAndColumns function is called to have the $rows and $columns global variables set appropriately based on the requested level. Because the function has a single parameter, WebAssembly will pop the top value off the stack (the level value) and will pass it to the function, as shown in the following snippet:

```
get_local $level
call $InitializeRowsAndColumns
```

To have the first and second card global variables reset to -1, the code calls the $ResetSelectedCardValues function. This function has no parameters, so nothing needs to be placed on the stack for this function call:

```
call $ResetSelectedCardValues
```

The function then determines how many cards are needed for the current level based on the values in the $rows and $columns global variables. These global variable values are placed on the stack, and then the i32.mul instruction is called. i32.mul pops the top two items off the stack, multiplies the values together, and pushes the result back onto the stack. Once the result is on the stack, set_local is called to put the value into the $count variable. The set_local call will pop the top item off the stack and place it into the variable specified. The following snippet shows the code that determines how many cards the current level has:

```
get_global $rows
get_global $columns
i32.mul
set_local $count
```

The next step is to determine the `$matches_remaining` value by dividing the `$count` value by 2. The `$count` value and `i32.const 2` are pushed onto the stack, and then the `i32.div_s` instruction is called. This instruction pops the top two items off the stack, divides them, and pushes the result back onto the stack. The `set_global` instruction is then called to pop the top item off the stack and put the value in the `$matches_remaining` global variable:

```
get_local $count
i32.const 2
i32.div_s
set_global $matches_remaining
```

The next thing that needs to happen in the function is for a block of memory to be allocated to hold the number of `i32` values based on the value in `$count`. Because `i32` values are 4 bytes each, the `$count` value needs to be multiplied by 4 to get the total number of bytes to allocate. You could use `i32.mul`, but it's more efficient to use the `i32.shl` (shift left) instruction. A shift left of 2 is the same as multiplying by 4.

Once the total number of bytes has been determined, the `$malloc` function that you imported from the Emscripten-generated module is called to have that number of bytes allocated. The `$malloc` function will return the memory index where the allocated memory block starts. You'll then call the `set_global` instruction to place that value in the `$cards` variable.

The following snippet shows the number of bytes being determined from the `$count` value and then being passed to the `$malloc` function, with the result being placed in the `$cards` variable:

```
get_local $count
i32.const 2
i32.shl
call $malloc
set_global $cards
```

Now that a block of memory has been allocated for your `$cards` array, you'll call the `$PopulateArray` function, passing it the number of cards that the current level has, as shown in the following snippet. The function will add pairs of values to the `$cards` array based on the number of cards there are for the current level (0, 0, 1, 1, 2, 2, for example):

```
get_local $count
call $PopulateArray
```

Finally, the function will call the `$ShuffleArray`, to have the contents of the `$cards` array shuffled:

```
get_local $count
call $ShuffleArray
```

Putting it all together, add the code in the next listing after the $ResetSelectedCard-Values node in your cards.wast file.

Listing 11.5   The $InitializeCards function for your cards.wast file

```
...

(func $InitializeCards (param $level i32)
  (local $count i32)

  get_local $level
  set_global $current_level        ⟵── Remembers the requested level

  get_local $level                      Sets the rows and columns global
  call $InitializeRowsAndColumns   ⟵── variables based on the current level

  call $ResetSelectedCardValues    ⟵──
                                        Makes sure the first and
  get_global $rows          ⟵──         second card values are reset
  get_global $columns
  i32.mul                       Determines how many cards
  set_local $count              there are for this level

  get_local $count          ⟵──
  i32.const 2                   Determines how many pairs of
  i32.div_s                     cards there are for this level
  set_global $matches_remaining

  get_local $count              Shifts left by 2 because each item
  i32.const 2                   in the array represents a 32-bit
  i32.shl            ⟵──         integer (4 bytes each)
  call $malloc       ⟵── Allocates the memory needed
  set_global $cards      by calling the malloc function

  get_local $count
  call $PopulateArray   ⟵── Fills the array with pairs of values

  get_local $count
  call $ShuffleArray    ⟵── Shuffles the array
)
```

The next func node that you'll need to define is the $PopulateArray function.

THE $POPULATEARRAY FUNCTION

Loop through the array, as shown in the following listing, adding pairs of values based on the number of cards there are for the current level (0, 0, 1, 1, 2, 2, for example).

Listing 11.6   The $PopulateArray function for your cards.wast file

```
...

(func $PopulateArray (param $array_length i32)
  (local $index i32)
  (local $card_value i32)

  i32.const 0
  set_local $index
```

```
i32.const 0
set_local $card_value

loop $while-populate
  get_local $index
  call $GetMemoryLocationFromIndex
  get_local $card_value
  i32.store
  get_local $index
  i32.const 1
  i32.add
  set_local $index

  get_local $index
  call $GetMemoryLocationFromIndex
  get_local $card_value
  i32.store
  get_local $card_value
  i32.const 1
  i32.add
  set_local $card_value

  get_local $index
  i32.const 1
  i32.add
  set_local $index

  get_local $index
  get_local $array_length
  i32.lt_s
  if
    br $while-populate
  end
  end $while-populate
)
```

Sets the memory value at $index
to the content of $card_value

Increments the index

Sets the memory value at $index
to the content of $card_value

Increments $card_value
for the next loop

Increments the index
for the next loop

If the index is less than
$array_length, loop again.

The next func node that you need to define is the $GetMemoryLocationFromIndex function.

THE $ GETMEMORYLOCATIONFROMINDEX FUNCTION

The $GetMemoryLocationFromIndex function has an i32 parameter called $index and an i32 return value. This function is called to determine the memory location of the index in the $cards array.

The function pushes the parameter value ($index) as well as an i32.const 2 value onto the stack. It then calls the i32.shl instruction (shift left), which pops the top two values off the stack, shifts the $index value by 2 (the same as multiplying it by 4), and pushes the result back onto the stack.

The function then calls get_global for $cards to push the start location of the $cards array in memory onto the stack. The i32.add instruction is then called; it pops the top two items off the stack, adds them together, and pushes the result back onto the stack. Because the function will be returning a value, the result of the `i32.add` operation is left on the stack to be returned to the caller.

Add the code in the following snippet after the `$PopulateArray` node in your cards.wast file:

```
(func $GetMemoryLocationFromIndex (param $index i32) (result i32)
  get_local $index
  i32.const 2
  i32.shl      ◁─── Shifts the index value left by 2

  get_global $cards
  i32.add   ◁───┐ Adds the start location of the
)              │ array to the index location
```

The next `func` node that you need to define is the `$ShuffleArray` function.

THE $SHUFFLEARRAY FUNCTION

The `$ShuffleArray` function has an `i32` parameter called `$array_length` and no return value. This function is called to have the contents of the `$cards` array shuffled.

> **INFO** The type of shuffling that will be used for this array will be the Fisher-Yates shuffle. You can find more information at https://gist.github.com/ sundeepblue/10501662.

This function first defines several local variables for use in the upcoming loop. It then calls the `$SeedRandomNumberGenerator` function that was imported from the Emscripten-generated module to seed the random number generator.

The `$index` value is initialized at 1 less than the `$array_length` value because the loop through the cards will be from the end of the array to the beginning. A loop is then started that will continue while the `$index` value hasn't yet reached zero.

Within the loop, a call is made to the `$GetRandomNumber` function that was imported from the Emscripten-generated module to get a random number from the range specified. The range specified is the current index adjusted to be one-based to get a random number between 1 and `$index + 1`. The random number received is then placed in the local `$card_to_swap` variable:

```
get_local $index
i32.const 1      │ Adds 1 to the value in $index
i32.add   ◁──────┘ to get a one-based index
call $GetRandomNumber
set_local $card_to_swap
```

Once the index of a random card to swap has been determined, the card's memory location at the current index and card to swap index is determined and placed in the `$memory_location1` and `$memory_location2` local variables, respectively.

After the two memory locations have been found, the value at the current index (`$memory_location1`) is read from memory by calling `i32.load`. This instruction will pop the top item—the memory location—off the stack and read the `i32` value from that memory location, placing it on the stack. Your function will then place the value in the local variable $card_value so that it isn't lost while the data from $memory_location2 is placed in $memory_location1, as shown in the following snippet:

```
get_local $memory_location1
i32.load
set_local $card_value
```

The next snippet can be confusing. The code pushes the value in $memory_location1 onto the stack (the current index) and then pushes the value in $memory_location2 (the card to swap index) onto the stack. It then calls i32.load, which pops the top item off the stack ($memory_location2—the card to swap index), reads the value from that memory location, and pushes that memory location's value onto the stack.

Because $memory_location1 (the current index) is already on the stack, and now the value from $memory_location2 is on the stack, the code can call the i32.store instruction. The i32.store call will pop the top two items off the stack and place the value in memory. The topmost item is the value to store, and the next item is the location in memory to store the value:

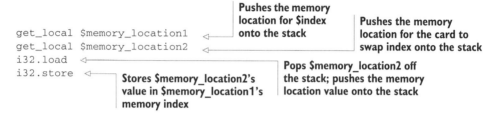

Now that the value from $memory_location2 is in $memory_location1, the code places the value that was in $memory_location1 into $memory_location2, as follows:

```
get_local $memory_location2
get_local $card_value
i32.store
```

The loop then decrements the $index value by 1. If the $index value is still greater than zero, the loop starts again.

Putting it all together, add the code in the next listing after the $PopulateArray node in your cards.wast file.

> **Listing 11.7 The $ShuffleArray function for your cards.wast file**

```
...

(func $ShuffleArray (param $array_length i32)
  (local $index i32)
  (local $memory_location1 i32)
  (local $memory_location2 i32)
  (local $card_to_swap i32)
  (local $card_value i32)

  call $SeedRandomNumberGenerator      ⟵  Seeds the random number generator
```

```
    get_local $array_length          The loop will start at the
    i32.const 1                      end of the array and
    i32.sub                          move to the beginning.
    set_local $index

    loop $while-shuffle
      get_local $index
      i32.const 1
      i32.add                        Determines a random
      call $GetRandomNumber          card to swap the item
      set_local $card_to_swap        at this index with

      get_local $index                    Determines the memory
      call $GetMemoryLocationFromIndex    location based on the index
      set_local $memory_location1

      get_local $card_to_swap             Determines the memory location
      call $GetMemoryLocationFromIndex    based on the card_to_swap index
      set_local $memory_location2

      get_local $memory_location1    Gets the card value from
      i32.load                       memory at the current
      set_local $card_value          index in the array

      get_local $memory_location1
      get_local $memory_location2    Pops $memory_location2 and pushes that
      i32.load                       memory location's value onto the stack
      i32.store
                                     Stores the value from
      get_local $memory_location2    $memory_location2 at
      get_local $card_value          $memory_location1
      i32.store

                                     Puts the card value into the memory
      get_local $index               where card_to_swap's value was
      i32.const 1
      i32.sub                        Decrements the index
      set_local $index               by 1 for the next loop

      get_local $index               If the index is still
      i32.const 0                    greater than zero,
      i32.gt_s                       then loop again.
      if
        br $while-shuffle
      end
    end $while-shuffle
)
```

The next `func` node that you'll need to define is the `$PlayLevel` function.

THE $PLAYLEVEL FUNCTION

The `$PlayLevel` function has an `i32` parameter called `$level` and no return value. This function is called to initialize the cards and then have them displayed for the player.

To initialize the cards, push the `$level` parameter value onto the stack and then call the `$InitializeCards` function. Because the function expects a single parameter, the top item on the stack is popped off and passed as the parameter to the function.

Next, you need to call the $GenerateCards JavaScript function so that the proper number of cards for the current level are displayed for the player. To do this, you push the global $rows and $columns values onto the stack and then the $level parameter value. Then call the $GenerateCards function. This function expects three parameters, so the top three items will be popped off the stack and passed to the function's parameters.

Add the code in the following snippet after the $ShuffleArray function in your cards.wast file:

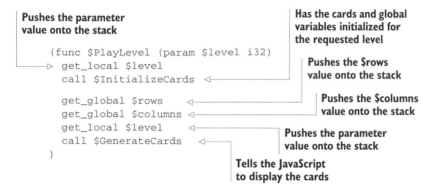

Pushes the parameter value onto the stack

Has the cards and global variables initialized for the requested level

```
(func $PlayLevel (param $level i32)
   get_local $level
   call $InitializeCards

   get_global $rows
   get_global $columns
   get_local $level
   call $GenerateCards
)
```

Pushes the $rows value onto the stack

Pushes the $columns value onto the stack

Pushes the parameter value onto the stack

Tells the JavaScript to display the cards

The next func node that you'll need to define is the $GetCardValue function.

THE $GETCARDVALUE FUNCTION

The $GetCardValue function accepts two i32 parameters ($row and $column) and returns an i32 result. This function is called to get the card value associated with a card at a specific row and column position.

The following equation is used to determine the index in the $cards array in which the requested row and column value resides:

```
row * columns + column
```

The next snippet shows the text format code that implements this formula. The parameter value $row is pushed onto the stack, and then the $columns global variable is pushed onto the stack. The i32.mul instruction pops the top two items off the stack, multiplies them together, and then pushes the result onto the stack.

The $column parameter value is pushed onto the stack, and then the i32.add instruction is called, which pops the top two items off the stack, adds them together, and pushes the result onto the stack, giving you the index within the array to find the card value:

```
get_local $row
get_global $columns
i32.mul       ⟵── Multiplies $row by $columns
get_local $column
i32.add       ⟵── Adds $column to the result
```

Once the array index has been determined, you need to shift the index left by 2 (multiply by 4) because each index represents a 4-byte, 32-bit integer. Then the start location of the `$cards` array in memory is added to the adjusted index to get the spot in the module's memory where that index resides. With the memory index now on the stack, the `i32.load` instruction is called, which pops the top item off the stack, reads the item from that memory location, and pushes the value onto the stack. Because this function returns an `i32` result, you just leave the result of the `i32.load` call on the stack, and it will be returned to the calling function when this function ends.

Add the code in the next listing after the `$PlayLevel` function in your cards.wast file.

> **Listing 11.8 The `$GetCardValue` function for your cards.wast file**

```
...

(func $GetCardValue (param $row i32) (param $column i32) (result i32)
  get_local $row
  get_global $columns          Multiplies the $row and
  i32.mul                      $columns values together
  get_local $column
  i32.add         ◁───         Adds the $column value to the
                               result of the multiplication
  i32.const 2
  i32.shl         ◁───         Shifts the index value left by 2
  get_global $cards            (multiplies by 4) because each
  i32.add                      index represents a 32-bit integer
  i32.load        ◁───
)
                               Reads the value from memory;
Adds the start position of the  leaves it on the stack to be
$cards pointer array to the     returned to the calling function
index position
```

The next `func` node that you'll need to define is the `$CardSelected` function.

THE `$CardSelected` FUNCTION

The `$CardSelected` function accepts two `i32` parameters (`$row` and `$column`) and doesn't return a value. This function is called by the JavaScript code when the player clicks a card.

As the following snippet shows, before this function does anything, it checks to see if the execution is paused. Execution will be paused if the player just clicked a second card and the module is giving them a short delay before either flipping the cards face-down or removing them. If execution is paused, the function exits by calling the return statement:

```
get_global $execution_paused
i32.const 1
i32.eq
if
```

```
   return
end
```

If execution isn't paused, the function will then determine what the card value is for the $row and $column specified in the parameter values by calling the $GetCardValue function. The card value determined is placed in the $card_value local variable, as shown in the following snippet:

```
get_local $row
get_local $column
call $GetCardValue
set_local $card_value
```

Next, the function calls the JavaScript $FlipCard function to have the card that was clicked flipped faceup:

```
get_local $row
get_local $column
get_local $card_value
call $FlipCard
```

The code then checks to see if the $first_card_row value is set to -1. If so, then the first card isn't yet faceup, and the then block of the if statement executes. If the value is not -1, the first card is already faceup, so the else block of the if statement executes, as the following snippet shows:

```
get_global $first_card_row
i32.const -1               $first_card_row's value is
i32.eq                     -1. The first card isn't
if                         faceup yet.
    ◁

else
         ◁
                           $first_card_row's value isn't -1.
end                        The first card is faceup.
```

In the then block of the if statement, the values of $row, $column, and $card_value are placed in the global variables $first_card_row, $first_card_column, and $first_card_value, respectively.

In the else block of the if statement, the code first checks to see if the $row and $column values belong to the first card by calling the $IsFirstCard function. If the player has clicked the same card again, the function exits, as shown in the following snippet:

```
get_local $row
get_local $column
call $IsFirstCard
if
   return
end
```

If the player has clicked a different card, the else branch places the values of $row, $column, and $card_value in the global variables $second_card_row, $second_card_column, and $second_card_value, respectively. The else branch code then gives the $execution_paused variable the value i32.const 1 to flag that execution is now paused and this function isn't to respond to clicks until execution is unpaused.

Finally, as the next snippet shows, the code in the else branch pushes the value i32.const 1024 onto the stack and then pushes i32.const 600 onto the stack. The 1024 value is the memory location of the string "SecondCardSelectedCallback" that you'll specify when you define the Data known section later in this chapter. The 600 value is the number of milliseconds for which you want the JavaScript code to pause execution.

Once the two values have been pushed onto the stack, the $Pause JavaScript function is called. The function expects two parameters, so the top two items on the stack are popped off and passed as the parameters to the function:

```
i32.const 1024
i32.const 600
call $Pause
```

Putting it all together, add the code in the next listing after the $GetCardValue function in your cards.wast file.

Listing 11.9   The $CardSelected function for your cards.wast file

```
. . .

(func $CardSelected (param $row i32) (param $column i32)
  (local $card_value i32)

  get_global $execution_paused        ◁──┐  Ignores clicks while
  i32.const 1                            │  the game is paused
  i32.eq
  if
    return
  end

  get_local $row                            Gets the value of the card
  get_local $column                         for the row and column
  call $GetCardValue     ◁──────────────    specified
  set_local $card_value

  get_local $row
  get_local $column
  get_local $card_value       Tells the JavaScript
  call $FlipCard    ◁──────   to show this card

  get_global $first_card_row
  i32.const -1
  i32.eq                  If no card has been
  if         ◁──────────  clicked yet...
    get_local $row    ◁──────────────    ...remembers the details about
    set_global $first_card_row           the card that was clicked
```

```
      get_local $column
      set_global $first_card_column

      get_local $card_value
      set_global $first_card_value
  else                          The first card is already shown.
      get_local $row
      get_local $column
      call $IsFirstCard
      if
        return
      end

      get_local $row               Remembers the second card's details
      set_global $second_card_row

      get_local $column
      set_global $second_card_column

      get_local $card_value
      set_global $second_card_value

      i32.const 1
      set_global $execution_paused

      i32.const 1024
      i32.const 600
      call $Pause
    end
  )
```

Annotations:
- **The first card is already shown.**
- **If the player clicked the first card again, exit the function.**
- **Remembers the second card's details**
- **Don't respond to clicks until the Pause function calls back into this module.**
- **Location in memory of the string "SecondCardSelectedCallback"**
- **Duration before the $SecondCardSelectedCallback function is to be called by the JavaScript**
- **Calls the JavaScript $Pause function**

The next func node that you'll need to define is the $IsFirstCard function.

THE $IsFirstCard FUNCTION

The $IsFirstCard function accepts two i32 parameters ($row and $column) and returns an i32 result. This function is called to determine if the $row and $column values are for the first card that's displayed to the user.

The function first checks to see if the $row parameter value matches the $first_card_row global value and puts the result in the $rows_equal local variable. In the same fashion, the function checks to see if the $column parameter value matches the $first_card_column global value and puts the result in the $columns_equal local variable.

The function next pushes the $rows_equal and $columns_equal values onto the stack and calls the i32.and instruction. This instruction pops the top two items off the stack and does a bitwise AND operation on the values to determine if they're both equal; it then pushes the result back onto the stack. Because this function returns an i32 result, you leave the result of the i32.and call on the stack; it will be returned to the calling function when this function ends.

Add the code in the next listing after the $CardSelected function in your cards.wast file.

Listing 11.10 The `$IsFirstCard` function for your cards.wast file

```
...

(func $IsFirstCard (param $row i32) (param $column i32) (result i32)
  (local $rows_equal i32)
  (local $columns_equal i32)

  get_global $first_card_row          Determines if the first
  get_local $row                      card's row matches the
  i32.eq            ◁───────          current row
  set_local $rows_equal

  get_global $first_card_column       Determines if the first
  get_local $column                   card's column matches the
  i32.eq            ◁───────          current column
  set_local $columns_equal

  get_local $rows_equal               A bitwise AND to determine
  get_local $columns_equal            if the rows and columns are
  i32.and           ◁───────          both equal
)
```

The next `func` node that you'll need to define is the `$SecondCardSelectedCallback` function.

THE `$SECONDCARDSELECTEDCALLBACK` FUNCTION

The `$SecondCardSelectedCallback` function doesn't have any parameters or a return value. This function is called by the JavaScript `$Pause` function when the timeout completes. It checks to see if the two cards that are selected are a match. If they are, the JavaScript function `$RemoveCards` is called to have the two cards hidden, and then the `$matches_remaining` global variable is decremented. If the two cards aren't a match, the JavaScript function `$FlipCard` is called for each card to have them flipped back facedown. The global variables indicating which cards have been clicked are then reset, and the `$execution_paused` variable is set to 0 (zero), indicating that the module isn't paused anymore.

The function next checks to see if the `$matches_remaining` value is at 0 (zero), indicating that the level is complete. If so, the memory for the `$cards` array is released by calling the `$free` function that's imported from the Emscripten-generated module. The `$LevelComplete` JavaScript function is then called to inform the player that they completed the level.

Add the code in the next listing after the `$IsFirstCard` function in your cards.wast file.

Listing 11.11 The `$SecondCardSelectedCallback` function for your cards.wast file

```
...

(func $SecondCardSelectedCallback
  (local $is_last_level i32)
```

```
get_global $first_card_value
get_global $second_card_value
i32.eq
if          <──────────────────── If the two selected cards match...
  get_global $first_card_row
  get_global $first_card_column
  get_global $second_card_row
  get_global $second_card_column
  call $RemoveCards  <──────────── ...tells the JavaScript to hide the two cards

  get_global $matches_remaining
  i32.const 1
  i32.sub
  set_global $matches_remaining  <────── Decrements the global variable by 1
else                            <────── The two cards were not a match.
  get_global $first_card_row
  get_global $first_card_column
  i32.const -1                         Tells the JavaScript to flip
  call $FlipCard  <────────────────    the first card facedown

  get_global $second_card_row
  get_global $second_card_column
  i32.const -1                         Tells the JavaScript to flip
  call $FlipCard  <────────────────    the second card facedown
end

call $ResetSelectedCardValues  <────┐ Sets the global variables for
                                    │ the selected cards to -1
i32.const 0
set_global $execution_paused  <───┐  Turns off the flag, allowing
                                  │  the $CardSelected function
get_global $matches_remaining     │  to accept clicks again
i32.const 0
i32.eq
if              <──────────── If there are no matches remaining...
  get_global $cards
  call $free  <────────────────┐ ...frees the memory used by
                               │ the $cards global variable
  get_global $current_level
  get_global $MAX_LEVEL
  i32.lt_s
  set_local $is_last_level  <──┐ Determines if the current
                              │ level is the last one
  get_global $current_level
  get_local $is_last_level
  call $LevelComplete  <──────┐ Calls the JavaScript function to tell the player they
end                          │ beat the level and whether there's another level
)
```

The next func node that you'll need to define is the $ReplayLevel function.

THE $REPLAYLEVEL FUNCTION

The $ReplayLevel function has no parameters or return value and is called by the JavaScript when the player presses the Replay button. This function simply passes the $current_level global variable to the $PlayLevel function.

Add the code in the following snippet after the $SecondCardSelectedCallback function in your cards.wast file:

```
(func $ReplayLevel
  get_global $current_level
  call $PlayLevel
)
```

The next `func` node that you'll need to define is the `$PlayNextLevel` function.

THE $PLAYNEXTLEVEL FUNCTION

The `$PlayNextLevel` function has no parameters or return value and is called by the JavaScript when the player presses the Next Level button. This function calls the `$PlayLevel` function, passing it a value that's 1 greater than the `$current_level` global variable's value.

Add the code in the following snippet after the `$ReplayLevel` function in your cards.wast file:

```
(func $PlayNextLevel
  get_global $current_level
  i32.const 1
  i32.add
  call $PlayLevel
)
```

The next `func` node that you'll need to define is the `$main` function.

THE $MAIN FUNCTION

The `$main` function has no parameters or return value. This function is called automatically when the module is instantiated because you specify it as part of the `start` node. It calls the `$PlayLevel` function, passing it a value of 1 to start the first level of the game.

Add the code in the following snippet after the `$PlayNextLevel` function in your cards.wast file:

```
(func $main
  i32.const 1
  call $PlayLevel
)
```

Now that you have all the functions defined for your core logic, your next step is to add in the `type` nodes.

11.1.10 The type nodes

As figure 11.13 shows, the Type known section declares a list of all unique function signatures that will be used in the module, including those that will be imported. When using the Binary Toolkit to generate a module, the `type` s-expression nodes are optional because the toolkit can determine the signatures based on the import function definitions and the defined functions within the module. Because you'll see the `type` s-expressions defined when viewing the text format in a browser's developer tools, you'll define them here also for completeness.

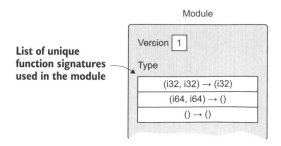

List of unique
function signatures
used in the module

Figure 11.13   The Type known section declares a list of all unique function signatures that will be used in the module, including those that will be imported.

A type is defined using an s-expression that has the label `type`, followed by an optional variable name, and then by the function signature. For example, the following would be a type definition for a function signature that has no parameters and no return value:

```
(type (func))
```

You can give a type any name you wish, but we'll follow Emscripten's naming convention, which is a variable name similar to `$FUNCSIG$vi`. The value following the second dollar sign indicates the function's signature. The first character is the function's return value type, and each additional character indicates the parameter types. The characters Emscripten uses are

- `v`—Void
- `i`—32-bit integer
- `j`—64-bit integer
- `f`—32-bit float
- `d`—64-bit float

The Type known section appears as the first section in the module, but you waited until now to implement it so that you could create the module's functions first. Now you can go through your functions and imports to put together a list of all unique function signatures.

ADDING THE TYPE NODES TO THE GAME

Looking over the imported functions and the function's you've built for this module, you have seven unique function signatures, shown in table 11.4.

Table 11.4   The seven unique function signatures this module uses

Return type	Param 1	Param 2	Param 3	Param 4	Emscripten signature
void	–	–	–	–	v
void	i32	–	–	–	vi
void	i32	i32	–	–	vii

Table 11.4   The seven unique function signatures this module uses *(continued)*

Return type	Param 1	Param 2	Param 3	Param 4	Emscripten signature
void	i32	i32	i32	–	viii
void	i32	i32	i32	i32	viiii
i32	i32	–	–	–	ii
i32	i32	i32	–	–	iii

With the unique function signatures determined in table 11.4, all that's left to do is create the `type` nodes for each signature. Add the `type` s-expressions from the following snippet to your cards.wast file before the `import` nodes and within the `module` s-expression:

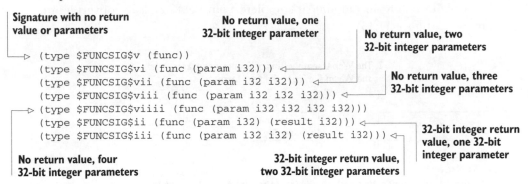

The final section that you need to define for this game is the Data section.

11.1.11 The data node

As figure 11.14 shows, the Data known section declares the data to load into the module's linear memory during instantiation.

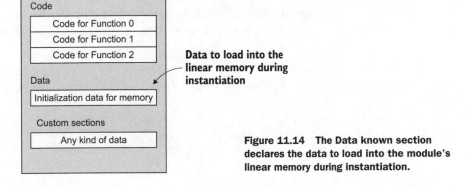

Figure 11.14   The Data known section declares the data to load into the module's linear memory during instantiation.

The `data` s-expression starts out with the label `data`, followed by an s-expression indicating where in the module's memory the data should go, and then by a string containing the data to place in memory.

You need to place the string `"SecondCardSelectedCallback"` into the module's memory. This module will be manually linked to an Emscripten-generated module at runtime, and Emscripten-generated modules sometimes place data of their own in the module's memory. As a result, you'll place the string at memory index `1024` to leave room in case the Emscripten-generated module wants to put something in memory too.

Add the code in the following snippet to your cards.wast file after the `func` s-expressions and within the `module` s-expression to have the string `"SecondCard-SelectedCallback"` placed at index `1024` in the module's memory:

```
(data (i32.const 1024) "SecondCardSelectedCallback")
```

Once your text format module is complete, your next step is to convert it into a binary module (figure 11.15).

2. The WebAssembly Binary Toolkit generates the Wasm file from the text format.

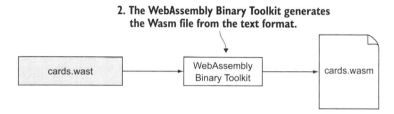

Figure 11.15   Generating a Wasm file from the WebAssembly text format

11.2   *Generating a WebAssembly module from the text format*

To compile the WebAssembly text format into a WebAssembly module using the wat2wasm online tool, go to the following website: https://webassembly.github.io/wabt/demo/wat2wasm/. As figure 11.16 shows, in the tool's top-left pane, you can replace the existing text with the text from your cards.wast file. The tool automatically creates the WebAssembly module for you. Click the Download button to download the generated WebAssembly file to your Chapter 11\source\folder, and name it cards.wasm.

Now that you've generated the WebAssembly module from the text format code, you can move on to the next step and create the Emscripten-generated module (figure 11.17).

1. Replace the contents of this pane with the contents of your cards.wast file.

2. Download the WebAssembly file.

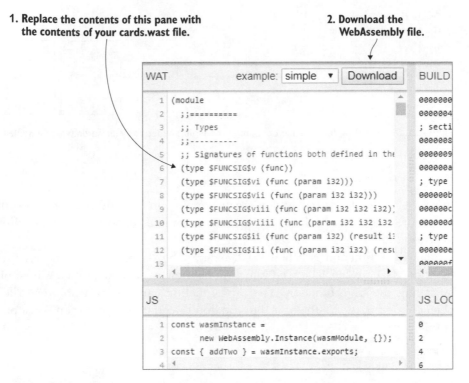

Figure 11.16 Replace the contents of the top-left pane with the contents of your cards.wast file. Then download the WebAssembly file.

3. Create the logic needed by the cards.wasm module.

4. Emscripten generates the WebAssembly files from main.cpp.

The standard C library functions will be included.

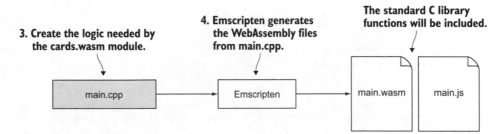

Figure 11.17 Creating the C++ file containing the logic needed for your cards.wasm module

11.3 *The Emscripten-generated module*

The Emscripten-generated module provides your cards.wasm module with the necessary standard C library functions, like `malloc`, `free`, and the random number generator functions `srand` and `rand`. The two modules will be manually linked at runtime. As shown in figure 11.18, now you'll create the C++ file.

3. Create the logic needed by
the cards.wasm module.

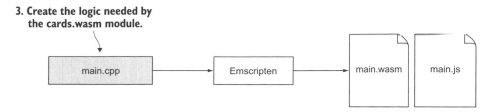

Figure 11.18   Creating the C++ file containing the logic needed for your cards.wasm module

11.3.1 *Creating the C++ file*

In your Chapter 11\source\ folder, create a main.cpp file, and open it with your favorite editor. You need to define two functions that will be exported for use by the game's logic module.

The first function is called `SeedRandomNumberGenerator` and passes the `srand` function a seed value. The seed value will be the current time, which will be obtained by calling the `time` function. The `time` function can accept a pointer to a `time_t` object to populate with the time, but you don't need that here, so you'll just pass `NULL`, as follows:

```
EMSCRIPTEN_KEEPALIVE
void SeedRandomNumberGenerator() { srand(time(NULL)); }
```

The second function that you need to create is called `GetRandomNumber`; it accepts a range and returns a random number within that range. For example, if the value for the range is 10, the random number will be between 0 and 9. The following is the `GetRandomNumber` function:

```
EMSCRIPTEN_KEEPALIVE
int GetRandomNumber(int range) { return (rand() % range); }
```

The logic module also needs access to the `malloc` and `free` functions, but the Emscripten-generated module will include those automatically. Add the code in the next listing to your main.cpp file.

Listing 11.12   The contents of the main.cpp file

```
#include <cstdlib>
#include <ctime>
#include <emscripten.h>

#ifdef __cplusplus
extern "C" {
#endif

EMSCRIPTEN_KEEPALIVE
void SeedRandomNumberGenerator() { srand(time(NULL)); }
```

```
EMSCRIPTEN_KEEPALIVE
int GetRandomNumber(int range) { return (rand() % range); }

#ifdef __cplusplus
}
#endif
```

Now that you've created your main.cpp file, you'll use Emscripten to turn it into a WebAssembly module, as figure 11.19 shows.

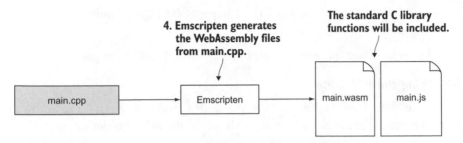

Figure 11.19   Using Emscripten to generate a WebAssembly module from main.cpp

11.3.2 Generating a WebAssembly module

To compile the code into a WebAssembly module, open a command prompt, navigate to the folder where you saved the main.cpp file, and then run the following command:

```
emcc main.cpp -o main.js
```

Your next step, shown in figure 11.20, is to copy the generated files to a location for use by the browser. You'll then create the HTML and JavaScript files needed for the web page to interact with the modules.

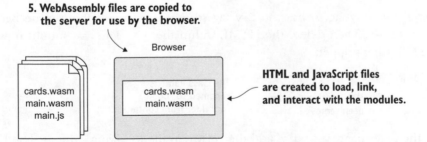

Figure 11.20   Copying the generated files to the server for use by the browser. You'll then create the HTML and JavaScript files needed for the web page to interact with the modules.

11.4   *Creating the HTML and JavaScript files*

In your WebAssembly\Chapter 11\ folder, create a frontend\ folder for the files that you'll use in this section. Then copy the following files from your source\ folder to your frontend\ folder:

- cards.wasm
- main.wasm
- main.js
- editproduct.html from your Chapter 4\4.1 js_plumbing\frontend\ folder; rename to game.html

You'll start building the game's web page by first adjusting the game.html file.

11.4.1   *Modifying the HTML file*

Open the game.html file in your favorite editor, and change the text in the `title` tag from `Edit Product` to `Wasm Match`, as shown in the following snippet:

```
<title>Wasm Match</title>
```

After the last `script` tag in the `head` tag, add the following `link` tag, which will load the CSS needed for styling the cards in the game:

```
<link rel="stylesheet" href="game.css">
```

> **NOTE**   The game.css file can be found with the source code for this book, which is available for download from the publisher's website at www.manning .com/books/webassembly-in-action. Add the game.css file to the same folder as your game.html file.

Modify the `body` tag so that it no longer has an `onload="initializePage()"` attribute. The `body` tag should now look like this:

```
<body>
```

Following the `body` tag, revise the `div` tag so that its class attribute value becomes `root-container`. Then delete the HTML within the `div`. The `div` should now look like the following snippet:

```
<div class="root-container">    ⟵——  The class name is
                                      renamed to root-
</div>    ⟵——  The HTML within the div       container from container.
                has been removed.
```

Within the `root-container` `div`, add the HTML in the following snippet. The HTML shows the name of the game on the web page as well as the current level that's being played. If the player decides to advance to the next level, the JavaScript will adjust the h3 tag to indicate the new level:

```
<header class="container-fluid">
  <h1>Wasm Match</h1>    ⟵——  Shows the name of the game on the web page
  <h3 id="currentLevel">Level 1</h3>    ⟵——  Shows the current level being played
</header>
```

After the `header` tag, and still within the `root-container` div, add the `div` tag shown in the following snippet. The game's cards will be placed within this `div` by the JavaScript code:

```
<div id="cardContainer" class="container-fluid"></div>
```

The next thing you need to do is add some HTML that will be presented to the player when they win a level. The HTML will indicate which level they completed and will give them the option to either replay the current level or play the next level (if there is a next level). Add the following HTML after the `cardContainer` div, and within the `root-container` div:

Not shown by default. The JavaScript will show this div if the player wins.

Will hold details about the level that was completed

Button the player can click to replay the current level

```
<div id="levelComplete" class="container-fluid summary"
    style="display:none;">
  <h1>Congratulations!</h1>
  <h3 id="levelSummary"></h3>

  <button class="btn btn-primary"
    onclick="replayLevel();">Replay</Button>

  <button class="btn btn-primary" id="playNextLevel"
    onclick="playNextLevel();">Next Level</Button>
</div>
```

Button the player can click to play the next level; hidden if there are no other levels

The final changes that you need to make to the game.html file are the `script` tag `src` values at the end of the file. You'll create a game.js file in a moment that will handle linking the two modules together and interacting with the module. Change the first `script` tag's value to `game.js` and the second `script` tag's value to `main.js` (the Emscripten-generated JavaScript code):

```
<script src="game.js"></script>        ⟵——— Was editproduct.js
<script src="main.js"></script>         ⟵——— Was validate.js
```

With the HTML now adjusted, the next step is to create the JavaScript that will link the two modules together and interact with the main logic in the cards.wasm module.

11.4.2 Creating the JavaScript file

In your frontend\ folder, create a game.js file, and then open it with your favorite editor. Add the global variables in the following code snippet to your game.js file to hold the module's memory and exported functions:

```
let moduleMemory = null;
let moduleExports = null;
```

Your next step is to create a `Module` object so that you can handle Emscripten's `instantiateWasm` function. This will allow you to control the process of downloading and instantiating the Emscripten-generated WebAssembly module. You'll then be able to download and instantiate the cards.wasm file, linking it to the Emscripten-generated module.

Within the `instantiateWasm` function, you need to implement the following:

- Place a reference to the `importObject`'s memory object into the `moduleMemory` global variable for use by your JavaScript later.
- Define a variable that will hold the instance of the main.wasm module once instantiated.
- Then call the `WebAssembly.instantiateStreaming` function, fetching the main.wasm file and passing in the `importObject` received from Emscripten.
- In the `then` method of the `instantiateStreaming` Promise, define the import object for the cards.wasm module, passing in functions from the main.wasm module as well as JavaScript functions from your own JavaScript code. Then call `WebAssembly.instantiateStreaming` to fetch the cards.wasm module.
- In the `then` method of the cards.wasm `instantiateStreaming` Promise, place a reference to the module's exports in the `moduleExports` global variable. Finally, pass the module instance of the main.wasm module to Emscripten.

Add the code in the next listing to your game.js file after your global variables.

Listing 11.13   The `Module` object in the game.js file

Emscripten's JavaScript will look for
this object to see if your code is
overriding anything.

Allows you to control the main
module's instantiation

```
...
var Module = {
    instantiateWasm: function(importObject, successCallback) {
        moduleMemory = importObject.env.memory;
        let mainInstance = null;

        WebAssembly.instantiateStreaming(fetch("main.wasm"),
            importObject)
        .then(result => {
            mainInstance = result.instance;

            const sideImportObject = {
                env: {
                    memory: moduleMemory,
                    _malloc: mainInstance.exports._malloc,
                    _free: mainInstance.exports._free,
                    _SeedRandomNumberGenerator:
        mainInstance.exports._SeedRandomNumberGenerator,
                    _GetRandomNumber: mainInstance.exports._GetRandomNumber,
                    _GenerateCards: generateCards,
                    _FlipCard: flipCard,
                    _RemoveCards: removeCards,
                    _LevelComplete: levelComplete,
                    _Pause: pause,
```

Keeps a reference to
the memory object for
use by your JavaScript

Downloads and instantiates
the Emscripten-generated
WebAssembly module

Keeps a
reference to the
main.wasm
module instance

Creates the import
object needed by the
cards.wasm module

Uses the same memory as
the main module instance

```
        }
    };

    return WebAssembly.instantiateStreaming(fetch("cards.wasm"),
        sideImportObject)
  }).then(sideInstanceResult => {
    moduleExports = sideInstanceResult.instance.exports;

    successCallback(mainInstance);
  });

  return {};
 }
};
```

Downloads and instantiates the cards.wasm module

Keeps a reference to the cards.wasm module's exports for use by your JavaScript

Passes the main module instance to Emscripten's JavaScript code

Because this is done asynchronously, passes back an empty object

When the cards.wasm module is instantiated, it will automatically start level 1 and call your JavaScript `generateCards` function to have the proper number of cards displayed on the screen. This function will also be called when the player chooses to replay the level or play the next level. Add the code in the next listing to your game.js file after the `Module` object.

Listing 11.14 The `generateCards` function in the game.js file

```
...
function generateCards(rows, columns, level) {
  document.getElementById("currentLevel").innerText
    = `Level ${level}`;

  let html = "";
  for (let row = 0; row < rows; row++) {
    html += "<div>";

    for (let column = 0; column < columns; column++) {
      html += "<div id=\"" + getCardId(row, column)
        + "\" class=\"CardBack\" onclick=\"onClickCard("
        + row + "," + column + ");\"><span></span></div>";
    }

    html += "</div>";
  }

  document.getElementById("cardContainer").innerHTML = html;
}
```

Called by the module to have the proper number of cards displayed

Adjusts the header section to indicate the current level

Will hold the HTML for the cards

Each row's cards will be in a div tag.

Builds the HTML for the current card

Closes the div tag for the current row

Updates the web page with the HTML

Each card displayed is given an ID based on its row and column values. The `get-CardId` function will return the ID of the card specified by the row and column values. Add the function in the following code snippet after the `generateCards` function in the game.js file:

```
function getCardId(row, column) {
  return ("card_" + row + "_" + column);
}
```

Whenever the player clicks a card, the module will call the `flipCard` function to have the card's face shown. If the player clicks a second card, and the cards don't match, then—after a brief delay so that the player can see the cards they clicked—the module will call the `flipCard` function again for both cards to have them flipped facedown. When the module wants the card flipped facedown, it will specify a `cardValue` of -1. Add the `flipCard` code in the following snippet after the `getCardId` function in your game.js file:

Called by the module to flip the card either faceup or facedown

Gets a reference to the card in the DOM

```
function flipCard(row, column, cardValue) {
    const card = getCard(row, column);     ◁────  Defaults the card
    card.className = "CardBack";     ◁────────────  to be facedown

    if (cardValue !== -1) {   ◁──────────────────  If a value was specified, then
      card.className = ("CardFace "                 the card needs to be faceup.
          + getClassForCardValue(cardValue));  ◁──
    }                                               CardFace is for the card and the
}                                                   value from getClassForCardValue
                                                    for the image.
```

The `getCard` helper function returns the DOM object for the card requested based on the row and column value specified. Add the `getCard` function after the `flipCard` function in your game.js file:

```
function getCard(row, column) {
  return document.getElementById(getCardId(row, column));
}
```

When a card is faceup, it includes a second CSS class name to indicate which image to display. The card values used in the game are 0, 1, 2, and up depending on how many levels there are. The `getClassForCardValue` function will return a class name starting with `Type` and with the card's value appended to the end (`Type0`, for example). Add the following code after the `getCard` function in your game.js file:

```
function getClassForCardValue(cardValue) {
  return ("Type" + cardValue);
}
```

When the player successfully finds two cards that match, the module will call the `removeCards` function to have those cards removed. Add the code in the following snippet after the `getClassForCardValue` function in your game.js file:

```
function removeCards(firstCardRow, firstCardColumn,
    secondCardRow, secondCardColumn) {                   Gets a reference to the
  let card = getCard(firstCardRow, firstCardColumn);  ◁──  first card in the DOM
  card.style.visibility = "hidden";     ◁──────────────
                                                         The card is hidden but still
  card = getCard(secondCardRow, secondCardColumn);       occupies the same space to
  card.style.visibility = "hidden";  ◁──                 prevent the cards from
}                                                        moving around.
          Hides the second card
```

Once the player has found all the matches for the current level, the module will call the `levelComplete` function so that the JavaScript can inform the player and offer the option to replay the current level. If the module indicates that there's another level available, the player will also get the opportunity to play the next level. Add the code in the next listing after the `removeCards` function in your game.js file.

Listing 11.15 The `levelComplete` function in the game.js file

```
...

function levelComplete(level, hasAnotherLevel) {
  document.getElementById("levelComplete").style.display
  = "";                  ⟵──────────────────────  Shows the level complete section

  document.getElementById("levelSummary").innerText =
      `You've completed level ${level}!`;        ⟵────  Indicates which level the
                                                         player just completed
  if (!hasAnotherLevel) {   ⟵────────────────
    document.getElementById("playNextLevel").style.display =
  "none";                                        If there are no other levels,
  }                                              then hide the button for
}                                                playing the next level.
```

When the player clicks a second card, the module will give the player a brief pause before either flipping the cards facedown if they don't match or hiding them if they do match. To pause execution, the module calls the `pause` JavaScript function, indicating which module function it wants the JavaScript to call once the timeout completes. It also passes the duration that it wants the timeout to be, in milliseconds. Add the code in the following snippet to your game.js file after the `levelComplete` function:

```
function pause(callbackNamePointer, milliseconds) {
  window.setTimeout(function() { ⟵────            Creates an anonymous
    const name = ("_" +                            function that will be called
        getStringFromMemory(callbackNamePointer)); ⟵  when the timeout completes

    moduleExports[name]();  ⟵────  Calls the function
  }, milliseconds);  ⟵───         that was specified    Gets the function's name
}                                                        from the module's memory
                              The timeout will trigger   and prefixes it with the
                              after the specified         underscore character
                              number of milliseconds.
```

The `getStringFromMemory` function that you'll create next is copied from the JavaScript code used by previous chapters to read a string from the module's memory. Add the code in the next listing after your `pause` function in the game.js file.

Listing 11.16 The `getStringFromMemory` function for the game.js file

```
...

function getStringFromMemory(memoryOffset) {
  let returnValue = "";

  const size = 256;
  const bytes = new Uint8Array(moduleMemory.buffer, memoryOffset, size);
```

```
let character = "";
for (let i = 0; i < size; i++) {
  character = String.fromCharCode(bytes[i]);
  if (character === "\0") { break; }

  returnValue += character;
}

return returnValue;
}
```

Whenever the player clicks a card, the card's `div` tag will call the `onClickCard` function, passing in the card's row and column values. Your `onClickCard` function needs to pass these values to the module by calling the `_CardSelected` function. Add the code in the following snippet after your `getStringFromMemory` function in your game.js file:

```
function onClickCard(row, col) {
  moduleExports._CardSelected(row, col);   ◁──┐
}
```
Tells the module that the card at this row and column position was clicked

When the player completes the level, they're presented with a button allowing them to replay the current level. The button will call your `replayLevel` function. In your function, you'll need to hide the level complete section and then tell the module that the player wants to replay the level by calling the `_ReplayLevel` function. Add the following code after your `onClickCard` function in your game.js file:

```
function replayLevel() {
  document.getElementById("levelComplete").style.display
➥ = "none";          ◁─────────────── Hides the level complete section

  moduleExports._ReplayLevel();   ◁──┐ Tells the module that the player
}                                      wants to replay the current level
```

Also, when the player completes the level, they'll see a button letting them play the next level (if there is one). When clicked, the button will call your `playNextLevel` JavaScript function. In this function, you'll need to hide the level complete section and then tell the module that the player wants to play the next level by calling the `_PlayNextLevel` function. Add the code in the following snippet after your `replayLevel` function in your game.js file:

```
function playNextLevel() {
  document.getElementById("levelComplete").style.display = "none";

  moduleExports._PlayNextLevel();   ◁──┐ Tells the module that the player
}                                        wants to play the next level
```

Now that all your files have been created, you can view the results.

11.5 Viewing the results

To view the results, open your browser and type `http://localhost:8080/game.html` into the address box to see the game's web page, shown in figure 11.21.

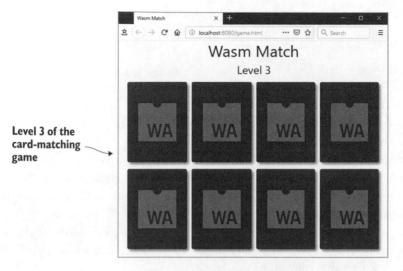

Level 3 of the card-matching game

Figure 11.21   The card-matching game looks like this when the player reaches level 3.

How can you use what you learned in this chapter in the real world?

Real-world use cases

The following are some possible use cases for what you've learned in this chapter:

- As you'll see in chapter 12, the text format is used by browsers when showing the contents of a WebAssembly module if source maps are unavailable. It's also possible to set a breakpoint and step through the text format code, which might be necessary to track down an issue if you can't reproduce it locally.
- As you saw in chapter 6 and will see again in chapter 12, you can include the `-g` flag with the `emcc` command to have Emscripten also output a .wast file. If you're receiving errors when trying to instantiate a module, or you're not sure why something isn't working, sometimes it helps to take a look at the contents of this file.

Exercises

You can find the solutions to the exercises in appendix D.

1 When using the WebAssembly Binary Toolkit to create a WebAssembly module, which s-expression nodes have to appear before the `table`, `memory`, `global`, and `func` s-expressions?

2 Try modifying the `InitializeRowsAndColumns` function in the text format code so that it now supports six levels rather than three:

  a Level 4 should have 3 rows and 4 columns.

  b Level 5 should have 4 rows and 4 columns.

  c Level 6 should have 4 rows and 5 columns.

Summary

In this chapter, you learned the following:

- There is a text equivalent of the WebAssembly binary format called the WebAssembly text format. This allows you to see and work with a module using human-readable text, rather than having to work with the binary format directly.

- The text format allows a browser user to inspect a WebAssembly module in much the same way they would inspect a web page's JavaScript.

- The text format isn't intended to be written by hand, but it's possible to do so using tools like the WebAssembly Binary Toolkit.

- The text format uses s-expressions to represent the elements of the module in a simple way. The root element is the `module` s-expression, and all other s-expressions are children of this node.

- There are s-expressions that correspond to the binary format's known sections. Only the `import` node's position matters; if it's included, it needs to appear before the `table`, `memory`, `global`, and `func` nodes. Also, the Function and Code known sections in the binary format are represented by a single `func` s-expression in the text format.

- The four value types supported by WebAssembly are represented in the text format as `i32` (32-bit integer), `i64` (64-bit integer), `f32` (32-bit float), and `f64` (64-bit float).

- To make working with the four types of data easier, the text format has an object for each type with that type's name (`i32.add`, for example).

- The code in a function acts as a stack machine in which values are pushed onto and popped off the stack. The code within a function can be written using either the stack machine format or the s-expression format. Browsers display a function's code using the stack machine format.

- If a function doesn't return a value, the stack must be empty when the function exits. Otherwise, an item of that type must be on the stack when the function exits.

- You can reference items by their index or variable name.

- A function's parameters are considered local variables, and their indexes come before any local variables defined in the function. Also, local variables must be defined before anything else in the function.

- At the moment, browsers display the get and set instructions for local and global variables in the format `set_local` or `get_global`. The WebAssembly specification was changed—the new format is `local.set` or `global.get`—but the way you make the calls remains the same as the original format.

Debugging 12

This chapter covers

- Various debugging methods for WebAssembly modules
- Error handling during compilation and at runtime
- Debugging with browser developer tools

At some point during development, you'll likely discover that your code isn't working as expected, and you need to find a way to track down the issue. Sometimes tracking it down is as simple as reading over the code. Other times, you need to dig deeper.

At the time of writing, WebAssembly's debugging options are a bit limited, but this will change as browser and IDE (integrated development environment) tooling improve. At the moment, you have the following options for debugging a WebAssembly module:

- You can make a small number of changes and then compile and test often so that if there's an issue, it's easier to track down. In this case, reading over your code changes might shed some light on the issue.
- If there are compiler issues, you can tell Emscripten to include verbose output by enabling debug mode. In this mode, debug logs and intermediate files are output. The EMCC_DEBUG environment variable or the -v compiler

flag are used to control debug mode. You can find more information about debug mode in the Emscripten documentation at http://mng.bz/JzdZ.

- You could output information from your module to the browser's console using an imported JavaScript function, one of Emscripten's macros, or functions like `printf`. Doing this allows you to see which functions are being called and what values the variables you're interested in hold at that point. With this approach, you start off by logging areas that you think may hold clues about the issue. You can add more logging as you narrow down the location. (Appendix C has more information about Emscripten's macros.)

- In some browsers, you can view the text format version of the WebAssembly module, set breakpoints, and step through the code. You'll learn how to use this approach to debug a module in this chapter.

- Emscripten has a number of -g flags (-g0, -g1, -g2, -g3, -g4) that include progressively more debug information in the compiled output. The -g flag is the same as using -g3. When using -g flags, Emscripten also generates a text format file (.wast) equivalent of the binary file that's generated, which is helpful if you're having issues with linking—for example, passing the proper items to the module during instantiation. You could check the text format file to see what it's importing to make sure you're providing the expected items. More information on -g flags can be found at http://mng.bz/wlj5.

- The -g4 flag is interesting because it generates source maps, allowing you to view your C or C++ code in the browser's debugger. This is promising as a future debugging option. But although this approach does show your C or C++ code in the debugger, and breakpoints are hit, the debugging doesn't work very well at the time of writing. For example, if your function has a parameter variable with a specific name, you can't do a watch on it because the text format might actually be using a variable like var0. Asking the debugger to step over the code might also take several tries because, under the hood, several text format steps are happening for that one statement, and the step-over call is happening per text format statement.

In this chapter, you'll put some of the debugging options to use as you add a feature to the card-matching game that you built in chapter 11.

12.1 Extending the game

Imagine that you're going to extend the card-matching game so that it keeps track of how many tries it takes the player to complete the level, as figure 12.1 shows. It's considered a *try* when the player clicks the second card, regardless of whether it's a match.

In this chapter, to learn about available debugging options, I'll have you make intentional mistakes so that you'll need to debug the code to determine where and what the issue is. Rather than making all these changes in the WebAssembly module

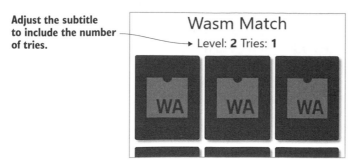

Adjust the subtitle to include the number of tries.

Figure 12.1   Level 2 of the card-matching game with the subtitle adjusted to include the number of tries

first and then adjusting the JavaScript, you'll make changes to both the module and JavaScript one function at a time.

Figure 12.2 graphically represents the following high-level steps you'll use to adjust the game to include the number of tries:

1   Adjust the HTML so that the subtitle includes a section for the number of tries.
2   Adjust the text format and JavaScript code to display the number of tries on the web page when the level starts.
3   Add the code to increment the number of tries and display the new value when the player clicks the second card.
4   Pass the number of tries to the summary screen when the player completes the level.

Your first step is to adjust the HTML so that it now includes a section for the number of tries.

12.2   Adjusting the HTML

Before you can adjust the HTML to include the number of tries, you'll need to create a folder for this chapter's files. In your WebAssembly\ folder, create a Chapter 12\ folder, and then copy the frontend\ and source\ folders from your Chapter 11\ folder.

In the frontend\ folder, open the game.html file in your editor. At the moment, your JavaScript code replaces the content of the h3 tag—your header tag—with the word Level followed by the level's value (Level 1, for example). You need to modify the h3 tag so that it also includes the number of tries:

- Remove the id attribute and its value from the h3 tag.
- Add the text Level: and then a span tag with an id attribute having the value currentLevel (id="currentLevel"). This span will now hold the current level.
- Add the text Tries: and then a span tag with an id attribute having the value tries (id="tries"). This span will display the number of tries.

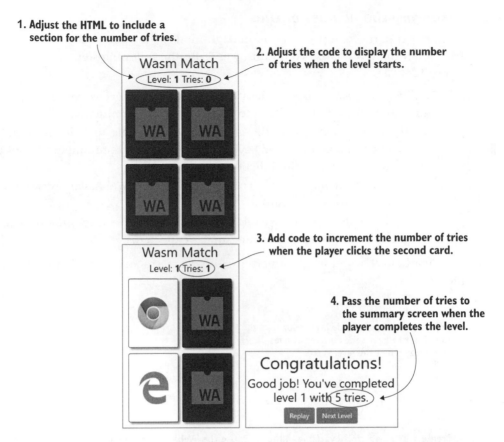

Figure 12.2 The high-level steps that will be used to adjust the game to include the number of tries

Your header tag in the game.html file should now match the code in the following snippet:

```
<header class="container-fluid">
  <h1>Wasm Match</h1>                          Removes the id attribute
  <h3>                          ⟵
    Level: <span id="currentLevel">1</span>
    Tries: <span id="tries"></span>
  </h3>
</header>
```

Now that the HTML has been adjusted, your next step is to modify the WebAssembly text format and JavaScript code to display the value for the number of tries when the level starts.

12.3   *Displaying the number of tries*

In the next part of the process, you need to modify the code to show the number of tries when the level starts. To do this, you'll use the following steps, also depicted in figure 12.3:

1 Adjust the `generateCards` JavaScript function to receive another parameter indicating the number of tries to display when the level starts.
2 In the text format, create the global `$tries` variable to hold the number of tries. Then modify the `$PlayLevel` function to pass the number of tries to the `generateCards` JavaScript function.
3 Use the WebAssembly Binary Toolkit to generate a WebAssembly module from the text format (cards.wasm).
4 Copy the generated WebAssembly file to the server for use by the browser, and then test that the changes are working as expected.

The first item that you need to modify is the `generateCards` function in the game.js file.

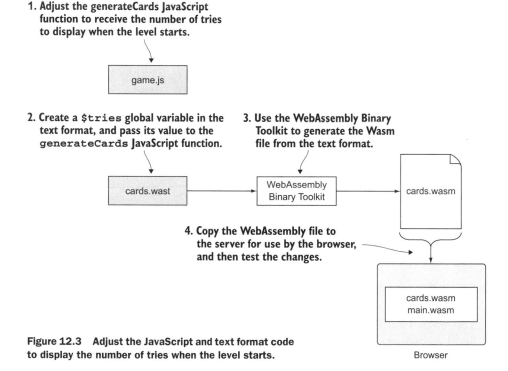

1. Adjust the generateCards JavaScript function to receive the number of tries to display when the level starts.

game.js

2. Create a `$tries` global variable in the text format, and pass its value to the `generateCards` JavaScript function.

cards.wast

3. Use the WebAssembly Binary Toolkit to generate the Wasm file from the text format.

WebAssembly Binary Toolkit

cards.wasm

4. Copy the WebAssembly file to the server for use by the browser, and then test the changes.

cards.wasm
main.wasm

Browser

Figure 12.3   Adjust the JavaScript and text format code to display the number of tries when the level starts.

12.3.1 The generateCards JavaScript function

Open the game.js file and locate the generateCards function. You need to add a fourth parameter called tries to the function, after the existing parameters. This parameter will be passed to this function by the WebAssembly module so that it can be displayed on the web page when the level starts.

Adjust the generateCards function in the game.js file to look like the code in the following listing.

Listing 12.1 The generateCards function in game.js

```
...
                                              Adds the parameter tries

function generateCards(rows, columns, level, tries) {
  document.getElementById("currentLevel").innerText = level;      Just passes
  document.getElementById("tries").innerText = tries;             the level
                                                                   value itself
  let html = "";
  for (let row = 0; row < rows; row++) {                    Add this line of code
    html += "<div>";                                        to update the number
                                                             of the tries element.
    for (let column = 0; column < columns; column++) {
      html += "<div id=\"" + getCardId(row, column)
           + "\" class=\"CardBack\" onclick=\"onClickCard("
           + row + "," + column + ");\"><span></span></div>";
    }

    html += "</div>";
  }

  document.getElementById("cardContainer").innerHTML = html;
}
...
```

As figure 12.4 shows, the next change that you need to make is to create a $tries global variable in the text format to hold the number of tries that the player makes. You then need to pass that value to the generateCards JavaScript function.

2. Create a $tries global variable in the text format, and pass its value to the generateCards JavaScript function.

cards.wast → WebAssembly Binary Toolkit → cards.wasm

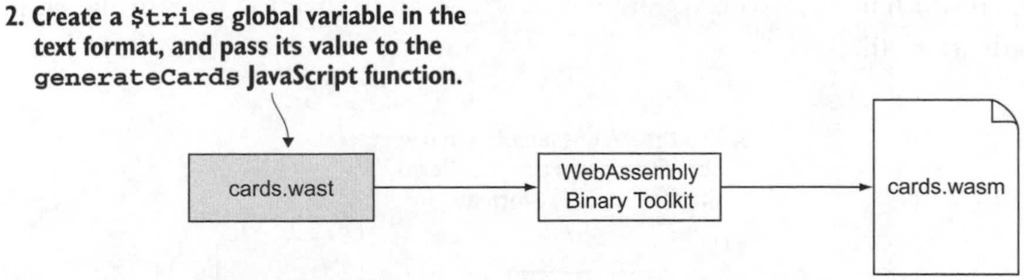

Figure 12.4 Create the $tries global variable in the text format code, and pass the value to the generateCards JavaScript function.

12.3.2 *Adjusting the text format*

In this section, you'll create a $tries global variable and pass it to the generateCards JavaScript function. Open the cards.wast file, and then navigate to the Global known section.

Add a mutable i32 global variable called $tries after the $matches_remaining global variable in your cards.wast file. The global variable should look like the following snippet:

```
(global $tries (mut i32) (i32.const 0))
```

Now that you've defined the global variable, you need to pass it as the generateCards JavaScript function's fourth parameter. Navigate to the $PlayLevel function, and put the $tries value on the stack as the fourth parameter to the $GenerateCards function call (between the $level variable and the call $GenerateCards line of code).

In your cards.wast file, the modified $PlayLevel function should now look like this:

```
(func $PlayLevel (param $level i32)
  get_local $level
  call $InitializeCards

  get_global $rows
  get_global $columns          The tries value is placed on the
  get_local $level             stack for generateCard's fourth
  get_global $tries    <────── parameter.
  call $GenerateCards
)
```

At the end of the $InitializeCards function, following the call $ShuffleArray line of code in your cards.wast file, add the following code to reset the $tries value every time a level is started:

```
get_global 6
set_global $tries
```

Once the text format code has been adjusted, figure 12.5 shows your next step, in which you'll use the WebAssembly Binary Toolkit to turn the text format code into the cards.wasm file.

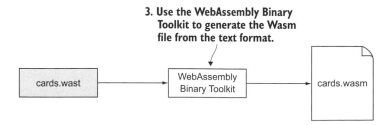

3. Use the WebAssembly Binary Toolkit to generate the Wasm file from the text format.

cards.wast → WebAssembly Binary Toolkit → cards.wasm

Figure 12.5   Use the WebAssembly Binary Toolkit to generate the cards.wasm file from the text format.

12.3.3 *Generating the Wasm file*

To compile the WebAssembly text format into a WebAssembly module using the wat2wasm online tool, go to the following website and copy the contents of your cards.wast file into the tool's top-left pane: https://webassembly.github.io/wabt/demo/wat2wasm/. Unfortunately, you'll see an error displayed in the tool's top-right pane, as figure 12.6 shows.

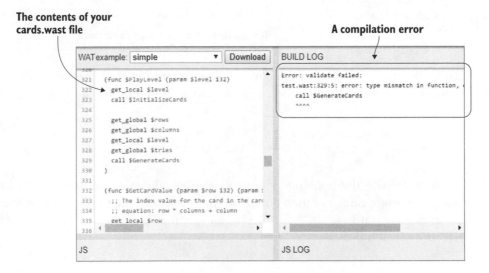

The contents of your cards.wast file

A compilation error

Figure 12.6   A compilation error with the contents of the cards.wast file

The following is the full error message:

```
test.wast:329:5: error: type mismatch in function, expected [] but got [i32]
call $GenerateCards
```

The error message is complaining about the $GenerateCards call.

Because the cards.wast file compiled without issue in chapter 11, and because the error message mentions the $GenerateCards function, the error probably has something to do with the change made in the $PlayLevel function. Look through the code for instances of the string $GenerateCards, and you'll likely discover what went wrong. In the Import known section, you have an import node for the JavaScript _GenerateCards function, but you didn't add the fourth i32 parameter to the function signature.

If you look at your $PlayLevel function, shown in the following snippet, it still thinks the $GenerateCards function needs three parameters. The result is that the top three items on the stack will be popped off and passed to the $GenerateCards function. This will leave the $rows value on the stack. When the $GenerateCards function returns, the $PlayLevel function will end with something still on the stack. The

`$PlayLevel` function isn't supposed to return anything, so having something on the stack throws the error:

```
(func $PlayLevel (param $level i32)        ◁
  get_local $level
  call $InitializeCards

  get_global $rows          ◁
  get_global $columns
  get_local $level
  get_global $tries
  call $GenerateCards       ◁
)
```

Doesn't return a value. The stack must be empty when the function ends.

Pushed onto the stack first. It will remain on the stack when $GenerateCards is called.

The top three items are popped off the stack and passed to $GenerateCards.

To fix this issue, navigate to the Import known section in your cards.wast file and add a fourth i32 parameter to the `$GenerateCards` function, as the following snippet shows:

```
(import "env" "_GenerateCards"
  (func $GenerateCards (param i32 i32 i32 i32))
)
```

Copy and paste the contents of your cards.wast file into the top-left pane of the wat2wasm tool again, and then download the new Wasm file to your frontend\ folder.

Now that you have the new cards.wasm file, figure 12.7 shows your next step, in which you test the changes.

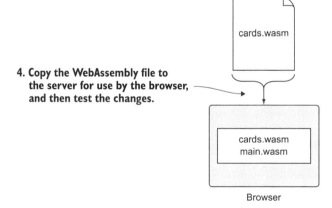

4. Copy the WebAssembly file to the server for use by the browser, and then test the changes.

cards.wasm

cards.wasm
main.wasm

Browser

Figure 12.7   Copy the cards.wasm file for use by the browser and then test your changes.

12.3.4 *Testing the changes*

When you modified the games.html file, you didn't place a value within the tries span tag; this means that if the changes don't work, the website will show only the text `Tries:` when the level starts. If the changes you made work, you'll see the text `Tries:  0` when the level starts. Open your browser and type `http://localhost:8080/game.html` into the address box to see the modified web page shown in figure 12.8.

Because a value is shown, you know that the changes you made are working.

Figure 12.8   The changes you made are working because a value of 0 is shown next to the Tries label.

Figure 12.9 shows the next step needed to implement the number of tries logic. When the player clicks the second card, the $tries global variable will be incremented and the web page updated with the new value.

3. Add code to increment the number of tries when the player clicks the second card.

Figure 12.9   The number of tries is incremented when the player clicks the second card.

12.4   Incrementing the number of tries

In the next part of the process, you need to increment the number of tries when the player clicks the second card. To do this, you'll use the following steps, which are also illustrated in figure 12.10:

1 Add a JavaScript function (`updateTriesTotal`) to the game.js file that will receive the tries value from the module and update the web page with the value.

2 Adjust the text format to import the `updateTriesTotal` JavaScript function. Have the text format increment the `$tries` value when the player clicks the second card and then pass that value to the JavaScript function.

3 Use the WebAssembly Binary Toolkit to generate a WebAssembly module from the text format (cards.wasm).

4 Copy the generated WebAssembly file to the server for use by the browser, and then test that the changes are working as expected.

Your first step is to create the `updateTriesTotal` function in the game.js file.

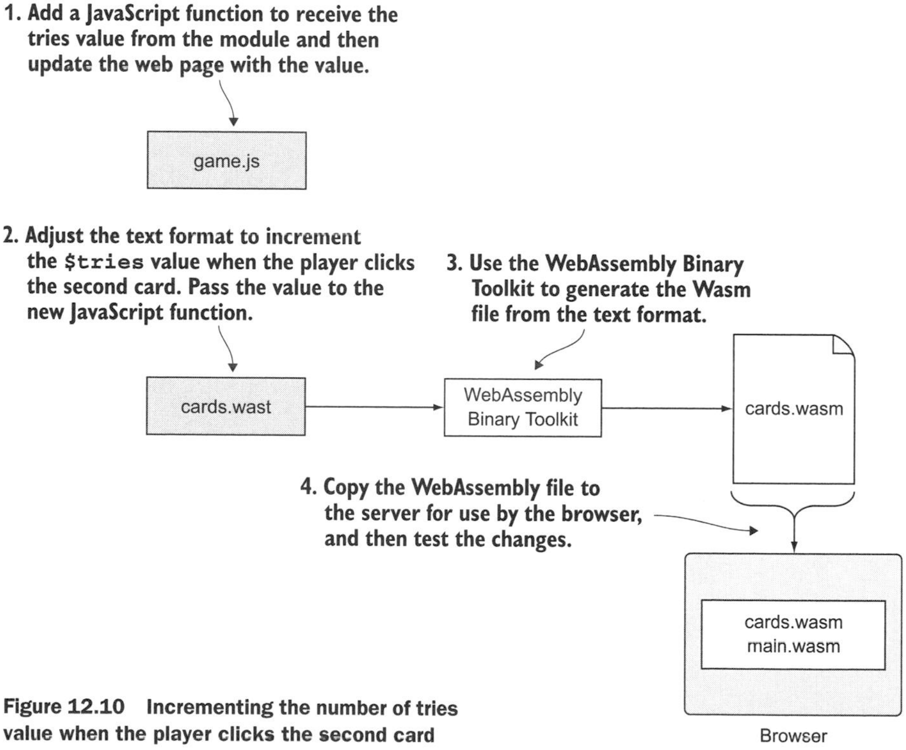

Figure 12.10   Incrementing the number of tries value when the player clicks the second card

12.4.1 *The updateTriesTotal JavaScript function*

In your game.js file, create an `updateTriesTotal` function that receives a `tries` parameter and updates the web page with the value. Place the function after the `generateCards` function, and then copy the `document.getElementById` line of code for the tries value from the `generateCards` function into the `updateTriesTotal` function.

Your `updateTriesTotal` function in the game.js file should look like the following snippet:

```
function updateTriesTotal(tries) {
  document.getElementById("tries").innerText = tries;
}
```

In the `generateCards` function of your game.js file, replace the `document.getElement-ById` line of code for the `tries` value with a call to the `updateTriesTotal` function:

```
updateTriesTotal(tries);
```

With the JavaScript modified, you can move to the next step, shown in figure 12.11, and adjust the text format code to increment the `$tries` value when the player clicks the second card. The new `$tries` value is then passed to the new JavaScript function.

**2. Adjust the text format to increment the `$tries`
value when the player clicks the second card.
Pass the value to the new JavaScript function.**

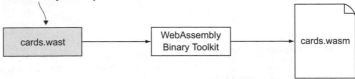

**Figure 12.11   The text format will increment the `$tries` value when the player clicks
the second card. You'll then pass the value to the new JavaScript function.**

12.4.2 *Adjusting the text format*

You need to add an `import` node for the `updateTriesTotal` JavaScript function so that you can pass the updated `$tries` value to the JavaScript code and have it displayed on the web page. In your cards.wast file, navigate to the Import known section and add an `import` node for the `$UpdateTriesTotal` function that receives one `i32` parameter. Place the `import` node after the `$GenerateCards` import node.

Your `import` node in the cards.wast file should look like the this:

```
(import "env" "_UpdateTriesTotal"
  (func $UpdateTriesTotal (param i32))
)
```

Navigate to the `$SecondCardSelectedCallback` function. This function is called after a short pause when the player clicks the second card so that they can see the card before it is either removed or flipped facedown, depending on whether the cards are a match.

After the `if` statement, increment the `$tries` global variable. Then pass the `$tries` value to the `$UpdateTriesTotal` function so that the JavaScript code updates the web page with the new value.

The code in the next listing shows the modifications made to the `$SecondCard-SelectedCallback` function in the cards.wast file. Some of the code in the function has been omitted in the listing to make it easier to focus on the changes.

Listing 12.2   The `$SecondCardSelectedCallback` function in cards.wast

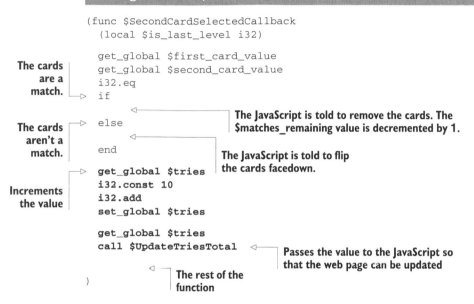

```
(func $SecondCardSelectedCallback
  (local $is_last_level i32)

  get_global $first_card_value
  get_global $second_card_value
  i32.eq
  if

  else

  end

  get_global $tries
  i32.const 10
  i32.add
  set_global $tries

  get_global $tries
  call $UpdateTriesTotal

)
```

The cards are a match.

The cards aren't a match.

Increments the value

The JavaScript is told to remove the cards. The $matches_remaining value is decremented by 1.

The JavaScript is told to flip the cards facedown.

Passes the value to the JavaScript so that the web page can be updated

The rest of the function

With the text format code modified, you can now generate the WebAssembly file from the text format, as figure 12.12 shows.

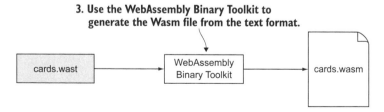

3. Use the WebAssembly Binary Toolkit to generate the Wasm file from the text format.

cards.wast → WebAssembly Binary Toolkit → cards.wasm

Figure 12.12   You'll use the WebAssembly Binary Toolkit to generate the WebAssembly file.

12.4.3 Generating the Wasm file

To compile the WebAssembly text format into a WebAssembly module using the wat2wasm online tool, go to the following website: https://webassembly.github .io/wabt/demo/wat2wasm/. Paste the contents of your cards.wast file into the top-left pane of the tool, as shown in figure 12.13. Then click the Download button to download the WebAssembly file to your frontend\ folder, and name the file cards.wasm.

Once you have your new cards.wasm file, figure 12.14 shows your next step, in which you test the changes.

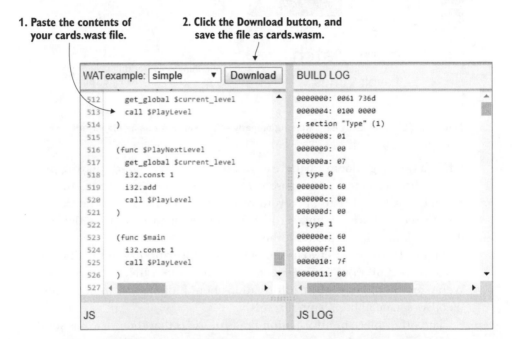

1. Paste the contents of your cards.wast file.

2. Click the Download button, and save the file as cards.wasm.

Figure 12.13   Paste the contents of your cards.wast file into the tool's top-left pane and then download the WebAssembly file, naming it cards.wasm.

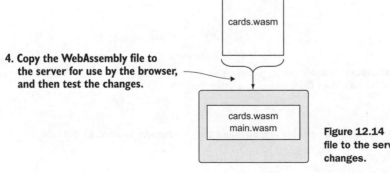

4. Copy the WebAssembly file to the server for use by the browser, and then test the changes.

Figure 12.14   Copy the cards.wasm file to the server, and test your changes.

12.4.4 *Testing the changes*

With the changes you've made to the JavaScript and text format, when you click the second card, the $tries value will be incremented by 1, and then the value will be updated on the web page. Open your browser and type `http://localhost:8080/game.html` into the address box to see that your changes are working as expected. Unfortunately, as figure 12.15 shows, something isn't working properly: your game isn't being displayed.

Something isn't working properly, so your game isn't being displayed.

Figure 12.15   Something isn't working properly—the game isn't being displayed.

When a web page doesn't behave as you'd expect—like not displaying properly in this case or not responding to mouse clicks, for example—sometimes the issue is a JavaScript error. Press F12 to open your browser's developer tools, and then view the console to see if there are any errors reported. As it turns out, as figure 12.16 shows, there's a JavaScript error about the _UpdateTriesTotal field.

Figure 12.16 gives us two useful pieces of information, with the first being the word *LinkError*. A LinkError is an error that's thrown when there's an issue instantiating a WebAssembly module. More information about LinkErrors can be found on the MDN Web Docs page at http://mng.bz/qXjx.

The other piece of information that's of use is that the error has something to do with the _UpdateTriesTotal field. _UpdateTriesTotal is the function name you gave

There's a JavaScript error about the _UpdateTriesTotal field.

Figure 12.16   A JavaScript error is logged about the _UpdateTriesTotal field.

to the `import` node to import a JavaScript function, as shown in the following snippet of the code you wrote earlier:

```
(import "env" "_UpdateTriesTotal"
  (func $UpdateTriesTotal (param i32))
)
```

Looking at the text format code, the `import` node appears to be correct. You were also able to compile the module without issue, so the problem doesn't seem to be with the module itself. If the problem isn't with the module, then you need to take a look at the JavaScript.

Open your game.js file. The `updateTriesTotal` JavaScript function shown in the following snippet has the proper signature (accepts a single parameter and doesn't return a value), so the function itself appears correct:

```
function updateTriesTotal(tries) {
  document.getElementById("tries").innerText = tries;
}
```

Because you have a LinkError, and it has to do with the cards.wasm file, take a look at the `WebAssembly.instantiateStreaming` section of code for cards.wasm. If you look at the `sideImportObject`, you'll notice that the `_UpdateTriesTotal` property hasn't been included.

In your game.js file, adjust the `sideImportObject` to have an `_UpdateTriesTotal` property for your `updateTriesTotal` function. Place the property after the `_Generate-Cards` property, as shown in the next listing.

> **Listing 12.3 The `sideImportObject` in your game.js file**

```
const sideImportObject = {
  env: {
    memory: moduleMemory,
    _malloc: mainInstance.exports._malloc,
    _free: mainInstance.exports._free,
    _SeedRandomNumberGenerator:
        mainInstance.exports._SeedRandomNumberGenerator,
    _GetRandomNumber: mainInstance.exports._GetRandomNumber,
    _GenerateCards: generateCards,
    _UpdateTriesTotal: updateTriesTotal,        ◁————┐  Passes the updateTriesTotal
    _FlipCard: flipCard,                              │  function to the module
    _RemoveCards: removeCards,
    _LevelComplete: levelComplete,
    _Pause: pause,
  }
};
```

Save the game.js file and then refresh the web page, and you should see that the Java-Script error is gone, and the page is displayed as expected.

When you click two cards, after the cards are flipped facedown or removed, you see the Tries value updated on the web page. Unfortunately, as figure 12.17 shows, something's not right because Tries is increasing in increments of 10.

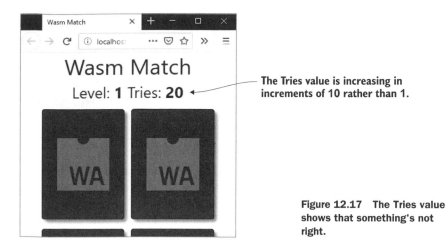

The Tries value is increasing in increments of 10 rather than 1.

Figure 12.17   The Tries value shows that something's not right.

To debug this issue, you'll step through the running text format code in the browser. If you're using the Firefox web browser, you can skip the following section and view the "Debugging in Firefox" section.

DEBUGGING IN CHROME

As figure 12.18 shows, to view the content of your WebAssembly modules in Chrome, you need to press F12 to view the developer tools and then click the Sources tab. Under the wasm section in the left pane, the modules are displayed in the order that they were loaded. In this case, the first module is main.wasm and the second is cards.wasm.

> **TIP**   Sometimes when you first open the developer tools, the wasm section isn't visible. Refresh the web page, and it should load.

When you expand the WebAssembly module, you'll see a list of each of the module's built-in functions, identified by their zero-based index. The imported functions aren't shown, but their indexes are before the built-in functions' indexes, which is why the indexes shown in figure 12.18 start at 10 and not 0.

When you click a function, you see its text format version in the right-hand pane. You can then click one of the line numbers in the right-hand pane to set a breakpoint. Once you have a breakpoint set, you just need to cause the web page to run that section of code, and the code will pause at that breakpoint, allowing you to step through the code to see what's happening.

With the text format, you can call functions and variables by their index, or you can use a variable name. Chrome's developer tools use indexes rather than variable names. This can make things confusing, so it's helpful to have the original code or text format open at the same time so that you can compare what you're looking at.

If you're using the Chrome web browser, you can skip the following section, which shows the areas of the Firefox developer tools when debugging a WebAssembly module.

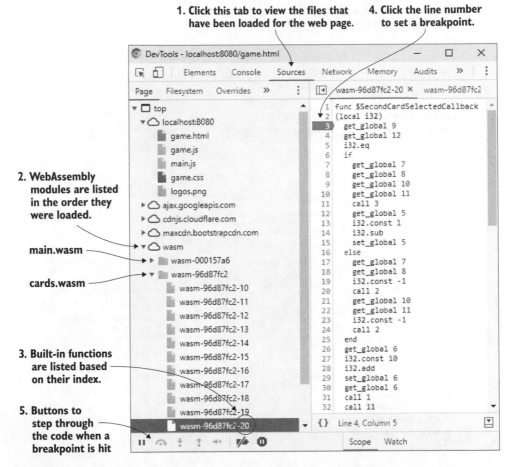

Figure 12.18 The areas of Chrome's developer tools for debugging a WebAssembly module

DEBUGGING IN FIREFOX

As figure 12.19 shows, to view the content of your WebAssembly modules in Firefox, you need to press F12 to view the developer tools and then click the Debugger tab. In the left-hand pane, click the WebAssembly file that you're interested in; the text format version of that file will be displayed in the right-hand pane.

You can then click one of the line numbers in the right-hand pane to set a breakpoint. Once you have a breakpoint set, you just need to cause the web page to run that section of code, and the code will pause at the breakpoint, letting you step through the code to see what's happening.

When looking at the function in figure 12.19, the variable names given aren't very helpful. If the code is referencing a local variable, that variable is either a parameter

Debugging a WebAssembly module using Firefox's developer tools

1. Click this tab to view the files that have been loaded for the web page.

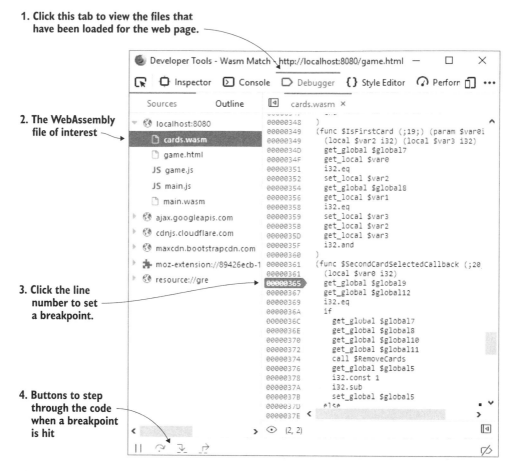

2. The WebAssembly file of interest

3. Click the line number to set a breakpoint.

4. Buttons to step through the code when a breakpoint is hit

Figure 12.19   **The areas of Firefox's developer tools for debugging a WebAssembly module**

or defined at the beginning of the function, so it's not that hard to determine what the value represents. Global variables, on the other hand, are defined at the beginning of the file, so variables like $global7 and $global12 are more difficult to understand. To make things easier, it's helpful to have the original code or text format open at the same time so that you can compare what you're looking at.

To determine the issue with the $tries value incrementing in values of 10 rather than 1, you'll debug the $SecondCardSelectedCallback function.

DEBUGGING THE $SECONDCARDSELECTEDCALLBACK FUNCTION

Before you start debugging the $SecondCardSelectedCallback function, it's helpful to know what each global variable index represents, because both Firefox and Chrome reference the global variables by their index in the function's code. Looking at your cards.wast file's Global known section, your global variables and their indexes are listed in table 12.1.

In your browser's developer tools, navigate to the $SecondCardSelectedCallback function and place a breakpoint on the first get_global line of code after the local variable declaration. For the rest of this section, we'll use the Firefox developer tools.

To trigger the breakpoint, click two cards. As figure 12.20 shows, one of the panes in the Debugger window is Scopes. If you expand the Block sections, you'll find that one of them shows you the values of the global variables for this function's scope. The first two get_global calls in the function are for global9 and global12, which, according to table 12.1, hold the first and second card values, respectively. The values for the global variables might differ from what you see in your browser's developer tools because the cards are randomly sorted. Here, the values for global9 and global12 hold 1 and 0, respectively.

Table 12.1　Global variables and their corresponding indexes

Global variable	index
$MAX_LEVEL	0
$cards	1
$current_level	2
$rows	3
$columns	4
$matches_remaining	5
$tries	6
$first_card_row	7
$first_card_column	8
$first_card_value	9
$second_card_row	10
$second_card_column	11
$second_card_value	12
$execution_paused	13

INFO　In Chrome's developer tools, the Scopes pane doesn't show the value of global variables. If you expand the *local* item in the Scopes pane, there's a *stack* item that shows you the values that are currently on the stack. Firefox doesn't show you what's on the stack. Depending on your debugging needs, you may need to use one browser's debugging tools in some cases and another browser's debugger in other cases.

The values in global9 (1, in this case) and global12 (0, in this case) are placed on the stack, and then i32.eq is called. The i32.eq call pops the top two values off the stack, compares them, and then puts a value on the stack indicating if they were equal. The if statement then pops the top item off the stack and enters the if block if the value was true. If the value was false, and if there's an else condition, the code will enter the else condition. In this case, the two global values aren't equal, so the code enters the else condition.

The code in the else condition puts the values from global7 and global8 (the first selected card's row and column values, respectively) on the stack along with a -1 value. It then calls the FlipCards JavaScript function. The -1 tells the FlipCards function to turn the card facedown. FlipCards is called again with the values from global10 and global11 to have the second card flipped facedown.

Viewing the values held by the global variables

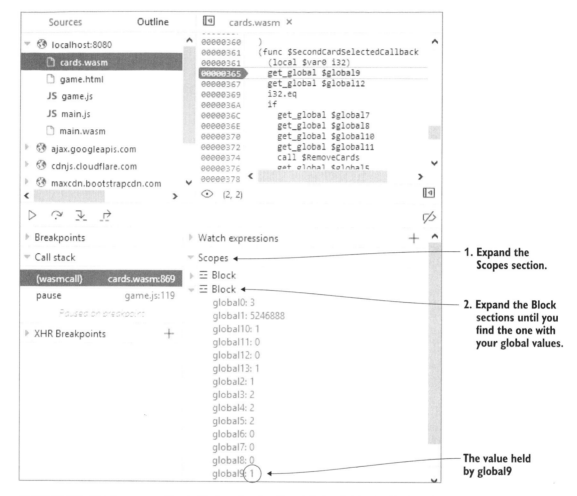

Figure 12.20   The Scopes section in Firefox showing the global variables in this function's scope

After the `if` statement, `global6` (the `$tries` counter) is placed on the stack along with the `i32.const` value of 10. The value in `global6` and the `i32.const` 10 are popped off the stack by the `i32.add` call, the two values are summed, and then the result is pushed back onto the stack, where it's then placed in the `global6` variable.

It turns out that the issue with the Tries value incrementing by 10 rather than by 1 is a typo in which `i32.const` 10 was used rather than `i32.const` 1. In your cards.wast file, locate the `$SecondCardSelectedCallback` function. Adjust the code that increments the `$tries` value so that it uses `i32.const` 1 rather than 10, as shown in the following code snippet:

```
get_global $tries
i32.const 1   ◁——— Change from 10 to 1.
i32.add
set_global $tries
```

REGENERATING THE WASM FILE

To compile the WebAssembly text format into a WebAssembly module, paste the contents of your cards.wast file into the top-left pane of the wat2wasm online tool: https://webassembly.github.io/wabt/demo/wat2wasm/. Click the Download button to download the WebAssembly file to your frontend\ folder, and name the file cards.wasm. Refresh the web page to verify that clicking two cards now increments the Tries value by 1 rather than by 10.

Now that the number of tries is updated every time the player clicks the second card, it's time to implement the last step. As figure 12.21 shows, you'll pass the number of tries to the summary screen when a level is completed.

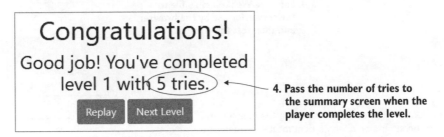

4. Pass the number of tries to the summary screen when the player completes the level.

Figure 12.21   The number of tries will be passed to the summary screen when the player completes the level.

12.5 *Updating the summary screen*

For the next part of the process, you need to update the congratulatory message to include the number of tries. To accomplish this, you'll use the following steps, also depicted in figure 12.22:

1 Update the `levelComplete` JavaScript function to accept another parameter for the number of tries. Then adjust the summary screen's text to include the number of tries.
2 Adjust the text format to pass the `$tries` value to the `levelComplete` JavaScript function.
3 Use the WebAssembly Binary Toolkit to generate a WebAssembly module from the text format (cards.wasm).
4 Copy the generated WebAssembly file to the server for use by the browser, and then test that the changes are working as expected.

Your first step is to modify the `levelComplete` function in the game.js file.

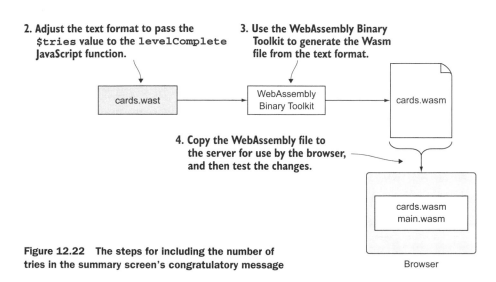

Figure 12.22   The steps for including the number of tries in the summary screen's congratulatory message

12.5.1   *The levelComplete JavaScript function*

In your game.js file, adjust the levelComplete function so that there's a tries parameter as the second parameter between the level and hasAnotherLevel parameters. Then adjust the text passed to the levelSummary DOM element so that it includes the number of tries. The levelComplete function in your game.js file should match the code in the next listing.

Listing 12.4   The levelComplete function in your game.js file

```
function levelComplete(level, tries, hasAnotherLevel) {          ◁——— Tries
  document.getElementById("levelComplete").style.display = "";        parameter
  document.getElementById("levelSummary").innerText = `Good job!      added
  ➥ You've completed level ${level} with ${tries} tries.`;      ◁———

  if (!hasAnotherLevel) {
    document.getElementById("playNextLevel").style.display = "none";
  }                                                    Text adjusted to include
}                                                       the number of tries
```

With the JavaScript adjusted, figure 12.23 shows your next step, in which you adjust the text format to pass the $tries value to levelComplete.

**2. Adjust the text format to pass the $tries value
to the levelComplete JavaScript function.**

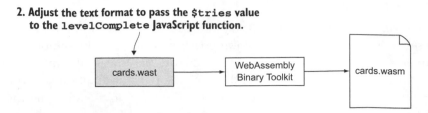

Figure 12.23   Pass the $tries value to the levelComplete JavaScript function.

12.5.2   *Adjusting the text format*

In your text format code, you need to adjust the logic so that it passes the $tries value to the levelComplete JavaScript function. Before you adjust the call to level-Complete, however, you need to adjust the import node signature for that function so that it has three i32 parameters.

In your cards.wast file, locate the import node for the levelComplete JavaScript function and add a third i32 parameter. The modified import node should now look like the code in the following snippet:

```
(import "env" "_LevelComplete"
  (func $LevelComplete (param i32 i32 i32))
)
```

The $LevelComplete function is called at the end of the $SecondCardSelected-Callback function, so navigate to that function in your cards.wast file. The $tries value is expected as the second parameter to levelComplete, so place a get_global call for the $tries value between the get_global call for the $current_level and the get_local call for the $is_last_level values.

In your cards.wast file, the call to the $LevelComplete function should now look like this:

```
get_global $current_level
get_global $tries    ⟵——— Pushes the value from $tries onto the stack
get_local $is_last_level
call $LevelComplete
```

Once the text format code has been adjusted, you can generate the WebAssembly file from the text format, as figure 12.24 shows.

**3. Use the WebAssembly Binary
Toolkit to generate the Wasm
file from the text format.**

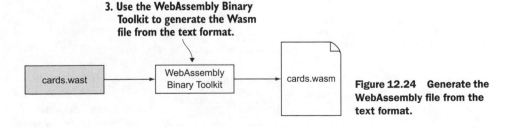

**Figure 12.24   Generate the
WebAssembly file from the
text format.**

12.5.3 *Generating the Wasm file*

To compile the contents of your cards.wast file into a WebAssembly module using the wat2wasm online tool, go to the following website: https://webassembly.github.io/wabt/demo/wat2wasm/. Paste the contents of your cards.wast file into the top-left pane of the tool, as shown in figure 12.25. Click the Download button, and download the WebAssembly file to your frontend\ folder. Give the downloaded file the name cards.wasm.

With your new cards.wasm file, you can move on to the next step, shown in figure 12.26, in which you test the changes.

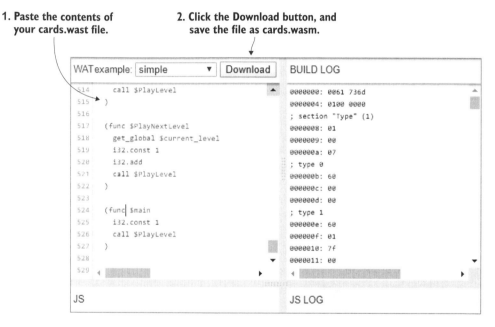

Figure 12.25   Paste the contents of your cards.wast file into the top-left pane, and then download the WebAssembly file. Give the downloaded file the name cards.wasm.

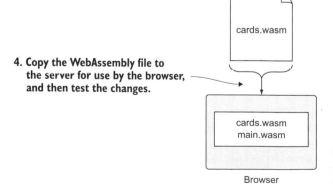

Figure 12.26   Copy the cards.wasm file to the server, and then test your changes.

12.5.4 *Testing the changes*

To test that the changes you made are working properly, open your browser and type `http://localhost:8080/game.html` into the address box. When you win the level, the summary screen will display the number of tries, as figure 12.27 shows.

The summary screen's message now includes the number of tries.

Figure 12.27   The summary screen with the number of tries included

Exercises

You can find the solutions to the exercises in appendix D.

1. In what two ways can you access a variable or call a function?
2. Something you might have noticed is that the Tries value doesn't reset when you replay the level or play the next level. Use the logging approach to locate the source of the issue.

Summary

In this chapter, you learned the following:

- Emscripten offers the `EMCC_DEBUG` environment variable and the `-v` flag to control debug mode. When enabled, debug mode causes logs and intermediate files to be output.
- Emscripten also has several `-g` flags to provide progressively more debug information in the compiled output. In addition to the increased debug information, Emscripten also outputs a text format equivalent version (.wast) of the generated binary file that can be helpful in tracking down issues.

- Logging information to the browser's console is one way to debug what's happening in your module.
- The -g4 flag can be used to instruct Emscripten to generate source maps so that your C or C++ code can be viewed in the browser. At the time of this book's writing, this feature still needs some work in the browsers.
- In some browsers, you can view the text format version of the binary file that was loaded. You can set breakpoints, step through the code, and, depending on the browser, either view the variable's value or view the values that are on the stack.
- At the moment, browser debugging features aren't uniform across browsers, so you might need to switch between browsers based on your debugging needs.

Testing—and then what?

This chapter covers

- Creating automated tests using Mocha
- Running your tests at the command line in Node.js
- Running your tests in the browsers you intend to support

There comes a point during project development when you need to test things to be sure they're working as expected. Doing manual tests at the beginning of the project might seem like it would suffice, but, as the code gets more and more involved, the testing steps need to become more detailed to ensure that there are no bugs. The problem with this is that testing becomes tedious—as focused as you try to be, it's easy to miss something, and a bug can slip through.

With manual testing, you're also dependent on your tester because tests can only be performed based on their availability. At times, testers can test only one thing at a time, and they can go only so fast before they start making mistakes.

When working with a product that needs to support multiple platforms, testing becomes even more involved because every time you make a change to your code, you need to repeat the exact same tests on every platform that you support.

Automated testing takes a bit of work up front to create the tests; but once you have them written, they have the following advantages:

- Depending on the type of test, they can run quickly.
- They can be run as often as you'd like. For example, you can run them before you check in your code to be confident that the change you just made didn't break something else in the system.
- You can run them at any time you'd like. For example, you can schedule longer-running tests to execute during the night and view the results in the morning when you return to work.
- They'll run exactly the same way every time.
- You can run the same tests on different platforms. This is helpful when writing WebAssembly modules for web browsers because you need to verify that the modules work as expected across several browsers.

Automated tests don't remove the need for manual testing but can handle the monotonous items, allowing you to focus on other areas.

You can implement several different types of testing when developing:

- *Unit tests* are written by the developer to test individual units (a function, for example) to ensure the logic is working as expected. Unit tests are designed to be fast because you write the test in such a way that the code under test doesn't depend on things like the file system, a database, or web requests.

  Unit tests are highly recommended as they help you catch bugs early in the development process. They also help you catch regression issues quickly if you make a change that impacts other areas.
- *Integration tests* verify that two or more areas are working together as expected. In this case, the tests might take longer to run because they may have external dependencies on things like a database or file system.
- There are many other types of testing, like *acceptance tests* to ensure the system satisfies the business requirements and *performance tests* to verify that the system performs adequately under a heavy load. The following website has more information on the different types of software testing available: https://en.wikipedia .org/wiki/Software_testing.

Suppose you've written a WebAssembly module, and now you'd like to create some tests to verify that the functions work as expected. You want to use a JavaScript framework that lets you run the tests from the command line so that you can verify that things are working as you write your code. But what works in one browser might not work exactly the same in another. In some cases, a feature in one browser won't exist in another, so you also want a JavaScript framework that will allow you to run your tests in a browser.

In this chapter, you'll learn how to write automated integration tests so that you can quickly and easily verify that your WebAssembly modules are working as expected. You'll also learn how to run those tests in the browsers you intend to support. This chapter gives you an overview of how you can test WebAssembly modules, but won't be a review of the different frameworks available or a deep dive of the chosen framework.

INFO There are many JavaScript testing frameworks available, with some of the more popular being Jest, Mocha, and Puppeteer, to name a few. Several frameworks are listed in the Medium article "Top Javascript Testing Frameworks in Demand for 2019" by Nwose Lotanna at http://mng.bz/py1w. For teaching purposes, we'll use Mocha in this book.

The first thing that you need to do is install the JavaScript testing framework.

13.1 Installing the JavaScript testing framework

For this chapter, you have two requirements for a testing framework:

- The tests need to run from your IDE, or command line, so that you can quickly test that everything is working as expected before you check in your code.
- The tests also need to run in a browser so that you can confirm that everything is working as expected in the browsers you intend to support.

Based on these two requirements, the framework I've chosen for this chapter is Mocha, which runs on Node.js when run from the command line and can also run in the browser. (If you'd like to learn more about Mocha, you can visit https://mochajs.org.)

If you're planning to use Mocha in only a Node.js environment, you can use the built-in Node.js `assert` module as your *assertion library*. An assertion library is a tool that verifies that the test result meets the expectation. For example, the following code snippet shows the code under test called and then the assertion library used to verify that the result is equal to 2:

```
const result = codeUnderTest.increment(1);
expect(result).to.equal(2);
```

The assertion library also does the verification in a way that's easier to read and maintain compared to a bunch of `if` statements throwing exceptions, as in the following example:

```
const result = codeUnderTest.increment(1);
if (result !== 2) {
  throw new Error(`expected 2 but received ${result}`);
}
```

In this chapter, because you'll be running the tests in both Node.js and in the browser, I chose Chai for consistency because it can be used in both locations. Chai also has several assertion styles, letting you use a style that you're most comfortable with. In this chapter, you'll use the Expect style, but you could also use the `Assert` style because it's also browser-compatible and very similar to the Node.js `assert` module. More information on the assertion styles available with Chai can be found at www.chaijs.com/api.

INFO Although Chai was chosen as the assertion library for this chapter, with Mocha, you can use any assertion library. A list of several available libraries can be found at https://mochajs.org/#assertions.

As mentioned, the Mocha framework runs on Node.js, which is convenient because Node.js was installed when you installed the Emscripten SDK. Node.js comes with a tool called *npm* (Node Package Manager), which is a package manager for the Java-Script language. It has a huge number of packages available (more than 350,000), including Mocha and Chai. (For more information, you can search npm's packages at www.npmjs.com).

In order to install Mocha locally for use with your project, you'll need a package .json file first.

13.1.1   *The package.json file*

To create a package.json file, you can use the `npm init` command. This command will prompt you with several questions about your project. If there's a default value for the question, the value will be indicated in parentheses. You can either enter your own value for the questions or press the Enter key to accept the default.

In your WebAssembly folder, create a Chapter 13\13.2 tests\ folder. Open a command prompt, navigate to your 13.2 tests\ folder, and then run the `npm init` command. Specify the following values:

- For `package name`, enter `tests`.
- For `test command`, enter `mocha`.
- For the rest of the questions, you can accept the defaults.

A package.json file will now exist in your 13.2 tests\ folder, with the contents shown in listing 13.1. The `test` property, under `scripts`, indicates which tool to run when you run the command `npm test` in your 13.2 tests\ folder. In this case, the `test` command will run Mocha.

Listing 13.1   Contents of the package.json file that was created

```
{
  "name": "tests",
  "version": "1.0.0",
  "description": "",
  "main": "tests.js",
  "scripts": {
    "test": "mocha"          ◁———  Mocha will be run when you use
  },                                the command npm test.
  "author": "",
  "license": "ISC"
}
```

Now that you have your package.json file, you can install Mocha and Chai.

13.1.2   *Installing Mocha and Chai*

To install Mocha and Chai for use with your current project, open a command prompt, navigate to your Chapter 13\13.2 tests\ folder, and then run the following command to add them as dependencies to your package.json file:

```
npm install --save-dev mocha chai
```

Once you have Mocha and Chai installed, you can move on to learning how to write and run tests.

13.2 Creating and running tests

Figure 13.1 graphically represents the following high-level steps you'll use to create and run tests for your WebAssembly modules:

1 Write the tests.
2 Run the tests from the command line.
3 Create an HTML page that loads your tests.
4 Run your tests in the browsers you intend to support.

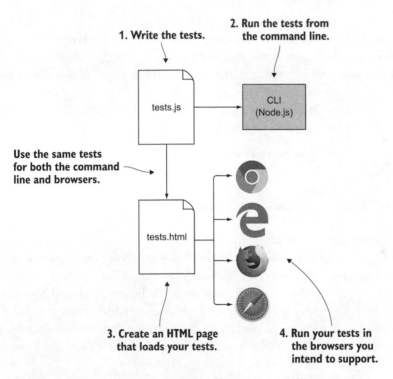

Figure 13.1 The steps for creating your tests and then running them at the command line and in the browsers you intend to support

13.2.1 Writing the tests

For this chapter, you'll write some tests for the WebAssembly module that you created in chapter 4, which validated the product name and category that were entered. In your 13.2 tests\ folder,

- Copy the validate.js and validate.wasm files from your Chapter 4\4.1 js_plumbing\ frontend\ folder.
- Create a tests.js file, and then open it with your editor.

Rather than creating two sets of tests, one for the command line and one for the browser, you'll create one set. This saves time and effort because you won't need to maintain two sets that test the exact same thing.

There are some differences between running the tests at the command line and in the browser, because Mocha uses Node.js for the former. The first thing that you need to do is write a line of code to test if Node.js is where the test is running. Add the following code snippet to your tests.js file:

```
const IS_NODE = (typeof process === 'object' &&
    typeof require === 'function');
```

Your tests need access to the Chai assertion library as well as the `Module` object created by Emscripten's JavaScript code. When running in Node.js, your tests will need to load these libraries using the `require` method within Mocha's `before` method (the `before` method will be explained in a moment). For now, you need to define the variables so that they're available to your code later.

Add the code in the following snippet after the `const IS_NODE` line in your tests.js file. You'll add code to the `else` condition in a moment:

```
if (IS_NODE) {   ◁────── Your tests are running in Node.js.
  let chai = null;
  let Module = null;
}
else {   ◁────── Your tests are running in a browser.
}
```

When you're running in a browser, the `chai` and `Module` objects will be created for you when you include those JavaScript libraries using the `Script` tag in your HTML. The `Module` object might not be ready to be interacted with if you include Emscripten's JavaScript file on the web page and then immediately tell Mocha to run. To ensure that the `Module` object is ready for use, you need to create a `Module` object that the Emscripten JavaScript will see as it's being initialized. Within the object, you define the `onRuntimeInitialized` function, which—when called by Emscripten's JavaScript—will tell the Mocha framework to run the tests.

Add the code in the following snippet within the `else` condition of the `if` statement you just created in your tests.js file:

```
var Module = {
  onRuntimeInitialized: () => { mocha.run(); }   ◁─┐
};
```
When Emscripten indicates the module is ready to be interacted with, start the tests.

Now that your tests know if they're running in Node.js or not, and the necessary global variables have been declared, it's time to start creating the tests.

THE DESCRIBE FUNCTION

Mocha uses a `describe` function to hold a collection of tests. The first parameter to the function is a meaningful name, and the second parameter is the function that executes one or more tests.

If you wish, you can have nested `describe` functions. For example, you might decide to use a nested `describe` function to group multiple tests for one of your module's functions.

Add the following `describe` function to your tests.js file after your `if` statement:

```
describe('Testing the validate.wasm module from chapter 4', () => {
});
```

With the `describe` function created to hold your collection of tests, you now need to set up a function to make sure your tests have everything they need when they run.

PRE- AND POST-HOOK FUNCTIONS

Mocha has the following pre- and post-hook functions that your tests can use to set preconditions so that they have what they need when they run, or to clean up after the tests have run:

- `before`—Runs before all the tests in the `describe` function
- `beforeEach`—Runs before each test
- `afterEach`—Runs after each test
- `after`—Runs after all the tests in the `describe` function

For your tests, you need to implement the `before` function to load in the Chai library and WebAssembly module if the tests are running in Node.js. Because the WebAssembly module's instantiation happens asynchronously, you need to define the `onRuntimeInitialized` function so that you're notified by the Emscripten JavaScript code when the module is ready for interaction.

> **INFO** If you return a `Promise` object from a Mocha function (the `before` function, for example), Mocha will wait until the promise completes before proceeding.

In your tests.js file, add the code in the following listing within your `describe` function.

Listing 13.2 before function

```
...
before(() => {            ◁─┐ Will be run before all the tests
    if (IS_NODE) {          │ in this describe function      Only do the following
        chai = require('chai');    ◁──────────────────────── if this is Node.js.
                                    ◁─────── Loads the Chai assertion library
        return new Promise((resolve) => {
            Module = require('./validate.js');    ◁─┐
            Module['onRuntimeInitialized'] = () => {  ◁─┐  Loads in Emscripten's
                resolve();   ◁─┐                           generated JavaScript
            }                  │
        });        Indicates that the              Listens for Emscripten's notification
    }              promise has completed           that the module is ready
});                successfully
```

Returns a promise — *(annotation)*

Now that everything is set up for the test, it's time to write the test itself.

THE IT FUNCTION

Mocha uses an `it` function for the tests themselves. The first parameter to the function is the name of the test, and the second parameter is a function that executes the code for the test.

The first test that you'll create will verify that the `ValidateName` function in the module returns the proper error message when an empty string is provided for the name. You'll use the Chai assertion library to verify that the message returned is the one you're expecting.

With test-driven development (TDD), you write the test before writing the code under test and watch the test fail because the feature hasn't been implemented yet. You then refactor the code so that the test passes, create the next test, and repeat the process. The test failures serve as a guide as you build out the feature.

In this case, because this is a book, the process is reversed, and implementation is performed before the tests. As a result, you want your tests to fail as a sanity check to ensure that they're testing the expected behavior when they pass. Once you run the test and verify that it fails, you can then correct the issue so that it passes. To cause this test to fail, you'll use the word `"something"` as the expected error message, but you can use any string you'd like as long as it doesn't match the one that gets returned.

Add the code in the next listing within your `describe` function and after your `before` function.

Listing 13.3   Testing the `ValidateName` function with an empty string for the name

```
...
                                          Defines the test itself
it("Pass an empty string", () => {    ◁─┘
  const errorMessagePointer = Module._malloc(256);
  const name = "";                          ◁──── Sets the name to an empty string
  const expectedMessage = "something";        ◁───────
                                                      The error message you're
  const isValid = Module.ccall('ValidateName',  ◁──    expecting; intentionally
      'number',                                        wrong so the test fails
      ['string', 'number', 'number'],
      [name, 50, errorMessagePointer]);            Calls the ValidateName
                                                   function in the module
  let errorMessage = "";
  if (isValid === 0)  {              ◁────────────────────────
    errorMessage = Module.UTF8ToString(errorMessagePointer);
  }
                                            If there was an error, reads
  Module._free(errorMessagePointer);        the error message from the
                                                   module's memory
  chai.expect(errorMessage).to.equal(expectedMessage);  ◁────
});
                                          Checks to make sure the
                                          message returned matches
                                          the one you're expecting
```

The second test that you'll create will verify that the ValidateName function returns the correct error message when the name is too long. To create this test, do the following:

- Make a copy of your first test, and paste this copy below the first one.
- Change the name of the it function to "Pass a string that's too long".
- Set the name variable's value to "Longer than 5 characters".
- Adjust the value passed for the second parameter of the ValidateName function from 50 to 5.

Your new test should now look like the code in the following listing.

Listing 13.4 Testing the ValidateName function with a name that's too long

```
...

it("Pass a string that's too long", () => {          ◁──── Adjust the name of the
  const errorMessagePointer = Module._malloc(256);          test to reflect what
  const name = "Longer than 5 characters";      ◁───        you're testing for.
  const expectedMessage = "something";
                                                  Provides a name
  const isValid = Module.ccall('ValidateName',    that's longer than
      'number',                                   5 characters
      ['string', 'number', 'number'],
      [name, 5, errorMessagePointer]);     ◁───  Tells the function that the maximum
  let errorMessage = "";                          length the string can be is 5 characters
  if (isValid === 0) {
    errorMessage = Module.UTF8ToString(errorMessagePointer);
  }

  Module._free(errorMessagePointer);

  chai.expect(errorMessage).to.equal(expectedMessage);
});
```

Congratulations! You've now written your first set of WebAssembly tests. Your next step is to run them.

13.2.2 Running the tests from the command line

Your next step is to run the tests from the command line. To run your tests, open a command prompt, navigate to your Chapter 13\13.2 tests\ folder, and then run the following command:

```
npm test tests.js
```

Figure 13.2 shows the results of the tests, which are listed with a number if they fail and a check mark if they pass. The tests that fail are also listed below the summary section showing details about why they didn't pass. In this case, all the tests failed because you intentionally provided the wrong values for the expected result.

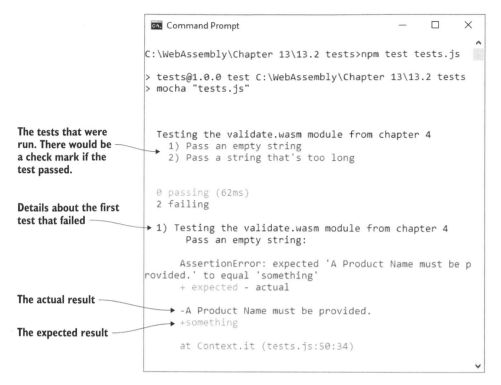

The tests that were run. There would be a check mark if the test passed.

Details about the first test that failed

The actual result

The expected result

Figure 13.2   The results of the tests at the command line. Both tests failed because you intentionally provided the wrong expected string of `'something'`.

Before you correct the tests so that they pass, you'll create an HTML page so that you can run them in a browser, too.

13.2.3 *An HTML page that loads your tests*

As figure 13.3 shows, in this section, you'll create an HTML page that will allow you to run your tests in a browser. You'll use the same tests in the browser that you used at the command line. Being able to use the same tests in both places saves effort because you don't need to maintain two sets of tests for the same thing.

In your 13.2 tests\ folder, create a tests.html file and open it with your editor.

> **INFO**   The HTML file that you're about to create was copied from Mocha's website and modified slightly. The original file can be found at https://mochajs.org/#running-mocha-in-the-browser.

When running in the browser, the Chai assertion library and WebAssembly module are loaded by including them in `Script` tags. When run in Node.js, they're loaded by using the `require` method. The areas that are changed from the Mocha HTML template are after the `Script` tag with the class `"mocha-init"`. The `Script` tags for

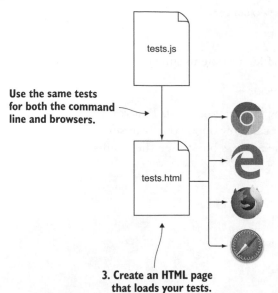

Use the same tests for both the command line and browsers.

3. Create an HTML page that loads your tests.

Figure 13.3 Your next step is to create an HTML page so that you can also run your tests in a browser.

test.array.js, test.object.js, and test.xhr.js and the class "mocha-exec" have been replaced with the Script tag for your test file tests.js and Emscripten's generated JavaScript file validate.js.

One thing to note is that your tests.js file needs to be included in the HTML before Emscripten's generated JavaScript file (validate.js). This is because you included code in your tests.js file to tell Emscripten to call the onRuntimeInitialized function when the module is ready. When that function is called, your code will have Mocha run the tests.

Add the code in the next listing to your tests.html file.

Listing 13.5 The HTML for your tests.html file

```html
<!DOCTYPE html>
<html lang="en">
  <head>
    <meta charset="utf-8" />
    <title>Mocha Tests</title>
    <meta name="viewport"
        content="width=device-width, initial-scale=1.0" />
    <link rel="stylesheet" href="https://unpkg.com/mocha/mocha.css" />
  </head>
  <body>
    <div id="mocha"></div>

    <script src="https://unpkg.com/chai/chai.js"></script>
    <script src="https://unpkg.com/mocha/mocha.js"></script>

    <script class="mocha-init">
      mocha.setup('bdd');
      mocha.checkLeaks();
    </script>

    <script src="tests.js"></script>
```

Your tests (must be included before Emscripten's generated JavaScript file)

```
    <script src="validate.js"></script>
  </body>
</html>
```

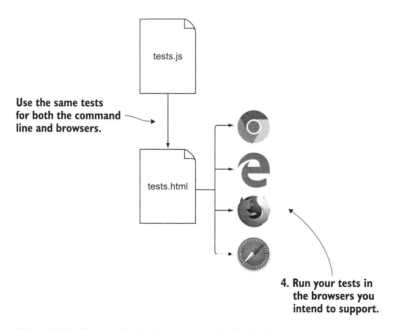 Emscripten's generated JavaScript file

Now that you have your HTML file, it's time to run your tests in a browser.

13.2.4   *Running the tests from a browser*

As figure 13.4 shows, you'll now run the same tests that you ran at the command line but this time in a browser. You can now open your browser and type `http://local-host:8080/tests.html` into the address box to see the results of your tests, as shown in figure 13.5.

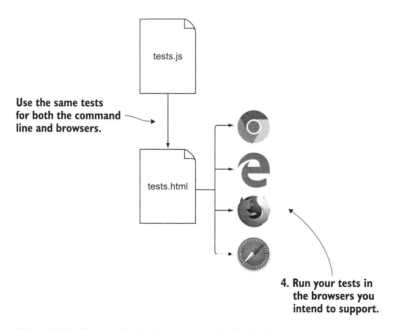

tests.js

Use the same tests for both the command line and browsers.

tests.html

4. Run your tests in the browsers you intend to support.

Figure 13.4   Your next step is to run your tests in a browser.

With your tests now running at the command line and in browsers, you can adjust them so that they pass.

13.2.5   *Making the tests pass*

Once you've verified that your tests run, you can adjust them so that they pass. Open your tests.js file, and make the following adjustments:

- In the `"Pass an empty string"` test, set the `expectedMessage` value to `"A Product Name must be provided."`
- In the `"Pass a string that's too long"` test, set the `expectedMessage` value to an empty string (`""`), and change the value passed as the second parameter to the `ValidateName` module function from 5 to 50.

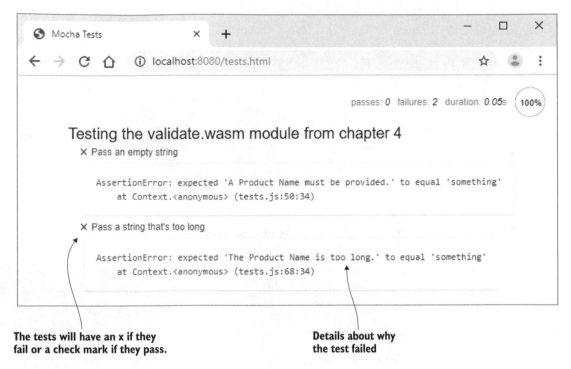

The tests will have an x if they
fail or a check mark if they pass.

Details about why
the test failed

Figure 13.5   The results of your tests running in a browser

Now you need to verify that your tests are passing. At the command prompt, navigate
to your Chapter 13\13.2 tests\ folder, and then run the following command:

```
npm test tests.js
```

The tests should pass, as figure 13.6 shows.

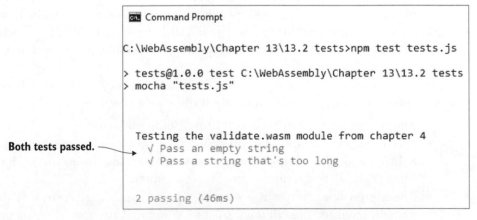

Both tests passed.

Figure 13.6   Both of your tests now pass when run at the command line.

Both tests now pass.

Figure 13.7   The results of your tests running in a browser show that the tests pass.

You can verify that your tests are passing in the browser, too, by typing `http://localhost:8080/tests.html` into the address box to see the results, as shown in figure 13.7.

13.3   *Where do you go from here?*

WebAssembly hasn't been sitting still since it entered MVP status in 2017. Since the MVP, the introduction of the `WebAssembly.instantiateStreaming` function brought faster compilation and instantiation, the ability to import or export mutable globals was added, the desktop version of the Chrome browser went live with pthread support, and improvements to the browsers continue to be made.

The WebAssembly Community Group is hard at work on features that will be added to WebAssembly to allow other programming languages to use it more easily and to open even more use cases. For a list of WebAssembly feature proposals and their current status, you can visit https://github.com/WebAssembly/proposals.

Work has also begun on a WASI specification to standardize how WebAssembly will work outside the browser. Mozilla has a good article introducing WASI: "Standardizing WASI: A system interface to run WebAssembly outside the web" by Lin Clark, at http://mng.bz/O9Pa.

Because WebAssembly will continue to improve and expand, the following are some options you can pursue to find help if you have an issue:

- Emscripten's documentation is at https://emscripten.org.
- If you find an issue with Emscripten itself, you can check to see if someone filed a bug report or knows how to work around the issue you're having at https://github.com/emscripten-core/emscripten.
- Emscripten has a very active community, with frequent releases. If there's a newer version of Emscripten available, you could try upgrading to the latest

version to see if that corrects your issue. Upgrade instructions are found in appendix A.

- The Mozilla Developer Network has good documentation on WebAssembly at https://developer.mozilla.org/en-US/docs/WebAssembly.
- Feel free to leave a comment in this book's liveBook at https://livebook .manning.com/#!/book/webassembly-in-action/welcome.
- Follow me on twitter (@Gerard_Gallant) and my blog as I continue to explore all that WebAssembly has to offer: https://cggallant.blogspot.com.

Exercises

You can find the solutions to the exercises in appendix D.

1 Which Mocha function would you use if you wanted to group several related tests together?
2 Write a test to verify that the proper error message is returned when you pass an empty string for the `categoryId` value of the `ValidateCategory` function.

Summary

In this chapter, you learned the following:

- Automated tests take a bit of time up front to write, but, once they're written, they can run fast, can be run as often as you'd like and at any time you'd like, will run exactly the same way every time, and can be run on different platforms.
- Automated tests don't remove the need for manual testing but can handle the monotonous items, letting you focus on other areas.
- Mocha is one of several JavaScript testing frameworks available and supports any assertion library. It can also run tests both at the command line and in the browser. When run from the command line, Mocha uses Node.js to run the tests.
- With Mocha, tests are grouped using a `describe` function, and the tests themselves use an `it` function.
- Mocha has several pre- and post-hook functions available (`before`, `beforeEach`, `afterEach`, and `after`) that you can use to set preconditions before the tests are run and to clean up afterward.
- When a promise is returned from Mocha's functions, Mocha waits for the promise to complete before continuing. This is helpful when you have asynchronous operations.
- If a test fails, details are given as to why it didn't pass.
- If a test passes, a check mark is shown in the output.

appendix A
Installation and tool setup

This appendix covers

- Installing Python
- Starting a local web server using Python
- Checking to see if the WebAssembly media type is configured for Python and, if not, learning how to configure it
- Downloading and installing the Emscripten SDK
- An overview of the WebAssembly Binary Toolkit

In this appendix, you'll install and set up all tools needed to follow along with the examples in this book. The main tool that you'll need is Emscripten. Originally created to transpile C and C++ code into asm.js, it has since been modified to also compile code into WebAssembly modules.

A.1   Python

You'll need to have Python installed on your system to run the Emscripten SDK installation. The minimum version of Python that's needed is 2.7.12. You can check

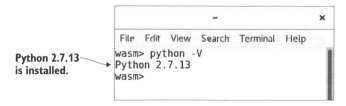

Python 2.7.13 is installed.

Figure A.1   Verifying that Python is installed

to see if Python is already installed and what version it is by running the following command in a console window:

```
python -V
```

If Python is installed, you should see a message similar to the one shown in figure A.1.

If Python isn't installed, you can download the installation from www.python .org/downloads/. If you're using a version of Linux that has APT (Advanced Package Tool), Python can also be installed by running the following command in a terminal window:

```
sudo apt install python-minimal
```

A.1.1   *Running a local web server*

Most of the examples in this book will require you to use a local *web server* because some browsers won't allow access to the file system to load other files by default. This will prevent some of the WebAssembly JavaScript API functions from working in certain browsers if the HTML file is run directly from the file system.

> **DEFINITION**   A web server is a special program that uses HTTP to pass files used by web pages to the caller (the browser, in our case).

Conveniently, Python can run a local web server, and there are two ways to start it, depending on the version of Python installed. For both approaches, you open a console window, navigate to the folder where the HTML file is located, and then run a command.

If you're using Python 2.x, the following command starts the local web server:

```
python -m SimpleHTTPServer 8080
```

For Python 3.x, the command is

```
python3  m http.server 8080
```

You'll see a message indicating that HTTP is being served on port 8080, as figure A.2 shows.

At this point, all you have to do is open a browser and set the address to `http://localhost:8080/`, followed by the HTML file name you wish to view.

Figure A.2   Python 2.x's local web server running on port 8080

The other option that's available is to use a tool called emrun that comes with Emscripten. Emrun starts Python's local web server and then launches the file specified in your default browser. The following is an example of using the `emrun` command to launch a test.html file:

```
emrun --port 8080 test.html
```

NOTE   For all three commands, the path where the files are served will be based on the directory that you're in when you start the local web server.

A.1.2   *The WebAssembly media type*

A *media type* was originally known as a MIME type. MIME stands for Multipurpose Internet Mail Extensions and is used to indicate the type of an email message's content and attachment. Browsers also use a file's media type to determine how to process the file.

Originally, WebAssembly files were passed to browsers using the `application/octet-stream` media type because a .wasm file is binary data. This has since been changed to a more formal media type: `application/wasm`.

Unfortunately, it takes time for new media types to be registered with IANA (the Internet Assigned Numbers Authority), which is responsible for standardizing media types. Because of this, not all web servers include the WebAssembly media type, so you'll need to make sure that it's defined for your web server in order for the browser to know what to do with the WebAssembly modules.

Python doesn't need to be used as the local web server if you prefer to use something else. Since it was installed for the Emscripten SDK, it's convenient if you don't have any other web servers installed on your computer. On a Mac or Linux, before trying to add the WebAssembly media type to Python's media types list, you can check and see if it already exists by running the following command:

```
grep 'wasm' /etc/mime.types
```

If the wasm extension hasn't yet been added to Python, nothing will be displayed. If the extension was already added, you should see something similar to the screenshot in figure A.3.

On a Mac or Linux, if the media type hasn't yet been added to Python, you can manually add it by editing the mime.types file. The following command uses gedit as

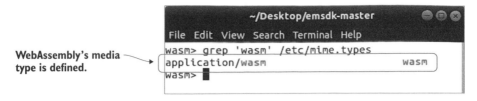

WebAssembly's media
type is defined.

Figure A.3   The WebAssembly media type is part of Python's list of media types on Ubuntu Linux.

the editor, but, if it's unavailable, most other editors can be substituted for gedit in the following command:

```
sudo gedit /etc/mime.types
```

Add the following to the list of media types and then save and close the file:

```
application/wasm    wasm
```

On Windows, to check if Python has the media type configured, you need to check the mimetypes.py file. If you open a console window and navigate to the Lib folder where Python is installed, you can check to see if the WebAssembly media type is in the file by running the following command:

```
type mimetypes.py | find "wasm"
```

If the wasm extension hasn't yet been added to Python, nothing will be displayed. If the extension was already added, you should see something similar to figure A.4.

WebAssembly's media
type is defined.

Figure A.4   The WebAssembly media type is also in Python's list of media types on Windows.

If the media type isn't in the file, then you'll need to edit the file. Open it in the editor of your choice. A search for the text types_map = { should bring you to the section of the file where you need to add the media type, as figure A.5 shows.

Add the following to the list in the types_map section and then save and close the file:

```
'.wasm'    : 'application/wasm',
```

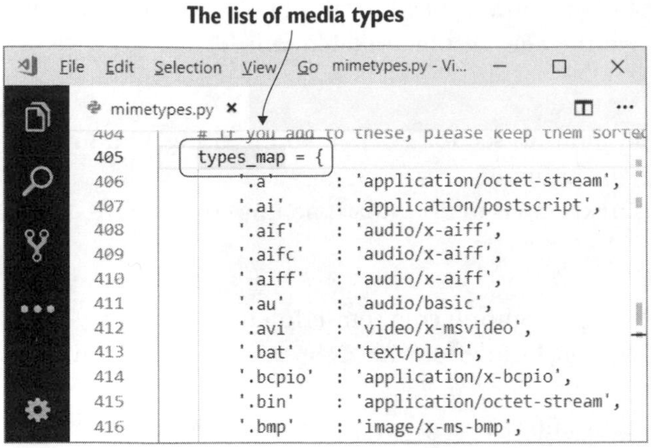

The list of media types

Figure A.5 The `types_map` section in the mimetypes.py file, opened with Visual Studio Code

A.2   *Emscripten*

At the time of this book's writing, 1.38.45 was the latest version of the Emscripten SDK. The toolkit is updated regularly, so you may have a newer version.

Before you go through the process of downloading and installing the SDK, you should check and see if it's already installed. To do this, you can run the following command in a console window to view the list of tools that were installed with the SDK:

```
emsdk list
```

If the SDK is installed, you should see a list similar to that in figure A.6. If the SDK is installed and is the version you need for this book (or higher), you can skip to section A.3.

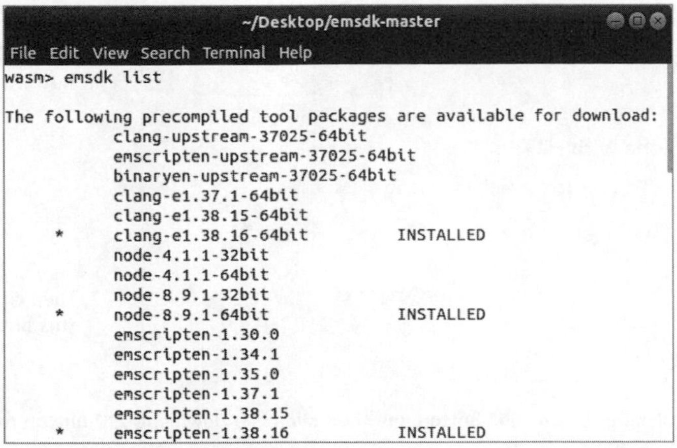

Figure A.6   The Emscripten SDK, version 1.38.16, is installed.

If the SDK is installed but isn't at the version you need for this book, run the following command to instruct the SDK to get the latest list of available tools:

```
emsdk update
```

You can skip the next section and jump to section A.2.2 if you're using Windows or section A.2.3 if you're using a Mac or Linux.

If the SDK isn't installed, your next step is to download the Emscripten SDK.

A.2.1   *Downloading the Emscripten SDK*

Navigate to the following website: https://github.com/emscripten-core/emsdk. Click the green "Clone or Download" button located on the right side of the screen, and then click the Download ZIP link from the pop up, as figure A.7 shows.

Extract the files to the desired location. Then, open a console window and navigate to the extracted emsdk-master folder.

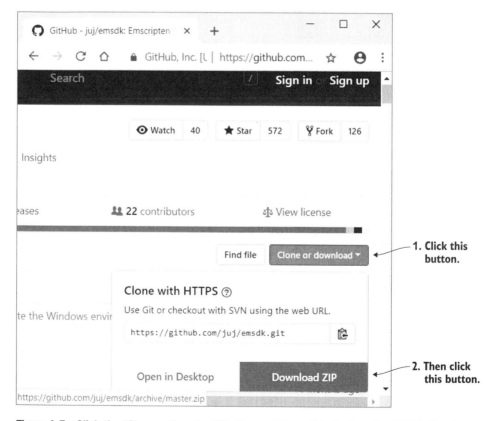

Figure A.7   Click the "Clone or Download" button and then click the Download ZIP button to download the Emscripten SDK.

A.2.2   *If you're using Windows*

The following command will download the SDK's latest tools:

```
emsdk install latest
```

Run the following command to make the latest SDK active for the current user. You may need to open the console window as an Administrator because the console will need to access the Windows registry when using the `--global` flag:

```
emsdk activate latest --global
```

> **INFO**   The `--global` flag is optional but is recommended so that the environment variables are also placed in the Windows registry. If the flag isn't used, the emsdk_env.bat file will need to be run every time a new console window is opened, to initialize the environment variables.

A.2.3   *If you're using a Mac or Linux*

Run the following command to download the SDK's latest tools:

```
./emsdk install latest
```

Run the following command to activate the latest SDK:

```
./emsdk activate latest
```

You'll need to run the following command so that the current terminal window knows the environment variables:

```
source ./emsdk_env.sh
```

The nice thing about running this command is that you no longer have to prefix the commands, like `emsdk`, with the `./` characters. Unfortunately, the environment variables are not cached, so you'll need to run the command every time you open a new terminal window. Alternatively, you can put the command into your .bash_profile or equivalent file. When adding the command to your .bash_profile or equivalent file, you'll need to adjust the path based on where the emsdk-master folder was placed.

A.2.4   *Working around installation issues*

If you run into installation issues, the following website has platform-specific instructions for installing Emscripten on Windows, Mac, and Linux that might be of some help: https://emscripten.org/docs/getting_started/downloads.html.

In some cases, downloading and installing the Emscripten SDK might not work due to conflicts with existing system libraries on your machine. In this case, you might need to build Emscripten from source. You can find the instructions for this at https://emscripten.org/docs/building_from_source/index.html.

A.3   *Node.js*

When you installed the Emscripten SDK, it installed several tools in addition to Emscripten, one of which was Node.js. Node.js is a JavaScript runtime built on the V8 engine, which is the engine that also powers the Chrome web browser. Node.js allows for JavaScript to be used as server-side code, and it also has a large number of open source packages available to help with many programming needs. It's possible to use WebAssembly modules in Node.js, so we'll include some examples for Node.js in this book.

WebAssembly support was added to Node.js in version 8, so that's the minimum version needed. Run the following command to see the list of tools that were installed when you installed the Emscripten SDK. You should see something similar to figure A.8, where the installed version of Node.js is pointed out:

```
emsdk list
```

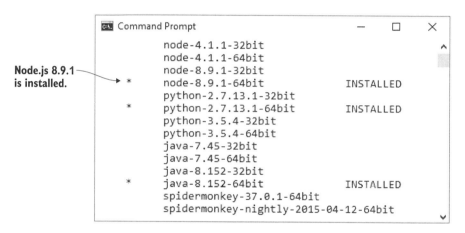

Figure A.8   Node.js version 8.9.1 was installed with the Emscripten SDK.

If the version of Node.js that was installed with the SDK isn't version 8 or higher, then you'll need to uninstall it from the SDK. To do this, at the command line, type `emsdk uninstall`, followed by the full name of the version of Node.js that's installed:

```
emsdk uninstall node-4.1.1-64bit
```

Once Node.js 4 has been uninstalled, you can use the `emsdk install` command to install Node.js version 8.9, which was listed as available for download when you ran `emsdk list`:

```
emsdk install node-8.9.1-64bit
```

A.4   *WebAssembly Binary Toolkit*

The WebAssembly Binary Toolkit contains the tools that will allow you to convert between the WebAssembly binary format and the text format. The wasm2wat tool converts from the binary format to the text format, and the wat2wasm tool does the opposite, converting from the text format to the binary format. There's even a wasm-interp tool, which allows the WebAssembly binary file to run stand-alone outside the browser, which can be useful for automated testing of the WebAssembly module.

Because browsers will use the WebAssembly text format if the user does a View Source, or for debugging if the WebAssembly module doesn't have source maps included, having a basic understanding of the text format is important. So, you'll work with the text format to build a game in chapter 11.

Source maps are files that map the current code—which may have been modified and renamed during the compilation process—to the original code so that debuggers can reconstruct the code being debugged to something closer to the original and make debugging easier.

There's no download of the WebAssembly Binary Toolkit executables. To get a copy, you need to clone the repository that's on GitHub and then build them. If you aren't comfortable using git, the toolkit's GitHub repository has some demos that you can work with using your web browser:

- The wat2wasm demo allows you to enter the text format and download the Wasm file: https://webassembly.github.io/wabt/demo/wat2wasm.
- The wasm2wat demo allows you to upload a Wasm file and view the text format: https://webassembly.github.io/wabt/demo/wasm2wat.

For the examples in this book, you'll simply use the wat2wasm-online demo, but you can download the source code for the toolkit and build the Wasm files locally if you wish. The instructions for cloning and building the toolkit can be found at https://github.com/WebAssembly/wabt.

A.5   *Bootstrap*

For a more professional-looking web page, instead of styling everything manually, you'll be using Bootstrap. Bootstrap is a popular framework for web development that includes a number of design templates to help make web development easier and faster. The examples in this book will simply point to files that are hosted on CDNs, but Bootstrap can be downloaded from the following location if you'd prefer to use a local copy: https://getbootstrap.com.

> **INFO**   A CDN, or content delivery network, is geographically distributed with a goal of serving the files needed as close to the device requesting them as possible. This distribution speeds up the process of downloading the files, which improves website load times.

Bootstrap depends on the jQuery and Popper.js libraries. jQuery is a JavaScript library that makes working with the DOM, events, animations, and Ajax simpler. Popper.js is a positioning engine that helps with the positioning of elements on a web page.

Popper.js is included with the bootstrap.bundle.js and bootstrap.bundle.min.js files, but jQuery isn't. You'll have to download jQuery, too, if you don't want to use the CDNs. You can do so from the following location: https://jquery.com/download.

appendix B
ccall, cwrap, and
direct function calls

This appendix covers

- Calling a module's function from JavaScript using the Emscripten helper functions `ccall` and `cwrap`
- Calling a module's function directly from JavaScript without using the Emscripten helper functions
- Passing arrays to a function

When working with Emscripten's generated JavaScript plumbing code, you have a few options for calling into a module. The most common approach is to use the `ccall` and `cwrap` functions, which help with memory management when passing and returning strings, for example. You can also call a module function directly.

B.1   *ccall*

The ccall function allows you to call a function in the WebAssembly module and receive the results. This function accepts four parameters:

- A string indicating the *name of the function* in the module that you want to call. When Emscripten creates a WebAssembly module, it will add an underscore character before the function name. Don't include the leading underscore character, as the ccall function will include that for you.
- The function's *return type*. The following values can be specified:
  - null if the function returns void.
  - 'number' if the function returns an integer, float, or pointer.
  - 'string' if the function returns a char*. This is optional and is here for convenience. If used, the ccall function will handle the memory management of the returned string for you.
- An array indicating the *data types of the parameters*. This array needs to have the same number of items as there are parameters to the function, and they needed to be in the same order. The values that can be specified are
  - 'number' if the parameter is an integer, float, or pointer.
  - 'string' can be used for a char* parameter. If used, the ccall function will handle the string's memory management for you. When using this approach, the value is considered temporary because the memory will be freed the moment the function returns.
  - 'array' can be used, but only for 8-bit array values.
- An array of *values to pass to the function*. Each array item corresponds to the parameters of the function and must be in the same order.

The third parameter's string and array data types are there for convenience, by handling the work of creating a pointer, copying the value into memory, and then freeing that memory once the function call has completed. These values are considered temporary and will be there only while the function is executing. If the WebAssembly module code saves the pointer for future use, it might point to invalid data.

If you want objects to live longer, then you need to allocate and deallocate the memory manually using the Emscripten functions _malloc and _free. In this case, you won't use string or array for the parameter type but rather number, because you'll be passing a pointer directly and not using Emscripten's memory management help.

If you need to pass an array that has values greater than 8-bit—for example, 32-bit integers—then you'll need to pass a pointer rather than the array type. Section B.3 shows how to pass an array to a module manually.

B.1.1   *Building a simple WebAssembly module*

To demonstrate the ccall function, you'll need a WebAssembly module. Create an Appendix B\B.1 ccall\ folder for your files. Create the file add.c in the folder, and then open it with your favorite editor. The following C code for an Add function will accept two values, add them together, and then return a result. Place this code snippet in the add.c file:

```c
#include <stdlib.h>
#include <emscripten.h>

EMSCRIPTEN_KEEPALIVE
int Add(int value1, int value2) {
  return (value1 + value2);
}
```

You'll reuse this module for the `cwrap` and direct call sections that follow. Because you'll want the `ccall` and `cwrap` functions available in the `Module` object of Emscripten's generated JavaScript, you'll need to include them as part of the `EXTRA_EXPORTED_RUNTIME_METHODS` command-line array. To compile the code into a Web-Assembly module, open a command prompt, navigate to the folder where you saved the add.c file, and then run the following command:

```
emcc add.c -o js_plumbing.js
➥ -s EXTRA_EXPORTED_RUNTIME_METHODS=['ccall','cwrap']
```

B.1.2 *Building the web page that will talk to the WebAssembly module*

You'll now need to create a simple HTML web page, and you'll also include the Java-Script to call the `Add` function in the web page rather than in a separate file. In your B.1 ccall folder, create an add.html file, and then open it with your editor. The web page will simply have a button that, when clicked, calls a JavaScript function that you'll create called `callAdd`. The JavaScript function will call the `Add` function in the module using the `ccall` Emscripten helper function and then display the result of the addition to the console window of the browser's developer tools. Add the code in the following listing to the add.html file.

Listing B.1　HTML for the add.html file

```html
<!DOCTYPE html>
<html>
  <head>
    <meta charset="utf-8"/>
  </head>
  <body>
    <input type="button" value="Add" onclick="callAdd()" />

    <script>
      function callAdd() {
        const result = Module.ccall('Add',          ⟵──── First parameter is the
            'number',                                ⟵──── name of the function
            ['number', 'number'],                    ⟵──── Return type is an
            [1, 2]);                                        integer in the module
```

Passes the values for the parameters ⟶ `[1, 2]`

```html
        console.log(`Result: ${result}`);
      }
    </script>
```

Displays the result ⟶ `console.log(`Result: ${result}`);`

Parameter types are both integers in the module

```
<script src="js_plumbing.js"></script>
    </body>
</html>
```
◁────── **The Emscripten-generated JavaScript file**

Now that you have the completed JavaScript code, you can open your browser and type `http://localhost:8080/add.html` into the address box to see the web page you just built. Open the browser's developer tools (press F12) to view the console and, then click the Add button to see the result of the call to the module's `Add` function, as figure B.1 shows.

Figure B.1   The result of calling the module's `Add` function using `ccall` and passing in the parameter values 1 and 2

B.2   cwrap

The `cwrap` function is similar to the `ccall` function. With the `cwrap` function, you only specify the first three parameters, which are identical to those of `ccall`:

- The function name
- The function's return type
- An array indicating the function's parameter types

Unlike with `ccall`, which executes the function right away, when you call the `cwrap` function, you're given a JavaScript function. In JavaScript, functions are first-class citizens and can be passed around like you would a variable, which is one of JavaScript's most powerful features. The JavaScript function can then be used to call the module's function, similar to how you'd call a normal function in which you specify the parameter values directly rather than using an array.

B.2.1   Adjusting the JavaScript code to use cwrap

To demonstrate using the `cwrap` function, create an Appendix B\B.2 cwrap\ folder for your files. Copy the add.html, js_plumbing.js, and js_plumbing.wasm files from Appendix B\B.1 ccall\ to Appendix B\B.2 cwrap\. Open the add.html file with your favorite editor so that you can adjust the `callAdd` function to now use the Emscripten `cwrap` helper function.

Because cwrap will be returning a function rather than the result of the module's Add function, the first change you'll want to make is change the const result variable to be const add. Also change Module.ccall to be Module.cwrap. Finally, remove the fourth parameter, in which you specified the values for the parameters, because the cwrap function only accepts three parameters.

Now that you've defined a function that can call the module's Add function, you need to actually call the function. To do this, you can simply call the add function that was returned from the cwrap call the same way you would any other function (you don't use an array). Replace the code in the callAdd function with the code from the following snippet:

```
function callAdd() {                          Return value of cwrap
  const add = Module.cwrap('Add',       ◁───  is a JavaScript function.
      'number',
      ['number', 'number']);                  Calls the JavaScript function,
                                              passing in the values directly
  const result = add(4, 5);             ◁───
  console.log(`Result: ${result}`);
}
```

With the changes to the callAdd function, you can open your browser and type http://localhost:8080/add.html into the address box to see the web page you just adjusted. If you click the Add button, you should see the result of the Add call in the console window of the browser's developer tools, as figure B.2 shows.

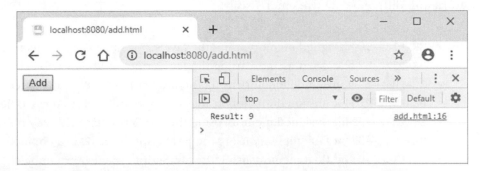

Figure B.2   The result of calling the module's Add function using cwrap and passing in the parameter values 4 and 5

B.3   Direct function calls

The Emscripten ccall and cwrap functions are typically the ones used when calling a function in a module because they help with things like memory management of strings when it's not necessary for the string to be long-lived.

It's possible to call the module's function directly, but doing so means your code will need to handle all the necessary memory management. If your code is already doing all the necessary memory management, or the calls involve only floats and integers, which don't require memory management, then this might be an approach for you to consider.

When the Emscripten compiler creates the WebAssembly module, it puts an underscore character in front of the function names. It's important to remember the following differences:

- When calling `ccall` or `cwrap`, you don't include the underscore character.
- When you call the function directly, you need to include the underscore character.

The following code snippet shows how to call the Add function in the module directly:

```
function callAdd() {
  const result = Module._Add(2, 5);    ◁─────── Calling the Add function directly. Don't
  console.log(`Result: ${result}`);             forget the leading underscore character.
}
```

B.4   *Passing an array to a module*

The `ccall` and `cwrap` functions accept an `'array'` type, but the automatic memory management is only for 8-bit values. If your function is expecting an array with integers, for example, you'll need to handle the memory management yourself by allocating enough memory for each element in the array, copying the contents of the array to the module's memory, and then freeing the memory after the call returns.

A WebAssembly module's memory is simply a typed array buffer. Emscripten provides several views that allow you to view the memory in different ways so that you can work with different data types more easily:

- HEAP8—8-bit signed memory using the JavaScript `Int8Array` object
- HEAP16—16-bit signed memory using the JavaScript `Int16Array` object
- HEAP32—32-bit signed memory using the JavaScript `Int32Array` object
- HEAPU8—8-bit unsigned memory using the JavaScript `Uint8Array` object
- HEAPU16—16-bit unsigned memory using the JavaScript `Uint16Array` object
- HEAPU32—32-bit unsigned memory using the JavaScript `Uint32Array` object
- HEAPF32—32-bit float memory using the JavaScript `Float32Array` object
- HEAPF64—64-bit float memory using the JavaScript `Float64Array` object

If you have an array of integers, for example, you'd use the HEAP32 view, which is really an `Int32Array` JavaScript object. To allocate enough memory for the array pointer, you'd call `Module._malloc`, passing in a value that's the result of multiplying the number of items in the array by the number of bytes for each item. The `Module.`HEAP32 object is the object for 32-bit integers, so you'd use the constant `Module.HEAP32`.BYTES_PER_ELEMENT, which holds a value of 4. Each heap object has a BYTES_PER_ELEMENT constant.

Once you have the memory allocated for the array pointer, you can use the HEAP32 object's `set` function. The first parameter of the `set` function is the array that's to be copied into the WebAssembly module's memory. The second parameter is an index for where the `set` function should start writing the data in the underlying array (the module's memory). In this case, because you're working with the memory's 32-bit view, each index refers to one of the groupings of 32 bits (4 bytes). As a result, you need to divide the memory address by 4. You can use standard division, but you may also see the use of the bitwise right-shift operator in some code, like the Emscripten JavaScript plumbing code. The following would be the same as a divide-by-four operation, but uses the bitwise right-shift operator `arrayPointer >> 2`.

The next listing shows how your JavaScript would pass an array of integers to a module.

> **Listing B.2   JavaScript passing an array of integers to a module**

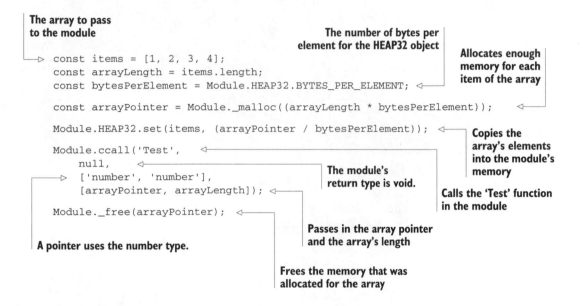

The array to pass to the module

The number of bytes per element for the HEAP32 object

Allocates enough memory for each item of the array

```
const items = [1, 2, 3, 4];
const arrayLength = items.length;
const bytesPerElement = Module.HEAP32.BYTES_PER_ELEMENT;

const arrayPointer = Module._malloc((arrayLength * bytesPerElement));

Module.HEAP32.set(items, (arrayPointer / bytesPerElement));

Module.ccall('Test',
    null,
    ['number', 'number'],
    [arrayPointer, arrayLength]);

Module._free(arrayPointer);
```

Copies the array's elements into the module's memory

The module's return type is void.

Calls the 'Test' function in the module

A pointer uses the number type.

Passes in the array pointer and the array's length

Frees the memory that was allocated for the array

appendix C
Emscripten macros

This appendix covers

- An overview of the `emscripten_run_script` series of macros
- The `EM_JS` Emscripten macro
- The `EM_ASM` series of Emscripten macros

Emscripten provides three types of macros that can help you talk to the host and can be quite helpful when you need to do things like debug issues with your code. Emscripten macros come in two flavors. The first type of macro is the `emscripten_run_script` series, and the other types are the `EM_JS` and `EM_ASM` series of macros.

C.1 emscripten_run_script macros

The `emscripten_run_script` series of macros executes JavaScript code directly using the JavaScript `eval` function. This function is a special JavaScript function that takes a string and turns it into JavaScript code. Using `eval`s in JavaScript is generally frowned upon—it's slower compared to the alternatives, but, more importantly, if the string you pass in contains user-supplied data, that data is turned into code that can do anything, which poses a serious security risk. Another disadvantage of using the `eval` function is that, depending on the browser's security settings, a browser may prevent `eval` from working altogether, and your code might not work as expected.

It's recommended that the `emscripten_run_script` series of macros never be used in production code and especially never with user-supplied data. The macros, however, could be of use for things like debugging. For example, as figure C.1 shows, if the WebAssembly module isn't working as expected, and a review of the code doesn't help narrow down the cause, you could drop in macros at specific points in your code. Perhaps you'd start by adding one macro per function to try to narrow down the source of the issue by displaying an alert or console message. You could add additional macros to further narrow down the source of the issue and then, once the issue has been identified and fixed, remove the macros.

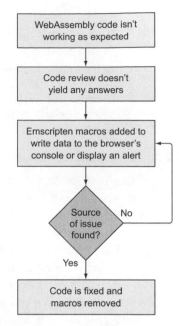

Figure C.1   Debugging a WebAssembly module using macros

The `emscripten_run_script` macro accepts a `const char*` pointer and return `void`. The following is an example of using `emscripten_run_script` to write a string to the console:

```
emscripten_run_script("console.log('The Test function')");
```

The `emscripten_run_script_int` and `emscripten_run_script_string` macros also accept a `const char*` pointer, but the difference between these two is their return types:

- `emscripten_run_script_int` returns an `integer`.
- `emscripten_run_script_string` returns a `char*` pointer.

C.2   EM_JS macros

The second type of Emscripten macro available to WebAssembly modules is the `EM_JS` and `EM_ASM` series. The `EM_JS` macro offers a way of declaring JavaScript functions right in your C or C++ code, whereas the `EM_ASM` macros allow for the use of inline JavaScript.

Although the JavaScript code for all these macros is within your C or C++ code, the Emscripten compiler actually creates the necessary JavaScript functions and calls those functions behind the scenes when the module is running. For this section, you're going to focus on the `EM_JS` macro; you'll see the `EM_ASM` macros in the next section.

The `EM_JS` macro accepts four parameters:

- The function's return type.
- The function's name.

- The arguments for the function surrounded by parentheses. If there are no arguments to pass to the function, empty opening and closing parentheses are still needed.
- The code for the body of the function.

WARNING One thing to keep in mind with this macro is that the first three parameters are written using C++ syntax. The fourth parameter, the body of the function, is JavaScript code.

C.2.1   *No parameter values*

The first EM_JS macro that you'll define is a JavaScript function that doesn't have a return value or parameters. To begin, you need to create an Appendix C\C.2.1 EM_JS\ folder for your files. Then create the file em_js.c in the folder, and open it with your favorite editor.

For the macro, you don't want a value returned from the function, so you'll specify void for the first parameter. The name of the macro will be NoReturnValueWithNo-Parameters, and because there won't be any parameters, the third parameter to the macro will simply be opening and closing parentheses. The JavaScript code itself will be a console.log call to send a message to the console window of the browser's developer tools indicating that the macro was called.

Once the macro is defined, calling the function is the same as a normal C or C++ function. You'll place the call to the function in a main function so that the code will run automatically when the module is downloaded and instantiated. Add the following code snippet to your em_js.c file:

```
#include <emscripten.h>

EM_JS(void, NoReturnValueWithNoParameters, (), {          ⟵  Declares the macro
  console.log("NoReturnValueWithNoParameters called");  ⟵┐ Logs a message to the
});                                                        │ browser's developer
                                                           │ tools console
int main() {
  NoReturnValueWithNoParameters();  ⟵┐ Calls the JavaScript
  return 0;                           │ function that you defined
}                                     │ with the EM_JS macro
```

There's no need to go through the process of creating a simple HTML page just to see the results of the macros in this appendix. Instead, you'll compile the code you create into WebAssembly modules and use the Emscripten HTML template.

To compile the code you just wrote, open a command prompt, navigate to the folder where you saved the em_js.c file, and run the following command:

```
emcc em_js.c -o em_js.html
```

INFO You may see a warning message that there were no arguments provided for the macro's function. You can ignore this warning.

Now that you've generated the WebAssembly file, you can open your browser and type `http://localhost:8080/em_js.html` into the address box to see the web page. If you open the browser's developer tools by pressing the F12 key, you should see the text `NoReturnValueWithNoParameters called` written to the console window, as figure C.2 shows.

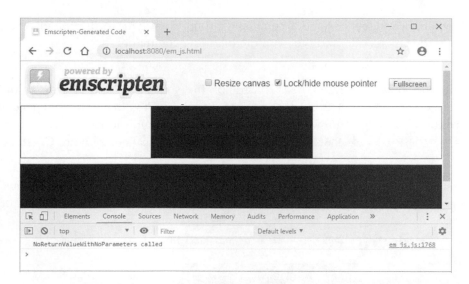

Figure C.2 The console window's output from the `NoReturnValueWithNoParameters` EM_JS macro

C.2.2 *Passing parameter values*

In this example, you'll look into how to pass values to the EM_JS macro and how the JavaScript code inside interacts with the parameters. In the Appendix C\ folder, create a new folder called C.2.2 EM_JS\, and then create a file named em_js.c in the folder. Open the file with your favorite editor.

Your macro won't return a value, so you'll set the first parameter to void. You'll give the macro the name `NoReturnValueWithIntegerAndDoubleParameters` because the function will receive an `int` and a `double` for the parameters. The JavaScript code will simply call `console.log` to display a message in the console window indicating that the function was called and what values were passed in.

You'll create a `main` function that will be called automatically when the module is instantiated. In the `main` function, you'll call your macro, passing in the `integer` and `double` the same way you would call a normal function.

Add the following code snippet to em_js.c:

```
#include <emscripten.h>

EM_JS(void, NoReturnValueWithIntegerAndDoubleParameters,
    (int integer_value, double double_value), {              ◁─────
  console.log("NoReturnValueWithIntegerAndDoubleParameters
  ➥ called...integer_value: " +
```

> The macro has two parameters, an int and a double.

```
      integer_value.toString() + "  double_value: " +
      double_value.toString());
});

int main() {
  NoReturnValueWithIntegerAndDoubleParameters(1, 5.49);
  return 0;
}
```

To compile the code, open a command prompt, navigate to the folder where you saved the em_js.c file, and then run the following command:

```
emcc em_js.c -o em_js.html
```

Now that you've generated the WebAssembly file, you can open your browser and type http://localhost:8080/em_js.html into the address box to see the web page. In the browser's console window, you should see the text indicating that the NoReturn-ValueWithIntegerAndDoubleParameters function was called, as figure C.3 shows.

Figure C.3   The console window's output from the NoReturnValueWithIntegerAndDoubleParameters macro

C.2.3   *Passing pointers as parameters*

Pointers can also be passed as parameters to the EM_JS macro. The thing to be aware of with this, however, is that WebAssembly code works only with integer and float data types. All other types, like strings, are placed in the module's linear memory. Although in your C or C++ code, it will feel like you're passing a string literal to the function, when the module is compiled, the WebAssembly code will now be pointing to a memory location and will be passing that to the function.

In the Appendix C\folder, create a new folder called C.2.3 EM_JS\and then create a file named em_js.c. Open the file with your favorite editor.

The macro won't return a value, will have the name `NoReturnValueWithString-Parameter`, and will accept `const char*` for the parameter. You'll use the `console.log` function to send a message to the browser's console window indicating that the macro was called and the string value that was received. Because the string will be in the module's memory, you'll use the Emscripten helper function `UTF8ToString` to read the string from memory. Add the following code snippet to your em_js.c file:

```
#include <emscripten.h>

EM_JS(void, NoReturnValueWithStringParameter,
    (const char* string_pointer), {          ⟵——— The macro accepts a const
                                                   char* for the parameter.
  console.log("NoReturnValueWithStringParameter called: " +
      Module.UTF8ToString(string_pointer));  ⟵——— Reads the string from
});                                                the module's memory

int main() {
  NoReturnValueWithStringParameter("Hello from WebAssembly");
  return 0;
}
```

Because the JavaScript code will need the `UTF8ToString` Emscripten helper function, you'll need to include that function in the `EXTRA_EXPORTED_RUNTIME_METHODS` array command-line flag when you build the WebAssembly module. The following is the command line to compile your code:

```
emcc em_js.c -s EXTRA_EXPORTED_RUNTIME_METHODS=['UTF8ToString']
  ➥ -o em_js.html
```

You can view the web page in your browser by typing `http://localhost:8080/em_js.html` into the address box. In the browser's console window, you should see the text indicating that the `NoReturnValueWithStringParameter` function was called and that it received the text `Hello from WebAssembly`, as figure C.4 shows.

C.2.4 *Returning a string pointer*

None of the `EM_JS` examples that you've created so far have returned a value. You can return values from the `EM_JS` functions, but, as with the parameters, you need to be mindful that WebAssembly code works only with integer and float data types. All other types, like strings, need to be placed in the module's linear memory.

In the Appendix C\folder, create a new folder called C.2.4 EM_JS\, and then create a file named em_js.c in the folder. Open the file with your editor.

For this example, you'll define a function called `StringReturnValueWithNo-Parameters` that will have no parameters and will return a `char*` pointer. In the Java-Script code, you'll define a string variable with a message to return to the module's code.

To pass the string to the module, you'll need to determine how many bytes it contains; to do this, you'll use the Emscripten helper function `lengthBytesUTF8`. Once you know how many bytes are in the string, you'll ask the module to allocate some of

Figure C.4   The console window's output indicating that the
`NoReturnValueWithStringParameter` macro was called

its memory for the string by using the standard C library function `malloc`. You'll then copy the string into the module's memory using the Emscripten helper function `stringToUTF8`. Finally, the JavaScript code will return the pointer to the string.

In the module's `main` function, you'll call the macro and receive the returned string pointer. You'll then pass the string pointer to the `printf` function so that the Emscripten plumbing code will log the message to the console window of the browser's developer tools, as well as to the text box on the web page.

> **NOTE**   The main thing to be mindful of is that, if you use `malloc`, you need to make sure to free the memory, or you'll end up with a memory leak. To release the memory, you use the standard C library function `free`.

Place the contents of the following listing into your em_js.c file.

Listing C.1   EM_JS macro that returns a string (em_js.c)

```
#include <stdlib.h>                        The string to return to the module
#include <stdio.h>
#include <emscripten.h>          Defines a macro that returns char*

EM_JS(char*, StringReturnValueWithNoParameters, (), {
  const greetings = "Hello from StringReturnValueWithNoParameters";
  const byteCount = (Module.lengthBytesUTF8(greetings) + 1);

                        Determines how many bytes are in the
                        string; adds a byte for the null terminator
```

```
const greetingsPointer = Module._malloc(byteCount);    ⟵┘  Allocates a section of the
                                                            module's memory for the string
Module.stringToUTF8(greetings, greetingsPointer, byteCount);  ⟵┐
                                                               Copies the string
return greetingsPointer;  ⟵┐  Returns the pointer to the string's   into the module's
});                            location in the module's memory       memory

int main() {
  char* greetingsPointer = StringReturnValueWithNoParameters();    ⟵

  printf("StringReturnValueWithNoParameters was called and it returned the
    ➡ following result: %s\n", greetingsPointer);    ⟵

  free(greetingsPointer);    ⟵

  return 0;      Frees the memory    Has the string displayed
}              that was allocated for  in the browser's console
               the string pointer     window on the web page
```

Calls the JavaScript function and receives the string pointer

Because the JavaScript code will be using the `lengthBytesUTF8` and `stringToUTF8` functions, you need to include them in the `EXTRA_EXPORTED_RUNTIME_METHODS` array command-line flag. The following is the command line to compile your code into a WebAssembly module:

```
emcc em_js.c -s EXTRA_EXPORTED_RUNTIME_METHODS=['lengthBytesUTF8',
➡ 'stringToUTF8'] -o em_js.html
```

> **INFO** You may see a warning message that there were no arguments provided for the macro's function. You can ignore this warning.

To view the web page in your browser, type `http://localhost:8080/em_js.html` into the address box. You should see the text indicating that the `StringReturnValueWith-NoParameters` function was called and that it received the text `Hello from String-ReturnValueWithNoParameters`, as figure C.5 shows.

C.3   EM_ASM macros

As mentioned in the previous section, the `EM_JS` macro offers a way of declaring Java-Script functions right in your C or C++ code. With the `EM_ASM` macros, you don't declare a JavaScript function explicitly. Instead, you write inline JavaScript in your C code. With both the `EM_JS` and `EM_ASM` macros, the JavaScript code isn't really within the C code. The Emscripten compiler actually creates the necessary JavaScript functions and calls them behind the scenes when the module is running.

There are several variations of the `EM_ASM` macro available:

- `EM_ASM`
- `EM_ASM_`
- `EM_ASM_INT`
- `EM_ASM_DOUBLE`

Figure C.5   The console window's output indicating that the
`StringReturnValueWithNoParameters` macro was called

The `EM_ASM` and `EM_ASM_` macros don't return a value. The `EM_ASM_INT` macro returns an `integer`, and the `EM_ASM_DOUBLE` macro returns a `double`.

C.3.1   *EM_ASM*

The `EM_ASM` macros are used to execute JavaScript that's specified within the macro's opening and closing parentheses. To demonstrate this, in your Appendix C\ folder, create a C.3.1 EM_ASM\ folder, and then create a file named em_asm.c in the folder. Open the file with your editor.

You'll create a `main` function and add a call to the `EM_ASM` macro to simply write a string to the console of the browser's developer tools. Add the following code snippet to your em_asm.c file:

```
#include <emscripten.h>

int main() {
  EM_ASM(console.log('EM_ASM macro calling'));
}
```

You can have Emscripten compile the code into a WebAssembly module and generate the HTML template by opening a command prompt, navigating to where you saved your em_asm.c file, and then running the following command:

```
emcc em_asm.c -o em_asm.html
```

You can view the web page in your browser by typing `http://localhost:8080/em_asm.html` into the address box. In the browser's console window, you should see the text `EM_ASM macro calling` written to the console, as figure C.6 shows.

Figure C.6 The console window's output from the EM_ASM function call

C.3.2 *EM_ASM_*

The EM_ASM_ macro is used to pass one or more values from the C or C++ code to the JavaScript code defined within the macro. Although the EM_ASM macro shown previously can also be used to pass values to the JavaScript code it contains, it's recommended that you use the EM_ASM_ macro instead. The advantage is that if the developer forgets to pass a value, the compiler will throw an error.

The first parameter of the EM_ASM and EM_ASM_ macros contains the JavaScript code, while any additional parameters are the values to pass from the C or C++ code to the JavaScript code within the macro:

- Each parameter passed in will be seen by the JavaScript code as $0, $1, $2, and so on.
- Each parameter passed into the macro can be only an int32_t or double, but pointers are 32-bit integers in WebAssembly, so they can be passed in as well.

Having curly braces around the JavaScript code in the EM_ASM macros isn't required, but it helps distinguish between the JavaScript code and the C or C++ values being passed in.

In your Appendix C\folder, create a C.3.2 EM_ASM_\folder, and then create a file named em_asm_.c. Open the file with your editor.

You'll now create a main function, and, within the function, you'll call the EM_ASM_ macro, passing in an integer value of 10. The JavaScript within the macro will simply write a message to the browser's console indicating the value that was received. Add the following code snippet to your em_asm_.c file:

```
#include <emscripten.h>
                                              Values are received as the
int main() {                               variables $0, $1, $2, and so on.
  EM_ASM_({
    console.log('EM_ASM_ macro received the value: ' + $0);  ◄——┘
  }, 10);    ◄——
}                          Only int32_t or double C/C++ values
                           can be passed to the JavaScript code.
```

To create the WebAssembly module, open a console window, navigate to the folder where your em_asm_.c file is located, and then run the following command:

```
emcc em_asm_.c -o em_asm_.html
```

As figure C.7 shows, if you type `http://localhost:8080/em_asm_.html` into your browser's address box, you should see the text indicating that the `EM_ASM_` macro received a value of `10`.

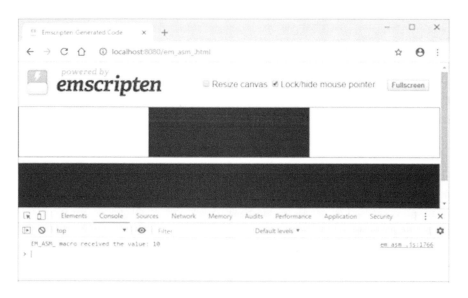

Figure C.7   The console window's output from the `EM_ASM_` function call

C.3.3   *Passing pointers as parameters*

In this example, you're going to pass a string to the JavaScript code of the `EM_ASM_` macro. The only data types that WebAssembly modules support are integers and floats. Any other type of data, like strings, needs to be represented in the module's linear memory.

Before you start, you'll need to create a C.3.3 EM_ASM_\ folder in your Appendix C\ folder and then create a file named em_asm_.c. Open the file with your editor.

You're going to create a `main` function. Within the `main` function, you'll call the `EM_ASM_` macro, passing in the string literal `"world!"`. Because WebAssembly modules support only integers and floats, when the code is compiled into a WebAssembly module, the string `"world!"` will actually be placed in the module's linear memory. A pointer will be passed to the JavaScript code within the macro, so you'll need to use the Emscripten helper function `UTF8ToString` to read the string from the module's memory before you can write the string to the console window of the browser's developer tools. Add the following code snippet to the em_asm_.c file:

```
#include <emscripten.h>

int main() {
  EM_ASM_({
    console.log('hello ' + Module.UTF8ToString($0));   ◁┘ Reads the string from
  }, "world!");   ◁─────┐ The string is being passed as a    the module's memory
}                       │ pointer to the JavaScript code.
```

Because the JavaScript code will be using the `UTF8ToString` Emscripten helper function, you'll need to include that function in the `EXTRA_EXPORTED_RUNTIME_METHODS` array command-line flag when you build the WebAssembly module. The following is the command line to compile your code:

```
emcc em_asm_.c -s EXTRA_EXPORTED_RUNTIME_METHODS=['UTF8ToString']
➥ -o em_asm_.html
```

Type `http://localhost:8080/em_asm_.html` into the address box of your browser to see your web page. As figure C.8 shows, in the browser's developer tools console window, you should see the text `hello world!`

Figure C.8   The console window's output from the `EM_ASM_` function call

C.3.4   *EM_ASM_INT and EM_ASM_DOUBLE*

There might be times when you need to call into JavaScript to request a value. To do this, you will use either the EM_ASM_INT macro, which returns an integer, or the EM_ASM_DOUBLE macro, which returns a double.

As with the EM_ASM_ macro, optional values can be passed from the C or C++ code to the JavaScript code. For this example, you'll call the EM_ASM_DOUBLE macro, passing in two double values as parameters. The JavaScript will sum the two values and return the result. You'll place the code in the main function and pass the result from the macro and Emscripten's JavaScript using the printf function.

In your Appendix C\ folder, create a C.3.4 EM_ASM_DOUBLE\ folder. Create a file named em_asm_double.c, and open it with your editor. Add the following code snippet to your file:

```
#include <stdio.h>
#include <emscripten.h>

int main() {
  double sum = EM_ASM_DOUBLE({
    return $0 + $1;
  }, 10.5, 20.1);

  printf("EM_ASM_DOUBLE result: %.2f\n", sum);
}
```

Open a command prompt, navigate to the folder where you saved the em_asm_double .c file, and then run the following command to create the WebAssembly module:

```
emcc em_asm_double.c -o em_asm_double.html
```

You can open your browser and type http://localhost:8080/em_asm_double.html into the address box to see the web page you just generated. In the browser's developer tools console window, and in the text box on the web page, you should see the text EM_ASM_DOUBLE result: 30.60 (figure C.9).

C.3.5   *Returning a string pointer*

It's possible to return a string pointer from the EM_ASM_INT macro because pointers are represented as 32-bit integers in WebAssembly. Memory management is required, however. To pass a string from the JavaScript code to the module, the string needs to be copied into the module's memory; then the pointer is returned to the module. When the module is finished with the pointer, it needs to free the memory that was allocated.

In your Appendix C\ folder, create a C.3.5 EM_ASM_INT\ folder. Create a file named em_asm_int.c, and open it with your editor.

In the EM_ASM_INT macro's JavaScript, you'll define a string and then use Emscripten's lengthBytesUTF8 helper function to determine how many bytes are in the string. Once you know this, you can ask the module to allocate the necessary amount of its linear memory to hold the string. To allocate the memory, you'll use the standard C library's malloc function. The final step is to copy the string into the

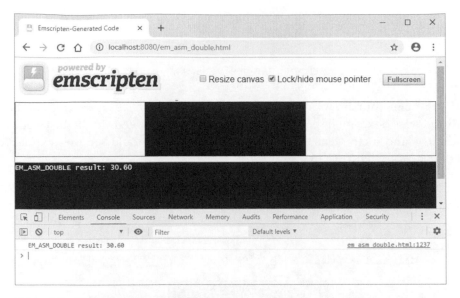

Figure C.9   The result of `30.60` from the call to the `EM_ASM_DOUBLE` macro

module's memory using the `stringToUTF8` Emscripten helper function and then return the pointer to the C code.

The code will be placed within the `main` function, and the result of the `EM_ASM_INT` macro call will be cast from an `integer` into a `char*`. The code will then pass the pointer to the `printf` function so that the Emscripten plumbing code will log the message to the console window of the browser's developer tools, as well as to the web page's text box. Before the `main` function ends, the memory that was allocated will be freed using the standard C library's `free` function:

```c
#include <stdlib.h>
#include <stdio.h>
#include <emscripten.h>

int main() {
  char* message = (char*)EM_ASM_INT({        Casts the integer
                                             return value to char*
    const greetings = "Hello from EM_ASM_INT!";
    const byteCount = (Module.lengthBytesUTF8(greetings) + 1);

    const greetingsPointer = Module._malloc(byteCount);
    Module.stringToUTF8(greetings, greetingsPointer, byteCount);

    return greetingsPointer;
  });
  printf("%s\n", message);        Displays the message in the
                                  browser's console window
  free(message);        Frees the memory that was
}                       allocated for the pointer
```

Because the JavaScript code will be using the `lengthBytesUTF8` and `stringToUTF8` functions, you'll need to include them in the `EXTRA_EXPORTED_RUNTIME_METHODS` array command-line flag. The following is the command line needed to compile your code into a WebAssembly module:

```
emcc em_asm_int.c
  -s EXTRA_EXPORTED_RUNTIME_METHODS=['lengthBytesUTF8',
  'stringToUTF8'] -o em_asm_int.html
```

If you open your browser and type `http://localhost:8080/em_asm_int.html` into the address box, you'll see the web page you just generated. In the browser's console window, and in the text box on the web page, you should see the text `Hello from EM_ASM_INT!` (figure C.10).

Figure C.10   The message from the `EM_ASM_INT` macro written to the console window of the browser's developer tools, as well as in the text box on the web page

appendix D
Exercise solutions

This appendix covers

- Solutions for the chapter exercises

D.1 Chapter 3

Chapter 3 has two exercises.

D.1.1 Exercise 1

Which four data types does WebAssembly support?

SOLUTION

32-bit integers, 64-bit integers, 32-bit floats, and 64-bit floats

D.1.2 Exercise 2

Add a `Decrement` function to the side module you created in section 3.6.1.

1. The function should have an integer return value and an integer parameter. Subtract 1 from the value received, and return the result to the calling function.
2. Compile the side module, and then adjust the JavaScript to call the function and display the result to the console.

SOLUTION

In your WebAssembly\ folder, create an Appendix D\D.1.2\source\ folder. Copy your side_module.c file from your Chapter 3\3.6 side_module\ folder into your new source\ folder.

Open the side_module.c file, and add the function shown in the following code snippet after your `Increment` function:

```
int Decrement(int value) {
  return (value - 1);
}
```

To compile your code into a WebAssembly module, navigate to your Appendix D\D.1.2\source\ folder and then run the following command:

```
emcc side_module.c -s SIDE_MODULE=2 -O1
➡ -s EXPORTED_FUNCTIONS=['_Increment','_Decrement']
➡ -o side_module.wasm
```

In your Appendix D\D.1.2\ folder, create a frontend\ folder and copy the following files into it:

- side_module.wasm from your source\ folder
- side_module.html from your Chapter 3\3.6 side_module\ folder

Open the side_module.html file in your editor. In the `then` method of the `WebAssembly.instantiateStreaming` call, change the variable value from `const` to `let`. After the `console.log` call, add a call to the `_Decrement` function, passing in a value of 4 and logging the result to the console. The `then` method's code should now look like the following snippet:

```
.then(result => {
  let value = result.instance.exports._Increment(17);
  console.log(value.toString());

  value = result.instance.exports._Decrement(4);
  console.log(value.toString());
});
```

D.2   Chapter 4

Chapter 4 has two exercises.

D.2.1   Exercise 1

What two options are there to have Emscripten make your functions visible to the JavaScript code?

SOLUTION

The two options are

- Include the `EMSCRIPTEN_KEEPALIVE` declaration with the function.
- Include the function names in the command line's `EXPORTED_FUNCTIONS` array when compiling the module.

D.2.2 Exercise 2

How do you prevent function names from being mangled when compiled so that your JavaScript code can use the expected function name?

SOLUTION

By using `extern "C"`

D.3 Chapter 5

Chapter 5 has two exercises.

D.3.1 Exercise 1

Which keyword do you need to use to define a signature in your C or C++ code so that the compiler knows the function will be available when the code is run?

SOLUTION

`extern`

D.3.2 Exercise 2

Suppose you need to include a function in Emscripten's JavaScript code that your module will call to determine if the user's device is online or not. How would you include a function called `IsOnline` that returns 1 for true and 0 (zero) for false?

SOLUTION

In your C code, you'd define the function as shown in the following snippet:

```
extern int IsOnline();
```

When needed, your C code calls the `IsOnline` function as it would any other function. For example,

```
if (IsOnline() == 1) { /* request data from the server perhaps */ }
```

To include your JavaScript function in Emscripten's generated JavaScript code, you use the `mergeInto` function. Web browsers have a navigator object that you can access to determine if the browser online or not by using the `navigator.onLine` method. If you'd like to know more about this method, you can visit the following MDN Web Docs page: http://mng.bz/yzZe.

In the JavaScript file that you'll specify at the command line (mergeinto.js), you'd have a function similar to the following:

```
mergeInto(LibraryManager.library, {
  IsOnline: function() {
    return (navigator.onLine ? 1 : 0);
  }
});
```

At the command line, you tell Emscripten to include your function in its generated JavaScript file by specifying the `--js-library` flag, followed by your JavaScript file with the `mergeInto` code, as the following example shows:

```
emcc test.cpp --js-library mergeinto.js -o test.html
```

D.4   *Chapter 6*

Chapter 6 has two exercises.

D.4.1   *Exercise 1*

Which two functions do you use to add and remove function pointers from Emscripten's backing array?

SOLUTION

addFunction and removeFunction

D.4.2   *Exercise 2*

Which instruction does WebAssembly use to call a function defined in the Table section?

SOLUTION

call_indirect

D.5   *Chapter 7*

Chapter 7 has two exercises.

D.5.1   *Exercise 1*

Using one of the dynamic linking approaches you've learned in this chapter, create the following:

1   A side module containing an Add function that accepts two integer parameters and returns the sum as an integer
2   A main module that has a main() function that calls the side module's Add function and displays the result to the console window of the browser's developer tools

SOLUTION FOR THE SIDE MODULE

In your WebAssembly\ folder, create an Appendix D\D.5.1\source\ folder. In your new source\ folder, create an add.c file, and then open it with your favorite editor.

Place the header file for Emscripten and the Add function shown in the following snippet in the add.c file:

```
#include <emscripten.h>

EMSCRIPTEN_KEEPALIVE      ◁──────────────    Alternatively, you could use
int Add(int value1, int value2) {                    the EXPORTED_FUNCTIONS
  return (value1 + value2);                           command-line array.
}
```

Next, you'll need to compile the add.c file as a WebAssembly side module. Open a command prompt, navigate to your Appendix D\D.5.1\source\ folder, and then run the following command:

```
emcc add.c -s SIDE_MODULE=2 -O1 -o add.wasm
```

The second part of the exercise is to create a main module that has a `main` function. Although the manual approach for dynamic linking using the WebAssembly JavaScript API can be used to link two modules together, that approach uses two side modules. The two approaches that use main modules are `dlopen` and `dynamicLibraries`.

In the `main` function, you need to call the side module's `Add` function and then display the result to the console window of the browser's developer tools. Let's look at the `dlopen` approach first.

SOLUTION FOR THE MAIN MODULE: DLOPEN

In your Appendix D\D.5.1\source\ folder, create a main_dlopen.cpp file. Add the code in the following listing to the file.

Listing D.1 The `dlopen` approach for the main module

```
#include <cstdlib>
#include <cstdio>                         Header file for dlopen and
#include <dlfcn.h>     ◁───────          related functions
#include <emscripten.h>
                                          Function signature for the Add
typedef int(*Add)(int,int);   ◁───────   function in the side module

void CallAdd(const char* file_name) {     ◁
  void* handle = dlopen(file_name, RTLD_NOW);        Callback function when
  if (handle == NULL) { return; }                    the add.wasm file has
                                                      finished downloading

  Add add = (Add)dlsym(handle, "Add");    ◁
  if (add == NULL) { return; }                       Gets a reference to
                                                     the Add function

  int result = add(4, 9);     ◁──────     Calls the Add function
                                          using the function pointer
  dlclose(handle);

  printf("Result of the call to the Add function: %d\n", result);   ◁
}                                                    Displays the result from
                                                     the Add function to the
int main() {                                         browser's console window
  emscripten_async_wget("add.wasm",      ◁
       "add.wasm",
       CallAdd,    ◁                          Downloads the add.wasm
       NULL);   ◁                             file to Emscripten's file
                                              system
  return 0;
}
```

Opens the side module (annotation pointing to `void* handle = dlopen(...)`)

Closes the side module (annotation pointing to `dlclose(handle);`)

Names the downloaded file add.wasm

No error callback function was provided in the event the download fails.

The CallAdd function will be called on a successful download.

Your next step is to compile the main_dlopen.cpp file as a WebAssembly main module and have Emscripten also generate the HTML template file. Open a command prompt, navigate to your Appendix D\D.5.1\source\ folder, and then run the following command:

```
emcc main_dlopen.cpp -s MAIN_MODULE=1 -o main_dlopen.html
```

If you chose to use the dynamicLibraries approach for the main module, let's take a look at how you could accomplish that.

SOLUTION FOR THE MAIN MODULE: DYNAMICLIBRARIES

The first step with this approach is to create the JavaScript file that will hold your JavaScript to update Emscripten's dynamicLibraries property of the Module object. In your Appendix D\D.5.1\source\ folder, create a pre.js file and open it with your editor. Add the code in the following snippet to your pre.js file, to have Emscripten link to the add.wasm side module during initialization:

```
Module['dynamicLibraries'] = ['add.wasm'];
```

The second step is to create the C++ for your main module. In your Appendix D\D.5.1\source\ folder, create a main_dynamicLibraries.cpp file, and open it with your editor. Add the code in the following listing to your main_dynamicLibraries.cpp file.

> **Listing D.2 The dynamicLibraries approach for the main module**

```
#include <cstdlib>
#include <cstdio>
#include <emscripten.h>

#ifdef __cplusplus
extern "C" {                           So the compiler knows the
#endif                                 function will be available
                                       when the code is run
extern int Add(int value1, int value2);  ◁─┘

int main() {
  int result = Add(24, 76);
  printf("Result of the call to the Add function: %d\n", result); ◁──
                                       Displays the results in the
  return 0;                            browser's console window
}

#ifdef __cplusplus
}
#endif
```

Calls the Add function → `int result = Add(24, 76);`

Your final step is to compile the main_dynamicLibraries.cpp file as a WebAssembly main module and have Emscripten also generate the HTML template file. Open a command prompt, navigate to your Appendix D\D.5.1\source\ folder, and then run the following command:

```
emcc main_dynamicLibraries.cpp -s MAIN_MODULE=1
➥ --pre-js pre.js -o main_dynamicLibraries.html
```

D.5.2 Exercise 2

Which dynamic linking approach would you use if you needed to call a function in the side module, but that function had the same name as a function in your main module?

SOLUTION

The dlopen approach

D.6 *Chapter 8*

Chapter 8 has two exercises.

D.6.1 *Exercise 1*

Suppose you have a side module called process_fulfillment.wasm: how would you create a new instance of Emscripten's `Module` object and tell it to dynamically link to this side module?

SOLUTION

```
const fulfillmentModule = new Module({      ◁─── Creates a new
  dynamicLibraries:                               WebAssembly instance
      ['process_fulfillment.wasm']      ◁──        of the main module
});
```

Creates a new WebAssembly instance of the main module

Tells Emscripten that it needs to link to the process_fulfillment side module

D.6.2 *Exercise 2*

What flag do you need to pass to Emscripten when compiling a WebAssembly main module in order to have the `Module` object wrapped in a function in Emscripten's generated JavaScript file?

SOLUTION

`-s MODULARIZE=1`

D.7 *Chapter 9*

Chapter 9 has two exercises.

D.7.1 *Exercise 1*

If you wanted to use a C++17 feature, what flag would you use when compiling your WebAssembly module, to tell Clang to use that standard?

SOLUTION

`-std=c++17`

D.7.2 *Exercise 2*

Test adjusting the calculate_primes logic from section 9.4 to use three threads rather than four to see how the calculation duration is impacted. Test using five threads, and place the main thread's calculation into a pthread to see if moving all the calculations off the main thread impacts the calculation duration.

SOLUTION FOR THREE THREADS

In your WebAssembly\ folder, create the Appendix D\D.7.2\source\ folder. Copy the calculate_primes.cpp file from your Chapter 9\9.4 pthreads\source\ folder to your new source\ folder, and rename it calculate_primes_three_pthreads.cpp.

Open calculate_primes_three_pthreads.cpp with your favorite editor. Make the following modifications to the main function:

- The `thread_ids` array will now hold three values.
- The `args` array will now hold four values.
- Adjust the `args_start` initial value to be 250000 (one quarter of the total 1,000,000 range).
- The `pthread_create` loop needs to loop while i is less than 3.
- Within the `pthread_create` loop, sets the `args[args_index].end` value to `args_start + 249999`. The `args_start` value at the end of the loop needs to be incremented by 250000.
- Adjust the `FindPrimes` call for the main thread so that the end value (second parameter) is 249999.
- The `pthread_join` loop now needs to loop while j is less than 3.
- Finally, the loop that outputs the prime numbers that were found needs to loop while k is less than 4.

Your main function should now look similar to the code in the next listing.

Listing D.3   The `main` function of calculate_primes_three_pthreads.cpp

```
...

int main() {
  int start = 3, end = 1000000;
  printf("Prime numbers between %d and %d:\n", start, end);

  std::chrono::high_resolution_clock::time_point duration_start =
      std::chrono::high_resolution_clock::now();

  pthread_t thread_ids[3];          ⟵——— Reduced to 3
  struct thread_args args[4];       ⟵——— Reduced to 4

  int args_index = 1;                        ⎤ The first thread's range
  int args_start = 250000;          ⟵——————⎦ will start at 250,000.

  for (int i = 0; i < 3; i++) {    ⟵——— Reduced to 3
    args[args_index].start = args_start;
    args[args_index].end = (args_start + 249999);  ⟵——┐
                                                       │ The end of the range is
    if (pthread_create(&thread_ids[i], NULL, thread_func,    now 249,999 after the
        &args[args_index])) {                                args_start value.
      perror("Thread create failed");
      return 1;
    }

    args_index += 1;
    args_start += 250000;   ⟵——— Increments by 250,000
  }

  FindPrimes(3, 249999, args[0].primes_found);   ⟵————┐
                                                       │ Increases the end
  for (int j = 0; j < 3; j++) {   ⟵——— Reduced to 3      value to 249,999
    pthread_join(thread_ids[j], NULL);
  }

  std::chrono::high_resolution_clock::time_point duration_end =
      std::chrono::high_resolution_clock::now();
```

```
std::chrono::duration<double, std::milli> duration =
    (duration_end - duration_start);

printf("FindPrimes took %f milliseconds to execute\n", duration.count());

printf("The values found:\n");
for (int k = 0; k < 4; k++) {        <———— Reduced to 4
  for(int n : args[k].primes_found) {
    printf("%d ", n);
  }
}
printf("\n");

return 0;
}
```

Your next step is to compile the calculate_primes_three_pthreads.cpp file and have Emscripten also generate the HTML template file. Open a command prompt, navigate to your Appendix D\D.7.2\source\ folder, and then run the following command:

```
emcc calculate_primes_three_pthreads.cpp -O1 -std=c++11
➡ -s USE_PTHREADS=1 -s PTHREAD_POOL_SIZE=3
➡ -o three_pthreads.html
```

A summary comparing these results with those from chapter 9 and the five threads solution is included after the five threads solution.

SOLUTION FOR FIVE THREADS

In your Appendix D\D.7.2\source\ folder, make a copy of the calculate_primes_three_pthreads.cpp file, and name it calculate_primes_five_pthreads.cpp. Open the file with your favorite editor, and make the following modifications to the main function:

- The start value will now be 0.
- The thread_ids and args array will both hold five values.
- Delete the int args_index = 1 line of code, and then adjust the args_start initial value to be 0.
- The pthread_create loop needs to loop while i is less than 5.
- Within the pthread_create loop
  - Set the args[args_index].end value to args_start + 199999.
  - The args_start value at the end of the loop needs to be incremented by 200000.
  - Delete the args_index += 1 line of code at the end of the loop. In the args[args_index] lines of code in the loop, replace args_index with i.
- Remove the FindPrimes call from the main thread (just before the pthread_join loop).
- The pthread_join loop needs to loop while j is less than 5.
- Finally, the loop that outputs the prime numbers that were found needs to loop while k is less than 5.

Your main function should now look similar to the code in the next listing.

Listing D.4   The main function of calculate_primes_five_pthreads.cpp

```
...
int main() {
  int start = 0, end = 1000000;   ⟵——— Set this to 0.
  printf("Prime numbers between %d and %d:\n", start, end);

  std::chrono::high_resolution_clock::time_point duration_start =
      std::chrono::high_resolution_clock::now();

  pthread_t thread_ids[5];   ⟵——— Set this to 5.
  struct thread_args args[5];

  int args_start = 0;   ⟵——— The first thread's range will start at 0.

  for (int i = 0; i < 5; i++) {   ⟵——— Loops while less than 5
    args[i].start = args_start;
    args[i].end = (args_start + 199999);   ⟵———————————————————┐

    if (pthread_create(&thread_ids[i], NULL, thread_func, &args[i])) {
      perror("Thread create failed");
      return 1;                             The end of the range is now 199,999
    }                                       after the args_start value.

    args_start += 200000;   ⟵——— Increments by 200,000
  }

  for (int j = 0; j < 5; j++) {   ⟵——— Set this to 5.
    pthread_join(thread_ids[j], NULL);
  }

  std::chrono::high_resolution_clock::time_point duration_end =
      std::chrono::high_resolution_clock::now();

  std::chrono::duration<double, std::milli> duration =
      (duration_end - duration_start);

  printf("FindPrimes took %f milliseconds to execute\n", duration.count());

  printf("The values found:\n");
  for (int k = 0; k < 5; k++) {   ⟵——— Set this to 5.
    for(int n : args[k].primes_found) {
      printf("%d ", n);
    }
  }
  printf("\n");

  return 0;
}
```

Your next step is to compile the calculate_primes_five_pthreads.cpp file and have Emscripten also generate the HTML template file.

Open a command prompt, navigate to your Appendix D\D.7.2\source\ folder, and then run the following command:

```
emcc calculate_primes_five_pthreads.cpp -O1 -std=c++11
 -s USE_PTHREADS=1 -s PTHREAD_POOL_SIZE=5
 -o five_pthreads.html
```

SUMMARY

The following table breaks down the results of performing the calculations using different numbers of threads. The tests were run 10 times each and the durations averaged out:

- Four pthreads and calculations also being performed on the main thread (chapter 9)
- Three pthreads and calculations also being performed on the main thread ("Solution for three threads")
- Five pthreads with no calculations on the main thread

Number of threads	Firefox (in milliseconds)	Chrome (in milliseconds)
4 pthreads + main thread	57.4	40.87
3 pthreads + main thread	61.7	42.11
5 pthreads (no processing on the main thread)	52.2	36.06

D.8   *Chapter 10*

Chapter 10 has three exercises.

D.8.1   *Exercise 1*

Which Node.js function do you need to call in order to load Emscripten's generated JavaScript file?

SOLUTION

require

D.8.2   *Exercise 2*

What Emscripten Module property do you need to implement in order to be informed of when the WebAssembly module is ready to be interacted with?

SOLUTION

onRuntimeInitialized

D.8.3   *Exercise 3*

How would you modify the index.js file from chapter 8 so that the dynamic linking logic works in Node.js?

SOLUTION

In your WebAssembly\ folder, create an Appendix D\D.8.3\backend\ folder, and then complete the following steps:

- Copy all the files except index.html from your Chapter 8\8.1 EmDynamicLibraries\frontend\ folder to your newly created backend\ folder.
- Open the index.js file with your favorite editor.

Because index.js can be called by either the Edit Product or the Place Order web page, you'll need to adjust the initialProductData object to have a Boolean flag (isProduct) indicating which form's data needs to be validated. You'll also need to add two new properties for the Place Order form's values (productId and quantity). The name of the object itself will need to be changed to better reflect its purpose.

Adjust the initialProductData in your index.js file to match the code in the following snippet:

```
const clientData = {           Renamed from
                               initialProductData
  isProduct: true,             Flag to indicate if the validation
  name: "Women's Mid Rise Skinny Jeans",   is for the Edit Product or Place
  categoryId: "100",           Order web page
  productId: "301",
  quantity: "10",
};           The Place Order form's     The Place Order form's
             quantity entered           selected product Id
```

Because the server-side code will be called to validate only one web page at a time, you don't need both the productModule and orderModule global variables. Rename the productModule variable to validationModule and then delete the orderModule line of code. Do a search of the code, and change all instances of productModule and orderModule to use validationModule.

Your next step is to have the Emscripten-generated JavaScript file (validate_core.js) loaded. To do this, add the require function call shown in the following snippet before the initializePage function in your index.js file:

```
const Module = require('./validate_core.js');
```

The validate_core WebAssembly module has been generated using the MODULARIZE=1 command-line flag. By using this flag, the Emscripten-generated JavaScript code doesn't run as soon as you load it. The code will run only once you've created an instance of the Module object. Because the code won't run as soon as you load it, you can't implement the Module['onRuntimeInitialized'] function as the starting point for your code in this case.

What you'll do instead is replace the contents of the initializePage function with the creation of the validationModule instance based on what the clientData object indicates needs to be validated. When you create an instance of the Module object, you'll specify the onRuntimeInitialized function at that point.

Adjust your `initializePage` function in your index.js file to match the code in the following snippet:

```
function initializePage() {
  const moduleName = (clientData.isProduct ?
      'validate_product.wasm' : 'validate_order.wasm');

  validationModule = new Module({
    dynamicLibraries: [moduleName],
    onRuntimeInitialized: runtimeInitialized,
  });
}
```

Determines which file will need to be linked to

Creates a new Module instance linking to the module with the validation logic you need

Calls runtimeInitialized once the module has been loaded

After your `initializePage` function, create the `runtimeInitialized` function that will call the `validateName` and `validateCategory` functions that are currently in the `onClickSaveProduct` function if you're validating the Edit Product web page data. Otherwise, the function will call the `validateProduct` and `validateQuantity` functions that are currently in the `onClickAddToCart` function if you're validating the Place Order form's web page data.

Add the code in the next listing to your index.js file after your `initializePage` function.

Listing D.5 The `runtimeInitialized` function in your index.js file

```
...
function runtimeInitialized() {
  if (clientData.isProduct) {
    if (validateName(clientData.name) &&
        validateCategory(clientData.categoryId)) {

    }
  }
  else {
    if (validateProduct(clientData.productId) &&
        validateQuantity(clientData.quantity)) {

    }
  }
}
...
```

The Edit Product web page data needs to be validated.

There were no issues. The data can be saved.

The Place Order web page data needs to be validated.

There were no issues. The data can be saved.

Your next step is to delete the following UI-specific functions from the index.js file:

- `switchForm`
- `setActiveNavLink`
- `setFormTitle`
- `showElement`
- `getSelectedDropdownId`
- `onClickSaveProduct`
- `onClickAddToCart`

When the Emscripten-generated JavaScript file was created in chapter 8, you had it include the `UpdateHostAboutError` function, which will read the error message from the module's memory and then call the `setErrorMessage` function in this file. Because the `UpdateHostAboutError` function is part of the JavaScript loaded by the `require` function call, its scope doesn't let it access the `setErrorMessage` function in this file. To let the `UpdateHostAboutError` function have access to the `setErrorMessage` function, you'll need to adjust the `setErrorMessage` function so that it's part of the `global` object. You also need to adjust the contents of the file to use `console.log` to output the error message.

Update the `setErrorMessage` function in your index.js file so that it matches the code in the following snippet:

```
global.setErrorMessage = function(error) { console.log(error); }
```

The final modification needed to the index.js file is to add a call to the `initializePage` function at the end of the file to have the validation logic start. Add the following snippet to the end of your index.js file:

```
initializePage();
```

VIEWING THE RESULTS

At the moment, the content of your `clientData` contains only valid data, so running the code right now won't show any validation errors. You can test the validation logic for the quantity, for example, by changing the `isProduct` flag to `false` and setting the quantity to `"0"` (zero).

To run your JavaScript file in Node.js, open a command prompt, navigate to your Appendix D\D.8.3\backend\ folder, and then run the following command:

```
node index.js
```

You should see the validation message `Please enter a valid quantity`.

D.9   *Chapter 11*

Chapter 11 has two exercises.

D.9.1   *Exercise 1*

When using the WebAssembly Binary Toolkit to create a WebAssembly module, which s-expression nodes have to appear before the `table`, `memory`, `global`, and `func` s-expressions?

SOLUTION

If included, the `import` s-expression nodes must appear before the `table`, `memory`, `global`, and `func` s-expressions.

D.9.2 *Exercise 2*

Try adjusting the InitializeRowsAndColumns function in the text format code so that it now supports six levels rather than three:

- Level 4 should have 3 rows and 4 columns.
- Level 5 should have 4 rows and 4 columns.
- Level 6 should have 4 rows and 5 columns.

SOLUTION

In your WebAssembly\ folder, create an Appendix D\D.9.2\source\ folder, and then copy in the cards.wast file from your Chapter 11\source\ folder. Open the cards.wast file.

In the $InitializeRowsAndColumns function, after the third if statement, add the code shown in the next listing.

Listing D.6   Additional code for the $InitializeRowsAndColumns function

```
...
(func $InitializeRowsAndColumns (param $level i32)
                                                       If statements for levels 1, 2,
  get_local $level   ◁——— If level 4 was requested    and 3 are here but not shown.
  i32.const 4
  i32.eq
  if
    i32.const 3
    set_global $rows   ◁——— Sets the rows to 3

    i32.const 4
    set_global $columns   ◁——— Sets the columns to 4
  end

  get_local $level   ◁——— If level 5 was requested
  i32.const 5
  i32.eq
  if
    i32.const 4
    set_global $rows   ◁——— Sets the rows to 4

    i32.const 4
    set_global $columns   ◁——— Sets the columns to 4
  end

  get_local $level   ◁——— If level 6 was requested
  i32.const 6
  i32.eq
  if
    i32.const 4
    set_global $rows   ◁——— Sets the rows to 4

    i32.const 5
    set_global $columns   ◁——— Sets the columns to 5
  end
)
...
```

To continue past level 3, one more change is needed. You need to adjust the $MAX _LEVEL global variable to now hold i32.const 6, as the following snippet shows:

```
(global $MAX_LEVEL i32 (i32.const 6))
```

To compile the WebAssembly text format into a WebAssembly module using the wat2wasm online tool, go to the following website: https://webassembly.github .io/wabt/demo/wat2wasm/. Replace the text in the top-left pane of the tool with the contents of your cards.wast file, and then download the WebAssembly module to your Appendix D\D.9.2\source\ folder. Name the file cards.wasm.

Create an Appendix D\D.9.2\frontend\ folder, and copy the cards.wasm file that you just downloaded into this folder. Copy all the files except cards.wasm from your Chapter 11\frontend\ folder to your Appendix D\D.9.2\frontend\ folder.

To view the results, you can open your browser and type `http://local-host:8080/game.html` into the address box to see the game's web page. The game should now allow you to continue to level 6.

D.10   Chapter 12

Chapter 12 has two exercises.

D.10.1 Exercise 1

In what two ways can you access a variable or call a function?

SOLUTION

You can access a variable or call a function by using its zero-based index. You can also use the item's name if one was specified for the item.

D.10.2 Exercise 2

Something you might have noticed is that the Tries value doesn't reset when you replay the level or play the next level. Use the logging approach to locate the source of the issue.

SOLUTION

In your WebAssembly\ folder, create an Appendix D\D.10.2\source\ folder, and then copy in the cards.wast file from your Chapter 12\source\ folder. Open the cards.wast file.

The first thing that you need to do is define an import s-expression for a logging function called _Log that takes two i32 parameters. The first parameter will be a pointer to a memory location for a string indicating which function the log value is coming from. The second parameter will be the $tries value.

The JavaScript will handle the logging, so the _Log function in the following snippet is added after the _Pause function import:

```
(import "env" "_Log" (func $Log (param i32 i32)))
```

A search of the code for every function that interacts with the $tries value results in the following functions:

- `$InitializeCards`
- `$PlayLevel`
- `$SecondCardSelectedCallback`

The data node at the end of the cards.wast file already has the function name for the SecondCardSelectedCallback, so you only need to add the other two function names. Add the characters \0 (zero—a null terminator) between the function names as a separator:

```
(data
  (i32.const 1024)
  "SecondCardSelectedCallback\0InitializeCards\0PlayLevel"
)
```

At the top of the $InitializeCards function, after the $count local variable declaration, place the value i32.const 1051 on the stack. This is the start location of the data node in memory (1024), plus the number of characters to get to the first character of the InitializeCards string (\0 is one character).

Add the $tries value to the stack, and then call the $Log function:

```
i32.const 1051
get_global $tries
call $Log
```

At the top of the $PlayLevel function, repeat what you did for the $InitializeCards function, but adjust the i32.const value to be at the start of the PlayLevel string:

```
i32.const 1067
get_global $tries
call $Log
```

At the top of the $SecondCardSelectedCallback function, add the $Log call, passing i32.const 1024 for the string location in memory:

```
i32.const 1024
get_global $tries
call $Log
```

With the text format modified, compile the WebAssembly text format into a Web-Assembly module using the wat2wasm online tool at the following website: https://webassembly.github.io/wabt/demo/wat2wasm/. Replace the text in the top-left pane of the tool with the contents of your cards.wast file, and then download the WebAssembly module to your Appendix D\D.10.2\source\ folder. Name the file cards.wasm.

Create an Appendix D\D.10.2\frontend\ folder, and copy the cards.wasm file that you just downloaded into this folder. Copy all the files except cards.wasm from your Chapter 12\frontend\ folder to your Appendix D\D.10.2\frontend\ folder, and then open the game.js file.

Adjust the sideImportObject to have a _Log function after the _Pause function, as shown in the following snippet:

```
const sideImportObject = {
  env: {

    _Pause: pause,        The other functions are
    _Log: log,            still part of the object
  }                       but aren't shown.
};
```

At the end of the game.js file, add the following log function that reads the string that's specified from memory and then logs information to the browser's console window:

```
function log(functionNamePointer, triesValue) {
  const name = getStringFromMemory(functionNamePointer);
  console.log(`Function name: ${name}  triesValue: ${triesValue}`);
}
```

If you run the game.html file and display the console window of the browser's developer tools, you'll see the function calls being logged. To narrow down the issue further, you could call the Log function in more spots.

Eventually, you'll discover that the source of the issue is at the end of the $InitializeCards function. The value of a global variable with an index of 6 is placed on the stack, and then the $tries global variable is given the value that's on the stack.

If you look at the global variables, you'll discover that the $tries global variable has the index of 6. Rather than a get_global 6 call, the stack should be given an i32.const 0 value to reset the $tries variable, as the following snippet shows:

```
i32.const 0
set_global $tries
```

With the issue tracked down, the calls to the $Log function can be removed from your cards.wast file.

D.11   Chapter 13

Chapter 13 has two exercises.

D.11.1 Exercise 1

Which Mocha function would you use if you wanted to group several related tests together?

SOLUTION

The describe function

D.11.2 *Exercise 2*

Write a test to verify that the proper error message is returned when you pass an empty string for the `categoryId` value of the `ValidateCategory` function.

Solution

In your WebAssembly\ folder, create an Appendix D\D.11.2\tests\ folder. Do the following:

- Copy the validate.wasm, validate.js, package.json, tests.js, and tests.html files from your Chapter 13\13.2 tests\ folder to your new D.11.2\tests\ folder.
- Open a command prompt, and navigate to your D.11.2\tests\ folder. Because your package.json file already lists the dependencies for Mocha and Chai, you can simply run the following command, and npm will install the packages listed in your file:

  ```
  npm install
  ```

- Open your tests.js file in your favorite editor.

After the `"Pass a string that's too long"` test, add the test in the next listing, which will intentionally fail.

Listing D.7 Testing `ValidateCategory` with an empty string for `categoryId`

```
                              New test added for the categoryId test of
...                               the ValidateCategory function

it("Pass an empty categoryId string to ValidateCategory", () => {   ◁
  const VALID_CATEGORY_IDS = [100, 101];
  const errorMessagePointer = Module._malloc(256);      The error message you're
  const categoryId = "";                                expecting; intentionally wrong
  const expectedMessage = "something";   ◁              so the test fails

  const arrayLength = VALID_CATEGORY_IDS.length;
  const bytesPerElement = Module.HEAP32.BYTES_PER_ELEMENT;
  const arrayPointer = Module._malloc((arrayLength * bytesPerElement));
  Module.HEAP32.set(VALID_CATEGORY_IDS, (arrayPointer / bytesPerElement));

  const isValid = Module.ccall('ValidateCategory',
      'number',
      ['string', 'number', 'number', 'number'],
      [categoryId, arrayPointer, arrayLength, errorMessagePointer]);

  Module._free(arrayPointer);

  let errorMessage = "";
  if (isValid === 0) {
    errorMessage = Module.UTF8ToString(errorMessagePointer);
  }                                                Checks to make sure
                                                   the message returned
  Module._free(errorMessagePointer);              matches the one
                                                   you're expecting
  chai.expect(errorMessage).to.equal(expectedMessage);   ◁
});
```

To run the tests, open a command prompt, navigate to your D.11.2\tests\ folder, and run the following command:

```
npm test tests.js
```

Your new test should fail.

Edit your test so that the expectedMessage variable now holds the value "A Product Category must be selected." If you run the tests again, they should now all pass.

appendix E
Text format extras

This appendix covers

- Working with `if` statements
- Working with loops
- The WebAssembly module's Table section and function pointers

As mentioned in chapter 11, the code execution in WebAssembly is defined in terms of a stack machine in which instructions push or pop a certain number of values onto and off the stack.

When a function is first called, the stack for that function is empty. The Web-Assembly framework will validate the stack when the function ends to ensure that, if the function is returning an i32 value, for example, the last item on the stack when the function returns is an i32 value. If the function doesn't return anything, then the stack must be empty when the function returns. If there happens to be a value on the stack, you can remove the item by using the drop instruction, which will pop the top item off the stack, as in the following example:

```
i32.const 1   ◁——— Adds the value 1 to the stack
i32.const 2   ◁——— Adds the value 2 to the stack
drop  ◁——— Pops value 2 off the stack
drop  ◁——— Pops value 1 off the stack
```

There might be times when you need to exit a function before it reaches the end. To do this, there's a `return` instruction that will pop the necessary items off the stack and then exit the function. The following example would pop two items off the stack if those are the only two on the stack, and the function is returning `void`:

```
i32.const 1          │ If the function returns void, the
i32.const 2          │ return instruction in this case will
return  ◁——————      │ pop the two values off the stack.
```

E.1   Control flow statements

WebAssembly has several control flow statements available, like `block`, `loop`, and `if`. Blocks and loops have no effect on the values on the stack and are simply constructs that have a sequence of instructions and a label. A block can be used to specify a label for use with the branching pattern the code needs.

E.1.1   If statements

Writing `if` blocks is interesting because there are multiple ways that they can be structured. Both the `then` and `else` branches of the `if` block are optional. When using the stack machine style, the `then` statement is implied. In both styles—stack or nested s-expression—you can use a `block` statement rather than the `then` statement because a `block` statement is just a series of instructions with a label.

   If statements pop an `i32` value off the stack in order to do their check. A value of 0 (zero) is considered false, and any `nonzero` value is considered true. Because the `if` statement needs to pop an `i32` value off the stack, with the stack machine style, you do a check, like `i32.eq`, before the `if` statement to put a Boolean value onto the stack. The nested s-expression style can do the check either before or within the `if` statement.

   Let's take a look at a stack machine style `if` statement.

STACK MACHINE STYLE IF STATEMENT

The example in the following listing is a module containing a function that uses the stack machine style to check whether the parameter's value is 0 (zero) or not. If a value is 0, the function will return the value 5. Otherwise, it will return 10.

> Listing E.1   Example of an `if/else` block written using the stack machine style

```
(module
  (type $type0 (func (param i32) (result i32)))
  (export "Test" (func 0))

  (func (param $param i32) (result i32)
    (local $result i32)
```

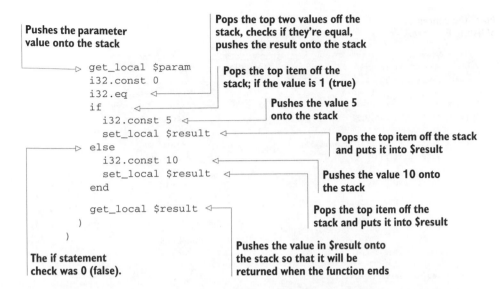

Pushes the parameter value onto the stack

Pops the top two values off the stack, checks if they're equal, pushes the result onto the stack

```
get_local $param
i32.const 0
i32.eq
if
    i32.const 5
    set_local $result
else
    i32.const 10
    set_local $result
end

get_local $result
)
)
```

Pops the top item off the stack; if the value is 1 (true)

Pushes the value 5 onto the stack

Pops the top item off the stack and puts it into $result

Pushes the value 10 onto the stack

Pops the top item off the stack and puts it into $result

The if statement check was 0 (false).

Pushes the value in $result onto the stack so that it will be returned when the function ends

You can test the code in listing E.1 by using the wat2wasm online tool.

TEST THE CODE

To test the code, go to the following website and copy the contents of listing E.1 into the top-left pane of the tool: https://webassembly.github.io/wabt/demo/wat2wasm/. As figure E.1 shows, in the tool's bottom-left pane, you can replace the contents with the following code snippet to load the module and call the Test function, passing in a value of 4. The result of the call to the Test function will be displayed in the bottom-right pane:

```
const wasmInstance = new WebAssembly.Instance(wasmModule, {});
console.log(wasmInstance.exports.Test(4));
```

You can adjust the value passed to the Test function to verify that passing 0 (zero) does indeed return 5, while all other values return 10. Let's take a look at a nested s-expression version of the if statement you just saw in listing E.1.

NESTED S-EXPRESSION IF STATEMENT: EQUALITY CHECK BEFORE THE IF STATEMENT

With the stack machine style, the equality check needs to happen before the if statement because the Boolean value needs to already be on the stack for the if statement. With the nested s-expression style, you can place the equality check before the if statement or within it. Listing E.2 shows the same code as in listing E.1, but using the nested s-expression style instead.

1. Place the contents of listing E.1 here.

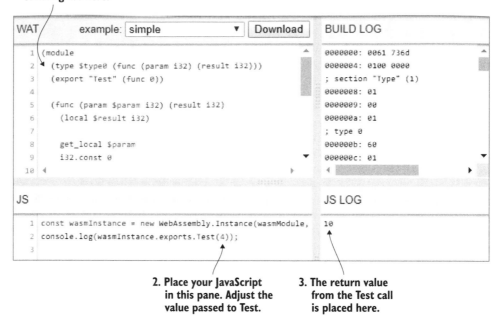

2. Place your JavaScript in this pane. Adjust the value passed to Test.

3. The return value from the Test call is placed here.

Figure E.1   The code from listing E.1 is placed in the top-left pane, and the JavaScript is placed in the bottom-left pane. The result of the function call is displayed in the bottom-right pane.

Listing E.2   Nested s-expression style with the equality check before the `if` statement

```
...

(func (param $param i32) (result i32)
  (local $result i32)

  (i32.eq              ⊲——————┐  Checks to see if the
    (get_local $param)        │  parameter value equals 0
    (i32.const 0)
  )
  (if            ┌———————————————  If the i32.eq check was 1 (true)...
    (then    ⊲———┘
      (set_local $result    ⊲——————  ...sets the return value to 5
        (i32.const 5)
      )
    )                   ┌———————————  The if statement check was 0 (false)...
    (else    ⊲——————————┘
      (set_local $result    ⊲——————  ...sets the return value to 10
        (i32.const 10)
      )
    )
  )                       ┌—————————  Places the return value on
                          │           the stack to be returned
  (get_local $result)  ⊲——┘           when the function ends
)
...
```

You can test this code by replacing the content of the top-left pane in the wat2wasm online tool. The JavaScript you used in the bottom pane for listing E.1 will work for this example code too.

Let's take a look at an example in which the equality check is within the if statement.

NESTED S-EXPRESSION IF STATEMENT: EQUALITY CHECK WITHIN THE IF STATEMENT
Although the layout of the if statement in listing E.2 makes sense based on how if checks work, writing if statements this way isn't typically how developers see them written. When using the nested s-expression style, you can modify the if statement to have the check within the if statement block, as the next listing shows.

> **Listing E.3 Example that has the value check within the if block**

```
...
(func (param $param i32) (result i32)
  (local $result i32)

  (if
    (i32.eq          ⟵——————    The equality check is now
      (get_local $param)        within the if statement.
      (i32.const 0)
    )
    (then
      (set_local $result
        (i32.const 5)
      )
    )
    (else
      (set_local $result
        (i32.const 10)
      )
    )
  )

  (get_local $result)
)
...
```

You can test this code by replacing the content of the top-left pane in the wat2wasm online tool. The JavaScript you used in the bottom pane for listing E.1 will work for this example code too.

If statements can use a block statement instead of a then statement.

NESTED S-EXPRESSION IF STATEMENT: BLOCK INSTEAD OF THEN
If you choose to have Emscripten output the text format equivalent of a module's binary, you'll notice that it uses block statements instead of then statements. To demonstrate a nested s-expression with an if statement that uses a block instead of a then statement, you'll modify the code in listing E.3 to set a default value of 10 for the $result value at the beginning of the function. Giving the $result variable a default value of 10 allows you to remove the else condition from the if statement.

Adjust the `if` statement to use the `block` statement instead of the `then` statement, as the following listing shows.

Listing E.4   Example of an `if` condition using a `block` statement instead of `then`

```
...
(func (param $param i32) (result i32)
  (local $result i32)
  (set_local $result      ◁──── Assigns a default value of 10
    (i32.const 10)
  )

  (if
    (i32.eq
      (get_local $param)
      (i32.const 0)
    )                        │ The then statement is replaced
    (block      ◁───────────┘ by a block statement.
      (set_local $result
        (i32.const 5)
      )
    )
  )

  (get_local $result)
)
...
```

The stack machine style of the `if` statement can also use a `block` statement instead of a `then` statement.

STACK MACHINE IF STATEMENT: BLOCK INSTEAD OF THEN

You can modify the code from listing E.4 to set the `$result` variable to a default value of 10 at the beginning of the function, allowing you to remove the `else` condition from the `if` statement. Within the `if` statement, you then wrap the `i32.const` and `set_local` lines of code with a `block` and `end` statement, as the next listing shows.

Listing E.5   Stack machine style of the previous code

```
...
(func (param $param i32) (result i32)
  (local $result i32)

  i32.const 10
  set_local $result      ◁──── Assigns a default value of 10

  get_local $param
  i32.const 0
  i32.eq       ◁──────┐ Checks to see if the
  if                  │ parameter value is 0
    block
      i32.const 5
      set_local $result
    end
```

```
   end

   get_local $result
)
...
```

The next control flow statements that you'll learn about are loops.

E.1.2   Loops

There are three types of branches available to WebAssembly code:

- br—Branches to the label specified
- br_if—Conditionally branches to the label specified
- br_table—A jump table to branch to the label specified

It's only possible to branch to a label that's defined by the construct that the branch is within, which means, for example, that you can't branch to the middle of a loop when the branch is outside the loop.

When in a loop, branches to a block effectively act like a break statement in high-level languages, whereas a branch to the loop acts like a continue statement. A loop is simply a type of block that's used to form loops.

To demonstrate how loops work, you'll build a GetStringLength function that receives an i32 parameter indicating where in the module's memory the string is that it needs to check. The function will return an i32 value for the string's length.

You'll build the function using the branch to a block approach *(acts like a break statement)* first, and then, in a later section, you'll modify the loop to branch to the loop instead *(acts like a continue statement)*.

NESTED S-EXPRESSION LOOP STATEMENT: BRANCH TO BLOCK

Before you create your function, you need to define memory that the module will use. Memory is defined by using an s-expression with the label memory, followed by an optional variable name, the initial number of memory pages desired, and, optionally, the maximum number of memory pages desired. Each page of memory is 64 KB (65,536 bytes).

For this module, one page of memory is more than enough, so your memory s-expression is shown in the following snippet:

```
(memory 1)
```

Once you've created this module, you'll create some JavaScript code for the wat2wasm online tool that will place a string in the module's memory and then call the Get-StringLength function. Because the JavaScript needs access to the module's memory, you'll need to export it. The following snippet shows the export statement needed for the memory. Because a variable name wasn't given to the memory s-expression, you'll specify the memory by its index:

```
(export "memory" (memory 0))
```

The GetStringLength function needs two local variables: one to keep track of how many characters are in the string so far ($count) and one to keep track of where in memory the function is currently reading ($position). When the function starts, $count will be set to a default value of 0, and $position will be set to the parameter value received, which is the start position of the string in the module's memory.

A block statement will surround the loop that you'll break out to if the character read from memory is the null terminator. The block statement will be given a variable name called $parent. Within the block statement, you'll have a loop statement with the variable name $while.

At the beginning of the loop, you'll load in the current character from memory based on the $position value using the i32.load8_s instruction. The value loaded by i32.load8_s is the decimal version of the character.

The i32.eqz instruction will then test the memory value to see if it's equal to zero (the null terminator; the zero ASCII character is decimal 48). If the value is zero, the br_if statement branches to the block ($parent), which exits the loop, and the code continues on after the end of the loop.

If the loop doesn't exit, the $count and $position variables are each incremented by 1, and then the br statement branches to the loop in order to loop again. After the loop ends, the $count value is placed on the stack to be returned to the calling function.

The next listing is the module containing the GetStringLength function.

Listing E.6   GetStringLength using nested s-expressions and breaking out of the loop

```
(module
  (type $type0 (func (param i32) (result i32)))

  (memory 1)

  (export "memory" (memory 0))
  (export "GetStringLength" (func 0))

  (func (param $param i32) (result i32)
    (local $count i32)
    (local $position i32)

    (set_local $count                    Will hold the number of characters
      (i32.const 0)                      in the string to return to the caller
    )

    (set_local $position                 The current position in the module's
      (get_local $param)                 memory that you need to read
    )
                                         The parent block that you'll use to break out
    (block $parent                       of the loop when you find a null terminator
      (loop $while
        (br_if $parent
          (i32.eqz                       Branches to the parent block, breaking out of
            (i32.load8_s                 the loop if 0 is found (the null terminator)
              (get_local $position)
            )
```

The start of your loop

Loads the current byte from memory and checks if the value is equal to zero

```
          )
        )
      (set_local $count      ◁──── Increments the character count
        (i32.add
          (get_local $count)
          (i32.const 1)
        )
      )
                                 Increments the memory position
      (set_local $position   ◁──┘ for the next iteration of the loop
        (i32.add
          (get_local $position)
          (i32.const 1)
        )
      )
                                 Branches to the top of the
      (br $while)    ◁──────────┘ loop so that it loops again
    )
  )
                                 Places the count on the stack
    (get_local $count)   ◁──────┘ to be returned to the caller
  )
)
```

You can test the code in listing E.6 by using the wat2wasm online tool.

TESTING THE CODE

To test the code, copy the contents of listing E.6 into the top-left pane of the wat2wasm online tool. In the bottom-left pane (figure E.2), replace the contents with the next code snippet, which will load the module and place a reference to the module's memory in a wasmMemory variable. A copyStringToMemory function is defined that accepts a string and memory offset and writes the string, along with a null terminator, to the module's memory.

The code calls the copyStringToMemory function, passing it a string. The module's GetStringLength function is then called, specifying the memory position where the string was written. The result of the call to the GetStringLength function is displayed in the bottom-right pane:

```
const wasmInstance = new WebAssembly.Instance(wasmModule, {});
const wasmMemory = wasmInstance.exports.memory;

function copyStringToMemory(value, memoryOffset) {
  const bytes = new Uint8Array(wasmMemory.buffer);
  bytes.set(new TextEncoder().encode((value + "\0")),
      memoryOffset);
}

copyStringToMemory("testing", 0);
console.log(wasmInstance.exports.GetStringLength(0));
```

You can adjust the string passed to the copyStringToMemory function to test and see what the various string lengths are.

1. Place the contents
   of listing E.6 here.

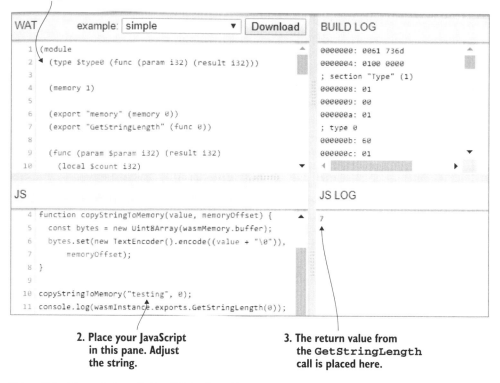

2. Place your JavaScript
   in this pane. Adjust
   the string.

3. The return value from
   the GetStringLength
   call is placed here.

Figure E.2   The code from listing E.6 is placed in the top-left pane, and the JavaScript is placed in the bottom-left pane. The result of the function call is displayed in the bottom-right pane.

Let's take a look at a stack machine version of the loop you just built.

STACK MACHINE LOOP STATEMENT: BRANCH TO BLOCK

The code in the next listing shows the same function as listing E.6, but written using the stack machine style.

Listing E.7   GetStringLength using stack machine style and breaking out of the loop

```
...

(func (param $param i32) (result i32)
  (local $count i32)
  (local $position i32)

  i32.const 0
  set_local $count

  get_local $param
  set_local $position
```

Will hold the number of
characters in the string

The current position in the
module's memory that you
need to read

```
block $parent
  loop $while
    get_local $position
    i32.load8_s      ◁────────  Loads the current byte from
                                memory and pushes it onto
                                the stack
    i32.eqz
    br_if $parent    ◁──────
                            │   If true, then you found the null
                            │   terminator. Branch to the parent
    get_local $count │──    │   block to break out of the loop.
    i32.const 1
    i32.add
    set_local $count

    get_local $position  ◁────  Increments the value in $position
    i32.const 1
    i32.add
    set_local $position

    br $while        ◁──
  end                   │       Branches to the top of
end                     │       the loop (loop again)

get_local $count     ◁──
)                       │       Places the count on the stack
...                     │       to be returned to the caller
```

Is the value equal to zero? — (points to i32.eqz / br_if $parent)

Increments the value in $count — (points to get_local $count / i32.const 1 / i32.add / set_local $count)

You'll now modify the loop to branch to the loop instead of a branch, which acts like a `continue` statement.

NESTED S-EXPRESSION LOOP STATEMENT: BRANCH TO LOOP

The logic within the loop will need to be modified to work using this technique, but a branch-to-loop approach doesn't have the surrounding `block` statement. If your code doesn't branch to the loop, then the loop ends. Your new loop will continue to loop while the current character isn't the null terminator.

Modify your listing E.6 code so that it no longer has a `block` s-expression around the `loop` s-expression. Replace the `(br_if $parent` statement with `(if` to do an `if` statement rather than a `branch` statement. Remove the closing parenthesis from the `br_if` statement that's just before the `(set_local $count` line of code. Place a closing parenthesis for the `if` statement after the `(br $while)` statement.

The `if` statement will check to see if the current character isn't equal to zero. Change the `i32.eqz` (equal to zero) statement to an `i32.ne` (not equal) statement, and then put the following s-expression after the `i32_load8` s-expression:

```
(i32.const 0)
```

After the closing parenthesis for the `i32.ne` s-expression, place a `(then` s-expression with the closing parenthesis after the `(br $while)` statement.

The next listing shows the modified loop using the `continue` approach.

Listing E.8 **GetStringLength** using nested s-expressions and continuing the loop

```
...

(func (param $param i32) (result i32)
```

```
    (local $count i32)
    (local $position i32)

    (set_local $count
      (i32.const 0)
    )

    (set_local $position
      (get_local $param)
    )                                    The start of the loop

    (loop $while    ◁───────────────┘
      (if        ◁──────── Replaces the br_if statement
        (i32.ne
          (i32.load8_s
            (get_local $position)            The value from the memory
          )                                  will be compared to zero
          (i32.const 0)    ◁─────────────┘   (null terminator).
        )
        (then    ◁──────────────┐
          (set_local $count      If the value from
          (i32.add             memory is not zero
            (get_local $count)
            (i32.const 1)
          )
        )

        (set_local $position            ◁──────── Increments $position
          (i32.add
            (get_local $position)
            (i32.const 1)
          )
        )

        (br $while)   ◁────────┐
        )                       Branches to the top of
      )                         the loop (loop again)
    )

    (get_local $count)
  )
  ...
```

Let's look at a stack machine version of the loop you just built.

STACK MACHINE LOOP STATEMENT: BRANCH TO LOOP

The next listing shows the same code as listing E.8, but in the stack machine style.

Listing E.9 Stack machine style of the previous code

```
...

(func (param $param i32) (result i32)
  (local $count i32)
  (local $position i32)

  i32.const 0
  set_local $count
```

Annotations in the left margin:
- Replaces i32.eqz → (i32.ne
- Increments $count → (set_local $count ... block

```
  get_local $param
  set_local $position

  loop $while
    get_local $position
    i32.load8_s                ──┐  New for the i32.ne check

    i32.const 0      ◁──────────┘
    i32.ne           ◁────── Replaces i32.eqz
    if               ◁──────┐
      get_local $count      └  Replaces br_if $parent
      i32.const 1
      i32.add
      set_local $count

      get_local $position
      i32.const 1
      i32.add
      set_local $position

      br $while
    end
  end

  get_local $count
)
...
```

The next area that you'll learn about is how to use the module's Table section for function pointers.

E.2　*Function pointers*

WebAssembly modules have an optional Table known section, which is a typed array of references, like functions, that can't be stored in memory as raw bytes for security reasons. If the addresses were stored in the module's memory, there would be a chance that a malicious module would try to modify an address to access data that it shouldn't have access to.

When a module's code wants to access the data referenced in the Table section, it asks for the WebAssembly framework to operate on the item at a specific index in the table. The WebAssembly framework then reads the address stored at that index and performs the action.

The Table section is defined with an s-expression that starts with a label using the word `table`, followed by an initial size, optionally followed by a maximum size, and finally followed by the type of data the table will hold. This is currently only functions, so `funcref` is the term used.

> **INFO** The WebAssembly specification has been adjusted to use the word `funcref` rather than `anyfunc` for the table's element type. When Emscripten outputs a .wast file, it uses the new name, and the WebAssembly Binary Toolkit can accept text format code that uses either name. At the time of this book's writing, developer tools in the browsers are still using the word

anyfunc when you inspect a module. Firefox allows you to use either word when constructing a WebAssembly.Table object in your JavaScript, but, at the moment, other browsers allow only the old name. Right now, for production JavaScript code, it's recommended that you continue to use anyfunc.

To demonstrate using the Table section, you're going to create a module that imports two functions. The module will have a built-in function that accepts an i32 parameter indicating the function's index in the Table section to call.

The first thing your module will need are two import s-expressions for the two functions, as shown in the following snippet:

```
(import "env" "Function1" (func $function1))
(import "env" "Function2" (func $function2))
```

Next you need to define the table s-expression with a size of 2 for the two functions:

```
(table 2 funcref)
```

After the table s-expression, you'll have your export s-expression for the function that the JavaScript will call to indicate which function needs to be called:

```
(export "Test" (func $test))
```

When the module is instantiated, you want the imported functions added to the Table section. To do this, you need to define an element s-expression. The items in this s-expression will be added to the Table section automatically when the module is instantiated.

The element s-expression starts with the label elem, followed by the start index in the table where the object references will be placed, and then followed by the items to place in the Table section. The following code snippet will add the two functions to the Table section starting at table index 0 (zero):

```
(elem (i32.const 0) $function1 $function2)
```

Your next step is to define your $test function, which receives an i32 parameter value and has no return value, as shown in the following snippet:

```
(func $test (param $index i32)
)
```

Within your $test function, you need to call the requested table item. To call an item in the Table section, you pass the index to the call_indirect instruction, but you also indicate the type (function signature) that you're calling, as the following snippet shows:

```
(call_indirect (type $FUNCSIG$v)
   (get_local $index)
)
```

⊲——— **$FUNCSIG$v is a variable name for a type s-expression (an index can also be used).**

Putting it all together, the module's code is shown in the following listing.

> **Listing E.10　Function pointer module using the nested s-expression style**

```
(module
  (type $FUNCSIG$v (func))          ◁─────  The signature of the two
                                            functions that will be imported

  (import "env" "Function1" (func $function1))
  (import "env" "Function2" (func $function2))

  (table 2 funcref)        ◁──────  Creates a table with
                                    an initial size of 2
  (export "Test" (func $test))

  (elem (i32.const 0) $function1 $function2)   ◁──  Has the two functions placed in
                                                    the table starting at index 0
  (func $test (param $index i32)
    (call_indirect (type $FUNCSIG$v)    ◁──  Calls the item in the table
      (get_local $index)                     using the index received
    )                                        in the parameter
  )
)
```

Now that you've created the module's code, you can test it.

E.2.1　Test the code

To test the code, copy the contents of listing E.10 into the top-left pane of the
wat2wasm online tool. In the bottom-left pane of the tool (figure E.3), replace the
contents with the following code snippet, which will define an importObject object
for the module containing the two functions to import. Each function will write a message to the console of the browser's developer tools indicating which function was
called.

Once you have an instance of the module, you can call the Test function, passing
in either 0 or 1 to have the functions in the Table section called:

```
const importObject = {     ◁──────────────────────────  Creates the importObject with
  env: {                                                 two functions for the module
    Function1: function() { console.log("Function 1"); },
    Function2: function() { console.log("Function 2"); },  ◁──
```

Writes to the browser's console
indicating that function 1 was called
                    Writes to the browser's console
                    indicating that function 2 was called

```
  }
};

const wasmInstance = new WebAssembly.Instance(wasmModule,
    importObject);

wasmInstance.exports.Test(0);    ◁──  Calls the Test function, passing
                                      in an index of 0 or 1
```

**1. Place the contents
of listing E.10 here.**

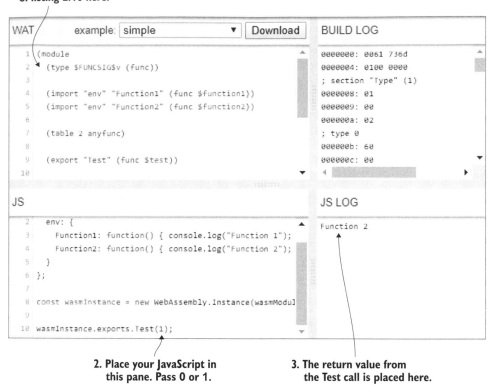

```
WAT        example: simple           ▼   Download      BUILD LOG
  1  (module                                          00000000: 0061 736d
  2    (type $FUNCSIG$v (func))                        00000004: 0100 0000
  3                                                    ; section "Type" (1)
  4    (import "env" "Function1" (func $function1))    00000008: 01
  5    (import "env" "Function2" (func $function2))    00000009: 00
  6                                                    0000000a: 02
  7    (table 2 anyfunc)                               ; type 0
  8                                                    0000000b: 60
  9    (export "Test" (func $test))                    0000000c: 00
 10                                              ▼

JS                                                    JS LOG
  2    env: {                                          Function 2
  3      Function1: function() { console.log("Function 1"); }
  4      Function2: function() { console.log("Function 2"); }
  5    }
  6  };
  7
  8  const wasmInstance = new WebAssembly.Instance(wasmModul
  9
 10  wasmInstance.exports.Test(1);
```

**2. Place your JavaScript in
this pane. Pass 0 or 1.**

**3. The return value from
the Test call is placed here.**

**Figure E.3   The code from listing E.10 is placed in the top-left pane, and the JavaScript is placed in
the bottom-left pane. The result of the function call is displayed in the bottom-right pane.**

index

X